The Canadian Press
STYLEBOOK

A Guide for Writers and Editors

Fully revised
and updated

Patti Tasko
Editor

The Canadian Press
The Last Word. First.

36 King St. East, Toronto, Ontario M5C 2L9
Telephone: 416-364-0321   Fax: 416-364-9283

Copyright © 1999 The Canadian Press
1st edition 1940
2nd edition 1947
3rd edition 1954
4th edition 1957
5th edition 1966
6th edition 1974
7th edition 1983
8th edition 1989
9th edition 1992
10th edition 1995
11th edition 1999

Canadian Cataloguing in Publication Data

The Canadian Press stylebook: a guide for writers and editors

11th ed.
Previously published under title: CP stylebook.
Includes bibliographical references and index.
ISBN 0-920009-20-4

1. Journalism – Style manuals. I. Tasko, Patti. II. Canadian Press.
III. Title: CP stylebook.

PN4783.C35 1999   808'.06607   C99-931052-6

Design and cover art by Sean Vokey, The Canadian Press.

Printed by Image Plus Graphics, Toronto.

Contents

The working journalist

Some useful tools

Illustrating the news

The CP news report

Introduction

The *CP Stylebook* began life as a modest little pamphlet more than a half-century ago. It was a sort of operator's manual for staff at The Canadian Press, Canada's national news agency.

It has blossomed since then into a comprehensive reference work used in newsrooms and business offices across Canada.

This new edition is an update from intro to index. Every chapter has been freshened or revised to reflect the priorities and sensitivities of today's world. We've also added colour photos to better illustrate and reflect today's news. The emphasis on getting real people and real pocketbook issues into the news, in a readable style, has not changed.

The stylebook is also designed to be friendly to the many outside CP who have come to consider it a standard reference. The language should be understandable to anyone who picks it up.

The stylebook has been organized into these main sections:

Policies: The standards that guide the work of collecting and distributing news. Basic journalism ethics, but also specific help with sensitive areas like racism, sexism, misquotes and anonymous sources.

General: Hard news and soft news, from news analysis to foreign reporting and sports coverage. CP's perspectives on the different types of basic news stories.

Legal: Libel. Copyright. Court coverage. Police searches of the newsroom. Contempt. The rights — and limitations — that govern the everyday work of reporters and editors.

The working journalist: Communicating clearly. Down-to-earth advice on writing and editing, with common pitfalls identified and lots of examples to illustrate each point.

Some useful tools: The nitty-gritty. In one subsection, punctuation, capitalization and other grammatical elements. In another, information on aircraft names, military ranks, weather and other technical matters. Also, a how-to guide for access-to-information laws and 20 pages of tricky words.

Illustrating the news: Pictures on the page. Practical information about getting photos and graphics into print.

The CP news report: Primarily for CP staff. Sets out procedures for advisories, packaging the news, coding and slugging of copy, the handling of corrections and other important elements of the agency's news report.

For those who judge a book by its cover, there's a fresh look, complete with our new logo. White space is provided throughout for notes and observations – particularly helpful at newspapers that modify or expand on CP style.

CP's basic style changes cautiously: evolution, not revolution. Thus, while this edition contains many changes of emphasis and detail, there are few departures from long-standing fundamentals. CP continually assesses its style to keep it up to date and sensible. Suggestions for improvement are always welcome.

What is CP?

Kevin Doyle tells a story in *Canadian Newspapers: The Inside Story* (Hurtig Publishers, 1980) that provides a perfect metaphor for the role Canada's national news agency has played in the lives of Canadians. It involves a 1950s publisher of the Charlottetown Patriot who watched in amazement one day as two CP reporters sent to Prince Edward Island to cover the provincial election set up a temporary shop in the Patriot newsroom, installing phones to collect results.

He finally took one of them aside and confided that he had a printer in his back room that, every election, spit out all the election results they would ever need.

The printer, of course, was the CP wire.

If a publisher of a newspaper – one of the owners of CP – could not understand the reach that the news agency has into the production and distribution of news, how can the average Canadian?

There is probably no other organization that has made such an ongoing contribution to Canadian life and yet has such a low public profile. Since it was founded in 1917, CP has been instrumental in telling Canadians about themselves. It has shaped the way Canadians see the world. It has played a crucial role in the growth of the Canadian news industry.

Yet the news organization remains largely anonymous to many of the people it serves. Those Canadians who read a newspaper over morning coffee, listen to a radio newscast on the drive home, watch The National before bed and pick up weekend sports scores on the Internet would likely be surprised to discover a lot of that news came from The Canadian Press.

CP was created by newspaper publishers to provide a flow of news across the sparsely populated regions of the country. Before 1917, newspapers exchanged news within regional associations and received international news from The Associated Press on north-south telegraph circuits. But there was no ready means of sending news east and west across Canada.

Then the First World War came along, and publishers were desperate to receive news of Canada's troops in Europe. Part of CP's early financing was a $50,000 federal grant to pay for telegraph circuits linking the Maritimes to Quebec and Ontario, Central Canada to the Maritimes and the Prairies to British Columbia. The government offered to help because of CP's potential to serve the cause of national unity during the war.

That funding ended in 1924 by mutual agreement and CP's founding publishers voted never again to risk the appearance of compromise by accepting government money for any news purpose.

Today, the logo (**CP**) appears on hundreds of newspaper pages every day. It can be found on Internet news sites. Stories from CP computer terminals end up in radio and television newsrooms across the country. Reports are picked up by other news agencies that rely on CP to cover Canada for the world. They are e-mailed to Canada's newsmakers, who are well aware of CP's reach.

What is CP? It is a news agency, co-operatively owned by Canada's daily newspapers. Those 95 or so newspapers control CP through a board of directors. They also pay fees to the agency based on their circulation and contribute news of their area to the common pool.

Since its early days this exchange of news via CP has been at the heart of the co-operative. During a major restructuring in the mid-1990s the importance of this news exchange role was reaffirmed, making CP the only major news agency in the world that relies so heavily on voluntary newspaper contributions.

How does the exchange work? The Montreal Gazette, for instance, takes on the responsibility of covering a major fire in its city for the co-operative. In return it gets coverage from the Halifax Chronicle-Herald about a waterfront strike. CP is the conduit, compiling reports from member papers and ensuring that the important news of the day is covered and delivered in time for deadlines that span six time zones.

From the beginning, CP has had reporters, editors and photographers based in bureaus across the country. But they cannot possibly cover the country to the extent that Canada's newspapers can, from Port Alberni on Vancouver Island to St. John's, Nfld., from Whitehorse in the Yukon to Windsor, Ont. Add into this mix news stories shared by the hundreds of radio and television stations that are clients of CP and its broadcast division, Broadcast News. The result is a Canadian news report that is unmatched for its depth, breadth, timeliness and diversity.

The CP report is not limited to Canadian news, but also includes full coverage from around the world. The bulk of the international report originates with The Associated Press and Reuters. CP World Desk editors fight their way through a massive file of AP and Reuters news every day, round-the-clock, looking for stories of particular interest to Canadians. CP reporters in Washington and London, as well as an extensive network of stringers, supplement this report.

A French-language service was established in 1951. In addition to providing an important service to French-language members, this service also serves as an important pipeline of news from Quebec. The best elements of this are translated into English for the CP members and the best elements of CP are translated into French for the Presse Canadienne service. This ensures that Quebecers are not isolated by language from important news from English Canada and that newspapers, radio and TV broadcasters in English Canada, likewise, are not isolated from important stories and issues in Quebec.

Since the early days of public and private radio, CP has served the broadcasting industry. An early task was preparing scripts for Lorne Greene and other well-known voices who read the latest dispatches from Second World War battlefronts over the fledgling Canadian Broadcasting Corp.

Currently, CP's Broadcast News division provides service to private television and radio broadcasters. BN microphone flashes are a common sight at major events as material is collected for the hourly newscasts and other information programming.

On the technical side, in 1973 CP became the first news organization in Canada to make extensive use of word processors to write and edit stories. In the mid-1980s, CP and BN switched from land circuits to satellite for delivery of stories, photos and audio reports. In 1997 the news agency started delivering news reports over the Internet to member newspapers and commercial subscribers. The following year a French-language service was added "en ligne" as well.

Past generations of CP journalists who practised their craft to the click of Morse code and the beat of teletype machines would find the modern CP newsroom a strange beast indeed. But some things would still feel comfortably familiar. It continues to be an organization driven by a quest for first-rate journalism. CP's mission hasn't changed. The goal continues to be to keep Canadians informed and help them understand and experience their world more fully. CP tells people the story of their country, every day, in all forms and from all corners of the land. In the 21st century of the global village the stories of our nation are a cornerstone of who we are and will become.

Eric Morrison

President

Notes

Why CP style is the way it is

The SWAT team moved in, frisking the rappers for crack.

Several words in that sentence would not have made sense to an average reader a generation ago. Most of today's readers would find the phrasing normal in a news report.

That's one of the reasons why stylebooks are needed. If a SWAT team turns up in a front-page story about a local hostage-taking, and again on the entertainment page in a movie review, the capitalization should be the same in both cases.

English is a fluid language, but it's bound by complicated rules of grammar. Working reporters and editors don't have time to research decisions on vocabulary and capitalization and grammar every time a problem arises. A stylebook presents such decisions in logical, handy form.

Whimsy is found in every stylebook. But style decisions overall are based on sound reasons. Most are basic grammar and common sense, with the stylebook simply a reminder. Other decisions involve choosing from among a range of valid alternatives, and at that point a number of factors come into play.

Among the ones that have influenced CP style over the decades:

Preferences of Canadian newspapers

The newspapers own The Canadian Press and most of them follow CP style in their handling of local news. It's only common sense to accept their preferences. And if there's an important style change being considered, the papers are consulted. The majority preference becomes CP style.

An example:

CP became the first western news agency to drop the courtesy titles **Mr., Mrs., Miss** and **Ms.** from all copy. Over the years, the use of such titles had become erratic. For men, the **Mr.** was omitted in stories from outside Canada as well as from sports and crime news. For women, the title tended to be dropped from sports and crime copy and in referring to some widely known celebrities, but it was retained in all other stories from Canada and abroad. The result was news columns with a **Mr.** here and not there, **Mrs.** and **Ms.** in stories where the **Mr.** was dropped and so on. Finally, most papers agreed the rules needed change, and the soundest course was to drop all such titles. Some papers continue to use them, either throughout the paper or in particular sections.

Consistency

A style that is full of exceptions is difficult to use. One goal of this stylebook is to keep exceptions to a minimum.

Maintaining consistency can be troublesome. In general, if there's an option, CP prefers lowercase initial letters to capitals. That meant CP did not capitalize federal and provincial government departments until fairly recently. However, with the naming of such departments as Environment Canada, and the proliferation of Crown agencies like the Canadian Wheat Board which demanded capitalization, it seemed inconsistent to keep using lowercase. Up they went.

Popular usage

News reporting is meant to inform the public, not to score points with language purists. Outdated expressions can get in the way of that goal. Some of the changes in the meaning of words may not be for the better, but if most readers are led to believe that **presently** means **right now**, rather than **soon**, there's no point in using the word in a news story and risking misunderstanding.

CP won't be the first to accept the misuse of a word, and occasionally we're a bit stubborn about changes that seem to debase the language. But eventually a misused form can take on a life of its own and CP bows to the inevitable. We have reluctantly accepted the word **gender** in such phrases as **gender politics** or **gender equality** although **sexual equality** makes more basic sense. (**Gender** is primarily the word used by grammarians to distinguish between masculine, feminine and neuter words; **sex** is what distinguishes males from females. But **gender** has gradually accumulated a variety of nuances in popular usage that go beyond the strictly grammatical.)

Sensitivity

Today's perfectly normal word can be tomorrow's flagrant example of sexism, racism or other abuse. In particular, people who feel put upon by society are likely to reject labels that seem to limit their potential or lock them into hurtful self-images.

People who are identified by certain words (**cripple, housewife, Indian**) can easily believe that the language is insensitive and prefer another description (**disabled person, home-maker, aboriginal**). In time, those labels may also fall out of favour.

CP believes that people's preferences should be respected when new forms are adopted by a significant number of those concerned and become familiar to the general public. But we don't want to be faddish, accepting words for routine use that are so *sensitive* that they have little clear meaning left — expressions like **developmentally challenged**. Nor will we go along casually with new labels that are politically controversial among the people most concerned.

Words like **spokesman** and **chairman** cause resentment, understandably, when applied to women. CP uses **spokeswoman** and **chairwoman**, as well as such forms as **salesperson, chairperson** and

spokesperson when appropriate. But the clumsy term **alderperson** does not seem to have gained wide acceptance, so CP prefers an alternative such as **councillor**.

"Our" spelling debate

In September 1998, The Canadian Press adopted the "our" spelling for words of more than one syllable in which the "u" is not pronounced. This came after 80 years of writing with **color, ardor** and **rigor.**

The change was made to reflect the spelling preferred by many readers and taught in most Canadian schools. A significant number of CP's member newspapers had already adopted the "our" spelling. A survey CP conducted showed that 77 per cent of its member newspapers wanted CP to use this style as well.

The "or" versus "our" spelling debate has long been a contentious one. For the "our" advocates, it is a matter of passion. "Or" is an Americanism, as huge a threat to the Canadian cultural identity as zee instead of zed.

The "or" proponents take the logical approach. They feel "or" is the more consistent, more modern spelling – there are many more words with "or" endings than "our" – and has been used in Canada long enough to be considered Canadian.

CP has been caught in the middle. On one hand, CP style is a strong advocate of distinctly Canadian spellings. At the same time, we stood behind "or."

The roots of the dispute go back to the 1700s, when written English – in Britain and elsewhere – began replacing "our" with "or" in such words as **governour, terrour** and **errour.** Then Americans began using "or" endings almost exclusively, and it became practically a matter of honour outside the United States to retain the remaining "our" spellings.

In Canada, Sir John A. Macdonald decided arbitrarily that Canada would use "our" endings in federal government documents, despite the fact that "or" endings were already in common use and that the Queen's Printer of the day spiritedly resisted the move.

But daily newspapers, which followed CP style, used "or" until recently when they started switching to "our" to reflect the preference of readers.

The complete list of "our" words can be found in the *Stylebook's* companion volume, *Caps and Spelling.*

When not to use CP spelling

Another style change takes effect with this edition of the *CP Stylebook.* When the spelling of the common-noun element of a proper name differs from CP style, CP will now use the spelling favoured by the subject. This applies to all proper names, including geographical places, and the titles of books, movies and the like.

This means it will be **U.S. Labor Department** (not U.S. Labour

Department); **Lincoln Center** (not Lincoln Centre); **Bar Harbor, Me.** (not Bar Harbour); **Color Your World** paint store (not Colour Your World); the book or movie **Primary Colors** (not Primary Colours).

Another troublesome area concerns capitalized or lowercased letters in proper names. These can be exploited for promotional purposes – an all-caps product name tends to jump out at the reader.

CP aims to spell names correctly, but for purposes of readability we do not go along with either all-capitals or all-lowercase names of corporations, products and cultural output. So it's **Scrabble** (not SCRABBLE); **Velcro** (not VELCRO); **Via** (not VIA) Rail.

One exception is the names of people and performing groups, where CP generally follows their preference, as long as it is consistent. So it is **k.d. lang** (not K.D. Lang) and **bp Nichol** (not B.P. Nichol).

➤ See **Capitalization**, page 187.

We don't expect everyone to agree with all of the style decisions we have made. They have been carefully thought out, but we welcome discussion of our style from the news industry and the public.

CP policies

Principles

When The Canadian Press was founded in 1917, it was for one reason: to serve the newspapers that owned it, and through them, the Canadian public. For decades, the only contact CP had with the public was through its member newspapers. But rapid changes in the communications industry have changed the way CP fulfils its mandate of keeping Canadians informed.

CP serves almost every daily newspaper in Canada, providing reliable and relevant news, photos and graphics. But beyond the traditional printed word, CP's role in new media continues to expand. Regardless of whether Canadians are getting their news from the Internet, cable TV, news tickers or info boxes on all-news television channels, there's a good chance much of the information comes from The Canadian Press. CP is truly Canada's No. 1 source for news – in French and English. News gathering is an imprecise science, but CP's formula is the envy of other news services around the world: a dedicated staff in bureaus and correspondent points across the country and in London and Washington; a working partnership with member newspapers; a connection to hundreds of TV and radio newsrooms through Broadcast News; and stringers around the world.

There's a difference between providing information and telling Canadians what is happening in their vast country – and how events beyond our borders affect them. Context and perspective are fundamental parts of the CP report. It's the goal of all CP reporters and editors to focus on real people – not just institutions – to show in human terms how events affect our lives. It's a busy world out there so every CP story needs to convince the reader that they should devote the time to read it. If the story doesn't strive to be interesting or tell the reader why they should care, the page will be turned or the channel changed.

Although our role continues to evolve, the principles that guide our work are unchanged. Everything that we do must be honest, unbiased and unflinchingly fair. We deal with facts that are demonstrable, supported by sources that are reliable and responsible. We pursue with equal vigour all sides of a story.

Accuracy is fundamental. Discovery of a mistake calls for immediate correction. Corrections to stories already published or broadcast must not be grudging or stingy. They must be written in a spirit of genuinely wanting to right a wrong in the fairest and fullest manner.

Our work is urgent. Speed must be a primary objective of a news service committed to the deadlines of newspapers and broadcasters in six time zones. But being reliable is always more important than being fast.

Good taste is a constant consideration. Some essential news is essentially repellent. Its handling need not be.

Staff responsibility

Responsibility for upholding CP standards rests with our reporters, editors and supervisors. So much individuality is involved in reporting, writing and editing news that it is impossible to have precise rules covering every eventuality. Being guided by proven practices is the surest way of meeting the standards that Canadians have come to expect from CP.

Among the most important of these practices:

1. Investigate fully before transmitting any story or identifying any individual in a story where there is the slightest reason for doubt. When in doubt cut it out. But never make this an excuse for ditching an angle without thorough checking. The doubt must be an honest doubt, arrived at after examination of all the facts.

Reporters, photographers and TV crews encircle Reform Leader Preston Manning after a rally of party members in Ottawa in 1993. Journalists will have opinions and a point of view, but these must not get in the way of balanced reporting.

(CP—Dave Buston)

2. Cite competent authorities and sources as the origin of any information open to question. Have proof available for publication in the event of a denial.

3. Be impartial when handling any news affecting parties or matters in controversy. Give fair representation to all sides at issue.

4. Stick to the facts without editorial opinion or comment. Reporters' opinions are not wanted in CP copy. Their observations are. So are accurate backgrounding and authoritative interpretation essential to the reader's understanding of complicated issues.

5. Admit errors promptly, frankly. Public distrust of the media is profound and troubling. The distrust is fed by inaccuracy, carelessness, indifference to public sentiment, automatic cynicism about those in public life, perceived bias or unfairness and other sins suggesting arrogance.

6. CP can help overcome such public attitudes through scrupulous care for facts and unwavering dedication to fairness. We must not be

quick to dismiss criticism and complaints, a trait journalists refuse to accept in others.

7.   The power of news stories to injure can reach both the ordinary citizen and the corporate giant. CP's integrity and sensitivity demand that supervisors and staff respond sympathetically and quickly when an error has been made. It doesn't matter whether the complaint comes from a timid citizen acting alone or from a powerful figure's battery of lawyers.

8.   Every story shown to be erroneous and involving a corrective must be drawn to the attention of supervisory staff. Each bureau is responsible for the copy it files whether it is written by its staff or by travelling staffers assigned to special events.

Ethical behaviour

Part of our responsibility as journalists is to ensure we don't do anything that demeans the craft or weakens our credibility. Because we deliver the bad news about politicians who turn dirty, caregivers who abuse their trust and business people who discard ethics for gain, we must observe stringent ethical practices, and be seen to be doing so.

It is impossible to raise all potential ethical challenges in this book. But the following guiding principles are offered in the spirit of wanting to advance, not restrain, our work.

1.   Pride in yourself and in the practice of journalism nourishes ethical behaviour.

2.   CP policy is to pay its way. Staff should not accept anything that might compromise our integrity or credibility.

Impartiality

Impartiality is somewhat like exercise. You have to work out regularly to build tone and strength.

The best exercise for impartiality is to stop regularly and ask yourself: "Am I being as impartial, honest and fair as I can be?"

Some other guides to impartiality:

Parties in controversy, whether in politics or law or otherwise, receive fair consideration. Statements issued by conflicting interests merit equal prominence, whether combined in a single story or used at separate times.

But always try to get opposing sides for simultaneous publication.

If an attack by one group or person on another has been covered, any authoritative answer is also carried. If a proper source cannot be reached, say so, and keep trying.

When a comparative unknown expresses controversial views, question his or her expertise on the subject. If there is no expertise, or the individual does not have an official position that puts weight behind the views, consider carefully whether the report should be carried.

Quotations

Quotes are the lifeblood of any story. They put rosiness into the cheeks of the palest stories. They add credibility, immediacy and punch.

They can also bring grief to writers and editors who play loose with them. Some news organizations permit liberties with quotes. CP takes a somewhat stern approach to any tampering with just what was said.

In general, we quote people verbatim and in standard English. We correct slips of grammar that are obvious slips and that would be needlessly embarrassing. We remove verbal mannerisms such as *ah*'s, routine vulgarities and meaningless repetitions. Otherwise we do not revise quotations.

While we don't routinely use abnormal spellings and grammar to indicate dialects or mispronunciations, they can have a place in helping to convey atmosphere.

Cleaning up this quote from a concerned unionized fisherman would have taken some of the heart out of the story:

"We don't want our money took to Toronto and not spent on behalf of our members," said Eric Miller. **"The few dollars that I makes, I want it spent on behalf of my family, my friends and my brothers and sisters in Newfoundland."**

And obviously Jimmy Durante's *Dese are de conditions dat prevail* would be worse for a quick tidy-up.

Quotes containing bafflegab are routinely paraphrased in plain English, no matter how eminent the speaker.

Other points to remember about handling quotes:

1. Getting exact quotes without shorthand or tape is not easy. When there is risk that a quote is not exact, for whatever reason, a paraphrase is safest.

2. When exactness is essential — if it's one person's word against another's — quote verbatim.

3. When a speaker uses what is obviously a wrong word, check back when possible. When a quote does not make sense, check back with the speaker or ditch it.

4. Misquotes result not only from tampering or carelessness. Failure to place a quote in context can have the same eroding effect on credibility. For instance: **"If our tax revenues allow it, I'll repave all secondary highways"** should not be parlayed into the bare reported statement that the speaker promised to repave all secondary highways.

Similarly, failure to indicate tone can skew a quote. A speaker's jocular comment may need to be reported with an explanatory **she said with a smile**. There are other occasions when the bare words benefit from addition of a brief description: **"I'm not guilty," he said, glowering at the jury.**

5.   When clear and concise, a full quote is preferred to a partial quote. But a partial quote can be useful for spicing a lead, setting off a controversial statement or giving the flavour of a speaker.

6.   Make only cosmetic changes to quotations from a text: changing spelling and capitalization to CP style, for example.

7.   If words are left out of a text or middle of a quotation, show the omission with an ellipsis.

8.   Long bracketed explanations and paraphrases should not be inserted at the beginning or end of a quote.

Not: **"(The new program) is imaginative, realistic and worth the time and money invested," Scott said.**

But: **The new program "is imaginative, realistic and worth the time and money invested," Scott said.**

9.   Guard against attributing one person's quote to several speakers.

Not: **Most retailers surveyed condemned the new tax, saying that "it will mean working half a day a week for the government."**

10. Do not include in a quote words that the speaker could not have spoken.

Not: **Davis said he "was delighted that the prize is going to the American."**

But: **Davis said he was "delighted that the prize is going to the American."**

Davis's words were **"I'm (not was) delighted."**

11. Provided the meaning is clear, use slang or other substandard language when it suits the context. Set it off with quotation marks only if it is to be explained. **He said he held up the bakery for "bread" — meaning money.**

Language

A reminder to be careful with translations. We should not imply that someone is speaking English when he is not.

In interviews and speeches, make clear what language is being used unless it is obvious. At a news conference where both French and English are used, specify when French was the original language. When reporting the shouts of a crowd or the wording of protest signs that are in other languages, specify that a translation is involved.

Readers are entitled to know when a direct or indirect quote is based on translation rather than the exact words used.

Obscenity

Casual obscenity, blasphemy and vulgarity are not wanted in the news report. Four-letter words shouted from a crowd or muttered by an angry demonstrator add nothing useful to a story.

There are few exceptions. A prominent figure who uses obscene language in a public situation is one. An interview subject may use obscenities in such a way that leaving them out would paint a false picture. Or a quote that includes a vulgarity might be the most effective way to connote certain emotions. But these are the exceptions, not the rule. Always consider other ways of getting across this element of the story before resorting to the use of obscenities.

Obscenities or vulgar language should always be flagged with the following slug:

EDS: Note language in para 3.

If the language or topic is exceptionally offensive, a **Borderline** slug is required:

BORDERLINE
Eds: Note language in para 3.

When an obscenity or vulgarity must be reported, do not use the prissy device of replacing some letters of the offensive words with hyphens. Put the questionable language in a separate paragraph that can be readily deleted by editors who do not want to use it.

Sensitive subjects

Potential for offence lurks in every news story. Age, race, sex, disabilities, religion are often pertinent to the news but must be handled thoughtfully.

Use fairness, sensitivity and good taste when identifying age, colour, creed, nationality, personal appearance, religion, sex and any other heading under which a person or group may feel slighted.

Aboriginal Peoples

In Canada, there are status (or reserve) Indians, non-status Indians (living outside reserves), Métis (people of mixed white and native origin) and Inuit. Collectively, they are known variously as Aboriginal Peoples, original peoples, aboriginals, indigenous peoples, the First Nations and other variations.

Some points concerning Aboriginal Peoples:

1. CP uses uppercase for **Aboriginal Peoples**, which includes all Indian, Métis and Inuit people in Canada. **First Nations** is also uppercase. Other variations – **indigenous people**, **aboriginals** (except for Aboriginals of Australia), **native peoples** – are lowercase.

2. In all references, be guided by the preference of those concerned.

3. Use **Indian** with discretion. Some people object to it because it originated with the European explorers' misconception that they had landed in India. Others, especially status Indians, prefer it to be used.

4. Use **native** advisedly. **Aboriginal** is more specific and is preferred by many in the community.

5. Where reasonable, prefer the actual name of the community – Cree, Mohawk, Blackfoot, Ojibwa – to a generality. For band names, use the spelling the band prefers, which is also the spelling used by the federal government.

6. The word tribe in its original sense was reserved for primitive peoples. Some natives use it casually and it need not be entirely avoided. But **community, people, nation, band, language group** are alternatives.

➤ See **Aboriginal Peoples**, page 247.

Age

Often age is relevant as part of a personal description or for identification. Ages also help readers to relate to people in news stories.

In general, give a person's age rather than imprecise and possibly derogatory terms such as **senior citizen, retiree, oldster, elderly, middle-aged, teenager, youngster**.

Put the age in the lead only when it is significant, such as in obituaries or when an 80-year-old is cycling across the country, or when a three-year-old child is missing. Guard against the formula lead — **a 30-year-**

old dentist; a 52-year-old fisherman; a 23-year-old convict . . .

Writing **Mario Lalonde, 30**, is usually preferable to the more cumbersome **30-year-old Mario Lalonde**.

If age is missing for an obituary, give an indication of it from the person's activities, such as year of graduation or year of retirement.

Males up to 16 are called **boys** and females to that age are **girls**. Use a phrase like **young people** for those of both sexes who are somewhat older.

First names may be used in subsequent references for those under 18, except in sports stories.

Youth in general includes both sexes: **the youth of Canada**. Applied to individuals, it usually means males. Try to avoid the latter use.

Disabilities

Be accurate, clear and sensitive when describing a person with a disability, handicap, illness or disease. They are people first; their disability is only one part of their humanity.

Mention a disability if it is pertinent. Never dismiss someone with an unqualified **disabled, crippled** or the like. Write **Romanov, whose hands are twisted with arthritis, . . .** And perhaps indicate to what extent a person has overcome a disability or how she copes with it: **Girushi uses a wheelchair once she leaves her studio.**

Be specific. **Afflicted with** suggests pain and suffering. It doesn't always apply. Nor does **suffering**. People who use wheelchairs are not necessarily **confined** to them. **Crippling** can be a temporary or permanent condition. People may be **deaf, slightly deaf** or **hard of hearing; blind** or have **poor eyesight**. A **patient** is someone under a doctor's care or in hospital. **Victim** connotes helplessness. A child who is **mentally retarded** (slow) is not necessarily **mentally disturbed** (ill). Epileptics have **seizures**, not **fits**.

Don't define people by their disorders: **the disabled, the blind, the retarded**. Writing **people with disabilities** emphasizes the human beings and not the disabilities.

Race

CP news reports should reflect the racial diversity of Canada in a natural way, free of explicit or unconscious racism.

Identify a person by race, colour or national origin only when it is truly pertinent. It is appropriate to report that a woman facing deportation is Polish. Similarly, the victim of hate mail may be referred to as a Jew. A full description, including colour, may be used if a person wanted by police is at large.

The appearance of racial minorities in news reports should not be confined to accounts of cultural events, racial tension or crime. A Korean shopkeeper's reaction to a sales tax is just as valid as a Scottish stockbroker's. Include comments from various races in matters of public interest such as federal taxes or national surveys on general topics.

Remember that what is obvious to a university-educated Christian of British stock might need explanation for persons from a variety of other backgrounds. And it should not be taken for granted that a Muslim ceremony needs explanation while the Roman Catholic mass does not.

Race is pertinent when it motivates an incident or when it helps explain the emotions of those in confrontation. Thus references to race are relevant in reports of racial controversy, immigration difficulties, language discussions and so on.

Race is not included when the context makes it obvious. Readers are safe to assume that people rioting in a predominantly black country are black.

When an incident cuts across racial lines, say so, as when a sizable number of whites join Pakistanis demonstrating against immigration procedures.

That a man found guilty of shoplifting is, say, an Indian is usually irrelevant and he should not be identified as such. However, revealing his race may be unavoidable, through giving a reserve as his address or identifying him as the son of a chief.

Race is pertinent in reporting an accomplishment unusual in a particular race: for example, if a Canadian of Chinese origin is named to the Canadian Football Hall of Fame.

Beware of playing up inflammatory statements at the expense of the main story. Be certain that a spokesman indeed speaks for a community or organization, and give a brief description of that organization, its aims and number of members.

Don't always turn to the same minority spokespeople and organizations for reaction. This can give unwarranted standing to groups that don't necessarily reflect the full range of views of their communities.

Let people speak for themselves. In particular, avoid stories about aboriginal people in which all or most of the talk is provided by white bureaucrats.

Arguing that humour was intended is no defence for a racial slur. Threadbare attempts at humour to be avoided include expressions such as **ah so**, **ugh** and **firewater**.

Use racially derogatory terms like **honky** and **nigger** only when part of a direct quotation and when essential to the story. Flag such a story:

BORDERLINE
EDS: Note racial slur in para 15.

Names of races

1. Capitalize the proper names of nationalities, peoples, races and tribes.

Aboriginal Peoples, Arab, Caucasian, French-Canadian, Inuit, Jew, Latin, Negro, Asian, Cree

2. Note that **black, mulatto, red, yellow** and **white** do not name races and are lowercase.

3. The term **black** is acceptable in all references in Canada and the United States. In the United States **African-American** is increasingly in use. In Bermuda, **coloured** is correct usage for both black and mulatto. In South Africa, the **Cape Coloured** are regarded as an ethnic group of mixed blood, and the term is capitalized. In the United States there is a National Association for the Advancement of Colored People, usually identified as the NAACP.

4. There is usually no need to use hyphenated descriptions such as **Polish-Canadian** or **Jamaican-Canadian**.

Sexism

Treat the sexes equally and without stereotyping. A woman's marital or family status — single, married, divorced, grandmother — is pertinent only to explain a personal reference or to round out a profile. The test always is: Would this information be used if the subject were a man?

Referring to a woman gratuitously as **attractive, leggy** or **bosomy** is as inappropriate as describing a man as **a hunk, hairy-chested** or **having great buns**. But there are stories beyond the routine in which it is appropriate to describe someone's appearance.

Never suggest surprise that a woman has talent. Not: **You would never guess from Adriana Hosek's appearance but she is a highly regarded brain surgeon.** Similarly, a woman who has achieved success in public life should not usually be referred to on first reference as **a housewife**.

Do not assume a woman uses her husband's last name. Check.

Use parallel references to the sexes. Not **the men and the ladies** but **the men and the women** or **the women and the men**. It's **husband and wife**, not **man and wife**. Do not treat **lady** as a synonym for **woman**, or **gentleman** for **man**.

Avoid stereotyping.

Shoppers (not **housewives**) are paying more. If statisticians speak of **a family of four**, don't translate it into **a worker with wife and two children**, unless that's exactly what is meant. More commonly, given the uncertainty about a family's source of income, it should be **husband and wife with two children**.

When writing in general terms prefer **reporter** to **newsman**, **police officer** or **constable** to **policeman**, **firefighter** to **fireman**, **mail carrier** to **mailman**, **flight attendant** to **air hostess** or **stewardess**.

But if sex is pertinent, masculine and feminine forms are proper: **postman, newswoman, policewoman, air steward**.

Use only established feminine variants ending in **-woman**.

Write **businesswoman, Frenchwoman, newspaperwoman, spokeswoman** but not **journeywoman, linewoman, second basewoman**.

Avoid other feminine variants unless they are so well established that a substitute rings false.

Thus it is proper to describe a woman as a **hostess, masseuse, princess, seamstress** or as an **author, comedian, Jew, murderer, poet, sculptor. Actor** and **actress** are both acceptable.

Avoid cumbersome coinages like **alderperson. Chairperson, salesperson** and **spokesperson** are in general use and can be used.

Often a plural construction solves the sex problem: **Retired officers are not usually referred to by their former rank.** Avoid: **A retired officer is not usually referred to by his or her former rank.**

There is not an entirely satisfactory substitute for **fisherman**, although **fisher, fish harvester, fish industry worker, fishing licensees** or the phrase **fishermen and women** are all possibilities.

Inuit women fishing for salmon with three-prong lances. The word "fishermen" isn't always inclusive enough – don't use it without checking whether it is an accurate description!

(CP—National Archive)

It is proper English to let **he (him, his)** stand as a word of common or indeterminate gender. Write **his or her** and the like only if there is a danger that women may seem excluded: **Whoever is promoted will have $50 added to his or her pay.**

The generic **man** is regarded by some as excluding women. Instead of **man** or **mankind**, you can write **people, human beings, humanity, human race.** Alternatives to **manmade** include **artificial, constructed, manufactured, synthetic.** But don't get carried away.

To write **human energy** or **human resources** to avoid **manpower**, or **person-eating tiger** to avoid **man-eating tiger** is being hypersensitive.

Gay may be used as an alternative for **homosexual**: **two gay men**. Some lesbians prefer the term **gay women** or **homosexual women**; follow an individual's preference when it is known. Prefer **sexual orientation** to **sexual preference**; gay people do not view their sexuality as an option. Don't refer to a gay **lifestyle** or suggest that the majority of homosexuals routinely live unorthodox lives; most don't. Consider using **same-sex** as an alternative to **homosexual** or **gay**.

Beware of leaving the impression that homosexuals alone, and not heterosexuals, are at risk to AIDS. Simply say that the disease is caused by a virus that attacks the body's immune system. It is spread most often through sexual contact, needles or syringes shared by drug abusers, infected blood or blood products and from pregnant women to their offspring.

When writing about abortion, the terms **pro-life** and **pro-choice** can be used if they are preferred by the person or organization involved. When writing about a movement in general, it is better to use a neutral phrase, such as **abortion-rights advocates** or **opponents of abortion**.

Sources

Cultivating knowledgeable sources who can provide the background and insight necessary for delivering a complete story is the trademark of the excellent reporter.

Without good sources — be they the town clerk in the small northern mining town, or the fast-moving executive assistant to a cabinet minister — CP cannot hope to craft a comprehensive daily picture of life in Canada and the world.

Getting and keeping good sources is hard work. It involves patient telephone work plus breaking free from our desks to get out and meet people.

CP reporters, editors and supervisors are encouraged to pull back from the front lines occasionally to spend time with people who know what's happening in the world beyond our own limited horizons. Special efforts should be made to develop contacts in non-urban areas, ethnic communities and other places beyond the bright spotlight of big-city journalism.

It is the job of journalists to meet a variety of people. We should all take a special interest in people and listen to what they have to say. Developing good sources is a way of living to the committed journalist.

When dealing with sources, remember that many people are not used to dealing with the media. Ensure they understand they are being quoted, and their words or picture may appear in many newspapers.

A cardinal rule with sources is to avoid close personal involvement. There is nothing wrong with social contact with sources, but close personal relationships can lead to conflicts of interest.

Unnamed sources

Democracy works best when someone with facts or opinions to make public is identified by the press by name and qualifications. Readers need to see named sources to help them decide on the credibility and importance of the information.

Regular use of unnamed sources weakens our news reports. CP should be firm in discouraging the quoting of sources who want to hide their identities. Leaks, especially in government and business, are sometimes designed to undermine new policies or to damage rivals.

There are of course many situations when people with information important to the public insist on concealing their identity for understandable reasons. CP would be foolish, and in some cases irresponsible, never to grant anonymity in news copy, but it can show leadership in working to stop misuse of unnamed sources.

Some guidelines:

1. Push sources hard to understand that putting their names to what they say is important to freedom of information. This is especially important in dealings with public servants who demand anonymity in routine circumstances.

2. Beat reporters should regularly test the willingness of their sources to be named.

3. Information from unnamed sources should be confirmed whenever possible by one or two other sources (always respecting the original source's anonymity, of course). Try to get supporting documentation. One-source stories are rarely acceptable these days.

4. Reporters writing stories containing unnamed sources must be able to demonstrate: (a) The information is of genuine public interest; (b) The information can be verified by at least one other source, even if unnamed; (c) The source is known to them; (d) There is no real possibility that the source is using CP for selfish purposes; (e) Normal standards of fairness and balance are followed.

5. Bureau supervisors must be consulted before a story with unnamed sources is released. Names of sources will be given to Head Office when requested.

6. Direct quotes should be avoided unless the actual words have unusual significance. This is especially important when opinion is being expressed and the sources might be tempted to use bolder language than if they were being named.

7. If the source is presenting one side of a controversy, the opposing side's views must be sought and presented fairly in the original story.

We don't have to tie every bit of information to a named source. Naming the airline employee who hands out a list of dead and injured in a plane crash adds nothing to the story. The government official who provides routine background or uncontestable fact need not always be named.

But always note names, just in case. And a reminder that prudent reporters always store their notes and tapes in safekeeping for one year at least. In extremely important matters, tapes and notes should be kept indefinitely.

Government officials often insist on anonymity at information briefings, such as in the locked room where reporters write federal or provincial budget stories in advance of delivery. CP abides by such restrictions if necessary, but will not go along with deliberate misrepresentation, such as when a cabinet minister wishes to pass as a civil servant.

Statements from such briefings should not be passed off as general knowledge or undisputed fact. The reader should be told as much as possible about the source and the circumstances should be described.

It is not unheard of for a source to give information confidentially, then deny it by name. If CP feels obliged to carry such a denial, it will identify the original source as the person denying it, provided we are confident the original story accurately reflected the source's information. Consult Head Office before proceeding.

Ethics and sources

When we do promise anonymity we must scrupulously respect that pledge. But it cannot be absolute and it is only fair to tell potential sources so. The courts may require reporters to disclose sources.

Verbal contracts with sources are enforceable in court. Make sure both you and your source understand precisely what that agreement is before you get the information. Do not make promises you cannot keep.

For instance, you can promise not to identify the source in your story and to not willingly make the identity known beyond your employer. You cannot promise to protect the source from any damages that result if the name does become known, through accident or through court order.

CP will not require or advise an employee to balk at the court's direction. It will provide counsel who can advise the employee and who will seek to persuade the court that the public interest does not require disclosure, or who will plead for a closed hearing.

Sources also should know that reporters must identify their sources to their supervisors. This could include anyone from a bureau News Editor to the President. This does not mean that everyone in the chain of command must know. A staffer in a delicate circumstance may go directly to the Editor-in-Chief or the President.

In extreme circumstances the President might have to inform the Chairman of the Board of a CP source because the member newspapers are legally responsible with CP for the CP news they publish.

If a source must be disclosed beyond the level of the President, senior management will make a concerted effort to advise the originating staffer in advance.

There may be cases where 100 per cent confidentiality is essential on an extremely sensitive news tip and CP is unable to confirm the information with other sources. In such a case senior management will consult the originating staffer. If the problem is insurmountable, CP will not carry the material.

Good reporting dictates that readers be given as much information as possible about the unnamed source's background. This helps readers judge why the story is worth their attention. Qualifications ascribed to the unnamed source must never be misleading. A bit of thought should produce a description helpful to the reader yet protective of the source.

It may be necessary to consult the source about the wording of such a description so the story can inform the reader without revealing the identity.

Other details should be clarified with sources. May all material be used, or must some be treated as only for the reporter's information and guidance (called *background* or *deep background* in the jargon of officialdom)? Are direct quotes permissible or only paraphrases?

Some phrases like **off the record** can have different meanings to different people. Be sure everyone is operating under the same meanings. Consult Head Office when someone proposes unusual restraints.

Some informants may provide information that may be attributed by name, then insist on anonymity for additional information. Attributing this confidential information is tricky: it would be misleading to specify that it came from someone else (**another Finance Department official, who asked for anonymity, said**). Usually it is preferable to rely on phrasing such as **It was also learned.**

Other guides to dealing with unnamed sources:

1.   Don't use others' unnamed sources as if they were CP's. Unnamed sources in stories picked up from newspapers or broadcast should be specifically tied to the paper or broadcaster: **The News quoted an unidentified official in the Energy Department as saying . . .**

2.   Stories should specify that the source requested anonymity and explain why.

3.   Spokespeople and officials should not be confused. A spokesperson puts forward the position of others; an official actually helps formulate that position.

4.   Where a fictitious name is being used — for instance, in the case of a juvenile in trouble or a family on welfare — or where a composite person is created to represent a variety of similar individuals, the artifice must be explained promptly. It is a device that cannot be used often without losing impact.

Involving Head Office

Stories from unnamed sources pack much potential for harm against an individual or an institution. Thoughtless journalism damages careers, personal lives, companies and public faith in the media. It also can hurt CP's reputation and its legal position in any suits that might arise.

Safeguards have been designed to help ensure that major stories with potential for harm get plenty of thoughtful evaluation before being rushed into print.

Bureaus with major news breaks involving unnamed sources and with legal and ethical implications must follow these steps:

1.   Have counsel review the story.

2.   After legal checks, the bureau supervisor must set up a telephone conference with the Editor-in-Chief and a Main Desk editor.

3.   The conference will answer questions such as:

(a) Who are the sources? How credible are they? What motives exist for a leak of information? Can further verification be obtained?

(b) What public good will the story serve? What are the legal risks? What ethical considerations are involved?

4. Every opportunity to respond must be given to the person or institution involved. Where conscientious effort does not produce a response, the story must detail the attempts made and the reasons why no response was provided.

A final caution: The source who does not want to be named in copy will rarely be available for CP's defence in the event of court action. This could leave us with no defence and lacking any ability to prove what we distributed for public consumption.

Describing unnamed sources

News sources given anonymity should be identified as specifically as possible.

Sources said is bare bones and lacks credibility. Also don't use the hackneyed or meaningless phrases **political observers** and **senior officials** and adjectives like **key, informed, veteran.**

Use specifics that give readers reason to read and believe the story: **An industry source who has been involved in the negotiations, a west European diplomat familiar with the case, a Finance Department official who worked on the draft.**

Internet sources

The Internet can be a quick source for a vast array of information in the form of raw data, official records and electronic mail.

There is no special protection when reporting information obtained online. And online sources can easily lie about their identity. Verify information obtained online just as vigorously as that obtained from other sources.

Don't use the Internet for a fishing expedition or to prove a point. Material gathered through electronic means, especially that of an anecdotal nature, should be the starting point, not the final word, on a story.

Women as sources

A balanced news report will provide a full range of voices and perspectives, including those of women. Reporters should make a conscious effort to broaden their usual lists of sources to include the women experts in every field. That means not just for topics like child care, equal pay and family violence but also the economy, sports, commodity trading, science, the law and all other news areas.

A well-equipped news desk should include the *Media Directory of Women* and other compilations of contact numbers for women in a variety of spheres.

Taste and tough calls

Today's public demands that the media do their work with more compassion, exhibit more good taste and intrude less on individual privacy. On the other hand, some segments of the public dote on gore and salacious detail.

How far to go in informing the public is a dilemma faced every day.

Do we publish the photo of the University of Montreal student slumped dead in her seat while a plainclothes police officer pulls down holiday decorations in the background?

Baseball player David Wells shows his displeasure with the media shortly after he was traded from the New York Yankees to the Toronto Blue Jays. Strong opinions arose about the publication of this photo. Several newspapers used it on the front page; others chose not to because they thought it would offend readers.

(CP – Frank Gunn)

Some newspapers did, arguing that the dramatic illustration made readers stop and think about the enormity of the Montreal massacre. Other editors said the photo intruded without sufficient cause on the privacy of the young woman's family and friends.

Were the bounds of decency overstepped by publishing the photos of Rajiv Gandhi's shattered corpse after the former Indian prime minister was assassinated with a bomb?

When a Pennsylvania civil servant, distressed by his own wrongdoing, puts a revolver in his mouth at a news conference and pulls the trigger, what restraints should we use in publishing the photos and in describing the scene?

What about the photo of the nude Vietnamese girl fleeing a napalm attack? Or the shocking photo of a South Vietnamese police chief executing a Viet Cong prisoner by shooting him in the head with a handgun?

These are tough calls, with strongly felt opinions on each side.

At CP we approach each tough call thoughtfully, relying on our experience, good taste and news judgment to help us make the right decision. We weigh carefully what the public needs to know and wants to know against what some might consider repugnant.

CP does enjoy some protection in that it does not transmit directly to the public except in its cable television, radio and online news operations. We expect that our member newspapers edit our stories and review our photos before deciding whether to publish them.

We must not act as their censors, rejecting material based on standards that are much more stringent than they, or their reading public, are willing to accept.

That said, our members pay us to select and edit and we must not abandon journalistic standards and principles on the premise that the final gatekeepers are the newspaper editors.

Some guidelines:

1.   An individual's grief is personal and private. CP respects privacy and does not exploit grief to enhance the news.

2.   That applies to funerals. Before covering any funeral, we must ask ourselves: What possible important information will we gain for the public by intruding on this intensely private event?

➤ See **Obituaries**, page 68.

3.   Flag questionable stories and photos with an editors' note to alert newspapers that the material might offend some readers.

4. When dealing with grieving sources, be respectful and understanding. Don't push your way in. Most people are willing to share their thoughts in situations involving grief, provided there is legitimate public interest. Don't ask people how they feel about a loss.

5.   Public interest must also be carefully weighed when deciding whether to publish the identity of a victim. Details of some crimes are so graphic that naming the victim can only cause more anguish to the innocent party. This can be especially harmful when publishing the victim's name serves no public purpose and adds nothing to the story.

Terrorism, hostage-takings

No news story is worth someone's life. Going for the scoop at any cost when lives are at stake belongs to a time long past.

A man holds a knife to the throat of a teenager as he talks to police during a hostage-taking incident in Quebec. CP has a clear policy on handling breaking news on hostage-takings.

(Journal de Québec – Benoit Gariepy)

That's why we treat terrorist incidents and hostage-takings with extreme caution: They are life-and-death situations.

We have a responsibility to report the news but we have an even greater responsibility to ensure that our actions in news-gathering and reporting do not endanger human lives.

We do not want to become an open publicity line for terrorists, give unwitting support to terrorist causes or impede anti-terrorist efforts.

Some specific guides for dealing with terrorist incidents and hostage-takings:

1.   Notify police immediately when you receive a phone call, fax or note about an unpublicized hostage-taking or other terrorist act. Make all information available to police.

2.   Do not move a story before checking a senior editorial supervisor at Head Office.

3.   If the story is approved, write that the information was given to **a news organization** without naming CP. Naming CP would risk having it become an outlet for terrorist publicity.

4.   Never telephone the terrorists or their hostages without the approval of a senior editorial supervisor at Head Office. If approval is received, consult the same supervisor again before moving a story.

5.   Do not detail police or security countermeasures or any other information that might aid the terrorists.

6.   We will not tailor or distribute terrorist demands or platforms without Head Office approval. Head Office will not give approval without consulting police or government, or both.

7.   Translate the language of terrorists and police for readers: use plain English such as **note** and **kill** for **communique** and **execute**.

8.   Also consult a supervisor on how to handle terrorism stories received from foreign agencies such as AP and Reuters. What's acceptable to other agencies might not fit CP standards and ethics.

9.   Keep our newspapers informed by advisories when policy restraints affect coverage.

For additional details consult the July 9, 1987, written policy on Reporting on Terrorism and Hostage-takings.

General

Analyses

The CP News Analysis tests the best qualities that reporters and editors can bring to the news report.

The writer must know the subject intimately to give the reader an informed, intelligent and reasoned assessment of the issues involved. Newspapers look to the CP News Analysis to give their readers a clear and unbiased understanding of what has happened or may happen — and why.

An analysis cannot be done on the run. It demands careful thought and unhurried discussion with a number of outside experts.

Most important: an analysis is not a soapbox. It can focus on a single perspective or point of view, but that perspective must be dispassionate and logical. Opposing views must not be neglected.

Some guidelines:

1. The CP News Analysis is usually built around a single thesis: the new tax will have little effect on consumer spending; the Opposition leader's staff is hurting her image. The thesis is supported by material marshalled in logical order. Objections can be noted, experts cited and secondary angles explored a bit. But the analysis should never lose sight of the main theme by jumbling it with distractions.

2. The analysis should open the reader's eyes, not belabour the obvious. Worthwhile analyses can be built on an unconventional viewpoint, a perspective that hasn't been explored much in the past, a prediction that seems calm when others are confused or even hysterical.

3. The analysis should strike the right balance and tone in the first paragraph. It should not be cute or hyper. Get right to the point:

CP News Analysis
By Robert Russo

WASHINGTON (CP) — An impressive American force is again being marshalled in the Middle East and a spasm of cruise missiles may soon be streaking over Saddam Hussein's head, but the aim of a limited strike against Iraq may be more psychological than strategic.

There is little doubt that anything short of a massive invasion of Iraq will not achieve the stated goal of restoring meaningful United Nations weapons inspection, several military analysts said.

---

4. The CP News Analysis is not a substitute for the CP Backgrounder. The analysis focuses more on perspective than on factual background while the backgrounder leans more toward straight-ahead treatment of the major issues in a complex news story.

5. Analyses do not float a writer's pet theory. They do not pass judgment. They do not offer the writer's solutions. These are CP News Analyses and writers should consider every line of them from that perspective. Some newspapers, in fact, remove individual bylines and attribute analyses to CP, period. CP must be able to stand behind every word of every analysis. That means editorializing — or anything that can be construed as editorializing — is out.

Unacceptable: Wilson, publicly crippled by his inability to get fellow Conservatives on side, now must start a new round of negotiations with special-interest groups.

Acceptable: Wilson must now resume negotiations with special-interest groups in the knowledge that his previous efforts failed to draw support from fellow Conservatives on this specific aspect of his tax-reform package.

Never try to build a case with adjectival powder when mortar in the form of facts and thoughtful opinion is lacking. Keep digging or abandon the story as a lost cause.

6. Keep loaded phrases and words out of analyses. They can turn a sound argument into instant rhetoric — and send a reader away.

Unacceptable: The decision to impose the GST during a recession was based strictly on political considerations, but it will haunt government candidates in the next election. (Two errors: CP is speculating on motivation and CP is making a hard prediction.)

Acceptable: Opposition MPs see pure political strategy behind the decision to impose the GST two years before an election even if it worsens the recession. Among government MPs, there is fear that even two years won't be long enough to soften voters' anger about the new tax. (The information is the same, but the sources for it are people in a position to say.)

7. Many analyses lend themselves to human touches. In a piece dealing with a major corporate shakeup, for example, a reader might wonder what elements in a new chief executive officer's background particularly qualify her for the top job. Who are the political winners and losers in a federal throne speech? What is the likely impact of a cabinet shuffle on the new or shifted ministers' prospects in the next election?

8. The one-voice *analysis* has no place in the CP news report. Instead, analyses should attempt to synthesize opinion and be as well sourced as news stories. They should give the reader a sense of the sources who have been consulted, even if they must be unnamed. In an analysis on aboriginal issues, for example, it makes a big difference whether the issues are looked at through the eyes of academics or aboriginals themselves.

9. Avoid over-attribution — a constant **he said, she said**. Often a general line early in an analysis can help.

. . . **interviews with several senior Liberal party members.**

This gives the reader a sense that the writer has done his homework.

10. The CP writer's own observations and conclusions can be helpful in shaping some analyses. For example, a reporter who has covered a major environmental story from its beginnings to a key development months later should have the background and understanding to assess the situation fairly and from all perspectives. More often, however, the analysis flows from exhaustive research, an uncluttered understanding of the issues involved and solid contact with sources on all sides of those issues.

11. Analyses should be written as close as possible to the news event to heighten their impact. Many papers use CP News Analyses on their front pages, sometimes as the main story.

12. A writer assigned to an analysis on a fixed time event, such as an election night, should not be assigned other duties. He or she will require an uncluttered mind (and desk) to concentrate on the event and its meaning for readers.

In these cases, it should usually be possible to rough out a couple of potential analyses based on different outcomes. If, for example, it appeared possible that the NDP could be elected for the first time in a province, some obvious questions could be explored in advance. What will an NDP government mean in everyday terms for everyday people in that province? Are the New Democrats likely to make major changes? Will people lose their jobs? Will the new government have difficulties dealing with the old-line parties in Ottawa? What has been the experience of other provinces with NDP governments?

13. No analysis should be distributed without being seen by a senior supervisor such as a News Editor or Bureau Chief.

14. Copy should be slugged **CP News Analysis**. There should always be a double keyword slug — one word indicating the subject, the other identifying the piece as an analysis. The label **CP News Analysis** is intended to be publishable. It goes directly above the writer's byline and below the headline.

BC-Filmon-Analysis, Bgt
Budget
See CP Photo WPG7

Vote-rigging scandal cuts close to premier

                        CP News Analysis
                        By Scott Edmonds

WINNIPEG (CP) — . . .

CP Backgrounders

When it's time to pull a maze of news threads together or to stand back from a particularly confusing story, the CP Backgrounder is the vehicle of choice — and a welcome friend to the reader.

Above all, the CP Backgrounder gives the reader the answers to basic questions: What's really going on here? What does it mean to me and my families and my neighbours?

CP Backgrounders, formerly known in-house as *situationals*, differ from CP News Analyses. Essentially, the analysis builds a structure of interpretation upon a foundation of factual material. The backgrounder focuses on the foundation stones through an orderly assembly of factual detail and perspective.

The backgrounder provides historical context, sets out the whys and wherefores of a complicated issue in the news, explores legal questions or lists the pocketbook impact of the development under review.

Where appropriate, the backgrounder will also quote knowledgeable authorities — or everyday people with first-hand experience in similar circumstances — about future implications for the lives of readers.

A strong sense of a key player's human side is usually needed to give the reader an understanding of the personalities involved.

There is no practical limit to the kinds of situations that can be served by a well-thought-out backgrounder:

• The history of Dr. Henry Morgentaler's battles with the legal system, as a scene-setter for his latest court test.

• How Prairie farmers are coping with a string of bad luck: drought, debt, coyotes and grasshoppers.

• How the premier has pulled her party together at the last minute to head into an election, with the story focusing on her persuasive personality and political savvy.

• Why some major corporations are lopping off subsidiaries after years of bigger-is-better thinking.

• What's behind a new NHL rule on facemasks, reviewing a rash of facial injuries from a doctor's perspective.

Effective backgrounders can often be worked up on matters that might otherwise receive only passing attention in the spot news report.

An example:

Business interests, local residents and nature lovers are locked in a battle over a proposed tourism development in the North. What is at stake? Why are the various sides in conflict? How have the battle lines been drawn?

The story could include interesting sketches of people on each side of the dispute, description and history of the area being fought over and some sense of the values being promoted — a rare breeding ground for song birds versus jobs in a high unemployment area, for example.

The writing approach to such stories is as wide open as the imagination of the writer. It often helps to focus on a specific element in a many-sided situation or on a single human being directly involved.

Be wary of the grab-bag lead that tries to gather in a large number of major components. It is an approach that rarely works.

Point form can be especially effective in setting out key issues or background to give the reader some fast and tidy context.

A backgrounder on the Atlantic provinces, for instance, could hit points like this high up in the story:

• The four provinces have 194 legislature members and 34,000 civil servants for a population of 2.2 million. Alberta, with a population of 2.4 million, has 83 legislature members and 12,000 civil servants.

• Newfoundland gets 47 cents of every government dollar from the federal treasury; P.E.I. 46 cents; New Brunswick and Nova Scotia 39 cents each.

• The cap on federal transfer payments has already cut $400 million from the amount the region had been counting on, and more cuts seem certain.

Style

The label **CP Backgrounder** is intended to be publishable. It goes directly above the writer's byline and below the headline.

AM-ENVIR-Tourism-Bkgrndr, Bgt
Budget
See CP Photo CPT17; CP Graphic CPT3

Town turns to tourism to help economy

CP Backgrounder
By Ian Bailey
SIOUX LOOKOUT, Ont. (CP) — . . .

Business news

Business news is about companies, industry, trade, commerce, finance and the economy. But ultimately it concerns people — their jobs, mortgages, bank accounts, investments and long-term prosperity.

Changes in economic conditions affect people. And people's behaviour can influence the economy.

- The merger of two companies, for example, may combine their strengths and improve production efficiency. But it may also mean lost jobs.

- Consumers continuing to spend despite signs of an impending recession may temporarily delay the start of the downturn.

- Higher interest rates could mean a higher Canadian dollar, which benefits someone travelling abroad but hurts exporters. Closer to home, higher interest rates may mean a bigger monthly mortgage payment, but savings in the bank may earn a bit more interest.

Business news deals with fluctuations in financial markets. As much as possible, business stories should explain what the price movements indicate. To what extent do they reflect investors' perception of economic conditions or a company's prospects? How much of the change is affected by political events? By sheer speculation? Is there a herd mentality at work? How about the interplay of greed and fear?

Like other news, business news occurs within the context of society. Bottom lines can be affected by developments in areas not traditionally associated with business. Environmental concerns, new standards of ethics and morality, the spread of AIDS, an aging population — these are some of the factors that can affect a company's prospects.

Similarly, business news in Canada is affected by what goes on elsewhere. A war in the Middle East could improve the economic outlook of oil-producing western provinces. The discovery of a cheaper and better substitute overseas may hurt the prospects of Canadian producers of, say, lumber or steel. Eventually, people who work in these industries feel the effect.

Business reporting

There is a great appetite for timely business news among newspapers, broadcasters, Internet news services, so-called day traders on the stock market and the corporate world. There are many news sources and services, all competing to be first with their stories.

While there's a premium on getting the story first, accuracy must always be the top priority. The business community is the biggest rumour mill around, and a rumour picked up by a media outlet can have a great effect on stock prices. Be careful. Check reports with more than one source.

Discard the assumption that business writing has to be staid, uninteresting and faceless. Business stories are often dynamic and colourful, driven by compelling personalities making their way through a constantly changing economic landscape.

Business writers should keep in mind two kinds of readers: general readers who want to keep up with what is happening in the business world; and business readers who want information on investments, the economy and developments in fields related to their own. But both audiences appreciate easy-to-read stories that are free of jargon.

Graphics can cover background or related information for which there is no room in a business story. This graphic presents statistics that give the reader useful background to help understand the main news announcement: the controversial privatization of a Crown-owned coal mine.

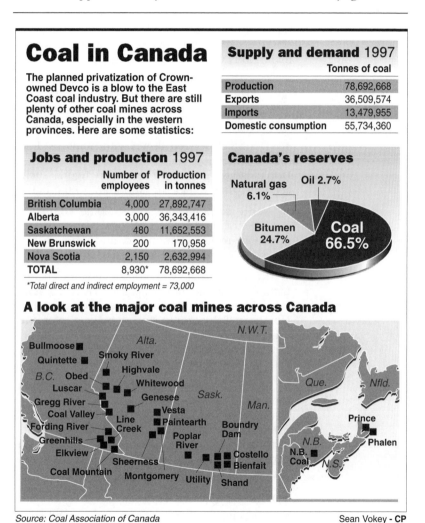

Coal in Canada

The planned privatization of Crown-owned Devco is a blow to the East Coast coal industry. But there are still plenty of other coal mines across Canada, especially in the western provinces. Here are some statistics:

Supply and demand 1997

Tonnes of coal

Production	78,692,668
Exports	36,509,574
Imports	13,479,955
Domestic consumption	55,734,360

Jobs and production 1997

	Number of employees	Production in tonnes
British Columbia	4,000	27,892,747
Alberta	3,000	36,343,416
Saskatchewan	480	11,652,553
New Brunswick	200	170,958
Nova Scotia	2,150	2,632,994
TOTAL	8,930*	78,692,668

*Total direct and indirect employment = 73,000

Canada's reserves

Natural gas 6.1%
Oil 2.7%
Bitumen 24.7%
Coal 66.5%

A look at the major coal mines across Canada

Bullmoose
Quintette
Smoky River
Highvale
B.C. Obed
Whitewood
Luscar
Genesee
Sask.
Gregg River
Vesta
Coal Valley
Line Creek
Paintearth
Man.
Fording River
Boundry Dam
Greenhills
Poplar River
Elkview
Costello
Coal Mountain
Sheerness
Bienfait
Montgomery Utility Shand
Alta.
N.W.T.
Que.
Nfld.
Prince
N.B.
Phalen
N.B. Coal
N.S.

Source: Coal Association of Canada   Sean Vokey - **CP**

Common pitfalls

•   Check all figures. One extra digit can throw a number off completely. A single letter turns million into billion.

•   Watch accounting terms. Net operating income and net income, for example, can be quite different things.

- Watch percentages. A statement that a company's profit is up 50 per cent isn't helpful without the raw numbers: $150 is 50 per cent more than $100, and $1.5 million is 50 per cent more than $1 million. Include actual figures.

- Don't make readers do the math in stories that compare numbers such as unemployment reports or corporate earnings. Include the current figure, the percentage increase or decrease, and last year's figure.

- Be wary of corporate self-interest in all aspects of business reporting. Remember that securities analysts are not unbiased observers of a company or sector. They work in an industry whose main job is to promote stock trading.

- Companies often use polls to increase brand awareness and market new products. Ask yourself if the poll provides newsworthy information. Question statistics to ensure they are not being used selectively by companies and lobby groups to advance their interests.

- Don't get bogged down with numbers. Use numbers that tell the reader something, such as net profit or revenues or earnings per share. Don't load the story with secondary figures such as cash flow or capital spending unless they are important to the news peg.

- Verify corporate identities. Some companies have similar names but are not directly related, or one may be a subsidiary of another. Appliance-maker **Camco Inc.** and uranium producer **Cameco Corp.** are in entirely different lines of business.

- Keep up to date with corporate name changes; **Northern Telecom Ltd.**, for example, now calls itself **Nortel Networks** to reflect its latest acquisitions and growth strategy, even though it's still incorporated as **Northern Telecom**. In stories, make a reference to what the company used to be called if the change was recent or the new name is not easily recognizable. Product names are also bought and sold – check with the company concerned.

- Be careful when using the term **bankruptcy**. A troubled company can ask a court for bankruptcy protection from creditors as it restructures and carries out business as usual. That doesn't mean it's bankrupt, although it can be called insolvent. If a court-monitored restructuring can't be done, creditors can petition the company into bankruptcy, which means its assets will be sold and the firm will go out of business.

Some suggestions

- Keep human faces high in the story whenever possible. It's a way of saying a corporate development affects people in real life. For example, if **Really Clean Inc.** announced a layoff of 150 employees, an effective approach to the story might be:

James Lee walked home from work to save bus fare. He and 140 of his co-workers at Really Clean received layoff notices Friday.

- Always ask how any development is likely to affect the reader. Some events, such as World Trade Organization negotiations, may have no immediate impact on readers but their long-term impact can be significant, affecting the Canadian economy and such things as egg and butter prices. Banking reforms in Japan may not directly affect Canada, but they may help boost the Japanese economy and lift demand for lumber, minerals and other products imported from Canada.

• When doing stories about economic predictions – especially bank and corporate forecasts of the coming year – try to include the previous year's forecast and how accurate it was. That helps readers decide how much weight to give the report.

• Concepts such as unemployment are hard to define statistically and can be measured differently in Canada and other countries. In Canada, the jobless numbers released each month don't include part-time workers or discouraged workers – people who have given up looking for work. That means the true jobless rate may be higher than the official count.

• Keep long corporate names or unfamiliar acronyms out of the first paragraph. Instead, use a short name that may be readily recognized, or a quick explanation of the type of business. The full name can be included a bit later in the story.

• It sometimes helps to mention a company's best-known products. For example: **Scott Paper, the company that makes White Swan tissue** . . .

• Complex corporate relationships, company holdings or a corporate history might best be laid out in a sidebar, a chart or a QuickFacts box. This allows the story to deal with the impact of a development.

• Translate business jargon into plain English. If a technical term must be included, explain what it means.

Tips for CP writers and editors

• Business stories on interest rates, company shutdowns, expansions or big shifts in stock markets and the dollar frequently find their way on to general news pages. Such stories should be filed as general news items and flagged: **Eds: Business interest.** A business designator should be used for all other items: routine company reports and annual meetings, a new twist in options trading, corporate takeovers, personal finance copy and the like.

• Some companies and organizations make the same announcement in two or more cities, or make a telephone conference call available to reporters from across the continent in hopes of getting many stories written on the same subject. As well, a company president will visit several places within a few days, delivering the same message to different groups. CP should avoid duplicating coverage of the same event. However, watch for regional angles that might be presented in one place only. If in doubt, check the archives or consult with the Business Editor or Main Desk.

• National reports can also yield important regional stories. Statistics Canada job figures that show British Columbia leading the country in growth could be developed by the regional bureau into a broader story explaining what's behind the numbers.

- Include stock symbols (in the **Index** line of slugging) in stories about companies listed on Canadian exchanges. This is valued information for readers who follow investment news closely.

- Good illustrations for business pages can be hard to come by and therefore are in great demand. Reporters should think about possibilities for a good graphic or photograph when they get their business-news assignment, so graphics editors can start planning. If a steel company is expected to report sharply lower year-end earnings in the next few days, alert the photo desk so a photographer can be sent out to get a shot of workers leaving the plant. This gives editors a livelier picture to work with than might otherwise be available on deadline. Annual meetings can be a good source of people pictures, whether of a reclusive chairman or an angry shareholder. Corporate Web sites can provide charts and other illustrations.

Business terms

Bonds, debentures
The buyer of **bonds** or **debentures** is a creditor who lends money to the company for a fixed term at an agreed interest rate.

Debentures are unsecured promises to repay the loan. Corporate **bonds** are ordinarily secured by fixed assets. Although government securities are often called bonds, they are actually debentures – guaranteed by the government but without assets being pledged. If a company goes out of business, secured creditors' claims on its assets have priority over claims of other creditors and preferred shareholders, who in turn are ahead of common shareholders.

Cash flow
Refers to a company's cash resources. Many companies like to focus on this figure in their earnings report. They usually call it EBITDA – earnings before interest, taxes, depreciation and amortization. Unlike earnings, cash flow includes interest, taxes, depreciation and amortization. It gives a more useful picture of a company's financial position.

Consolidated statement
A financial statement that includes the results of subsidiary companies. This is usually done when the parent company owns 50 per cent or more of a subsidiary. For example, when Imasco Ltd. of Montreal issues financial reports, it consolidates results from its major operating units – Imperial Tobacco, the Shoppers Drug Mart chain, Canada Trust and real estate developer Genstar.

Extraordinary items
Year-over-year comparisons of net profit can be distorted in a year when, for example, plants and equipment are sold or the value of investments or assets is written down because they have lost market value. A big layoff or restructuring will also dramatically affect a company's bottom line because of severance and restructuring costs. In general, focus on the figures that give a true picture of a company's performance. BCE Inc. might say it had an annual profit of $1.4 billion from operations but wrote off $2.9 billion in assets, posting a net loss

of $1.5 billion. But that doesn't mean BCE is in trouble, since the writeoff was an accounting measure and not a loss of cash.

For a meaningful comparison from year to year, it is usually necessary to look as well at **net profit** before **extraordinary items,** generally referred to as operating profit or profit from operations. Whenever possible, try for longer-term comparisons such as a five-year range or average. Figures should be given for comparable earlier periods.

Financing
Equity financing means raising money through the sale of common shares. The buyer becomes a part-owner of the company.

Debt financing means raising money through bonds and debentures. The buyer lends money to the company, which promises to repay the amount in the future with interest.

Net profit, net income, net earnings
The three terms means the same thing – a company's profit (or loss) after all expenses and taxes have been paid. It is out of **net profit** that dividends are paid – first to preferred shareholders, then to common shareholders.

Net operating profit
Money earned from a company's operations – the sale of its products or services. It should not be confused with **net profit,** which includes both income from operations and non-operating sources like rents, interest and investments.

Net earnings per share
Obtained by deducting from net profit any amount paid to preferred shareholders, and dividing the resulting amount by the number of common shares outstanding. It is a key figure that investors, analysts and other players in the financial industry consider in determining the performance of a company. Companies often take a beating in the stock market when their earnings per share fall short of analysts' predictions.

Revenues
A company's overall sales and money earned from other sources. This should not be mistaken for profits. The cost of doing business, including wages, is subtracted to get profits.

Share, stock
A part-ownership of a company obtained by providing capital to the business. **Common shareholders** have the right to vote in the company. If the company performs well, shareholders benefit from the rise in the value of the shares. The term **a share** refers to a common share unless otherwise stated.

Preferred shares entitle the holder to a fixed dividend from net profit before common shareholders are paid. Preferred shares generally carry no voting privileges as long as promised dividends are paid.

Company meetings and reports

Some Canadian companies like Hudson's Bay Co. and Molson Cos. Ltd. played important roles in the country's economic development. Other firms have been the economic bedrock of their community, providing both employment and tax dollars. Some occupy pivotal positions in their sector of the economy. Their financial health and future plans are often news of wide interest.

Company meetings and reports can provide information on how these companies are doing and where they are going financially. Company Web sites can supply many of these documents.

Stories based on company reports need not be dry recitals of statistics. Many companies explain in their reports why profits are small or sales have increased. This kind of information, along with background on the company and its products, can brighten the story and give it depth.

Foreign currencies

In stories from most parts of the world it is best to convert amounts into Canadian dollars. (The daily item slugged **BC-Tab-Foreign-Exchange** can be used to convert many foreign currencies into Canadian dollars.) Allied agencies usually provide U.S. dollar figures. Convert them and use phrases like **the equivalent of $500 Cdn** to avoid giving the impression that people elsewhere use the Canadian currency. The **Cdn** is usually necessary only on first reference.

Note: In these days of fluctuating currency levels, when doing conversions it is often a good idea to keep the original currency amount in the story, especially in items concerning major takeovers and acquisitions. This makes it easier for editors using the story as background later to determine the exchange rate that was used.

Conversions are not done in the following cases:

1. U.S. dollar figures may be kept in copy with U.S. placelines. Specify the currency on first reference:

NEW YORK (CP) – Seagram Co. Ltd. said Monday it will spend more than $10 billion US to buy PolyGram, the world's biggest record company. The deal will also mean Seagram will put its juice division up for sale, for about $3 billion.

2. Most of the world's commodities – gold, oil, nickel, lumber and pulp and paper – are traded on world markets in U.S. dollars. In business copy and routine financial items it is acceptable to keep U.S. dollar prices. In broader stories, it may be desirable to include a Canadian dollar equivalent in one or two examples.

Note: In stories where U.S. and Canadian dollars are both used, add an Editors' Note: **EDs: The following figures are in Canadian dollars unless otherwise stated.**

Precise figures

Precise figures are preferred in routine financial items but should be rounded off in business stories.

VANCOUVER (CP) – MacMillan Bloedel Ltd., one of the country's biggest forestry companies, reported a net profit of $42.1 million last year, a big turnaround from a loss of $367.9 million the year before.

Two daily items that need precise figures are: **BC-Earnings**, a roundup of financial results (three months, six months, nine months and annual) reported by publicly traded Canadian companies; and **BC-Dividends**, as declared by Canadian companies.

BC-Earnings
By The Canadian Press
Canadian earnings declared Wednesday:
MacMillan Bloedel: Year ended Dec. 31, 1998, $42,000,000, $0.29 a share; 1997 net loss $368,000,000, net loss $2.99 a share. Revenue: 1998, $4,183,000,000; 1997, $4,521,000,000.

BC-Dividends
By The Canadian Press
Corporate dividends declared Monday (quarterly unless otherwise indicated):
Extendicare Inc.: Class II Pref. Series 1, $0.113. Payable March 15. Record Feb. 26.
First Australia Prime Investment Co.: Common, $0.08. Payable March 15. Record Feb. 26.

Note: If an extra dividend is declared, say so.

Elections

Public-opinion polls and clever election strategists have dramatically changed the election process in Canada. So have skeptical and savvy voters.

Fund-raising has become an art, candidates' personalities are carefully polished, campaigns are stage-managed for maximum television exposure, news is manipulated. And yet the voters grow ever more wary of elections and intolerant of manipulative politics.

News coverage must adapt to the changes, looking for more effective ways of describing the process and involving the voters. Television has become a more influential factor in campaigns, but print reporting still has an important role.

Quebec Premier Lucien Bouchard greets supporters after being re-elected in 1998. There is always tremendous pressure to get photos out in time for newspaper deadlines on election nights.

(CP – Tom Hanson)

Some of CP's criteria for an effective news report on an election:

1. **Let the voters, not the politicians, decide what the issues are.**

Campaign coverage that is focused heavily on candidates' travels and statements may be irrelevant to readers. For example, if all the major parties are concentrating on constitutional issues, where does that leave voters worried about their jobs or the air they breathe or the fact that their kids have trouble reading?

Political reporters need to recognize that getting the *tough* one-liner snapped off by a cabinet minister with an eye on the 6 o'clock TV news is often less important than spending 20 minutes talking to voters in the minister's riding.

If reporters listen to what's on the voters' minds, and put those concerns to the candidates, readers may decide the media are worth paying attention to.

The alternative is to allow politicians to decide what's news.

A sound election file can be built by focusing on the party leaders and the apparent issues in the first week or two of the campaign. From then until the final days, the focus should shift to pinpointing what's bothering the voters, explaining the background to the big issues and clarifying the parties' stands on voter concerns.

2. **Be prepared.**

Surprise elections are rare. Supervisors and political reporters aware of an impending election will (a) set up a clear organization for covering the campaign; (b) establish their news priorities; (c) put profiles of the party leaders and other basic backgrounders *in the bank* for use when the election is called.

As the campaign unfolds, measure out special takeouts on the issues dear to the voters' hearts. Some regional issues become important enough to swing whole areas, so they need sensitive explanation. Some unlikely candidates will come on strong and need profiling. Issues like party funding, television ads, all-candidates debates, minor parties and historical trends are often worth looking at.

Election campaigns are also a test of CP's relationship with newspapers and broadcasters. Getting their news supervisors on side ahead of time can mean timely reports on major developments and a consistent supply of spot and feature material from all over a bureau's region.

Being prepared also means recognizing that the general public has lots of other interests besides politics. Campaign coverage shouldn't deprive readers of other news that's important to them.

3. **Don't forget the libel laws.**

Statements are sometimes made in the heat of an election campaign that in other circumstances would be pretty good grounds for a libel suit.

Some basic legal ground rules:

a) A fair and accurate report of public statements made at a meeting that's open to the general public isn't usually risky. But that may not apply if only some members of the public (say, one party's members) are allowed into the meeting. And if a person attacked at the meeting wants to respond, the response must be reported.

b) Potentially libellous statements made in other circumstances — even a radio broadcast — are not safe to publish. Get legal advice.

c) Some provincial and federal laws limit certain forms of campaigning and advertising just before voting day. Check election laws for pitfalls.

4. **Provide context, colour, detail.**

Reporting on campaign activities means making sense of the political statements. It also means bringing the campaign to life.

Context: What would the promise of a new housing policy mean for house prices? Construction jobs? Increased government debt and taxes? How does the new policy compare with past promises, the other parties' positions? What do outside experts think of it? Not all such questions will be worth answering, but few political statements of any importance should be left to stand alone.

Colour: Most politicians are scarcely known to the public. They often need to be described in action, gesturing and raising their voices to emphasize a point or laughing at the hecklers or making small talk on the street. The towns and crossroads where they campaign should be sketched. The campaign audiences should be shown responding or watching skeptically.

In both context and colour, be specific.

Not: The premier promised to cut government spending.

Instead: For the farm crowd in Ruralia, the premier promised to cut loan guarantees for big business. At the Middleton Rotary Club, she said there would be fewer tax concessions for shopping malls. Back in the capital, she worried about the cost of irrigation projects and secondary roads.

5. **For election night, again be prepared.**

Smooth, comprehensive coverage of election results depends on thorough advance work. It's too late to look for background information when the voting results are flooding in.

Prepare: profile material on the leaders and any candidates important to the overall coverage; background on the major issues and how the parties stood on them; the range of public-opinion poll results; the best of the campaign anecdotes to lighten up the stories.

Also: statistical histories of which parties have formed the government and when; figures on the size of majorities for past governments; information on minority governments, the defeat of governments and their leaders, the national situation for each major party.

(Most newspapers and broadcasters depend on CP for detailed results, gathered progressively at a single election centre. The results are delivered in ready-to-use formats from a computer programmed to make instantaneous adjustments in vote totals, winners and losers, party votes and other categories. The material is invaluable for those writing lead stories and separates at CP and other media.)

6. **Down with hype.**

The frenzy of election night can be the enemy of clear thinking.

It's common in Canadian elections for one party to win a substantial majority of seats with barely 40 per cent of the votes. That doesn't constitute a **landslide** of popular support. Stories about the result need precise wording.

And sweeping statements about the voters' feelings or intentions are risky. Each voter in a federal or provincial election makes a choice among local candidates, period. Each constituency result is probably influenced by broader issues and the popularity of the party leaders, but they aren't on the ballot.

It's stretching things to write baldly that voters **rejected a spending freeze** or **punished the government for failing to cut unemployment**. The effect of all those individual votes will be a government with some stated commitments. That's the surest way to describe the election result. Informed political observers can help keep the influence of national or provincial factors in perspective.

7. **The cleanup.**

Election campaigns don't end on election night. The days immediately following an election bring some of the most significant stories.

Supervisors need to ensure that fresh staff is available for two or three days after an election to complete reporting on how the results will affect voters.

Working from notes left over by election-night supervisors, the next-day staff should clean up loose ends — late polls, possible recounts, missing ballot boxes.

They can also concentrate on reaching the experts who will help make better sense of the results. They can examine the detailed results more closely for victories and defeats that were overlooked. And CP staff can exploit newspaper material that was neglected in the rush of election night.

8. **Plan for the next one.**

The start of good coverage of the next election begins with a thoughtful file on this one. Before the ink is dry on coverage of any election, a file should be opened that includes:

• Careful notes from supervisors on everything that went well and everything that went wrong — and why.

• Notes from reporters and deskers on how to improve election coverage. Everyone who took part should have something to contribute.

• Examples of the best and the worst stories from the campaign, your own or others'.

• Copies of all the memos, circulars, letters and other paperwork that will be needed as reminders the next time.

Entertainment

Entertainment is a catch-all title covering a broad range of activities and interests. For so-called popular tastes, there are television and radio, pop music and movies, circuses and standup comedy. For the highbrows, there are books and plays, operas and concerts, museums and balls.

Each of these categories can produce a hard-news story on any given day — everything from a fund-raising crisis at the art gallery to the arrest of a prominent actress. On other days, they'll merit a profile or feature.

Or they may be dealt with in a review or column.

News

It's often regarded as soft news, but basic principles of journalism apply to entertainment coverage.

1. **Look for hard news:** Ask the TV actor if and when he plans to move on from his current sitcom. When the tour of a controversial rap group is announced, ask police whether they'll have extra patrols when the musicians hit town. Ask the author of the new best-seller her opinion of sales taxes on books.

2. **Strive for balanced coverage:** If a songwriter complains that music royalties in Canada are tiny, check copyright laws and how royalties compare with those in other countries. When an author trashes a celebrity in a book, get comment from the star or his representatives. In articles about the state of a particular art form in Canada, include representatives from across the country.

3. **Avoid single-source stories:** When the artistic director of a theatre announces a new stage season, some insightful comments may be provided by actors, directors or even academics and drama critics about the choices. In a profile of a sexually provocative singer, talk to others — his parents, perhaps? — about his image.

4. **Inject colour and personality:** Don't say **Madonna wore a bathing suit and shoes when she entered the press room.** Say **The former Material Girl wore very little of it, except for the teeny weeny polka-dot bikini, black spike heels and a gleaming white smile.** In reviews of new works, describe the atmosphere in the hall and the reaction of the opening night audience. If a usually suave young actor trips and falls at your feet when you come to interview him, don't brush it off — include it in your article.

Think pictures and graphics. Nothing sells a story like a good illustration.

Keep section deadlines in mind. Deliver a time-sensitive story well in advance of deadline to help editors making up pages. Keep editors advised of late-breaking or short-notice material they can expect soon.

Awards

Industry awards are among the highest profile entertainment events. There are so many of them, the challenge is to determine how much and what type of coverage to give each awards event and how to develop lively, interesting copy from it.

Actors Sandra Oh and Don McKellar pose after winning Genie awards in 1999. Entertainment awards are popular with both readers and the entertainment industry.

(CP – Kevin Frayer)

Entertainment awards tend to be self-serving. Major events such as the Emmys, Grammys, Oscars, Junos, Geminis and Genies are of interest to the average reader and merit extensive coverage. Lesser-known events may warrant little or no coverage.

A little homework in advance can be valuable. For example, research may turn up that the director of a film on long-distance running suffered polio as a child.

Complete lists of winners are an important companion to stories on the event. The list should give the category first, preferably in boldface. Then on a separate line, indented, the name of the winner.

Top Female — Country
Shania Twain

Some category titles may have to be shortened to fit a single column. **Outstanding Performance by a Lead Actor in a Drama Series** might be changed to **Best Actor – Drama.**

Features

Entertainment feature-writing generally allows more freedom to inject colour, personality and imaginative writing.

Colourful metaphors or similes can sometimes paint a vivid mental image. **Rock music on television is a lion in a cage. The BMW on Rodeo Drive glistened like a well-buffed Gucci loafer.**

Summing up a well-known person in a choice phrase can do two things: distil the subject's personality for the reader, plus set a tone for the article. **The artistic film director is a 32-year-old bundle of neuroses.**

While actors may make for identifiable hooks for a story, producers and directors are often more articulate about a project and can provide fresh insight. A good entertainment story often mixes the creative insights with the star quality of a Hollywood figure.

Reviews

In a world teeming with entertainment choices, the thoughtful review is especially important to help readers decide how to spend their leisure time.

Basically, a review gives the reader a synopsis of the work with some commentary on its artistic merit or entertainment value.

Full-time reviewers have more credibility and leeway than part-timers — who would do well to approach the assignment as a news event, describing it and getting audience comment or quoting newspaper reviewers.

Reviewers should avoid cheap shots or gush. While someone like George Bernard Shaw could get away with a demolishing review, readers can be turned off by harshness or apparent unfairness.

Commentary needs to be grounded in specific detail. Saying a rock band's show was atrocious means nothing. Rather: **The lead singer was off-key on three numbers, the lighting failed during another and people at the rear of the hall complained they couldn't hear the lyrics.**

Give readers a signpost: **The band conjures up the driving rhythm of the early Rolling Stones.**

When reviewing drama or books, reveal only as much of the plot as necessary to set the scene for the review. Readers will be annoyed to have the ending revealed by a thoughtless reviewer.

Resist adopting the vocabulary of the industry. Terms such as **genre** and **film noir** smack of trendiness and they're not used by the average reader.

Flashbacks

The key to Flashbacks is to make clear why the events were important when they happened and why they deserve to be remembered now.

Newspapers always seem to have space for a nicely written historical piece on anything from Louis Riel to the October Crisis, especially one sprinkled with human touches and appealing anecdotes.

1. Flashbacks tied to anniversaries should note that connection somewhere in the first two or three paragraphs: **It was 60 years ago this week that** . . .

2. The successful Flashback starts with a strong idea, usually in one of these two categories:

a) Recognizable historical events like Prohibition and the conscription crisis, tied to a specific anniversary, or an event like the Korean War that is tied to a veterans reunion.

b) All-but-forgotten happenings that can be successfully revived for today's reader — events like the Frank landslide of 1903 that killed at least 70 people in the territory that in 1905 became Alberta.

3. Flashbacks on historical figures should usually be tied to a specific anniversary as well (birth, death, special honour, etc.) — the anniversary of Sir John A. Macdonald's first election, for example.

Lesser-known individuals can serve as the focus point for Flashbacks on major events — the security guard who was on duty the night the mine exploded; the woman whose car was lifted during the tornado.

4. Look for topics with some direct effect on people — then or now.

5. Try to find someone who was around at the time. That will be impossible in some cases, of course, so it will mean a trip to an archive or a library — public, university or newspaper — to search for contemporary accounts or comments on the incident being recalled.

6. Opportunities for colour are rife in such stories. Sometimes personal scrapbooks or letters can be helpful. Quoting the flowery language of the day can bring a dusty piece of history to life.

7. If the subject is controversial, check at least three different sources to ensure you're not quoting someone with an axe to grind.

The label **CP Flashback** is intended to be publishable. It goes directly above the writer's byline, separated by a space from photo and other service slugs. See page 41 for a comparable example.

Labour

General

Most people spend more of their waking hours at work than at anything else, including time for friends, family or leisure. They can have strong opinions about work.

That's one of the factors that make reporting on work and the workplace so demanding. There are many other complications that increase the need for accuracy and fairness.

For instance, relations between employee and employer, between labour and management, tend to be complex and sensitive.

And despite its reputation, work isn't always something people perform numbingly. For many, work is how they define themselves. For others, it's something they regularly discuss with friends and family and continually contemplate.

Workers go through periods of great ambition and satisfaction and swings of unproductiveness and discontent. They are often part of a business or profession that can boom one year and go bust the next.

And they are an increasingly transient and adapting force. Where a generation ago someone had a lifelong career, this generation of workers can expect to have two or more different careers, sometimes at the same time.

That means workers, and people seeking work, must be thoughtfully portrayed. Stories about work need to reflect that work is a focal point for many and a diversion for others. Stories need to vividly represent work's role in society and examine the many aspects of the work environment.

The new workforce

1. Although contract disputes provide the most drama, coverage of work needs to go far beyond the union-shop floor. The rapid growth of service industries, small businesses and self-employed enterprises has fuelled job creation in the last decade. Most of these workers do not have a contract and are not part of a union. Indeed, roughly 60 per cent of the workforce is not unionized.

2. Two-income families are the norm, not the exception, and the two-worker phenomenon has as much to do with economic necessity as it does with career aspirations. Having a job doesn't mean having economic security — a significant number of people using food banks in cities are the working poor.

3. An increasing number of skilled workers and skill-seeking businesses are looking for ways to alter the employee-employer relationship. With initiatives like *flex time*, more people would work from home, more would have flexible or reduced work hours, more would share jobs, more would take leaves of absence for retraining and professional development. Workplaces increasingly offer such benefits as on-site child care or fitness centres.

4. At either the urging of employees or the concession of employers, a number of highly prized workers are engaging in the process called *downshifting*, named after the tactic a Formula One driver uses to go around a hairpin curve. By reducing hours of work or taking less demanding jobs, they are trying to get out of the rat race.

5. There has been steady growth in the number of term contract employees — people hired for a specific function for a specific time. They are often paid a lump sum in lieu of benefits or pensions.

The new workplace

1. If the nature of labour is changing, so is the nature of management. Experts say more duties are being delegated, more decisions are being made by workers and more ideas are working their way up to the boardroom from the office or factory floor.

2. Consultation between workers and managers is becoming more common. The *us-against-them* approach is slowly breaking down, and partnerships among business, labour and governments in industrial and professional risk-taking have begun to appear.

3. These changes in turn produce other changes in traditional practice. Workers make concessions on salaries in exchange for bonuses tied to performance. Managers make concessions on professional leaves even if that creates short-term expertise problems.

Coverage of news about work and the workplace has to reflect such changes.

But even when covering more traditional union-management situations, the goal should be perspectives that are tied to human beings: how someone is making ends meet during a strike; how a local merchant is coping with a lockout; what prompted someone to become active in the labour movement.

Conditions of work

The basic document governing conditions for employees and workers in unionized plants and offices is the contract. Non-unionized workers generally live under more casual arrangements. Complicated economic times bring complex work arrangements that require careful, clear explanations.

Some general guides:

1. **Wages:** In contracts, always compare the previous basic or average wage with the new rate, using a recognizable job (a bricklayer in the construction industry, a production line employee in an auto plant, a senior reporter at a newspaper). When wage changes vary according to the job category, the range should be specified.

When using percentage changes in wage stories, always use actual examples of change. And compare like elements: report a $50 weekly increase in a $700 weekly salary, not a 50-cent hourly increase in a $700 weekly salary. Beware of baldly totalling percentage increases. An increase of 10 per cent now and 10 per cent next year is not a 20 per cent increase; compounded, it is 21 per cent. Don't make readers do math.

2. **Dates:** In contract stories, spell out the starting date to indicate how much retroactivity is involved in a contract settlement. Spell out the dates of further changes in the contract during its identified full term. Don't say a new contract gives workers $4 an hour more, when in fact it gives $2 now and $2 in two years' time.

3. **Inflation protection:** Mention when wage arrangements provide for additional increases if inflation is a specified rate, commonly called **indexation** or a **cola (cost-of-living-allowance) clause**, terms to be avoided except in quotes and to be explained no matter what.

4. **Job protection:** Summarize measures that shield workers from unemployment, including advance notice of layoffs or plant closings, guaranteed payments for those laid off, retraining programs, pension protection, offers of corporate transfers to other communities.

5. **Worker concessions:** In contract stories, summarize changes that might limit strikes or other activities to protest work conditions, or agreements to limit salary increases in order to protect jobs or increase the workforce.

6. **Pay equity:** Roughly defined as **equal pay for work of equal value**, pay equity is part of some provinces' legislation. It compels employers to pay women the same as men for similar work. Many contracts now feature a catch-up clause for women in specific jobs; any breakthroughs in this area should be mentioned.

7. **Non-statutory holidays:** Mention should be made of companies that provide workers with a fixed number of days off to be taken in observance of their religious or ceremonial holidays.

8. **Non-monetary issues:** Some contracts are now fought over conditions of work, including the flexibility of work hours, the ability of workers to curtail their work hours or to share jobs, the amount of continual worker training a company will provide, or health and safety issues.

These should be highlighted as interesting elements for readers with similar or contracted jobs. When estimates of the value of these benefits are carried, the source of the estimate must be given: **The company says the new child-care provisions are worth $50 a week per employee.**

When neither workers nor companies mention these aspects of a contract, try to get the information independently.

Labour organizations and affiliations

Federations

Unions are grouped in national and regional groups but have a large measure of autonomy within them. The main federations are:

Canadian Labour Congress, with 2.6 million members, formed out of the 1956 merger of the Trades and Labour Congress of Canada and the Canadian Congress of Labour. The CLC counts among its affiliates more than 50 international organizations, 20 national, three provincial and 80 directly chartered local unions. Affiliated secondary bodies include 12 provincial federations, 120 local labour councils and one labour committee. CLC headquarters is in Ottawa.

People are members of the CLC only through their affiliated unions. In larger provinces, such unions are grouped in provincial federations — the Saskatchewan Federation of Labour, for example. CLC unions also maintain local labour councils in most urban areas.

It is correct to describe the CLC as the **Canadian counterpart** of the American Federation of Labor-Congress of Industrial Organizations, but the CLC is autonomous and doesn't regard itself as affiliated with the AFL-CIO.

Confederation of National Trade Unions — in French, **Conseil des syndicats nationaux** — formerly the Canadian Catholic Confederation of Labour. The CNTU developed in Quebec from a Roman Catholic labour movement into a broad-based organization with 243,000 members. It has member unions in Newfoundland, New Brunswick and Ontario as well as Quebec, and headquarters in Montreal.

Centrale de l'enseignement du Quebec is a federation representing teachers and others in French-language Roman Catholic schools and junior colleges in Quebec. It represents 113,000 members in more than 130 affiliated units and has headquarters in Quebec City.

Centrale des syndicats democratiques, an independent federation formed in 1972 by unions that broke away from the CNTU. It represents 73,000 members in 490 unions and is based in Quebec City.

Confederation of Canadian Unions, a federation that often clashes with CLC affiliates that are U.S.-based. It consists of about 20 member unions with 17,000 members, mostly in British Columbia, and has headquarters in Toronto.

Unions

Large unions in Canada, especially those spread over a wide area, are usually broken down into locals. For example:

Canadian Union of Public Employees — 389,000 members in 2,400 locals, with headquarters in Ottawa.

National Union of Public and General Employees — 309,000 members in 1,200 locals, with headquarters in Ottawa.

National Automobile, Aerospace, Transportation and General Workers Union of Canada — 220,000 members in 280 locals, with headquarters in Toronto.

United Food and Commercial Workers International Union — 200,000 members in 875 locals, with headquarters in Toronto.

United Steelworkers of America — 180,000 members in 140 locals, with headquarters in Toronto.

Independents

Independent unions are occasionally regular labour organizations, but many are company sponsored and were organized to keep out regular trade unions.

Note: When writing about a union that has a French name only — **Syndicat des fonctionnnaires provinciaux du Quebec**, for example — avoid using the French name unless the story requires it. Paraphrase the nature of the membership — **Quebec civil servants union** — rather than invent a capitalized English name.

Union membership

Specific terms describe the various forms of union membership.

Closed shop: an employer may only hire people who are members of the union.

Union shop: an employer may select employees but all are obliged to join the union within a specified time.

Maintenance of membership: employees must retain membership for the duration of the contract.

Open shop: employees are free to join or not join a union. Workers who don't join are commonly called **free riders**, a term to avoid.

Rand formula: named after Justice Ivan Rand, who arbitrated a 1945 Ford strike. It requires all members of a bargaining unit to pay union dues but makes membership in the unit voluntary.

Checkoff: The employer acts as a collecting agent for a union by deducting dues from the employee's pay.

Laws and courts

Labour relations in Canada are divided into federal and provincial jurisdictions, each governed by a labour code.

The Canada Labour Code covers employees of federally chartered companies like banks, Crown corporations and those in such regulated businesses as transportation and communications that have interprovincial dealings. Provincial codes cover all others.

The federal code is enforced by the Canada Labour Relations Board, a quasi-judicial body that investigates and rules on union accreditations and violations of the code, such as illegal strikes and lockouts, unfair labour practices and inter-union membership raids.

Similar bodies exist in the provinces. Such functions in Quebec are filled by a labour court.

Federal civil servants are governed by the Public Service Staff Relations Board and disputes are regulated by a special act.

Conciliation

When the federal government intervenes in a dispute, there are several stages:

Stage 1: A conciliator is appointed who tries to get the sides talking.

Stage 2: A conciliation commission, often the original conciliator, is next appointed. The commission studies the issues and, unless it is felt the sides are too far apart for agreement, writes suggestions for a settlement.

Stage 3: A mediator goes back and forth to the parties and tries to craft a report for a vote by management and union membership.

Stage 4: An arbitrator can be brought in to devise a binding settlement. Arbitrators are also used in grievance procedures and, on occasion, for contract negotiations.

Provincial governments intervene in different ways, and a reporter covering a dispute under provincial jurisdiction should be aware of specific procedures that apply.

Strikes and lockouts

Strikes are the cessation of work to press the workers' position. Lockouts are the closure of all or part of an establishment to counter a work slowdown, to gain concessions from workers or to resist their position. Always distinguish between the two.

The reasons for a dispute must always be at the top of a story. Every story should say how long the strike or lockout has been in effect and the number of employees involved. Specify the average or base wage before the dispute — preferably the average.

As with any labour story, reporters should seek out the human elements when strikes or lockouts occur. There are economic consequences from a prolonged dispute for both the workers and their industry, and occasionally there are moments of violence and high drama. Less well explored are the psychological impacts for healthy workers to be away from their jobs and for managers to be in open conflict with employees.

Vocabulary

Labour-management reporting is loaded with pejoratives, so tread warily.

1. People are not **terminated** and workforces are not **downsized** or **consolidated**. People are **laid off** or **fired** and workforces are **cut**. (Avoid the term **cutbacks**. It's simply **cuts**.) Always say whether layoffs are temporary or permanent.

2. Employees are not **engaged in study sessions** or **job actions**. They have **stopped work** or **slowed work**.

3. **Scab**, a term used since 1777 for a worker who refuses to join a strike or who takes over the work of strikers, is permissible only in direct quotes; even so, use with discretion. **Strikebreaker** is a vague, rarely accurate term — a strike is seldom broken by the hiring of people to replace striking workers. A more accurate term — even though it doesn't reflect the hostility of strikers that can accompany such hiring — is **replacement worker**. In Quebec, companies are forbidden to hire outside workers to do the jobs of strikers.

4. Avoid **company offer** and **union demand**. **Proposal** and **counter-proposal** are neutral terms.

5. A **picket**, borrowed from the military term for a small body of soldiers on guard duty, is a force of workers stationed outside an establishment to dissuade customers or workers from going in. A **sympathy picket** involves people outside the bargaining unit joining in. A **demonstration picket** is a temporary form of protest by workers about employment conditions or bargaining talks. An **electronic picket** involves a striking union tying up all incoming lines to an establishment relying on telephones for business.

Avoid the term **honour a picket line**. It implies some legal obligation which may not exist. Report that someone or some group **refused** or **declined to cross a picket line**. Similarly, do not write that pickets **barred access** to a struck establishment unless someone was actually prevented from entering.

6. Avoid the term **union bosses**. Union leaders in some cases may not legally order members to walk off the job. Strike decisions and executive appointments in unions depend by law on a majority vote of union members or of members present and voting at a union meeting.

7. A **wildcat strike** is a strike for which union leaders disclaim responsibility.

8. A number of specialist terms deal with workforce reduction. **Attrition** involves reduction through normal retirement, leaves of absence and resignation. A **buyout** involves a company offer to pay special compensation — improved pension, generous severance or the like — to employees who will retire early or quit. In some cases, if attrition or a buyout doesn't achieve the desired workforce reduction, **layoffs** would be the next step. But a buyout is not a layoff.

Lifestyles

Lifestyles coverage should be a mirror on how our society is changing — how we take care of ourselves, how we relate to each other, what we eat, wear, do for fun.

It is a broad field that includes health, fitness, medicine, food, fashion, leisure, human interest, gardening, homes, psychology, social affairs and science.

Lifestyles stories are not fluff. They are often tied to the day's news and can hit page 1.

A graphic like this puts information in a convenient and useful form. A good Lifestyles graphic can end up clipped by readers and posted on refrigerator doors.

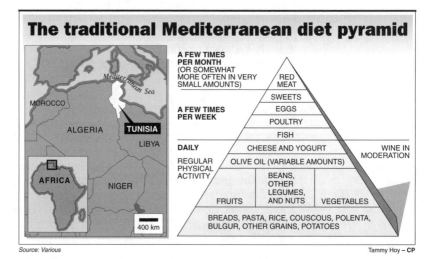

Source: Various   Tammy Hoy – CP

An inquest into the death of someone following liposuction, for example, calls out for an article outlining the procedure. The closing of a department store chain's fur salons could be accompanied by a story examining trappers who relied on the stores for their livelihoods. A piece on gardening trends could focus on concerns about pesticides.

In short, basic rules of journalism apply in lifestyles coverage: Watch for the hard-news angle; keep copy tight; strive for balance; avoid single-source stories.

Aim for QuickQuotes, QuickFacts and graphics that can help an editor lay out a page attractively.

On an ongoing topic, always seek a new angle or twist. A look at the dangers of suntanning may turn up an angle that some sunscreens do little to decrease the dangers of skin cancer.

Remember to include cross-sections of society — both sexes, various age and racial groups, geographical regions and income levels.

Avoid stereotypes. Not all grandmothers are silver-haired matrons in aprons.

Write in simple language. When technical terms must be used, explain them in plain English. Don't talk about **in vitro** fertilization if most people are more likely to understand **test-tube babies**.

Lifestyles basically breaks down into two types of stories: the exotic and the everyday.

Trends

While readers want to keep abreast of the latest trends, guard against inventing trends by exaggerating their scope. Two or three men seen wearing eye makeup doesn't mark a trend toward men wearing women's cosmetics.

On the other hand, keep an eye out for larger changes in society that narrowly focused writing may overlook. Changes in the family unit, living arrangements, family size and division of work are constant. These changes are worth writing about and should also influence writing on society as a whole.

Use personal observation as a tipoff, then seek out research material and Statistics Canada data to gauge how widespread a trend may be.

Promotion

Guard against promotion. Manufacturers and retailers have an outlet for promoting new goods and services — it's called advertising.

Be wary of the public relations practitioner's sales pitch. Some new products or services are newsworthy. Others are not. Be wary of claims for health treatments, parapsychology, the latest How-To books and so on. The litmus test is: Who will benefit from the story — the source or the reader? Always aim to include comments from outside sources.

Obituaries

Survey after survey has shown strong reader interest in obituaries.

Readers are attracted to obits for many reasons, some of the main ones being simple curiosity; wanting to learn the secret of the person's success, happiness or failures; or wanting to know what kind of person society has lost.

Obituaries are stories about life — about recognizing a life for what it was and what it meant.

They should be portraits, with brush strokes provided by friends, family, colleagues or acquaintances who can provide insights into the person's personality and life. Sharp quotes add colour and depth.

But the portraits should be exact, with no attempt to brush out wrinkles and warts. Resist the tendency to canonize the departed; very few are true saints.

Some general guidelines:

1.   Report deaths of newsworthy people. Don't limit obits to lawyers, politicians and other automatically prominent members of society. Be on the lookout for the deaths of average folk: the waitress who worked 30 years at the town's most popular diner to put seven foster children through university; the amateur philosopher who operated a downtown newsstand for many decades.

2.   Often an obituary item of 50 to 100 words will suffice, but it should include a significant fact or two about the person and his or her life.

3.   Unsavoury details may be pertinent as part of a life story but should be kept in perspective.

4.   The spot story opens with the simple facts — the name, other identification, notable achievements, cause of death and particularly age — the first questions that a reader wants answered.

Glenn Gould, the world-famous Canadian concert pianist, died early today in hospital, a week after a stroke from which he did not regain consciousness. He was 50.

5.   After the lead paragraphs, details of the subject's life are given in inverted-pyramid style rather than chronologically. The early years and schooling are rarely as interesting as later accomplishments.

6.   For a next-cycle story, a featurish top may be the best approach in the absence of worthwhile developments.

Glenn Gould was remembered Monday as a child prodigy who could read music at age three, as a 21-year-old pianist who recorded Bach "the way the old master himself must have played," and as an eccentric who wore gloves the year round.

7. The   length   of   an   obituary   depends   on   the   person's newsworthiness. In addition to the lead information, longer obituaries

should include biographical facts, the names of survivors and funeral arrangements.

8.   For unusually prominent public figures, as well as for people in the news business, include precise details of funeral arrangements.

9.   At some point — but preferably not in the lead where it might confuse readers — include the full name of the subject: **Alexander Young Jackson** for the painter usually known as **A.Y. Jackson**.

10. The identifying feature in the first paragraph should be the one that best highlights the subject's life and career. Often it is something that happened years ago.

A.Y. Jackson, a father of modern Canadian painting and last survivor of the original Group of Seven artists, died today in a nursing home at age 91.

11. In reckoning age, take into account the birth month and day. A person born Dec. 27, 1927, who died Oct. 1, 1987, was 59, not 60. To say **She was in her 60th year** is correct but confusing.

12. When the precise age is not available, give some indication of it from the person's activities, such as the year of graduation or the setting up of practice in law or at the newsstand.

Cause of death

1.   The cause of death should be given, except when the story makes plain that death resulted from the complications of old age. When the cause is not available, say so, and why.

2.   Never speculate about the cause. If information doesn't come from someone clearly in a position to know, it is irresponsible to speculate.

3.   When the cause is suspected to be a disease like AIDS, which carries certain connotations, respecting the wishes of the family can normally be justified. However, in the case of someone clearly in public life, the right to privacy in such matters can be outweighed by the public's right to know. If in doubt, consult Head Office.

4.   In listing the cause of death, prefer a plain term to medical jargon: **heart attack** and **heart disease** rather than **coronary thrombosis** or **coronary occlusion**.

5.   Explain unfamiliar scientific terms: **Hodgkin's disease — an uncommon disorder of the lymph nodes and spleen**.

6.   Taste and redundancy often rule out detail when death resulted from violence.

7.   When suicide is suspected but not officially confirmed, it may be possible to report that a note or a gun or an empty barbiturate bottle was found near the body.

Language

1. Write **die, bury, coffin** and **undertaker** or **funeral director** rather than **pass away, inter, casket** and **mortician**. Do not use **resting** for the dead, or other euphemisms.

2. Write **die of**, not **from**, an illness.

3. Use **widow** and **widower**, but **wife** and **husband** until after the funeral. Guard against the redundant **widow of the late**. Write **wife of the late** or **widow of**.

4. Do not describe people as **late** when referring to something they did while alive. Not: **The late doctor fought the epidemic alone.**

5. In general, use **the late** only of a person who died recently. It is not needed, for instance, in **the late John Lennon.**

6. Beware of such common non sequiturs as **Born in Calgary, she was an ardent skier.** The two ideas are not linked by meaning and do not belong in the same sentence. Better: **She was born in Calgary. Six years later, the family moved to Collingwood, Ont., where she soon developed a taste for skiing.**

Prepared obits

1. When an obit shows up in a newspaper's electronic return news, always check with the paper by telephone. The story may be one prepared in advance.

2. Each bureau prepares biographical sketches of its most prominent citizens. The Main Desk in Toronto keeps copies on disk.

3. As with spot obituaries, prepared obits are made interesting by quotations and anecdotes bringing out the character of the subject.

4. To make an obit stand up for use at any time, avoid past tenses except when tied to a specific date or time. Include religious affiliations or activities if newsworthy.

Funerals

1. On those rare occasions when CP does staff funerals, do not sentimentalize the dearly departed. Plain language is best, avoiding any attempt at tear-jerking.

2. Do not suggest that the remains are in any way the person.

3. There is generally little need to staff show funerals, such as the funeral of a police officer killed on duty, except through photographs.

Polls

Public-opinion polls are like snapshots: it's not always obvious what they're showing. Is that woman on the right smiling or grimacing? Is she the mother of the young girl in the centre with the same blond hair? Some mysteries there, and opportunities for misinterpreting the scene — particularly if you try to speculate that the snapshot is typical.

There's another similarity between polls and snapshots: there are too many of them, but no one wants to be the first to give them up. CP reports on reputable polls dealing with topical issues, leaving it to individual newspapers to decide when they've had enough.

By canvassing the opinions of a relatively small group of people, pollsters are able to calculate how a larger population feels about a topic. But reputable pollsters would never state that the smaller group's views exactly mirror the larger one's, nor that there isn't a possibility of being wildly wrong once in a while.

1.   Stories about polls should use verbs like **indicate** and **suggest**, rather than **show** or **report**.

TORONTO (CP) — Liberal support appeared to be holding stable across Canada in March as measured by the Angus Reid polling organization.

Reid's poll, published Tuesday in the Toronto Star, suggested little change from February for any of the major national parties among voters with an opinion: Liberals 38 per cent support versus 39 the previous month, Conservatives 32 (35), NDP 28 (26).

---

2.   An essential qualification is called the *margin of error*. It needs to be spelled out in stories on polls and its significance explained. Where changes in comparative figures are smaller than the margin of error, public opinion cannot be said with any certainty to have moved up or down.

Angus Reid said the poll was reliable within 2.5 percentage points 19 times out of 20. That means, when applied to the population at large, Liberal support in March could have been as high as 40.5 per cent or as low as 35.5 while Tory strength could range between 29.5 and 34.5 per cent. In one case in 20, the figures could be substantially different.

Changes from February figures that are smaller than the margin of error have no polling significance. The apparent drop in Liberal support, for instance, is meaningless.

---

3. A national census is the ultimate poll. An election is a close second: it registers the opinion of all who vote. Comparing a poll on party popularity with the most recent election result is sound practice. When comparing one poll with earlier polls on the same topic, however, don't assume that similar results make the polls more accurate. They don't.

4. Polls, like snapshots, show a moment in time. By the day after the questions were asked, people have already begun to change their minds. So it's wrong to suggest that a poll result can predict how people will behave — for example, a June political poll that's used to forecast an October election result. And it's wrong to take polling figures from the past and write about them in the present tense as if they are still just as valid.

5. National poll figures will usually be out by no more than two to four percentage points. But when the national figures are broken down into regions, the risk of error is much greater. The difference needs to be explained.

> By regions, the poll indicated NDP support was at a peak of 38 per cent in Ontario and a low of 12 per cent in Prince Edward Island. However, since the poll's accuracy depends on the number of people surveyed, the Ontario figure might range anywhere from 32 to 44 per cent while the P.E.I. sample was too small to be considered reliable.

6. There's a big difference between **per cent** and **percentage points**. The poll is accurate within 2.5 percentage points, not per cent. A political party whose support has apparently gone from a level of 16 per cent to 24 per cent has registered an increase of eight percentage points but its support has increased 50 per cent.

7. Statistical studies produced by Statistics Canada and other reputable organizations are routinely based on a sampling of the general population. They are polls. That means they may not accurately reflect what's happening in the population as a whole; the margin of error needs to be specified and explained, just as in a political poll. And **suggest,** not **show,** is still the verb of choice.

➤ See **Statistics,** page 85.

8. Some published polls cover a wide range of issues. In reporting on them, it's better to sacrifice polling results on secondary questions than to skip over essential information about the basic poll and its accuracy. Take a narrower focus and do it right. Consider using a Quick-style box to summarize some of the secondary results.

Some other pitfalls

Public-opinion researchers recognize a number of other elements in polling that can affect the accuracy of a poll's results.

1. The sponsor of a poll may influence the questions asked and other aspects. The story should say if the poll was paid for by a political party, a lobby group or someone else with a vested interest in the outcome. And results from two different polling organizations can't be compared unless they were asking the same questions: for example, about the popularity of **the Liberals** rather than **Jean Chrétien's Liberals.**

2. The dates a poll was taken can affect the outcome. If there was a significant event before or after the poll that could have coloured the result, say so.

3. A poll that requires members of the public to make a specific effort is likely to attract those who feel strongly about an issue. Specify whether the poll was conducted by personal interview, by phone or by mail. Phone-in or mail-in polls are of dubious value.

4. If the people polled aren't a random selection — that is, with every person having an equal chance of being picked to respond — the results may be skewed. If there were a disproportionate number of middle-class people sampled on the question of income tax rates, the poll might not give a true picture of society's attitudes as a whole.

5. The question asked can influence the result. Polls suggest most Canadians don't support abortion on demand, but a majority believe a woman whose health is at risk should be able to get an abortion. Depending on the question, poll results can claim to support almost any position in the abortion debate.

6. If 40 per cent of a random selection of people can't be contacted, or refuse to answer a particular question, or don't know the answer, the significance of the remaining responses is reduced. They may not represent society at large. This aspect needs increasingly careful attention since polling organizations report that the growth in answering machines and people's irritation with phone canvassing are leading to more difficulty getting accurate samples.

Profiles and Newsmakers

Profiles and Newsmakers tell people about people. They put human beings into news pages.

Profiles usually deal with people who may not be in the public eye but whose lives, jobs, hobbies or thoughts are interesting and appealing. Newsmakers focus on people in the day's news — the new leader of a national native organization, the provincial cabinet minister whose public statements have caused a furore, the unlikely hero of a Stanley Cup championship game.

Except for the time element — or *peg* — Profiles and Newsmakers have much in common. At their best, they leave the reader with a sense of knowing the subjects as individuals — the next best thing to meeting them in person.

Like all CP stories, the Profile and Newsmaker must be fair and in good taste. They should never be a vehicle for cheap shots, sexist comments, irrelevant detail or clumsy description that can be embarrassing to CP as well as the subject.

These stories should skilfully blend background, colour, personality touches and newsy tidbits about the subject. They should avoid logjams of detail and gratuitous information. Good quotes which convey the mood or personality of the subject are particularly helpful.

Stories such as Profiles and Newsmakers offer a great opportunity to take the reader where the TV camera can rarely go. They also go beyond the canned biography of *Who's Who*.

Look for telling actions that would probably not take place before the cameras: a federal cabinet minister gets upset when he can't get into his hotel room because he's misplaced his key; a notoriously tough football coach spends his days off as a volunteer art instructor for inner city youngsters.

The keen-eyed reporter can also sketch things a TV viewer might miss: the politician's aide always wears red neckties and combs his hair exactly like his mentor; the baseball player warming up for the all-star game keeps a jealous eye on the television camera.

Profiles and Newsmakers should be tight and bright. They should tell readers something about who the subjects are, how they got where they are, a little about what makes them tick. Friends and colleagues can be helpful in providing perceptive insights and anecdotes. So can enemies, but only if they're named.

Did the subject grow up on a farm and save egg money to buy books? Did she run three newspaper routes at the same time to buy a bicycle? Does she read books for blind people at a seniors home?

Let the reader in on your subject's home surroundings, revealing his likes, dislikes and interests.

Reform party Leader Preston Manning laughs as MP Deborah Grey takes him for a ride on her motorcycle during the 1997 federal election. Often people have interests that can lend colour to a Newsmaker or Profile.

(CP – Frank Gunn)

Roy Romanow, the well-groomed Saskatchewan premier, has steadfastly refused to divulge his age. Reform MP Deborah Grey likes riding a motorcycle. So does Al Duerr, the mild-mannered mayor of Calgary, who lists Born to be Wild, the biker's anthem from the movie Easy Rider, among his favourite songs.

Interesting mannerisms, speech patterns and habits can speak volumes about a subject. Singer Rita MacNeil performs in front of thousands but is painfully shy and reluctant to talk about herself offstage. Joe Clark frequently punctuates what he is saying with air-chopping hand motions.

Colour and description

1. Description should be fresh, imaginative and relevant. It should help the reader get a sense of the subject's appearance and personality or to feel what it was like to be at the news scene.

2. A string of generalized adjectives is usually less effective than active and specific words.

Not: He laughed heartily as he watched the Three Stooges on TV in his wood-panelled library.

But: His laughter rumbled so forcefully as he watched the Three Stooges on TV that a photograph of his yacht wobbled on the wall of his wood-panelled library.

3. A basic description of physique or character should be provided when it is pertinent to the news event. The lined faces and baggy eyes of the first ministers were worth noting during the endless Meech Lake talks in 1990. But readers do not need to be told that Brian Mulroney has a prominent chin or that Lucien Bouchard has one leg.

4. Description should always serve a purpose. Saying that a

businessman wore a pinstripe suit will seem unimaginative unless there is a specific reason — for instance, a former athlete's deliberate attempt to create a new image.

5. Watch for chances to use a description that will work better than a bald statement:

Not: The prime minister was angry.

But: The prime minister's face tightened with anger as he spun on his heel and strode quickly off the platform.

6. It sometimes helps to encourage subjects to talk about themselves. Ask lots of questions about childhood, hobbies, former jobs, dreams and hopes. Many people will be refreshingly open when given the chance.

Sometimes even the well-known public figure will reward the reader with something new and different. For instance, Jerzy Urban, the official spokesman for the former hardline Communist government in Poland, was asked in an interview what the worst day of his life was. He replied it was when his sombre weekly news conferences were cancelled and he ceased being "a TV star."

7. Subjects who are naturally reserved and taciturn are particularly challenging. So is the individual who dislikes media attention. Look for body-language from such people. Some of them convey a wealth of information even though their actual answers may be sparse or even gruff.

A media-hating tycoon whose speech is closely clipped can still leave a trail of visual images.

He's big and rough-looking, a yep-and-nope type who seems to shun even those monosyllables if a shrug or nod will do for an answer.

8. Comparisons can be helpful in giving the reader a mental image. *Lincolnesque*, for instance, implies tall and craggy.

Or compare a person's appearance or character to natural objects: granite-jawed; reed-like; limbs like oak; built along the lines of a water buffalo.

9. Technical references can even be helpful: nimble as a Porsche; he was well put together, like a neatly constructed Lego man.

10. When it comes to effective use of colour and description, one trick is working it in without making it look forced. A paragraph devoted entirely to colour to the exclusion of news, quotes or anything else to inform the reader will seem distracting. Laborious descriptive clauses are also discouraging.

11. Colour should be woven into a story in a natural way:

The judge who will recommend how much time Albert Walker ought to spend in prison for murdering Ronald Platt denounced the convicted Canadian on Monday as a callous and ruthless man who used people for his own selfish ends.

Walker, 52, blinked twice when the foreman of the eight-woman, four-man jury announced the guilty verdict after two hours of deliberation.

Later, as he was led down the stairs of the dock into the holding cells, the composure Walker maintained throughout the trial appeared on the verge of collapse. His eyes were reddening and his facial muscles seemed ready to give way.

12. But don't fall into the trap of tediously substituting bits of background for the person's identity:

Para 1:   John Simpson said Tuesday . . .

Para 2:   . . . the former Vancouver engineer added.

Para 3:   The lanky, grey-haired bureaucrat insisted . . .

Instead, consider giving readers an early mental image that can stay with them as they read on:

Simpson, lanky and grey-haired, is a former Vancouver engineer who in 1986 joined the federal Transport Department and rose quickly to the No. 2 spot. In that job he is now insisting that the harbour project be shelved.

Slugs

The word Profile or Newsmaker is included in the first slugline:

BC-Sorensen-Profile
code:3
SEE CP Photo CPT27
Canadian woman faces test Down Under

By Lorrayne Anthony
          TORONTO (CP) — It's been nearly six solitary months . . .

PM-Scott-Newsmaker, Bgt
code:3
Budget
Home-town crowd willing to forgive Scott

By Chris Morris
          FREDERICTON (CP) — When Andy Scott was named Canada's solicitor general . . .

Sports

General

1. The standards of good general-news writing apply with equal force to the coverage of sports. People are the focus of reader interest. Bare results are the preserve of the agate page.

2. The sensitive sports writer should know when a cliché has become threadbare. While athletes still profess to be *taking it one game at a time* and *giving it 110 per cent*, the days of reporting such mundane quotes are over.

3. When writing game copy, be concise. There's no need to describe every scoring play. Focus on the key play or performer and build the story around it. Pull together the remaining scoring plays into a paragraph or two. Sometimes, one sentence listing the remaining goal-scorers for each team in a hockey game, for example, will suffice. The reader who wants more can find it on the agate page.

Limit game-over stories to 400 words; papers seldom have space for more. If developments warrant, do an add or spin it off into a sidebar. All vital elements of the game must be contained in that initial 400-word story.

4. Make sure the blinkers are off. Sports is more than what unfolds on the playing field. Capture the mood and size of the crowd and its impact on the game. Were the fans raucous, or sedate? Did they display banners or signs vilifying the visitors?

Watch for the interaction at the bench between players and coach, as well as between teammates. If the coach berates the star defenceman for giving the puck away on the decisive goal, let the reader in on it.

➤ See **More than a game**, page 80.

5. Be mindful of the competition for sports-page space and write accordingly. Tight writing is particularly needed on weekends when there is a glut of copy for Monday editions. Overwriting hurts a story's chances for publication.

6. Finally, don't forget something so simple it's often neglected in stories: Was it a good game? Was it well-played? Was it entertaining?

Points to watch

1. The sport involved must be identified early in every story.

2. City names used as team names take singular verbs; team titles, even singular ones, usually require plural verbs: **Vancouver is last** . . . but **The Canucks are last. Miami played its first game** . . . but **the Heat played their first game.**

3. Avoid unnecessary possessives. Write **The Canadiens centre stole the puck** not **The Canadiens' centre** . . . However, the possessive is required in the following: **The Canadiens' three straight losses are a season record.** When you are unsure whether the possessive is necessary, mentally substitute the city for the team nickname. By substituting **Montreal** in the examples given, it's quickly apparent which requires the possessive.

4. Avoid nicknames unless they are long-standing. If a person is known to readers by a given name and nickname, put the nickname in parentheses on first reference: **boxer Thomas (Hit Man) Hearns.** Usually, however, when a person is commonly known by a nickname, it is unnecessary to provide the given name as well: **baseball outfielder Chili Davis** and **tennis player Gigi Fernandez,** not **Charles (Chili) Davis** and **Beatrice (Gigi) Fernandez.**

5. Long-established and well-known leagues such as the National Hockey League, the Canadian Football League, the National Football League and the National Basketball Association may be referred to in first reference as **the NHL, the CFL, the NFL** and **the NBA.**

Initials are permissible on second reference for well-known minor leagues such as the American Hockey League **(AHL)**, the International Hockey League **(IHL)** and Canada's three major junior hockey leagues. Otherwise, avoid initials even on second reference.

All leagues named in newspapers and other stories that might end up on non-sports pages should be spelled out in full.

6. Capitalize major events and trophies such as **the Olympic Games, the Olympics, the Pan Am Games, the Commonwealth Games, the Canada Games, the World Series, the Canadian Open, the Grey Cup, the Super Bowl, the Queen's Plate** and **the Vezina Trophy.** On second reference, refer to them simply as **the Games, the Open,** etc.

National and world championships are not capitalized. Write **the Canadian wrestling championships** and **the world hockey championship.**

7. Use the plural of proper nouns advisedly. Write **Boston is a five-time winner of the Stanley Cup** not **Boston has won five Stanley Cups.** Similarly, if referring to baseball's two major leagues, write **The presidents of the American and National leagues** (lowercase *l*) . . .

8. The word *final*, meaning the last round of a competition, is singular. Write **Pittsburgh reached the Stanley Cup final** not **finals.** An exception: **Five swimming finals were scheduled Tuesday.**

9. Don't expect the reader to have a medical dictionary next to the newspaper. What's an *anterior cruciate ligament* and why is it preventing Eric Lindros from playing hockey? Make sure any medical jargon is explained and the extent of the disability is clear.

Sports . . . More than a game

1.   A sports writer who reports only what happens on the field or rink and ignores what takes place off it is being negligent.

2.   On many sports pages today, the daily game is often summarized in a few paragraphs or worked into a roundup. Line stories tend to be analyses, backgrounders and profiles, or else they focus on trades, drafts, salaries, racism, substance abuse and legal problems.

3.   Certain stories invite a blind eye: substance abuse, racial tension, disciplinary problems. These are not merely personal questions for publicly acclaimed athletes. Writing about these issues may require legal advice, but it should be part of the sports beat.

Wayne Gretzky wipes a tear during a news conference announcing his trade from the Edmonton Oilers to the Los Angeles Kings in 1988. This picture dramatically showed how the business of sports takes a human toll.

(CP – Ray Giguere)

4.   Sports pages must reflect the evolution of the multibillion-dollar sports entertainment industry. Every sports writer takes time to interview a team's general manager about a new prospect or a hot trade rumour. But a good sports writer will also get to know a team's business manager to write about attendance, television revenue and taxes.

5.   Don't leave the business end of sports out of so-called amateur events. Members of Canada's national teams are no longer amateurs. Appearance money is now the main criterion for most track meets, so don't ignore it in the story.

6. As well, Canada's amateur sports federations are part of a substantial bureaucracy and should come under the same journalistic scrutiny as any government department.

7. The only true amateurs left in sports are people like weekend softball players and neighbourhood joggers. While recreational athletes aren't usually newsworthy, the sports they play are. Keep a close eye on trends in recreational sports. Why are people willing to spend hundreds of dollars on running shoes? How many weekend warriors are seriously injuring themselves on the softball diamond?

Women in sports

1. Sports pages tend to be filled with stories about male athletes. Despite that, a survey by the National Hockey League found more than 40 per cent of its fans are women. The crowd at any major sports event can show a similar ratio.

2. Sexist language, stereotypes and references have no more place in sports pages than in any other part of the newspaper.

3. A few anachronisms survive in sports: **the Ladies Professional Golf Association**. But generally, female athletes are no more *ladies* than males are *gentlemen*.

Beware of sports stereotypes. This picture is proof that hockey – and wrestling – aren't just for men. Team Canada forward Danielle Goyette puts a Team China player into a headlock during a women's hockey game at the 1998 Winter Olympics in Nagano, Japan.

(CP – Frank Gunn)

4. There are sports where women excel — tennis, cycling, athletics, golf, to name a few. The complete sports report includes full, well-written stories about such events.

5. There's no justification for always leading with the men's competition in events, such as marathons, where both sexes compete. If separate stories aren't warranted, the most competitive, exciting race deserves the lead — and that's not always the men's event.

6. Be on the lookout for sexism in sports. Female athletes, particularly in golf and tennis, get a disproportionately smaller share of prize money compared with men. If an amateur program seems to be devoting more resources to male athletes, find out why.

7. Physical descriptions of athletes — male and female — are sometimes appropriate, and their personalities and gestures will enliven quotes. But avoid gratuitous descriptions that have sexist undertones. The simple test: Would this type of thing be written about a male athlete?

8. Finally, any male sports writer who refers to a female gymnast as a **pixie** or a basketball player as an **amazon** is not relying on a cliche, but is being sexist. Don't patronize. Be thoughtful and tasteful in your use of language.

➤ See **Sexism**, page 22.

Thinking visuals

1. When developing a story, think immediately about illustrations. Discuss the story with a staff photographer or photo editor. Rely on their talents to make your story more complete.

2. The same holds for graphics. Many sporting events leave writers with more statistics than should be used in a story. The unused stats can make a timely graphic. Sports lends itself to graphics and a good one can sell a story to editors and readers.

Information that would be boring and hard to understand if presented in a story can be used as the basis for an eye-catching graphic.

1998 Toronto Molson Indy

Toronto's Molson Indy is the 11th race of the 1998 CART FedEx Championship Series. The track is a temporary street course at Exhibition Place on the shores of Lake Ontario.

RACE FACTS
Circuit name: Exhibition Place.
Length: 2.77 km.
Direction: Clockwise.
Course type: Temporary street course.
When: Sunday 1:30 p.m. EDT.
TV: CBC.
Last year's winner: Mark Blundell (PacWest Racing)

DRIVER STANDINGS	
1. Alex Zanardi	155
2. Greg Moore	96
3. Jimmy Vasser	92
4. Adrian Fernandez	85
5. Michael Andretti	68
5. Dario Franchitti	64
7. Gil de Ferran	63
8. Scott Pruett	56
9. Bryan Herta	54
10. Bobby Rahal	43

Sean Vokey - CP

3.   As well, QuickSketches, QuickFacts and QuickQuotes are welcome complements to sports stories. They can spell out essential background material, leaving more room for colour and personality in the story.

Sponsorship in sport

Sponsorship has crept into every corner of sports, making it difficult to separate the commercial sponsor from the event title.

National and world championships are usually identified as such in first reference, with the sponsor's name given later, because the reader is probably more familiar with the name of the championship. This is especially true in cases where the sponsorship changes from year to year. There are exceptions: the **Labatt Brier** probably carries more reader recognition than the **Canadian men's curling championships.**

Sports are inevitably an advertising vehicle, but the sponsorship should have a legitimate connection to the event in order to rate being mentioned. References to the sponsorship should not be unduly emphasized.

Metric, measurement and numbers

1.   CP generally uses metric to measure distances and calculate speeds. However, some sports — golf, football, horse racing and certain classes of auto racing, for example — are reported in imperial. (For departures from the metric rule, see sections dealing with individual sports.)

Orlando Merced of the Toronto Blue Jays narrowly misses snagging a long ball at the 100-metre (328-foot) outfield sign. CP uses metric measures in many sports, including baseball.

(CP – Moe Doiron)

Today's youth have been brought up on metric and to persist needlessly in imperial measures is to risk turning away potential readers. Unless precise imperial field demarcations are involved, as in football, or race distances, such as the Indianapolis 500, use metric wherever it's a sensible option.

Although fence signs in most baseball parks still list the distance from home plate in feet, there is no logical reason why the distance a batted ball carries can't be given in metres. Write **Wilson's drive barely cleared the fence in left-centre field, about 110 metres away.** Should the actual distance sign be pertinent to the story, put the metric equivalent in parentheses: **Wilson doubled off the 360-foot sign (about 110 metres) in left-centre field.**

Similarly in hockey, there's no need to write about a **30-foot slapshot** when **a slapshot from the top of the faceoff circle** or **a 10-metre slapshot** is just as descriptive.

Note: Many figures, imperial or metric, are rough estimates. When translating imperial to metric, don't use exact conversions unless precision is essential, such as in field events at an athletics meet. Round figures off.

2.   Personal measurements continue to be imperial. When referring to heights, write **The centre stood six foot three**; as an adjective, it's **the six-foot-three centre.** If it's clear from the context, it's permissible to say **Jones, 6-3, 220 pounds, came to the Blue Bombers . . .**

Don't mix imperial and metric in one sentence: **The six-foot-three forward shot from 10 metres out.** Rephrase it or use separate sentences.

3.   When measurements consist of two or more elements, do not use commas. Write **She stood five foot three** and **She was timed in two hours 15 minutes 35 seconds.**

4.   In times, a colon is used between hours, minutes and seconds; a period before decimal fractions of a second. Write **0:27** (27 seconds), **0:27.7** (27.7 seconds), **2:00.1** (two minutes one-tenth of a second), **3:47:39.67** (three hours 47 minutes 39.67 seconds). Note that times involving only seconds include a zero before the colon.

5.   When not expressing fractions in decimal terms, write **8-100ths of a second** and **3½ minutes**, but **two-thirds of an inning.**

6.   Odds are listed as **20-1**, not **20 to 1** or **20-to-1**.

➤ See **Numbers**, page 215.

Records

When records are established, put them into perspective:

• Compare a national standard with the world mark.

• Try to explain why the previous record had been one of long standing or why it has been broken three times in the last year.

Statistics

Statistics can be pillars of the day's news. They are also the devil's playground, luring reporters into errors of interpretation, assumption and fact.

Some of the problems with statistics would diminish if the news media would regularly treat them with the care — and the skepticism — they need. The quote credited to Benjamin Disraeli is deservedly famous: **"There are . . . lies, damned lies and statistics."**

The value of statistics, intelligently used, can hardly be overstated. They help to give substance to stories on hundreds of topics. But there are pitfalls:

1. Some statistical reports rely on actual counts: the number of new cars sold in Vancouver in March, based on sales reports from all dealerships. Some are estimates: the number of unemployed in Canada in August, based on extensive samplings of households. These poll-based statistics are subject to error and reporting on them needs some of the same care applied to writing about public-opinion polls.

➤ See **Polls**, page 71.

2. Some statistical reports are issued on a preliminary basis, subject to adjustments later. The federal government's figures on international trade are one example. Some of the later adjustments can be substantial. That means the figures must always be described as preliminary, and early in the story the importance of the adjustment process needs to be spelled out each time. When the final figures are available, they should be reported and comparisons made with the preliminary figures. Since the preliminary figures are tentative, it doesn't make sense to attribute great significance to the precise numbers. If that makes a story less interesting and less authoritative, so be it.

3. Statistics are usually relevant only for the time period concerned. There can be substantial changes from one year to the next in all sorts of statistics. An obvious example: a poll on the number of homes with Internet access in 1995 says very little about how many families had jumped on the Net by 1999.

4. Comparisons of statistical studies on the same topic can be useful in detecting trends, such as employment in the manufacturing sector over a few months or even years. However, comparisons between one time period and an earlier one should take account of how the population and other crucial factors have changed in the interim. A 25 per cent increase in auto thefts from 1989 to 1999 might actually represent a decline in the **rate** of thefts, if population and car ownership figures are taken into account. (Rates are more telling when they're available: the number of murders per 100,000 population.) Similarly, comparisons of value over time must take into account the decline in purchasing power of the dollar.

5. The bases of comparison shouldn't be decided routinely. Comparing January retail sales figures with December's can be meaningless because of the Christmas rush; comparing them with the previous January's is usually best. But when the economy is reaching a peak or a trough, a year-over-year comparison may not be as revealing as month-over-month or some other comparison thoughtfully chosen.

6. The significance of statistics can't be safely stretched. If Canada's overall cost-of-living index goes up mainly because of higher taxes in Ontario, many Canadians will not be affected and a story should make that clear from the start. If a provincial study reports that the number of homeless people in the province has declined eight per cent from a year earlier, that alone can't be taken to suggest declines in other provinces.

7. Similarly, it's risky to assume that American statistical studies are equally valid in Canada. Some academics find it hard to resist using the floods of American studies to buttress arguments about conditions in Canada, adding casually that "there's no reason to think the same figures don't apply in this country." Don't believe it. Check some authorities; there are numerous differences between the two societies.

8. Phrases like **seasonally adjusted, gross domestic product** and the like may be understood by specialists, but the ordinary reader can use help. The methods of calculating changes in such basic measurements as the consumer price index or the unemployment index should also be explained from time to time. When available, sample size — 700 of the 2,000 sporting goods stores, for example — should be mentioned. People want to know how reliable these indicators are.

Travel

Travel stories share many of the requirements of other features: effective use of quotes and people, a lively writing style, a good lead that grabs the reader's interest.

But more than most other features, travel stories must usually convey a sense of place. The writer draws a picture for the reader by selecting vivid detail and using description effectively.

1. Travel writers need to make their stories interesting — a mere listing of information from travel brochures and government tourist boards won't do.

The airily upbeat style more common in promotional travel literature doesn't work either.

2. The proper approach is somewhat sharper and reflects the writer's personal observation.

What is it about a particular place that is distinctive, that catches the writer's senses?

What do the city streets look like? What do the people wear? What is striking about the markets, the countryside?

The writer should try to get one or two real people into the story — a street vendor, a passerby, a museum guide. Anyone but the overused taxi driver or hotel desk clerk.

3. The best travel stories will capture the genuinely interesting aspects of a destination without glossing over harsh reality: poverty, inefficient transportation, anti-tourist sentiment. Experienced travellers expect some discomfort but they also want practical information on what to be prepared for.

At times, the need for plain-speaking will be paramount. When travel is likely to be affected by political developments, earthquakes or floods, terrorist threats or other newspage developments, a travel-page report can hardly ignore it.

4. Good travel topics include an offbeat site, a new attraction, any interesting destination.

Trends that affect tourists are also worth considering: the modernization of British pubs, the renovation of cathedrals in France.

A narrow focus often provides the best opportunity for colourful writing — for example, a market street in Lima, a festival in Barcelona, a museum on cats in Malaysia. But a large-topic story — travel in eastern Europe, London in summertime, cruising the Caribbean — is also worthwhile.

If the reporter can add some perspective — a sense of familiarity with the country and the people — all the better.

5. Business people make up a large part of the travelling public. They want information that can help them travel more efficiently — tips on getting through airports, facts on practical matters like packing, food, ground transportation, foreign customs.

6. Unlike some magazine material, travel stories for newspapers must be punchy and concise. Interesting historical background can be woven in judiciously.

Facts on accommodation, food, prices and other similar information may be appropriate, especially when organized into an **If you go** Quick.

7. The use of the first person is occasionally acceptable when giving a personal account of an unusual adventure, but it should not be overdone.

Include people or animals in travel shots to liven up street scenes or pictures of buildings. They also help give a sense of scale. Generally, keep the sun behind you and take lots of pictures.

(CP—Jim Fox)

8. The most useful length for travel stories is usually 500-600 words. Photos are essential, and a map may be handy to locate offbeat sites.

9. Travel stories do not need exotic placelines. Many people want ideas on cheaper or shorter holidays within Canada.

World news

Canadians play an active role in world affairs: as peacekeepers in trouble spots; as diplomats advancing Canada's objectives within international agencies; as business people getting a share of the global market. CP tries to ensure that the Canadian angle receives appropriate attention in the constant flow of news and photos from abroad.

Canadian Forces soldiers hand out water to victims of hurricane Mitch in Honduras in 1998. CP photographers and writers travelling aboard can bring home stories that are of particular interest to Canadians.

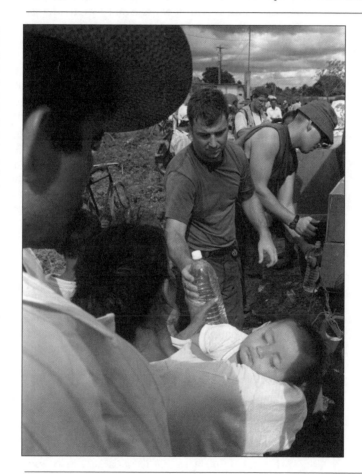

(CP – Tom Hanson)

CP has its own network of staff and freelance correspondents around the world to report on stories with particular significance for Canadian readers. Staffers from the CP World Desk in Toronto and bureaus across Canada actively pursue the Canadian connection in foreign stories by phone, e-mail and faxes, or travel outside the country to cover such events.

Together, these efforts by CP personnel add a distinctly Canadian dimension to the world report selected from major international news agencies such as The Associated Press and Reuters. Copy is delivered directly into CP computers, and co-ordinated and edited on the World Desk by people who are experienced in making sense of complicated foreign developments.

The international agencies offer a comprehensive view of key developments around the world. While they use a cosmopolitan mix of reporters and editors and maintain a high standard of journalism, their stories are not written with a Canadian readership in mind. CP tries to make world news relevant to Canadians, who have their own history and perspective. Canada's interests don't exactly coincide with those of any other country; we have a different political system, different trade and cultural traditions, and different internal tensions and problems. As often as not, we respond to international events in our own way. Canadian reporters abroad and their editors back in Canada are more likely to notice parallels of interest to Canadian readers. They can make foreign developments understandable in Canadian terms.

CP makes sure that the Canadian perspective is at the core of a rich menu of international news covering not just politics and disasters, but also business, entertainment, medical, scientific, lifestyles and human interest issues. International news is not only the doings of world leaders along with some riots and civil wars. It is also ordinary people doing extraordinary things anywhere in the world. It is the small triumphs and defeats of the human spirit. It is social and cultural trends that can reach across borders and continents. And sometimes, Canadians are in the middle of these developments and deserve coverage.

At the same time, CP ensures that Canada's influence and accomplishments on the international stage are seen in the proper context. For example, the activities of the Canadian delegation at a major international conference are certainly worth reporting in detail, but a balanced story should contain the most important overall developments spearheaded by other countries, and the most thoughtful or provocative positions at the conference.

A complete world report includes stories on how other nations try to solve issues that Canadians also face. A report on how problems such as health care, pollution and taxation are handled abroad can provide Canadians with fresh alternatives to consider.

And in the same way that Canada isn't just Mounties and snow, other countries are more than their folklore and stereotyped eccentricities. CP aims to provide a world report that goes beyond the cliches to shed light on the fascinating complexities of different societies.

Chasing world news

The CP World Desk relies on stringers, correspondents and allied news services around the world to help keep tabs on international events. But the phone is also a prime tool in tracking down news involving Canadians abroad. Some tips:

- A Foreign Affairs Department booklet of Canadian ambassadors and other representatives abroad is an invaluable resource. It includes business phone, fax and e-mail addresses as well as some home phones.

- The Internet, especially e-mail, is another invaluable tool. It is quickly becoming the preferred way to communicate with newsmakers and correspondents in the field, as well as a reliable way for correspondents to file material. It helps overcome the time-zone barrier too. Stories are often planned when overseas correspondents are asleep, and filed in the middle of the night when editorial supervisors are asleep. With e-mail, editors can assign stories when they are being planned and correspondents can receive instructions before they head out to the assignment, even if that it is in the middle of the night, Toronto time.

- Remember when calling abroad that almost anyone you reach is likely to know more about the country and its information sources that you do. Ask them who they would call if they were trying to get the information you need. And always ask the person you've managed to contact for the names and numbers of anyone else who might also be able to help.

Editing world news

- Keep in mind the changing complexion of Canada's population. Most newcomers now come from China, Hong Kong, the Philippines, South Korea and other countries outside the traditional European sources. Their interest in their birthplaces should influence the selection of news for CP's world report.

- Stories from abroad frequently include currency figures, usually expressed in U.S. dollars. For Canadian readers, the figures should normally be translated into Canadian currency and rounded off. Style is to use **Cdn** and **US** immediately after the currency figure, without periods.

- Keeping the news report free of legal problems presents special challenges for World Desk editors. After hours spent looking at copy on American crime cases in which the accused is all but convicted before charges are laid, it takes an alert eye to recognize the legal risks of a similar story that has Canadian elements. U.S. libel laws, in particular, permit statements that would be extremely dangerous in Canada. U.S. police seem free to blacken the reputations of arrested people before they come to trial. The rules: Check with a supervisor or legal counsel before releasing doubtful material. Kill any story found to be dangerous. Withhold any story that has given rise to legal questions.

➤ See **Legal,** page 94.

Legal

Legal

Although this section provides general information on journalism and the law, it is written for CP editors and reporters and reflects the news agency's needs. The guidelines and policies in this section do not represent an agreed professional standard; nor do they represent the practices of all newspapers. Its main focus is to alert CP staff to situations that may require advice from legal counsel. It is not a substitute for such advice and should not be used in that way.

Engraved in the memory of every reporter and editor should be:

1. Carelessness and bad judgment on legal questions can ruin people's lives. Every journalist must weigh this responsibility when working.

2. It is dangerous to publish statements that damage a person's reputation or livelihood unless the statements are provably true or unless the law clearly provides a special exemption.

3. It is particularly dangerous to suggest criminal conduct unless it has been proved in the courts.

4. Every person charged and before the courts is entitled to be presumed innocent and to receive a fair trial. It is forbidden to publish anything that passes judgment on an accused or that could hinder a fair trial unless it has been admitted in court as evidence. (Of course, the court's judgment is publishable.)

5. Juveniles involved with the law — accused, witnesses or victims — must not be identified, even indirectly, without legal advice.

Follow these rules:

1. Check legal authority before writing anything legally doubtful.

2. Cut out anything that looks legally questionable until it can be cleared for use.

3. If legal doubts arise after a story has been distributed, order the story killed or withheld immediately until the doubts can be resolved.

Crime

Reporting on crime

No area of reporting requires greater care than crime.

People's reputations and livelihoods are at stake. Concepts of fairness that are at the core of Canadian democracy come regularly into play.

On the other hand, a justice system that deals effectively with criminals is a legitimate goal of every democracy. And one of the bases of an effective justice system is public scrutiny: the public must see justice being done, if not in person then through the media.

Courtrooms are natural theatres of human drama and good court reporting takes the reader to the heart of the drama – but always with fairness and objectivity in the recording of testimony and the description of witnesses.

Reporters and editors should make themselves familiar with the entire legal section of the *CP Stylebook* in a general fashion. The subsections are set out in such a way that those working on a specific step in the legal process can refer to the portion dealing with that step. The worst pitfalls are highlighted at the start of each subsection.

However, the law is complex. A stylebook is no substitute for legal counsel on doubtful issues.

Criminal cases

Some general rules:

1.   Court reporting must be fair and accurate to be legally protected. Otherwise, the protection is lost. That means straightforward coverage of testimony, even-handed descriptions of accused or witnesses, balance between Crown and defence cases, no plain or implied taking of sides.

2.   Coverage must also be contemporaneous. It is risky to report well after the fact on a criminal proceeding, particularly if the accused was acquitted. It can seem like an attempt to blacken the accused's name needlessly. Consult counsel before reporting on an old proceeding.

3.   Give the exact charge in a criminal case, not a generality. If the charge is sexual assault, don't write **attack**.

4.   Don't refer casually to a defendant's religion, race, political party, profession or other qualification unless it's directly relevant. Beware of categorizing an accused in a way that could reflect on an entire group of people.

5.   Identifying alleged victims or other witnesses in sexual assault cases and some other sensitive areas may be banned by the court. Even if not banned, such details should be published only after carefully weighing the possible hurt to those who have already been victimized.

6. In important cases, provide the possible penalty, but also mention that the maximum penalty is rarely imposed and prison terms are rarely served in full.

7. When substantial prison terms have been imposed, specify promptly how much time must be served before parole can be considered.

8. Don't total concurrent sentences (**sentenced to a total of 120 years**). Report the individual sentences on various charges and the actual maximum prison term.

9. Don't attempt to pull together two or more court cases into one story unless they were linked in court. Such natural linkages are rare anyway, but on days when a number of parallel cases are going on in different courts — say, concerted disturbances by activists — publishing a roundup can risk influencing a sitting jury or potential jurors.

Some general background:

1. Criminal offences are generally of two types, **summary conviction** (less serious) and **indictable** (more serious). Some offences such as theft under $1,000 may be prosecuted either summarily or by indictment, at the discretion of the Crown.

2. Summary conviction offences are dealt with in a streamlined procedure under which the accused goes directly to trial without a preliminary hearing. Examples include causing a disturbance, indecent exhibition in a public place or being found in what are called **common gaming-houses** or **bawdy-houses**.

3. Summary conviction offences are tried by a justice of the peace or by the lowest of a province's courts. There are no jury trials at this level.

4. Indictable offences generally involve a choice of courts, at the discretion of the Crown, and sometimes a choice of trial with or without jury, at the discretion of the accused.

5. For many indictable offences — including armed robbery, breaking and entering, forgery and arson — the options are:

a) Trial by provincially appointed judge (lower courts) without jury and without first undergoing a preliminary inquiry.

b) Trial by federally appointed judge in a provincial superior court without jury but with a preliminary inquiry.

c) Trial by a federally appointed judge with jury in a provincial superior court. Such courts have a variety of names in different provinces: Court of Queen's Bench, Supreme Court, Superior Court, Court of Quebec, general division of Ontario Court.

6. For the most serious indictable offences, such as murder or treason, there is no option. They must be tried in a superior court. And they must be heard by a jury unless the accused and the provincial attorney general both agree otherwise.

7. Appeals of convictions for indictable offences are heard by provincial courts of appeal. Appeals for summary conviction offences are heard by a variety of courts depending on the province.

8. The Supreme Court of Canada hears criminal appeals only if a point of law is involved and if leave to appeal is granted by a panel of three justices or by a provincial appeal court. Leave to appeal is not necessary if a provincial appeal court has reversed an acquittal won in the trial court; if at least one justice has dissented in the appeal court's decision; or if a co-accused, having been tried jointly, has had an acquittal sustained on appeal.

Before charges are laid

Dangers:

1. Naming a person before formally charged.
2. Providing past criminal record.
3. Linking a suspect to a crime.

Police take an interest in many people. Often nothing comes of it. But to write that someone **is under investigation** for a criminal offence can cast a cloud over the person's life. The courts consider a false allegation of criminal conduct among the worst forms of libel.

Therefore, special care must be taken with any story identifying a person being investigated but who has not been charged or has not appeared in court to answer a charge.

CP does not normally name individuals until they face formal charges. There may be exceptions depending on particular legal circumstances and news value, but the exceptions are rare.

Always check supervisors or seek legal advice before using doubtful information. With that caution, following are some general comments and examples:

1. Contempt of court — appearing to influence a criminal proceeding — usually becomes a risk only when the case is actually about to proceed in court (**sub judice**).

2. Even if not contemptuous, a report that police are **investigating** a specific person, or **considering charges** against a specific person, can be libellous in some cases.

3. Depending on the circumstances, it may be permissible to report that **an investigation is under way** or **searches have been carried out**.

4. It is proper to publish the fact that a warrant has been issued for the arrest of a named person, or that he or she has in fact been arrested, or has received a summons to appear in court, or has signed a promise to appear.

5. The exact nature of the charge can be stated if the person has appeared before a judge, or if the charge is outlined in a warrant, summons or other document. It is probably dangerous to go into further detail without documentary evidence or testimony in open court.

6. Occasionally, the criminal record or other background of the accused is virtually inseparable from the description of the crime. A breakout or a riot at a prison or detention centre, for example, is committed by people who either have a criminal record or are held without bail for trial.

7. Trickier is the case of a murder committed by someone on parole. If the suspect's previous conviction was also for murder, a strong editorial case could be made for reporting that fact on grounds of public interest, although legally the information would be totally prejudicial. If the previous crime was petty theft, the record is irrelevant.

8. Under these and other circumstances, it may be OK to refer to the criminal record of an accused at the time of arrest. But Toronto Main Desk, which can consult counsel in tricky cases, must check all stories that make such references. Contempt is a real risk. The references need to be relevant and in the public interest, and the information must be presented concisely and fairly. Unless there are special circumstances, such references to a past record should be dropped after the first few stories done at the time of arrest and shortly after. Don't continue to carry such information later in the legal process without getting the approval of counsel.

9. Even when it's permissible to mention the background, a story must never imply that the suspect's record means he or she is guilty of the new offence.

10. Occasionally, a criminal comes before the courts who's so notorious that virtually anything may safely be written about the person's past and character until trial is imminent. Resist the temptation to abuse this liberty. If the criminal is truly notorious, the public doesn't need constant reminders of the reasons. And such stories can send the wrong signal about the media's concern for fair play.

11. On rare occasions — a hostage-taker who surrenders, a bank robber wounded in the act — the suspect's identity may be obvious even before being charged. In such cases, write only that a named person has been arrested or is in custody, without going into detail.

12. A suspect must be kept separate from the crime. For example, it may be all right to say: **A robbery was committed. John Doe is being held.** It is never all right to say: **John Doe committed a robbery.** Similarly, it is not acceptable to write: **A drug ring was broken today with the announcement of charges against three people.**

13. Witnesses can be interviewed when a crime is committed, but their statements should not be used to link a specific suspect to actions that could be disputed later in court. Witnesses must not be interviewed once a suspect has come before the courts.

14. Reporting police statements carries no immunity from the risk of libel or contempt. Such statements have to be weighed as carefully as any other information and checked for accuracy when possible. Whether a particular police force can be depended upon for fairness

and accuracy is a matter of past experience. It is no defence against a libel or contempt charge to say the police were thought to be trustworthy.

Inquests

Dangers:

1. Publication bans.
2. Later use of incriminating evidence.

---

1. Coroner's inquests — or as they are increasingly known, **fatality inquiries** — are held to investigate the cause of a violent death and make recommendations designed to avoid future deaths. They are presided over by a judge or coroner, depending on provincial law.

2. Inquests are usually open to media and public. The general rule holds that public hearings may be reported fairly and accurately.

3. However, the person presiding may order the inquiry closed, temporarily or permanently, because of possible prejudice to a potential accused, national security, public safety or intimate testimony, depending on provincial law. In such cases, whether evidence from the inquiry becomes public later is a matter for the presiding officer and/or provincial law.

4. An inquest may hear evidence that would be inadmissible at a later court proceeding, such as a confession. It may be reported at the time, unless the presiding officer directs otherwise, but it should not be repeated without legal advice once the case is before the courts.

5. Inquest juries are usually forbidden to make any finding of civil or legal responsibility. However, their investigations can sometimes lead to questions of who might have committed a crime, in a way not normally open to the courts, and that could lead to criminal charges. It's unwise to speculate about such possibilities without legal advice, however.

6. Inquest juries, like those at criminal trials, are forbidden by law from disclosing any information about their deliberations.

7. In Quebec, among things the law forbids:

a) Publishing a photograph of the dead body without consent.

b) Publishing any identifying information about a witness under 18 years of age implicated in the events.

c) Publishing autopsy reports.

Pré-enquête

Danger:

1. Reporting testimony.

1. A pré-enquête is a rare form of private inquiry by a judge to determine whether a charge should be laid. It is sometimes used when a public figure is implicated, to limit potential damage should the evidence not support a charge. The judge may hear witnesses in private before deciding whether to proceed to a preliminary inquiry or another step in the judicial process.

2. Procedure can be one-sided (**ex parte**), without cross-examination under oath and other legal safeguards. Thus, testimony may not be reported if it somehow becomes available. It is permissible to report that the hearing is being held, to name the persons against whom charges are being considered, and to report the decision on whether to proceed with charges.

3. The pré-enquête should not be confused with a preliminary hearing, a later step used in many criminal cases at which the judge decides whether a person already charged should be sent to trial.

Arraignment and bail hearing

Dangers:

1. Violating publication ban.
2. Reporting confession or criminal record.

1. Arraignment is normally the first step in a criminal court proceeding. It usually involves just an appearance by the accused before a judge, reading of the charge, making a plea and selecting a trial option. It's not essential that the accused enter a plea; the court may record a plea of **not guilty** if no plea is entered.

2. The court may hear evidence from a psychiatrist or other qualified person and order a psychiatric examination to test the accused's fitness to stand trial. The judge usually orders a ban on publication of such evidence; if not, it may be reported. There are normally no other restrictions on reporting arraignments.

3. A decision on bail may be made at arraignment, or at a separate bail (or **interim release**) hearing. If the accused requests a ban on publicity, the judge must grant it. It is then forbidden to publish testimony or the judge's reasons for granting or denying bail. The fact of whether bail was granted, and any conditions for release, may be reported.

4.   Even without a publication ban, no confession offered in evidence by police or other witnesses may be reported at this stage without legal advice. There should be no mention of a criminal record without approval from a supervisor or counsel.

Change of venue

Danger:
1.   Reporting court decision.

1.   When a criminal case becomes so notorious in a community that it would be almost impossible to find jury members who could be impartial, a change of location (**venue**) can be ordered by the court to ensure a fair jury trial for the defendant. The change is usually to a community well removed from the scene of the crime.

2.   Since the point of changing location is to find untainted jury members, the court may order severe limitations on what can be published about the case.

3.   On occasion, the court may ban publication of anything about the change of location — including the fact that a change of venue has been requested or granted.

4.   When the trial begins in the new location, the court can order a ban on reporting that a change of venue has taken place. The ban remains in effect until a verdict has been handed down or the trial otherwise ends.

Preliminary inquiry

Dangers:
1.   Violating a publication ban.
2.   Reporting a confession.

1.   A preliminary inquiry is held to determine if there's enough evidence to warrant a trial. The accused usually asks for a ban on publicity. The judge is required to grant it on request, and no evidence may then be reported.

2.   What may be reported:

a)   Whether the accused is sent to trial.

b)   The exact charge on which the accused was brought to preliminary hearing and, if appropriate, on which he or she was sent to trial.

c)   The number of witnesses heard.

d) Any comment by the lawyers, or the accused, or any part of the judge's decision not referring to the evidence heard.

3. Even without a publication ban, the Criminal Code prohibits reporting any confession — by the accused at the hearing (rare) or mentioned in evidence by police or other third parties at this stage — at risk of a fine of up to $2,000 or up to six months in jail, or both.

4. A confession in this context can mean a literal admission of guilt or any statement or action implying guilt. For example, if police testify that the accused led them to the body in a murder case, it should be avoided as an implied admission of guilt.

5. Any publication ban remains in effect until the conclusion of any subsequent trial, defined as the point at which a verdict is reached, regardless of intention to appeal. At that point, testimony at the preliminary hearing becomes publishable.

6. If the accused is discharged at the end of a preliminary hearing for lack of sufficient evidence, the banned testimony becomes publishable. An exception is a confession offered as evidence by police but not admitted by the judge; in such cases, consult a supervisor or counsel.

Trial

Dangers:

1. Reporting what the jury hasn't heard.

2. Evidence of criminal record.

---

1. The general rule is that any evidence admitted by the judge at a public trial can be reported. This includes confessions and other evidence that may have been excluded at previous stages, if the evidence is presented again in open court.

2. It is dangerous to resurrect any other previous submissions made at a preliminary inquiry until the trial ends.

3. Evidence or arguments presented with the jury absent should not be reported, except in the rare cases where the jury has been sequestered. For example, no reference should be made to evidence at a hearing (**voir dire**) held to determine whether certain evidence, such as confessions or wiretaps, may be legally presented to the jury.

4. If such evidence is admitted by the judge, it can be reported when presented to the jury. If not admitted, it may not be reported until after the trial, and then only with consent of supervisors or counsel.

5. Statements ordered struck from the record by the judge may still be reported. The judge's ruling has the effect of erasing the statements only from the trial record.

6. Any reporter who starts to cover a trial part way through must confirm that there is no voir dire or other restriction on what may be reported.

7. Evidence of previous convictions is usually not admitted at trial. If an accused presents evidence intended to show good character, he or she may then be asked about any prior criminal record.

8. On rare occasions, the public is excluded from all or part of a trial:

a) Trials of young people under the federal act dealing with youth crime.

b) Trials in which there is risk of disclosing information affecting national security or defence, international relations or the public interest.

c) Cases where the judge orders a trial closed in the interests of maintaining order or the proper administration of justice. No testimony may then be reported, but the verdict can be.

9. If the public is excluded to maintain order but the media are allowed to remain, the proceedings may be reported unless the judge directs otherwise.

10. Immediately after a verdict in a criminal trial has been rendered — and even if one of the parties plans to appeal — it is permissible to report fair and accurate comments by editorial writers, columnists and legal experts on the facts of the case, the parties, their lawyers, the judge's conduct and the administration of justice.

11. There is increasing leeway now to criticize the administration of justice, including the conduct of judges and the validity of their judgments. But to suggest unworthy motives by a judge is courting a contempt citation.

Appeals

Danger:

1. Suggesting bias.

1. Normally, anything and everything said at an open appeal court hearing can be reported.

2. Appeal court judges are generally considered to be above being prejudiced by the publication of comment or opinion about a case being heard on appeal.

3. Nonetheless, to suggest bias or prejudgment on the part of a judge — appeal court or otherwise — is tempting fate.

4. And of course the normal rules of court reporting — fair and balanced coverage — apply to appeal court hearings.

Retrials

Dangers:

1. Recalling previous verdict.
2. Recalling previous evidence.

---

1.   When a trial ends in a hung jury, or when a conviction or acquittal has been overturned on appeal, a new trial may be ordered. That means that for the accused, the slate has in effect been wiped clean. It is as if the first trial did not take place.

2.   The appeal court's decision may be reported at the time with full background. But well before a new trial begins there must be the same restraint in reporting on evidence or testimony as would have applied before the first trial, especially if a jury trial is possible.

3.   Unless specifically banned, it is permissible to report at any time that a previous trial ended in a hung jury, or that the verdict of the previous trial was overturned on appeal. When retrial is imminent, it is not normally permitted to report what the previous verdict was, since that could influence the new jury.

Young persons

Note: In early 1999, the federal government proposed major changes to the way the justice system deals with people under age 18. The material in this section does not include details on these changes, which are primarily concerned with sentencing.

1.   A federal act covers how the justice system deals with people from their 12th to their 18th birthdays.

2.   The act prohibits publication of the names or other identifying characteristics of young people as persons who appear or are to appear at a hearing, adjudication or appeal under the act. The prohibition applies to the accused, witnesses and victims, unless a victim is dead.

3.   Among the characteristics that could serve to identify a young person under the act — and are therefore forbidden to be published — would be names of family members, a home location, a sports team, or the name of a school attended or of the institution in which a young person has been detained.

4.   The publication ban applies also to adults who were under 18 at the time of an offence.

5.   The ban also applies to a young person who is said by witnesses or police to have committed an offence. It is risky, for example, to quote a witness as saying a named young person was speeding when an accident occurred.

6.   When a young person is suspected in a crime involving members

of his or her own family, no story may include *both* the victims' names *and* their relationship with the suspect. That would amount to identifying the suspect. When the first news of such a crime becomes available:

a) Do not either name the victims or describe their relationship with the suspect until it is clear from accumulating details where the chief news interest will lie: in the relationship or in the stature of the family.

b) Try to develop a consensus with other media on what to publicize — the names or the relationship.

c) Once a decision is made on which element to publicize, do not switch tracks without consulting counsel. Anyone putting together the names from one story and the relationship from the other can identify the suspect.

7. The court can order all or part of a youth court hearing closed to media and public at any time to protect those involved, in the interest of public morals or maintenance of order.

8. Some young people dealt with by the act may be identified in some cases involving serious offences.

9. Occasionally, police are given permission by a judge to issue a public appeal for a wanted young person, by name, where there is thought to be danger to others. Such court orders are valid *only for 48 hours*. Before publishing anything based on such an order, it's essential to verify that publication won't occur after permission has lapsed. CP news stories must include an editor's note at the top, giving the deadline.

10. Don't refer to accused people as **young offenders**. That phrasing automatically convicts the defendants.

11. The entire issue of young persons and the law is particularly treacherous because of the sweep of the current law and uncertainties about its application. Whenever there is doubt about a particular case, consult a supervisor or legal counsel.

Child protection laws

Care must be taken when handling stories that deal with proceedings under provincial laws on child custody and guardianship. These acts restrict reporting in order to shield children from harmful publicity.

The rules vary from province to province, so check before running a story that identifies children in custody cases.

In British Columbia, for instance, it is up to the courts to decide if the children can be identified. In Ontario, the Child and Family Services Act prohibits the identification of children involved in proceedings or hearings. It also prohibits identifying the child's parents, foster parents or other family members. It is OK to identify a couple in court on drug trafficking charges, and to say they have a daughter. But it contravenes the act to include that the daughter was taken into protective custody by the Children's Aid Society. A proceeding under the Child and

Family Services Act begins as soon as a child protection worker intervenes to take a child to a place of safety. No court need be involved.

Sensitive cases

1.   In cases involving sexual offences, extortion or usury, a judge must ban publication of the identity of victims or a juvenile witness if asked to do so by either the victim, the witness or the Crown.

2.   In such cases, it is forbidden not only to name the victim or witness but also to provide any information that could disclose their identity.

3.   Among information that could reveal their identity would be a family relationship, address, place of employment or other characteristic that could allow some members of the community to make an identification.

4.   Even where no ban is in effect, it is usually wrong to identify alleged victims of sexual assault without their active consent. CP does not name minors who are victims of sexual assault, even with the consent of their parents.

5.   In rare cases, a victim's name somehow becomes widely known in the community and publication of the name is not banned. Nevertheless, editors should still weigh whether using the name will send a signal to readers that the press is indifferent to the problems of sexual assault victims in general.

6.   Reporting on divorce and annulment proceedings is subject by law to restraints. Generally, only a bare identification of those involved, the main issues and the judgment can safely be reported.

7.   Generally, provincial legislation that requires the reporting of communicable diseases also provides for strict confidentiality. It is therefore risky to breach the anonymity of those with a sexually transmitted disease, AIDS or other reportable infection without their consent.

8.   Certain offences are regarded by the law as relatively minor, subject to small fines at most. But publicly naming those accused of communicating with a prostitute, indecent exposure or similar offences can have ruinous consequences. It should be done rarely.

9.   The law, not just ethics, can determine what gruesome or indecent details to publish in court cases. The law forbids reporting on indecent matters or indecent medical details that could injure public morals — phrases that are vague enough to require legal advice when in doubt.

Civil cases

While criminal cases involve society's attempt to control wrongdoing or protect the public good, civil cases involve disputes between private individuals or corporations. Society provides the court structure and a set of laws designed to make the settlement of grievances an orderly process.

Civil cases require the same care and dispassion of reporters as criminal cases do.

Vocabulary:

1. In civil cases, there is no **prosecutor**. Nobody is said to be **charged**. At the end of a court hearing, no one is **convicted** or **acquitted**, nor found **guilty** or **not guilty**.

2. The person initiating a civil case is the **plaintiff** or **petitioner**. The process involves **bringing suit** or **taking action** or **seeking damages**. The other party is the **defendant** or **respondent**.

Claims

1. Small claims are heard in a variety of lower courts depending on the province. The upper limit for the amount claimed in such cases also varies with the province.

2. Small claims are usually heard directly by a judge, without lawyers acting for the contesting parties.

3. Intermediate claims are heard at lower or intermediate court levels, with lawyers representing the parties. Jury trials are rare.

4. The largest civil claims are heard in provincial superior courts, by judge alone or with jury.

5. Jury trials are no longer provided for in Quebec for civil suits.

Other civil cases

1. Surrogate or probate courts exist in some provinces to deal with wills and estates. In other provinces, such cases are heard by the courts that handle other civil actions.

2. The Federal Court of Canada has jurisdiction over citizenship, taxation, immigration, copyright, trademark and patent cases, judicial review of federal administrative tribunals, and claims brought against the government of Canada.

Appeals

1. Appeals in civil cases are heard by the appeal division of a provincial superior court or court of appeal. Leave to appeal must almost always be sought from the higher court.

2. The appeal division of Federal Court hears appeals from decisions of that court.

3. The Supreme Court of Canada hears appeals on civil cases if there is a matter of public importance or an important point of law at issue.

Examination for discovery

1. Before trial of a civil suit, a process called examination for discovery is normally held. It allows the parties to examine each other's case and to clarify the issues to be resolved at trial.

2. Although the testimony is recorded and those testifying are under oath, the evidence at examination for discovery is not subject to all the normal safeguards of a courtroom.

3. Such examinations are not considered public hearings and cannot be covered by reporters. The transcripts are not public documents and are not normally accessible to the media. Publication of such evidence should not be considered without legal advice.

Damage suits

Dangers:

1. Quoting from one-sided documents.

2. Referring to amount claimed.

1. When one party files suit for damages against another, a writ or statement of claim is issued. A fair and accurate account of what is in the writ normally may be carried, but the story should strive for balance by:

a) including comment from principals named in the writ;

b) making clear the writ consists of allegations that are still to be tested in court.

A report on a statement of claim could present a libel risk if the above conditions are not met. In cases where a writ contains extremely defamatory information, it is prudent to seek counsel's advice before filing a story.

2. When a jury is hearing a civil suit for damages, it is not supposed to be informed about the amount of damages sought, for fear it will be misled. There is no real limit to the damages a person can claim and the amount may be ridiculous. As a working (but not infallible) rule, don't report the amount of damages sought during a jury trial or for a month before such a trial. Once a case has been decided, there is no such restriction.

3. The restriction does not apply to cases heard by a judge alone, nor to civil cases in Quebec where there are no longer jury trials in civil suits.

Contempt of court

Every journalist must be on guard against contempt of court in reporting on crimes, investigations and court cases.

Contempt of court doesn't mean despising a judge or the justice system. It's an old usage of the word **contempt**, meaning to **interfere** with the administration of justice or **disobey** the courts.

Controlling contempt is intended to protect a person's right to a fair trial, a cornerstone of democracy.

General guidelines

Dangers:
1. Defendant's confession.
2. Previous convictions.
3. Speculation.
4. Ignoring publication bans.

1. When a story is known to be in contempt, kill it at once. If contempt is suspected, withhold the story from publication, check it with counsel and keep editors advised.

➤ See **Libel**, page 111.

2. It is a basic rule that nothing must be published that interferes with the proper course of justice. That particularly includes anything that impairs an accused person's right to a fair trial.

3. Even if a statement is true and not libellous, it may be in contempt of court if it hurts a person's right to a fair trial.

4. A statement made in a legislature, court or other place of privilege is not protected from contempt. If an MP makes a statement in the Commons that could be prejudicial, it should not be published without consulting counsel.

5. There is a particular risk of prejudice in reporting on a defendant's confession unless it has been accepted as evidence in open court.

6. Check counsel before referring to previous convictions unless they are mentioned in open court. Such information is not necessarily admissible at trial.

7. The publication or repetition of a statement in contempt of court is itself contempt. The source of the statement or its accuracy doesn't matter.

8. Guilt or innocence should not be imputed to any party in a court case. It is also dangerous to speculate on possible motive for a crime,

the credibility of witnesses or the likely outcome in a jury trial.

9. Do not report testimony or other material from previous stages of a criminal proceeding — preliminary hearing, death inquiry or the like — unless it is introduced again in open court.

10. At a jury trial, it is a crime to report evidence heard by a judge at a *voir dire,* a hearing held to determine whether certain evidence will be presented to the jury. Such hearings are always held with the jury excluded. However, publication of voir dire evidence may be allowed when it involves a case being tried by judge alone or in those rare cases where a jury is being sequestered. If in doubt, check counsel.

11. Any restriction imposed by a court on publication remains in effect until the court sets it aside.

12. It is a crime in Canada for jurors to disclose any information on their deliberations. While there's no law forbidding reporters to interview jurors, the reporter could be charged with inducing a juror to break the law by encouraging the juror to reveal protected information.

13. Once a case has ended, it is usually permissible to report criticism of the administration of justice or the conduct of a judge. It is risky to suggest the judge had improper motives. In some provinces, a statement may also be in contempt if it vilifies a court or judge. Check counsel when in doubt.

Foreign cases

1. Exercise care on any story from abroad that includes out-of-court statements by police or others about Canadian individuals or businesses if a subsequent trial is likely to take place in Canada.

2. In particular, beware of assuming that U.S. laws and legal procedures apply in this country. Statements about an accused person from police and other authorities of a kind that are routine in the United States can be considered contempt in Canada.

Libel

Remember:

1.   Statements damaging to reputation must never be published unless there is a clear legal basis for doing so.

2.   Anyone who repeats a libel is fully responsible for the libel, no matter what its source.

3.   A libel can cause great damage to a person's life.

4.   Individual reporters and editors can be sued along with their employers for libels they permit to be published.

Libel is the publication of a false and damaging statement. It is part of the broader legal category known as **defamation**, covering **slander** (ordinary conversation) and **libel** (published or broadcast).

Defamation is a statement that tends to lower a person in the opinion of others, or exposes the person to hatred, contempt or ridicule. Defamation is also a statement that injures another's reputation in a way that affects that person's livelihood — work, trade or profession — or financial credit.

When a story is known to be libellous, **kill** it at once.

> **BULLETIN**
>   EDITORS: Kill Moncton PM-Accusation. No charge laid yet. Story is possibly dangerous. Will be no sub.
>   **CP Halifax**

When even a slight doubt exists, **withhold** the story from publication immediately while a check is made.

> **URGENT**
>   EDITORS: Withhold Brandon AM-Wheat from publication. Contains possibly dangerous quotes. CP is checking with counsel.
>   **CP Winnipeg**

Then either kill it or release it promptly. If a kill is needed, advise whether a sub will be sent. If the story is approved as sent, release it urgently in an advisory.

Note: Don't blame libel or libellous material for a kill or withhold. It might weaken CP's defence against a subsequent suit.

General information

Key points:

1. Truth difficult to prove.

2. Public interest must be weighed.

1. Libel has serious potential to harm not only CP and its employees, but any newspaper or broadcaster using the material. A plaintiff can sue everyone, or pick and choose arbitrarily — even to the point of aiming at the weakest links, those with the smallest resources who are most likely to pay to settle a libel suit without contest.

2. Libel involves an untrue report. Truth is a **complete defence** against a libel suit. A true statement of fact is not vulnerable even if it is damaging. But the one who publishes a damaging statement is responsible for proving the truth of the statement, and that is often extremely difficult. In some cases it may be impossible. It's not up to the plaintiff to prove the statement is false.

3. In Quebec, in addition to truth, the Civil Code requires that publication be in the **public interest** and **without malice**.

4. **Public interest** and **lack of malice** are not specified by law elsewhere in Canada. However, professional ethics dictate that before publishing a truthful but damaging statement, the press will weigh carefully whether the public interest is served by publication. And absence of malice must be a foregone conclusion in the publication of any news report.

5. The Canadian Press and other media whose reports reach an audience within Quebec must take into account Quebec's legal requirements when considering publication of potentially libellous material from elsewhere in Canada, particularly if the report concerns a Quebec resident.

6. Consent can be used as a defence in a libel suit, but it requires proof that:

a) the person defamed has been informed defamatory information will be published, and

b) the person knows what he or she is consenting to, and

c) the person consents to publication.

If consent is to be used as a defence, the proof of it will have to meet certain standards that stand up in court. A signed formal statement or an audio tape of an interview may be called for. Consult with counsel beforehand to work out details.

7. Except in Quebec, it is virtually impossible to libel the dead. And a libel suit launched by someone who subsequently dies is normally dropped. However, it could be dangerous to defame a dead person in a way that affects the living: for example, suggesting a man sexually abused his children before he died.

Privilege

Key points:
1. Fair, accurate, no malice.
2. Right to rebuttal.

1. Privilege means **protection from legal action**, even when defamatory material has been published. Privilege is based on two traditional assumptions:

a) It would be in the public interest for every citizen to attend certain events or read certain reports. Failing that, all citizens should have access to fair and accurate reports of such events.

b) In some cases, the public good is better served through unrestrained debate and the free communication of information than it is through a normal concern about accuracy or defamation.

2. Privilege is never absolute. At its most fundamental, it still requires that any report be **fair, accurate** and **without malice**:

a) **Fairness** means lack of bias, not taking statements out of context.

b) **Accuracy** means reporting the facts correctly. A report need not be textual or complete; it can be a fair synopsis.

c) **Lack of malice** means there is no dishonest or hidden motive nor reckless disregard for the truth.

3. The protection of privilege is also lost as a defence in a libel action if there has been a refusal to publish a reasonable statement of explanation or contradiction despite a request from the person defamed to do so.

4. Privilege does not extend to matters of contempt. Statements that could interfere with a person's right to a fair trial risk contempt even if made by an elected representative during an open session of a legislature. A fair and accurate account of a court case could be in contempt as well if it prejudices another case.

What's protected

Key points:
1. Legislative bodies, courts.
2. Quasi-judicial bodies.
3. Meetings, reports.
4. Public proceedings.
5. Notices to the public.

1. The common law — that is, traditional rights recognized by the courts — and the Civil Code in Quebec provide general principles for the protection known as privilege.

2. In addition, all provinces have specific statutes dealing with libel and privilege. The statutes vary; in tricky cases, get legal advice. However, the following may be considered privileged:

a) Debates and committee meetings of the House of Commons, the Senate and provincial legislatures, as well as public reports and documents issued by these bodies.

   Note: The privilege doesn't extend to statements made outside of a chamber or committee hearing, such as in a scrum.

b) Proceedings heard in public before any court exercising judicial authority, and reports issued by courts. The privilege doesn't extend to hearings from which public and press are excluded, nor to any matter on which the court has banned publication. If a report is not contemporaneous, consult counsel.

c) Death inquiries or coroner's inquests, royal commissions and other commissions of inquiry are not strictly courts but their proceedings and reports or documents are generally privileged.

d) Hearings of federal and provincial regulatory agencies and administrative tribunals, such as labour relations boards, and their reports or documents.

e) Meetings and reports of local government bodies and their agencies, such as municipal councils, municipal planning boards, school boards, boards of health.

f) Public meetings. This broad category can be tricky. It is usually defined as a meeting open to the general public, lawfully convened, to discuss a matter of public interest. It probably doesn't cover a news conference, nor a political meeting to which only supporters of one party have been invited. When in doubt, check counsel.

g) Any bulletin, report, notice or other document issued for the information of the public from any government office or department, medical officer of health or local board of health. This would include, for example, a warning that a particular product is dangerous to health.

h) Any notice or report issued by any government or municipal official, commissioner of police or chief constable for the information of the public, and published at that person's request. The most common example is a police appeal for public help in locating a fugitive or missing person.

Provincial statutes

Key points:

1. Professional, business, sports bodies.

2. Right of rebuttal.

3. Retraction, apology.

1. Each province in Canada has some form of libel legislation, dealing with issues of defamation and protection from legal action under certain conditions.

2. In addition to the categories of privilege listed previously, most provincial laws extend privilege to the findings and proceedings of professional, business and sports organizations that are formed in Canada. Included would be the disciplinary proceedings of law societies, medical associations, trade and business associations and sports leagues.

3. However, provincial law states that refusal to carry a reasonable statement of explanation or contradiction from the complainant, if asked to do so, will wipe out the privilege.

4. The law also specifies that a full and fair retraction for a defamatory story, if published with equal prominence to the orginal story and within *three days* of receiving legal notice, will reduce damages. The provision doesn't apply to a story that suggests a criminal offence was committed.

5. Damages may also be reduced if a full apology is published either before legal action was started or promptly afterwards.

6. The Quebec Press Act, in addition to most of the above, also extends privilege to the reports of the provincial ombudsman when tabled in the legislature, and to reports by the government or an authorized person about the financial solvency of companies or the value of certain stock and bond issues.

7. The Quebec law provides for reduced damages by apology, but that doesn't apply when a criminal offence is suggested. Nor does it apply when the defamation involves a candidate for Parliament, the national assembly or municipal office and when it is published in the period extending from three days before nomination day until election day.

Special concerns

1. People in certain areas of society make outrageous statements as a matter of course. Politics and sports are prime examples.

2. Public statements from people in these fields are routinely harsh, overstated and malicious. If such statements were made by others under different circumstances, the courts would be much busier.

3. The fact that political or sports comments rarely result in libel claims does not mean there is no need for caution in reporting them. Libel is libel. Check counsel before taking chances.

4. A separate concern involves non-Canadians who have business or other interests in Canada. Such people can sue for libel in this country if news from abroad is published in Canada which affects their reputation or livelihood in Canada. Thus, for example, a report from somewhere in the United States that alleges drug-taking by a football player now in the Canadian Football League — or even with CFL prospects — would be dangerous. So would a report from abroad that damages the reputation of a Hong Kong businessman with Canadian business interests.

Good faith

1. If a statement is false, it is no defence to claim that it was thought to be true at time of publication.

2. However, the damages awarded in a libel suit may be reduced because of absence of malice and evidence of good faith:

a) if there were reasonable grounds for believing the defamatory statement was true, and

b) if an apology was published when the statement was discovered to be false.

Fair comment

Key points:
1. Honest opinion.
2. Based on provable fact.
3. Public interest.

1. Commentary involves questions of opinion and interpretation. A different test is applied to commentary than to factual reporting. Comment or opinion (**the government's program is ruining the economy**) need not be proved true in the sense that an objective fact (**the government has increased the sales tax**) is true.

2. The defence of fair comment has often been applied to editorials and to artistic criticism such as book, film or theatre reviews. But it isn't limited to such material. It can be used to defend any story that mixes factual material with interpretation and analysis.

3. To be defensible, comment must meet these criteria:

a) It must express an opinion honestly held. It can't be presented maliciously or out of a hidden motive.

b) Most important, it must be based on facts *presented in the story* that can be proved to be true. An honest opinion based on false information cannot be defended.

c) It must relate to a matter of public interest, not a purely private matter.

4. Public interest is roughly parallel to news value. But publication in one province on the grounds of public interest could be libellous in another province.

5. The basic rule holds: When in doubt, get legal advice.

Copyright

Dangers:

1. Substantial quotes without OK.
2. Permission not in writing.

1. Copyright is what gives the creator of an original work the exclusive right to benefit from it.

2. Copyright covers such creations as books, films, songs, articles and essays, letters, diaries, pictures or anything else that's original and in some permanent form. It can even extend to distinctive titles.

3. The copyright owner controls the right to reproduce the work, in whole or in substantial part.

4. For the press, this means there can be no substantial quotations from copyrighted material without written permission of the copyright owner. Giving a mere credit to the copyright owner isn't sufficient.

5. *Substantial* has different meanings for different works. A complete stanza from a short pop song could be substantial. Generally, copying the heart of a work would be against copyright law. Check counsel when in doubt.

6. An exception is made for quotations used in a review or critique, but it must be a bona fide review and the quotes should be no more than needed to make a critical point.

7. Generally, government documents, speeches and most other material used in daily journalism are not copyright.

8. Over time, copyright protection is lost and the work falls into the public domain. In Canada, literary and artistic copyright expires 50 years after the author's death. Copyright on photographs expires 50 years after the negative has been processed.

9. Information cannot be copyrighted, only the form in which it is presented. Although newspapers frequently identify a story as being copyright, the actual news in the story cannot be protected. Someone else using an original method of expression may reproduce the information. Making a few changes in expression is not sufficient; the presentation must be substantially original.

10. The Canadian Press has first right to use staff-written local news from newspapers that are part of the co-operative news agency, whether or not the newspaper declares it to be copyright.

11. However, worked-up exclusives or news from beyond the newspaper's normal coverage area cannot legally be distributed in their original form by CP without permission from the managing editor or other senior officer at the paper. Giving credit to the paper is not a substitute for getting permission if there are to be substantial quotes or reproductions from the original. Permission can be assumed if the paper has transmitted the story to CP electronically

12. Like anyone else, in the absence of permission, CP may distribute a report based on the information in the copyright story. It must use substantially different words and it should be brief — no longer than needed to report the substance of the story. Direct quotes of more than a sentence or two are not allowed.

13. CP may also not normally use a published feature created by a freelance, even if it involves local news. Freelance work is usually identified by a different credit line (e.g., **Special to the Mirror**) than staff work. Ignoring the copyright owned by a freelance can be costly.

14. The copyright in a Letter to the Editor is held by the letter writer, who automatically gives a right of publication to the newspaper that receives the letter. To reproduce all or part of the letter elsewhere would require written permission from the copyright holder, in strict legal terms. But in practical terms, verbal permission from the newspaper will do. (Few letter writers are likely to sue because their views have been given a wider audience, and if they won a suit the damages would likely be minimal.)

15. Freelance photographers hired by CP negotiate in advance the ownership and resale rights for their film. The work of newspapers' regular freelance photographers is available to CP. In most instances of spontaneous photography — the bystander's shots of a hot news event — the freelance is told by the paper to negotiate directly with CP.

➤ See **Pictures**, page 336.

Privacy, wiretaps

Dangers:
1. Disclosing others' communications.
2. Broadcasting private conversations.

1. Anyone may record their own conversations, without the permission of the other party, whether in person or on the telephone or other circumstance.

2. However, it's illegal to intercept or record conversations or private communications of other people without the consent of one of the other parties.

3. It's also illegal to broadcast on radio (but, oddly, not on TV) any part of one's own conversation with someone else without the consent of the other person. An exception is when the other person has phoned in to participate in the broadcast.

4. And it's illegal to use or disclose anything about others' private communications without the consent of one of the parties.

Press and police

Police in Canada have shown a disturbing tendency to turn to the print and broadcast media for information and evidence in recent years. They have demanded the use of photographs and film to document charges against possible rioters and others involved in public disturbances, and have made other demands on news people to support police work.

The media have generally resisted. If people come to view the media as an arm of the justice system, they will lose confidence in the media as an intermediary between ordinary citizens and authorities.

Following are normal guidelines for dealings with police:

Public notices

1. The press normally co-operates when police ask for publicity about the hunt for suspects or lost persons. Accuracy in identification is essential. Racial description and other characteristics — not usually part of a news report — are a normal part of such published identification material.

2. Do not casually refer to a person as dangerous. The description would be prejudicial if referring to someone whose jury trial is imminent. It should be based on a *written* release from police intended for the public.

Co-operation with police

1. There is normally no objection to providing police with copies of stories or photographs that have already been published, or other routine material of a non-confidential nature, as a matter of courtesy.

2. However, reporters' notes, unpublished film, background files, electronic mail and other material dealing with ongoing stories or anything of a private or confidential nature should not be provided to police unless they produce a search warrant.

3. Material gathered by reporters and other employees in the course of their work is the property of the employer. No employee has the right to turn over such material to police without permission from a senior supervisor.

Newsroom searches

1. Police will sometimes provide advance notice that they intend to present a search warrant. In any case, police arriving in a newsroom with a search warrant — with or without notice — must not be delayed, obstructed or resisted. They are not obliged to wait until legal counsel is on the scene.

2. However, police should be referred immediately to a senior supervisor, and legal counsel should be informed immediately by phone.

3. The warrant should be inspected closely to ensure that

a) all factual references (address, name of company or person, date) are accurate;

b) a suspected offence is specified;

c) it is properly signed by a justice of the peace.

4. If there are errors, the police should be asked to leave. If there aren't, the supervisor can watch any search being conducted. Others on staff can observe and, if necessary later, serve as witnesses about the way the search was conducted, but only the supervisor should talk to police.

5. While not obliged to assist searchers, the supervisor may decide it is best to direct them to a specific desk or area and otherwise help them if the alternative is a wide sweep that could uncover unrelated confidential material elsewhere in the newsroom.

6. The supervisor should ask permission to photocopy any material that is to be seized. If the request is refused, legal counsel should be consulted immediately.

7. If the searchers intend to take confidential material relating to sources, or unpublished material, the supervisor should insist that it be placed in a sealed envelope until the question of privilege can be decided in court.

8. Legal counsel should be consulted promptly about any question that arises as a result of being served with a search warrant.

Legal vocabulary

The language of courts and lawyers is extremely precise, but it can be distant from plain speech. Latin terms and jargon abound. Legal language may find its way into a story legitimately for effect or precision, but in most cases a plain substitute or clear explanation is best.

Some standard legal terms:

affidavit: sworn written statement to be used as evidence.

arraign: charge before the courts.

bawdy-house: archaic term still used in Criminal Code for brothel.

common law: unwritten law based on ancient custom and judicial precedent.

> **common-law marriage**: relationship based on living together without legal recognition. **Note:** It is not usually necessary to specify if a relationship is common-law.

concurrent: at the same time; of a number of jail sentences, to be served simultaneously (as opposed to consecutively).

contempt (of court): not disdain for the judge, but interference with justice or disobedience of court order.

copyright: protection of exclusive use of original work.

ex parte (Latin for *from one party*): one-sided; submission by one party in legal dispute without contest from other side.

habeas corpus (Latin for *You have the body*): writ requiring person be brought before court, usually to test whether person's detention is legal.

in camera (Latin for *in a room*): private(ly); hearing with public excluded.

indeterminate sentence: of no fixed term, dependent on prisoner's conduct.

indict, indictment: formally accuse of crime; formal accusation or charge.

> **indictable offence**: more serious level of criminal charge (less serious is called summary offence).

interim release: term increasingly used instead of **release on bail**.

leave: permission, as in **leave to appeal**.

open custody: assignment of offender to group home or other lightly supervised environment, usually for juveniles.

plaintiff: person who brings complaint to court in civil case.

pré-enquête (*pre-inquiry*): rare form of private hearing by judge or justice of peace to decide whether charge should be laid.

privilege: immunity granted under certain conditions to speak without fear, or to report such speech.

sub judice (Latin for *under a judge*): before the courts; for the court alone to decide.

subpoena (Latin for *under penalty*): writ commanding presence in court.

venue (change of): location; move trial to another community to avoid prejudice against accused.

voir dire (Old French for *say the truth*): hearing within a trial, with jury excluded, to test admissibility of confession or other evidence.

writ: court order requiring specified act or giving authority to someone to have act done.

> **writ of certiorari** (from Latin for *inform*): demand from higher court for records from lower court.

> **writ of mandamus** (Latin for *We command*): command to inferior court, or to person to perform legal duty.

young person: in law, male or female between 12th and 18th birthdays.

> **child**: person under 12.

Canadian courts

Each province has different names for its courts. Here is a list, including federal courts, with upper courts listed first (capitalization is in CP style):

Federal:
Supreme Court
Federal Court of Appeal
Federal Court
tax court

Alberta, New Brunswick, Manitoba:
Court of Appeal
Court of Queen's Bench
provincial court

British Columbia:
Court of Appeal
Supreme Court
provincial court

Newfoundland:
Supreme Court (Court of Appeal and trial division)
unified family court
provincial court

Nova Scotia:
Court of Appeal
Supreme Court
provincial court (city court in Halifax)
family court

Ontario:
Court of Appeal
Superior Court of Justice (formerly general division)
Ontario court of justice (formerly provincial division)

Prince Edward Island:
Supreme Court (appeal division and trial division)
provincial court

Quebec:
Court of Appeal
Superior Court
Quebec court (provincial)

Saskatchewan:
Court of Appeal
Court of Queen's Bench
unified family court
provincial court

The working journalist

Breaking news

Battle stations!

The call to action in a CP newsroom when a major story breaks is like a ringing command across the deck of a warship steaming into action.

The fast-breaking story goes to CP's very heart. The Canadian news industry — print, radio and TV — fixes its eyes on the CP computer queue when major news erupts.

CP faces a potential deadline every minute. It must deliver at breakneck speed.

But absolute accuracy and precise attribution rank ahead of speed in handling breaking news.

Slow down, step back, check and recheck if there is any risk of inaccuracy.

Getting organized

There is no textbook on handling the spot news break. Circumstances in any two breaks are never the same.

There may be official sources such as the police to help. But there may not be — at least in the early stages.

Improvisation and resourcefulness are the standards. So are clear-cut organization, precise individual roles, steady direction and cool heads.

Confusion at the scene of events like a plane crash, prison riot or tornado is the norm. Expect it but don't get caught up in it. Officialdom may be in a dither. The *official* version of what has happened may change in minutes. And then change again. Damage estimates and death tolls can swing wildly.

But disorder has no place in a newsroom when a big story is breaking.

Some basic guidelines:

1. Respond immediately to a tip of a major break. Assign someone to concentrate on getting it confirmed or denied. Notify Main Desk and a bureau supervisor so planning can begin immediately on staff assignments: on-site staff, main lead writer, other writers, chasers, editors; and on logistics like rental cars and chartered aircraft (see *Equipment* below). Main Desk will tip the other services, including BN, CP Pictures and CP Online. If a report cannot be confirmed immediately, send an advisory to say CP is checking an unconfirmed (*repeat, unconfirmed*) report or angle, and include the gist of what is involved. If the report is confirmed, send a NewsAlert, Bulletin or Urgent immediately and work on the advisory next.

Note: Don't dredge up the relic *copy will be expedited*. That goes without saying. Do say as precisely as possible when copy is expected. Then deliver it on time. Or, in rare cases, send another note saying why it has been delayed. Never leave editors hanging.

➤ See **Advisories**, page 354.

2.   Never move a story on a major break that isn't nailed directly to an identified source. That can be anyone from the prime minister announcing a declaration of war to a tow-truck driver at the scene of a multi-vehicle pileup. Move a Bulletin or Urgent as soon as the report is confirmed. Get the attribution in the first paragraph. Every detail must be secure. Hold back if there is even the slightest doubt about a new development. But don't sit on a hot angle or wait for official sources to return calls. Move immediately to get it confirmed or denied. Nail down all sources. Ask them to spell their names — twice if there is any possibility of error. Ask for precise ranks or titles. This takes only seconds. Corrections take minutes and disfigure the report. Hold on to tapes or original notes of who said what and when.

A typical opening story:

PM-Crash
code:1

BULLETIN

   REGINA (CP) — An unidentified airliner plunged into a farmer's grain field and exploded in a huge fireball today near the community of Gravelbourg in rural south-central Saskatchewan, the farm's owner told radio station CXYZ.

MORE

Note: The **MORE** slug promises further information in the form of a 1st add (see page 395) within 10 minutes.

3.   Move a coverage advisory as soon as plans are firm:

PM-Crash-Advisory
code:1
   Eds: CP reporter Martin O'Hanlon has left Regina for Gravelbourg, Sask., where an eyewitness has told a radio station that an unidentified airliner has crashed and exploded. O'Hanlon should reach the area at about 11:30 a.m. CST. A further advisory on other coverage plans, including photos, will move within 20 minutes.
   CP EDMONTON

---

4.   Quickly pin down the location, including the nearest town if the site is remote. Tip Graphics so a newsmap can get rolling. Keep the location high in all subsequent leads.

5.   Don't wait for local authorities to get back from the scene. Chasers should not stop pressing while waiting for a promised call-back from an official source.

Each bureau should have current telephone listings for every community in its region. CD-ROM or Internet phone listings can be a great help. Scour listings for likely unofficial sources — the local service station or general store. Or if there is nothing obvious, take a stab at random listed numbers. Chances are most people in the area will know something. Or know someone who does.

Note: Long before authorities were saying anything for the record, an eyewitness to the 1989 University of Montreal massacre told a CP reporter that a man carrying a gun had burst into a classroom.

"Someone asked him if it was a joke and the guy started firing," the eyewitness said.
Another said: "It was a human hunt and we were the quarry."

Caution: Don't say witnesses or sources when only one person is being quoted.

6.   Move adds in short takes of a paragraph or two. Aim for a 1st Writethru within 20 minutes of moving an Urgent such as the reported plane crash above. Official confirmation or direct word from a reliable witness may rate a Bulletin:

AM-CRASH, 1st Writethru
code:1
Eds: UPDATES with police confirming airliner has crashed.
BULLETIN
   REGINA (CP) — An unidentified airliner described by a farmer as "silver with a green tail" crashed in a fireball today in a grain field near Gravelbourg in south-central Saskatchewan, police said. An officer at the scene said there were no signs of survivors.

---

7. Don't bury the news when new — but less important — information becomes available. Survivors found staggering from the scene or casualties on the ground belong at the top. But don't leapfrog the real news with secondary information such as an RCMP announcement of a news conference on the plane crash. That sort of information is vital for the media — but not the reader.

8. Try for fresh information for the top of Writethrus, but it must be pertinent to the main news. If necessary, stay with the original lead and keep later secondary information lower.

Here is an example of a lead that keeps the essentials at the top:

**By Penny MacRae
and
Peter Lowrey**

MONTREAL (CP) — A gunman who yelled "you're all a bunch of feminists" went on a deadly rampage Wednesday at the University of Montreal, shooting 14 female students before committing suicide with his own weapon.

The gunman, who was in his early 20s and wore hunting garb, also inflicted bullet wounds on 13 others — nine women and four men — in the bloodiest mass shooting in Canadian history.

"I saw death close up and I shook," said Vanthona Day, 22, one of scores of horrified students who streamed out of the building after the carnage.

Not all breaking news comes as a surprise and a writer can benefit from advance preparation:

By Chisholm MacDonald

ST. CATHARINES, Ont. (CP) — Helmuth Buxbaum, millionaire businessman, womanizer and patron of dubious drug-pushers, has moved to an even darker level of life — a prison cell for at least 25 years.

Convicted Thursday of first-degree murder in the contract slaying of his wife Hanna, his partner in nursing-home enterprises and marriage for 23 years, Buxbaum insisted to the end that he had nothing to do with her death.

But a jury of 10 men and two women decided it was he — not his drug supplier — who masterminded the murder plot in which the 48-year-old mother of six children was pulled from the Buxbaums' car on a roadside and ruthlessly shot in the head.

---

9. Give a wide berth to generalized and vaguely attributed statements, especially related to death tolls and damage estimates:

Not: Witnesses at the scene estimated about 20 people were killed and 40 or more injured.

But: "I counted 20 or 21 bodies and there must have been twice that many people who were showing some sign of life," said Jackie Lo, one of the first to reach the scene.

If the figures prove badly out of line, it was Lo who was wrong — not those reporting her words:

The official toll — 11 dead and 46 injured — was provided by RMCP Sgt. Laura Bridges and coroner Luis Alvarez. Earlier, one of the first volunteer rescuers to reach the area said she had counted 20 or 21 bodies.

Guard against slipping into the present tense on breaking stories, especially when picking up material from radio or TV. Writing in the past tense has two advantages: the story can be quickly led without having to change the tensing of the original; and the story stands up even if the situation changes after a paper has gone to press.

First steps

Major news breaks at any hour of the day. A solo CP staffer who gets word on such a break should:

1. Brief Main Desk.

2. Move an Urgent, NewsAlert or Bulletin, as appropriate.

3. Alert local supervisors who can call in reinforcements and start making plans for getting staff to the scene.

4. Send an advisory on coverage plans, even if it has to be tentative.

Organizing chaos

As noted, no two big news breaks are alike. But there are some tried and proven procedures to follow:

1. Get a strong lead writer in place immediately and let that person stick with the job. The writer knows what information has been placed where in the story, where figures are first reported and where sources are first named, where new information can be smoothly blended in and where pickups should naturally occur.

2. The lead writer should be assigned an editor who can work directly with the writer, checking content, smoothing the flow, setting up slugging, coding and headers, and moving Completes. The writer and editor keep the copy moving. A last-minute detail or appealing touch of colour can go in the next lead. The editor ensures the writer knows about any major changes being made in the story.

3. The writer and editor should **not** be involved in any other news while handling the big break. Their undivided attention is needed.

4. A bureau supervisor decides how much other copy is to be handled. Depending on available staff, or if the story is big enough, everything else may have to be put on hold. Often, though, the best course is to free one reporter-editor to handle all unrelated copy, likely in bare-bones form.

5. A supervisor, consulting with the writer and editor, decides what angles need chasing, who should go where and what information is needed for the next main lead or sidebars. If others are providing quotes or other details for the main story, remember this from the Old Lead Writer's Creed: *Don't tell me — write it.*

6. One supervisor or senior staff member should be the bureau funnel, dealing with Main Desk, the Picture Service, BN supervisors at Head Office and other media to ensure the bureau is getting everything it can from newspapers and radio stations in the area. The lead writer and editor should not be answering phones and worrying about logistics and other details.

7. An editorial assistant may be able to help the lead writer by chasing down a piece of background, checking a map for spelling or digging into Newstex or the morgue files. This staffer may also help Pictures and Graphics if a file photo needs to be transmitted or information is needed for a locator map or cutline.

Equipment

Proper equipment and fast action on logistics like transportation are critical when big stories break. Editorial and Communications supervisors should ensure:

1. That cellular telephones, tape recorders and portable computers are in top shape, fully charged and ready for action at all times. Company credit cards should be available for staff on short notice. There also should be some system in place for supplying cash in off hours.

2. That each bureau has at hand the after-hours phone numbers for at least two charter plane companies in the bureau's area. Phone immediately and get a quick estimate of cost and availability. Competition for charter aircraft can become intense when a big story breaks. It is often wise to make a tentative booking. Check other local media quickly about possible cost-sharing.

3. That reporters and photographers have current passports. Even entry to the United States has become stickier. St-Pierre-Miquelon lie just off Newfoundland but belong to France.

Common faults

The most common faults in news writing are lack of imagination, muted curiosity, and a deaf ear and closed eye for the reader's interests.

These faults lead straight to news stories that are predictable, unfocused and boring.

By turn or together, they may confuse readers with conflicting information, leave them gasping for missing facts or infuriated at what they know is misinformation.

Such stories can puzzle readers with fog and bafflegab, and have them wondering what the news means to them and their everyday lives.

Bluntly put, they turn readers off.

Unanswered questions

Never leave basic questions unanswered.

Not: The price of two litres of milk is going up five cents in New Brunswick today.

But: The price of two litres of milk in New Brunswick is going up today by five cents to $3.10 a carton or two-bag plastic pack. It is the second five-cent increase in just over seven months.

Not: She was sentenced to life in prison.

But: She was sentenced to life in prison with no chance of parole for 17 years.

Not: A police officer was shot Friday as two men sped away from the scene of a bank holdup in downtown Brandon.

But: A police officer was shot in the chest and seriously wounded as two men sped away ...

Not: Canadian shoe manufacturers say a federal government plan to lift import quotas on leather footwear will deliver a severe blow to the industry.

But: Canadian shoe manufacturers say a federal government plan to lift import quotas on leather footwear will ultimately lead to higher shoe prices for Canadians, especially women. It will also mean hundreds of Canadians will lose their jobs in shoe factories, they said.

Dig for treasure

Search a story for hidden angles that would snatch a reader's attention if even a hint of the buried treasure were woven into the lead.

Not: A local man faces three counts of attempted murder and four counts of assault with a weapon causing bodily harm after a hotel brawl at a wedding reception sent seven men to hospital, six with knife wounds, early Saturday morning.

But: A brawl at a wedding reception between friends of the bride and friends of the groom left seven men hurt and a country lodge with a heap of shattered furniture, antiques and chandeliers early Saturday.

Sentences and paragraphs

Readability has never been more important. People are busier and have less time than ever to read newspapers. They will quickly bail out from a story that is heavy and dull.

One key factor in readability is sentence length.

A sentence is more likely to be clear if it is short and conveys one idea:

People with near-death experiences agree about details to a remarkable extent.

A longer sentence which closely connects several ideas also works:

Many of them say they float out of their bodies, encounter God or a spirit figure, meet deceased relatives, review their past lives, feel great peacefulness and finally return to their bodies.

That sentence runs to 32 words, but its meaning never falters because everything relates to the same subject and the language is simple.

Try to begin sentences with words that have punch and power. Avoid starting with phrases, longer clauses or attribution.

Keep paragraphs short and active. Paragraphs of two or three tight sentences are inviting. Long, grey blobs of print are not.

Active vs. passive

Think of active verbs as power words — words that drive your sentences, keep the reader's attention and move her briskly along.

Not: The economy experienced a quick revival.

But: The economy revived quickly.

Not: At first light there was no sign of the ship.

But: The ship vanished in the night.

Use the passive when a switch in emphasis is helpful, for instance, to put the news ahead of the source:

Not: A grievance board has ordered the reinstatement of a counsellor fired for kicking a patient.

But: A counsellor fired for kicking a patient has been ordered reinstated by a grievance board.

And the passive may lighten a sentence by removing secondary information that can wait: **A banker wanted for questioning in the disappearance of $1 million is believed to have flown to Mexico, police said today.** (But be sure a later paragraph gives reasons for the belief.)

More than words

Tell the reader what has happened, certainly. But also help the reader understand why and how it has happened in terms that strike home:

Not: The hurricane caused widespread damage to buildings, farm equipment, trees and hydro lines.

But: The hurricane's winds lifted roofs off houses and barns and flipped over cars, tractors and even lumbering dump trucks used to carry grain. Almost every fruit and shade tree in the region was knocked over, and linemen said about 3,000 hydro poles had been snapped off.

Trippers

Be alert for words, phrasing and sentences that will cause a reader to stumble:

Not: Manness said he met with trucking industry officials earlier this year who said they were concerned about taxes.

But: Manness said he met earlier this year with trucking industry officials who said they were concerned about taxes.

Not: After dining on hundreds of pet cats and dogs, the provincial Environment Ministry has decided to round up coyotes and ship them to remote parts of the province.

But: Coyotes have killed dozens of pet cats and dogs, so the provincial Environment Ministry has decided to round up the predators and ship them to remote parts of the province.

Not: The bears were destroyed when they would not leave a tree in which they were munching leaves.

But: The bears were shot when they could not be coaxed out of a playground tree where they were munching leaves.

Front-end loading

Avoid it like the plague.

Not: United States envoy Herman Cohen said in London after meeting government and rebel representatives at peace talks that the two sides had agreed to a ceasefire.

But: The two sides have agreed to a ceasefire, United States envoy Herman Cohen said after ...

Not: In a telegram to Prime Minister Jean Chrétien urging that the offices Canada Post plans to eliminate be retained, the union said it was appalled by the proposed measures.

But: The union said it was "appalled" by Canada Post's plans to close the offices. It urged in a telegram to Prime Minister Jean Chrétien that all the post offices be retained.

Not: An official of the Nova Scotia Environment Department, who was at the scene on the Annapolis River near the small community of Paradise about 170 kilometres west of Halifax, said both tractor-trailer units were spilling chemicals into the river.

But: Both tractor-trailer units were spilling chemicals into the Annapolis River near the small community of Paradise, a Nova Scotia Environment Department official said from the scene, about 170 kilometres west of Halifax.

Not: British Columbia and Yukon Birders Association executive director Anne-Marie Sheehey will be the featured speaker.

But: Executive director Anne-Marie Sheehey of the British Columbia and Yukon Birders Association will be the featured speaker.

Overloads

The overloaded lead is sure to turn the reader off:

Not: The family and friends of William John Fortune have raised enough money to rescue the stranded Canadian tourist and, with the help of volunteers from the Barbados police department, will send an airplane on Tuesday to lift him and his two daughters, Louise and Samantha, from a tiny sandspit north of the Caribbean island, longtime friend Lorne Pulsifer said today.

But: An airplane will head for a tiny Caribbean sandspit north of Barbados on Tuesday to rescue a stranded Canadian tourist and his two daughters, a family friend said today.

The overblown statement is another turnoff:

Not: Once the wind was at his back, the home-town quarterback wreaked as much havoc on the defence as Hurricane Hugo did in the Caribbean.

But: The home-town quarterback, with the wind now at his back, threw touchdown passes on three consecutive drives.

Overwriting weakens stories and repels readers:

Not: The legislation was greeted with howls of protest.

But: One opposition member after another criticized the legislation, calling it ill-conceived and dangerous.

The facts are best presented in plain conversational style with deft phrasing, touches of human interest, significant details and strong quotes.

Avoid overcharged words: **blast, charged, chastise, flail, flay, lambaste, enraged, lash** and **slam**.

Simply report in an even tone what was said:

Not: Labor leader Bob White launched a bitter attack on the company offer.

But: "It is the most preposterous company offer I've seen in the last 15 years," said labor leader Bob White.

The formula lead

It needs no introduction.

Not: BARRIE, Ont. (CP) — Three men suffered minor injuries when their light plane crashed into a field after striking hydro lines Friday.

But: BARRIE, Ont. (CP) — A light plane hit power lines while taking off in a rainstorm Friday, flipped and crashed upside down in a farmer's potato field. The three men aboard escaped with minor injuries.

Jargon

Bureaucratese and other forms of bafflegab have become an epidemic. Some experts and academics seem bent on smothering readers in phrases like **problemize binary opposition, conceptual signage** and **rethink categoricalism** which frustrate translation.

As if this weren't stifling enough, newspaper people have their own self-inflicted verbiage in the form of *journalese:* MPs **blast** each other; inquiries **probe**; rescuers are **grim-faced**.

Inside language of a profession or any other specialist group should be translated into understandable English. But the translation needs care.

Not: "The bullet lodged in the cerebrum," the doctor said.

But: The bullet lodged in the upper front part of the brain, the doctor indicated.

Not: There was "a severe loss of separation" between the two aircraft, the air traffic controller said.

But: The two planes nearly collided, the air traffic controller suggested, explaining that is what he meant when he used the term "a severe loss of separation" in his report.

Not: Police withheld his identity pending notification of next-of-kin.

But: Police withheld his name.

Abstract nouns, especially ones ending in *-ion* and strung together with prepositions, often signal foggy writing. Passive verbs can be culprits as well.

Short words tend to be concrete, standing for people, places, objects and acts.

Not: Medically speaking, the inhalation of the toxic substance is considered capable of the creation of psychological compulsions resulting in his criminal behavior.

But: Doctors said breathing the poison may have affected his mind and driven him to kill.

Everyday words

Treat the reader to words and phrases that are short and familiar.

About, not **approximately**

Met, not **held a meeting**

Instructor or **teacher**, not **resource person**

Improve, never **ameliorate**

Plan or **program**, not **initiative** or **strategy**

Lazy words

Cast an inquisitive eye on words like **colourful, controversial** and **zany**. An editor who asks why Mayor Horsefall is **colourful** may learn Horsefall once ate his hat on the town hall steps when he lost a hockey bet with the mayor of a rival town. Tell the reader.

Say and variants

Early CP stylebooks described **say** and **said** as honest and inconspicuous. They are also not to be toyed with.

Say and **said** should be attached to words and ideas that exactly mirror the speaker's, not an interpretation or extension. Words like **indicate** or **suggest** may be appropriate where **said** is not and are mandatory in stories on opinion polls.

Not: The poll shows fewer than 10 per cent of Canadians believe . . .

But: The poll suggests fewer than 10 per cent . . .

Many substitutes for **say** and **said** are risky or, at best, vague:

Admit implies confession, **affirm** states a fact, **assert** declares strongly, **claim** and **maintain** hint of doubt, **confide** implies a confidence, **declare** states explicitly, **disclose** and **reveal** presume earlier concealment.

Be especially wary of **explain, point out, claim** and **note.** They all imply that what is being said is fact. **According to** and **said she believes** may question the speaker's credibility.

Words like **recalled** and **predicted** can be tricky. Make sure they fit the circumstances.

Attribution

Avoid the hackneyed **told reporters.** That the speaker said something after her speech, or after her statement in the Commons, or after a news release was issued is always sufficient.

Told The Canadian Press or **The Canadian Press has learned** should be used sparingly, such as when:

• The same person has said different things to different media and it seems appropriate to spell out the differing versions.

• CP has an exclusive interview with the prime minister or some other high official.

• An interview is obtained from an unusually distant or hard-to-reach point such as a submerged submarine or the tip of Mount Everest.

• Exclusive material has been gained through the Access to Information Act or similar legislation.

Arithmetic

Writers should mind their math when dealing with statistical percentages and other figures. Never make the reader do the arithmetic.

Reporting that the number of flagpole-sitters in Canada has increased 100 per cent in the last year is meaningless without the base figure. An increase from five flagpole-sitters to 10 is 100 per cent but the percentage figure alone suggests a population explosion.

Take care as well in phrasing changes in percentage statistics. A poll that suggests a drop in government support to 25 from 50 per cent does not mean a 25 per cent drop. It's a change of 25 percentage points.

Headline language

Keep headline language out of news copy.

Not: Bell inked a six-year contract.

But: Bell signed a six-year contract.

Not: The commission will launch a three-pronged probe into the fire.

But: The commission will investigate the fire in three ways.

Short general-purpose words may fit in a headline, but not in a story. Avoid words like:

Ban, beef up, bid, boost, cop, ink, ire, laud, lash, pact, probe, quiz, rap, shun, vow

The headline-writer's practice of dropping **a, the, of** and the like to save space leads to lumpy sentences in the body of a story.

Not: He was intrigued by Canadian Imperial Bank of Commerce chairman John Hunkin's defence of Dome Petroleum's rescue.

But: He was intrigued by the defence of Dome Petroleum's rescue offered by John Hunkin, chairman of the Canadian Imperial Bank of Commerce.

Verbs ending in -ize

Trendy verbs ending in -ize strike many readers as ungainly.

Accessorize, capsulize, decimalize, definitize, prioritize, therapize

Accept them cautiously or only when there is no satisfactory alternative.

Time element

Put the time element where it falls naturally in speech, usually right after the verb or at the end of the sentence.

Not: Transport Minister Doug Young Thursday said the new policy . . .

But: Transport Minister Doug Young said Thursday the new policy . . .

Try to put the time element at the end if putting it directly between the verb and its object is awkward:

Not: Finance Minister Paul Martin announced Wednesday a $2-billion job program.

But: Finance Minister Paul Martin announced a $2-billion job program Wednesday.

There are situations where the time element is at home either in the middle or at the end.

Dawn Coe came out of the pack Saturday to score a five-shot victory in the Canadian women's golf championship (Saturday).

That

Dropping **that** often makes for smoother reading, especially in shorter sentences.

She said (that) she wanted to be alone.

But retain it to avoid misleading the reader even momentarily.

Carr said that **on May 1 he was in Halifax;** Justice Minister Allan Rock warned that **the government would step in.**

That should also be retained and repeated with two or more clauses.

He promised that **the singer would appear** and that **the evening would be a success.**

That-which

When it comes to introducing a clause in the middle of a sentence, there's sometimes confusion about whether **that** or **which** is correct. **Which** sounds grammatical somehow, so it ends up being used too often.

That is generally used when the clause is essential to the noun it defines or narrows the topic: **The movie that opened at the Roxy last week.** (It's not just any movie, it's the one that opened last week at a specific theatre.)

Which clauses give a reason or add a new element: **The movie, which cost $4 million to make, has done landslide business.** (The assumption here is that the reader already knows which movie is being discussed, and its cost is an added bit of information.)

A helpful distinction: **which** clauses generally need commas, **that** clauses don't. Read the clause over in your mind. If it makes sense using **that** instead of **which**, chances are **that** is the right word to use.

Who and whom

Correct usage of these two eluders can be determined by dividing a sentence in two. Use **who** when it stands for **he, she** or **they.** Use **whom** when it stands for **him, her** or **them.**

The police issued a public alert for a man who **they said was armed and dangerous.** (They said **he** was armed and dangerous so **who** is correct.)

She took refuge with her next-door neighbour whom **she had trusted in the past.** (She trusted **her** so **whom** is correct.)

Clichés

Tired expressions are indeed tiresome. No one needs to read about a hurler who **toed the slab** or the **red-faced MP** who got a **tongue-lashing** from the opposition.

But use a cliché if it expresses your meaning exactly and if it will spare the reader some cumbersome second choice. It would be hard to improve on such gems as **sour grapes**, **cry wolf** or **tip of the iceberg** which sum up complex ideas in a few words.

Avoid the automatic or lazy cliché:

Grind to a halt, unveil, in the wake of, launch, seriously consider

And the fad term:

Ambience, downsize, peer group, quantify, underachievers, wannabe

And the fossil that no longer raises the faintest image:

Moot point, short shrift, at loggerheads, by the same token

Word order

Words out of order can create chaos.

Not: Having been born in France 24 years ago, Montreal baseball fans wasted little time picking up on Charlie Lea's French connection.

But: Charlie Lea was born in France 24 years ago and Montreal fans wasted little time picking up on his French connection.

Not: She has a six-figure income as a model, a horse and a Jaguar.

But: Modelling has given her a six-figure income, a horse and a Jaguar.

Mind-reading

Reporters and editors should not consider themselves mind-readers who can somehow measure others' true feelings.

Not: Genereux believes the government is corrupt.

But: Genereux said he believes the government is corrupt.

Not: Iroshima is furious about the layoffs.

But: "We're not taking this lying down," Iroshima said, shaking with anger and smashing his clenched fist into the factory fence.

Splits and prepositions

The normal position for an adverb that modifies a compound verb (**is missing, was reached**) is between the parts of the verb: **The plane is still missing. Agreement was soon reached.**

Split an infinitive (**to satisfy, to keep**) rather than create a confusing or unnatural sentence: **The discovery is expected to more than satisfy investors. Godfrey told him to kindly keep his opinion to himself.** But don't split infinitives unnecessarily: **The parents asked the babysitter to quietly leave by the back door.**

If a preposition falls naturally at the end of the sentence, leave it there: **Reuben wants to know which team he'll be on.**

Locating the news

1. Today's reader is more interested than ever in knowing exactly where the news is happening, both in Canada and abroad. Few Canadians live their full lives in the area in which they were born and brought up. Career moves take them from one part of the country to another and sometimes to still another. And, of course, thousands of Canadians have come here from other parts of the world.

2. Name well-known streets or areas in stories about major fires and the like. In Halifax it might be: **a block from Barrington Street in the restored Historic Properties district of the waterfront beneath Citadel Hill.** In Hong Kong: **in the heart of the Central District within sight of the Bank of China Tower and just three blocks from the Star Ferry Pier.**

3. Readers interested in entertainment and celebrities want to know where events are held. In a review of a show or coverage of an event involving a big-name star, try to set the scene for the reader: **the cast met for an after-show dinner at the Bayshore Inn, on Burrard Inlet facing the mountains of West Vancouver.**

4. But keep in mind as well those readers who are unfamiliar with even the biggest cities. Pause early in the story to set the scene: **highrises on the Toronto harbourfront with a view over boat-dotted Lake Ontario and out to the greenery of the Toronto Islands; the shooting at the University of Montreal, whose Art Deco administration tower atop Mount Royal can be seen from all over the city.**

5. Don't assume readers know precisely where familiar mid-size cities are. Give places like Moncton, Kitchener, Prince Albert and Kelowna a physical presence and geographical location when that would help readers picture an event.

6. Pinpoint the location of news in remote areas, as well: **The two tankers collided at the tiny community of Purple Springs on Alberta Highway 3 just east of Taber and about a 40-minute drive from Lethbridge; The power station is near Gillam in a rugged area of northeastern Manitoba inland from Hudson Bay and about 14 hours by road from Winnipeg.**

7. Sometimes referring back to the story's placeline helps: (Glenwood, Nfld.) — **this central Newfoundland logging town about 300 kilometres west of St. John's**; (Mahim, India) — **this seaside town just outside Bombay.**

A graphic can help a reader quickly understand where the story is taking place.

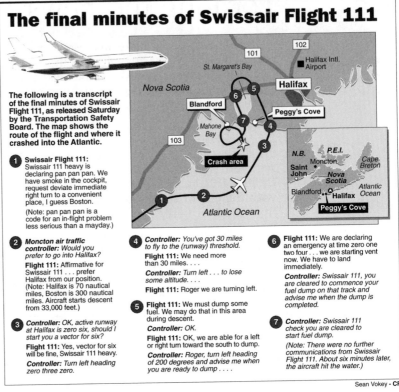

The final minutes of Swissair Flight 111

The following is a transcript of the final minutes of Swissair Flight 111, as released Saturday by the Transportation Safety Board. The map shows the route of the flight and where it crashed into the Atlantic.

1 Swissair Flight 111: Swissair 111 heavy is declaring pan pan pan. We have smoke in the cockpit, request deviate immediate right turn to a convenient place, I guess Boston.

(Note: pan pan pan is a code for an in-flight problem less serious than a mayday.)

2 Moncton air traffic controller: Would you prefer to go into Halifax?

Flight 111: Affirmative for Swissair 111 . . . prefer Halifax from our position. (Note: Halifax is 70 nautical miles, Boston is 300 nautical miles. Aircraft starts descent from 33,000 feet.)

3 Controller: OK, active runway at Halifax is zero six, should I start you a vector for six?

Flight 111: Yes, vector for six will be fine, Swissair 111 heavy.

Controller: Turn left heading zero three zero.

4 Controller: You've got 30 miles to fly to the (runway) threshold.

Flight 111: We need more than 30 miles. . . .

Controller: Turn left . . . to lose some altitude. . . .

Flight 111: Roger we are turning left.

5 Flight 111: We must dump some fuel. We may do that in this area during descent.

Controller: OK.

Flight 111: OK, we are able for a left or right turn toward the south to dump.

Controller: Roger, turn left heading of 200 degrees and advise me when you are ready to dump . . . .

6 Flight 111: We are declaring an emergency at time zero one two four . . . we are starting vent now. We have to land immediately.

Controller: Swissair 111, you are cleared to commence your fuel dump on that track and advise me when the dump is completed.

7 Controller: Swissair 111 check you are cleared to start fuel dump.

(Note: There were no further communications from Swissair Flight 111. About six minutes later, the aircraft hit the water.)

St. Margaret's Bay
Nova Scotia
Halifax Intl. Airport
Halifax
Blandford
Peggy's Cove
Mahone Bay
Crash area
Atlantic Ocean

N.B.   P.E.I.
Moncton   Cape Breton
Saint John   Nova Scotia
Blandford   Halifax   Atlantic Ocean
Peggy's Cove

Sean Vokey - **CP**

8. Don't assume the placeline is going to give the reader a clear geographic sense of where the news has happened. For example, a story from Edmonton that says a force of specially trained police officers has been set up to give immediate emotional support to battered women must make clear where the force will function. In Edmonton alone? In all major Alberta centres? Or throughout Alberta? Watch phrases like *city police* and *the provincial department* which may be adequate for local newspapers but rarely for CP. Usually it is better to name the city and province in first references.

Writing

The first page of one of the early CP stylebooks had this to say about writing news:

"Every story worth printing can be written for The Canadian Press."

That remains the case, although much about writing news has changed.

No longer is the role of the news writer merely to inform. Readers (call them news consumers, if you will) are bombarded with information.

But what many modern-day messengers fail to provide are context, background, balance and the sights, smells and sounds of the news. Things that tell readers why this is important and what it means, in terms that strike home.

Newspapers are fighting to attract new readers and hold the ones they have. Some of the forecasts are chilling and the fight seems far from over. To help, reporters and editors must present news stories that are uniformly appealing.

Readability has always been an issue in the newspaper business, but never more than in today's reality: Fewer people are reading newspapers. Those who are reading papers spend less time at it.

Readability is often tied to sentence length. Sure signs of trouble: too many ideas, too many subordinate clauses.

It's possible to write brightly and clearly in sentences that run to 30 words and more. Possible — but not probable.

Be human

Stories must be human, specific, clear, concise, imaginative and factual.

1. Write about people. Personal words like **father, pilot, nurse, welder** put life into news stories:

An ice fisherman trudging along the edge of an isolated lake found the wreckage.

A power failure crippled most of Quebec's electricity network Tuesday afternoon. It left about six million people without heat and light in freezing temperatures.

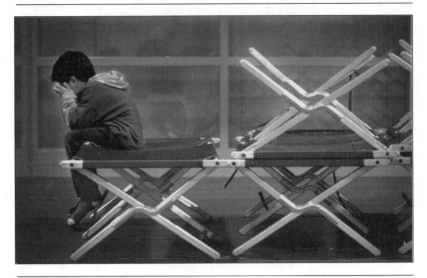

A boy cries while sitting on an army bunk at a shelter in Montreal. He was one of more than a million Quebecers left without power during a 1998 ice storm. The photo brings a huge news story down to a human scale. Try to do that in every story.

(Montreal Gazette – Pierre Obendrauf)

Look for the human angle in every story: the sheet-metal worker replaced by a robot, the single parent whose rent has doubled, the teller robbed by a gunman with a shaking hand. A roundup on unemployment could open this way:

> Like anyone buying insurance, Donald Good hoped he wouldn't need it. He insured himself last March against being laid off. As it turned out, he did need it.

Put things in real-people terms:

Not: An Alberta provincial court judge has thrown out charges against two men, ruling that the six days they spent in a Camrose jail constituted cruel and unusual punishment.

But: Two young Alberta farmhands were freed from jail after telling a judge their cell had a broken window and was so cold the water pipes to the sink and toilet froze for days on end.

2. Relate the news to the reader's life whenever possible, which is often:

> Air-fare negotiations between Canada and the United States broke down Wednesday, dashing the hopes of thousands of travellers for bargain flights over the Labour Day weekend.

Scientists believe they have detected the deadly chemical dioxin in the lake, but they say the levels appear too low to harm cottagers who drink its water or swim in it.

The ruling means the plant workers will be eligible to apply for unemployment benefits within a week.

3. Enliven the story with quotes that set the scene, capture the flavour of the news or provide insight:

"He burst through the swinging door and ran straight to the checkout counter," she said. "He waved this baseball bat he was carrying over his head and kept saying: 'Give me the money — all the money.'"

"I've dealt with the Raineys ever since I've been a cop," said Ephraim H. Branton, the affable deputy sheriff of the Lake County police and a 24-year veteran.
"A lot of 'em came from ol' river rats. I've dealt with 'em on everything from runnin' moonshine to huntin' gators illegal."

4. Perk up stories that are devoid of anything human, except perhaps some unnamed *spokesman* or *official*. Season them with examples that bear directly on readers' lives:

Just when you thought you had finally caught up with the Joneses, along came Statistics Canada on Tuesday announcing that 367,000 families have backyard swimming pools.

Be specific

1. Give the reader specific details. Ask yourself: How does this look? sound? feel?

ASTOR, Fla. (CP) — Inland from the shimmering beaches and swaying palm trees featured on garish postcards is where many locals say you will find the real Florida.
Swampy bogs and inky rivers are stealthily patrolled by alligators. Snakes slither across the sun-baked asphalt greased by constant humidity. And every kind of criminal has come here to either ply their trade or escape from the law.

2. Get interesting human nuggets into the lead:

A prison guard killed in the Archambault Penitentiary last July "was looking at pictures of his family and crying like a baby" when convicts burst in on him, a murder trial was told Tuesday.

In the land they poignantly call Next Year Country, Prime Minister Brian Mulroney promised drought relief for farmers and a rosy, free-trade future for agriculture.

Simon Reisman paced the halls like an expectant father on Saturday night. And when the news of the delivery came through, he acted like one pleased pop.

Quebec's language law, better known as Bill 101, led Eaton's and the Bay to rename themselves Eaton and La Baie. On many menus, hamburgers became hambourgeois and hot dogs became chiens chauds.

3. Paint word pictures:

Not: The accused were overjoyed.

But: The accused kissed and hugged each other.

Not: The northern cod is found in huge numbers off Newfoundland.

But: The northern cod, a grey-green fish with a barb under its chin, is found in teeming abundance in the chilly waters around Newfoundland.

Not: The MPs showed disgust at a rape scene in one of the Playboy films.

But: The MPs winced as the Confederate soldiers grabbed and raped a black slave in one of the Playboy films.

Be clear

1. Always organize the story in your mind before you start writing.

Decide what the news is and put that in your lead. Stories with leads like these stand a good chance of flowing smoothly:

A convicted 50-year-old rapist whose record for violent crimes stretches back to 1963 was sent to jail for at least 35 years Monday. The judge said he was so "sickened" by the case that he would ignore sentencing guidelines.

> American daredevil Maxie Anderson has decided to give up trying to fly around the world in a balloon after his third attempt came to an abrupt end Monday in the trees of a southern Ontario peach grove.

2. But there are other ways to a reader's heart as well:

> The old Tory tune played in Alberta again on Thursday, but a lot fewer people got up to dance.

> Liberal party policy seems a lot like Scottish weather. If you don't like it, wait a few minutes — it's bound to change.

> Lotteries. Those spine-tingling, dream-inducing, pot-of-gold-at-the-end-of-the-rainbow lotteries are everywhere.

3. Use plain words, but always the right words. Make it **wicked**, not nefarious; **remaining**, not residual; **tone down**, not modulate.

4. Use specific words when details are useful. Write **hamburger and french fries**, not food; **shouting and laughing**, not making a noise; **a man of 87**, not an elderly man.

Be direct

1. Don't write **a number of cars** if you can say **five cars**; a six-figure income if you can say **an income of $115,000**; a long dry spell if you can say **37 days without rain**.

2. Don't use lazy terms for unknown quantities: **fairly, really, pretty, few, quite, very**.

3. Translate pompous phrases.

Not: A poor public response.

But: Only a quarter of the tickets were sold.

Not: There is a doctor availability problem in the health delivery system.

But: There are not enough doctors in hospitals and private practice.

4. Avoid putting more than one thought in a sentence. In general, the contents and structure rather than length itself make sentences hard to understand.

Not: Union leader John Dickerson declared, "I have no regrets and would do the same again" as he entered prison today to begin serving a three-month sentence imposed last week for defying the legislature and refusing to call off a strike of civil servants angered by wage rollbacks.

But: Union leader John Dickerson said he had "no regrets and would do the same again" as he entered prison today to begin serving a three-month term.

Dickerson was sentenced last week for defying the legislature and refusing to call off a strike of civil servants angered by wage rollbacks.

5. Beware of too many dependent clauses, especially in mid-sentence where they break the flow. Each clause adds more ideas to the sentence, making it harder and harder to grasp.

Not: The U.S. vice-president flew into Berlin from Bonn, along with the German chancellor, with whom he held talks Monday on disarmament strategy on the first stop of a seven-country tour.

But: The U.S. vice-president flew into Berlin from Bonn on the second stop during his seven-country tour. With him was the German chancellor, with whom he held talks Monday on disarmament.

6. Keep introductory phrases and clauses short and simple.

Not: Noting spirited and repeated suggestions from the floor that the group should press Ottawa for a higher salmon quota for British Columbia fishermen who have complained bitterly about competition from foreign fishing fleets, especially the Japanese and American, but to some extent the Russians, association vice-president Hedley Evansson said ...

But: As for higher salmon quotas, Evansson said ...

7. Sentence length can grow comfortably when the sentence is simply a list of closely linked ideas referring to the same subject:

The Blue Jays pulled off the first triple play of the major league season when shortstop Manuel Lee stabbed what looked like a sure hit to left field by Oakland's Mark McGwire, stepped quickly on second base to double off Harold Baines and then drilled the ball to third baseman Kelly Gruber, catching Dave Henderson as he tried to get back to the bag.

Be concise

Keep your story tight in content as well as phrasing. Stick with the truly significant angles. A *full* report can often mean a dull report.

Be aware that a 1,000-word story in standard newspaper print would cover the back of a corn flakes box. Ask if the story would really hold a reader through an entire bowl of cereal.

If a story threatens to run long, consider whether some of the material could be broken out as highlights, a chronology or a point summary.

Clutter chokes meaning. Simplify:

1.   Ditch the long word that says no more than the short: **attempt** (try), **approximately** (about), **preponderance** (most), **consequently** (so), **substantiate** (prove), **initiative** (plan).

2.   Ditch the laborious phrase: **despite the fact that** (although), **at this point in time** (now), **in the event that** (if), **ahead of schedule** (early), **in the majority of cases** (usually).

3.   Ditch ponderous euphemisms and gobbledegook: **correctional facility** (prison), **job action** (strike, slowdown), **depressed socio-economic area** (slum), **in a classroom setting** (in a classroom), **resource centre** (library or lab), **lower rates of infant mortality** (fewer baby deaths).

4.   Ditch words that aren't doing any work: **He said** (that) **the cut**(back)**s in** (the) **health care** (field) **have put hospitals in a crisis** (situation).

5.   Consider whether the fad word works before using it: **parameter, overview, trendy, viable, motivation, inoperative, strategy, interface, prioritize, supportive.**

Next-trick stories

AMs newspapers are increasingly turning to more analytical approaches on stories, especially staged news events, as a way to attract readers who are likely to have already heard the facts from last night's TV newscast, a 24-hour news channel or a brief radio report. This puts next-day afternoon editions in a tight spot as they seek even fresher angles. Copy for these papers must keep alive a story that may have already been reported for more than 24 hours. Try to avoid past-tense wording as much as possible: **Canada can no longer export goods to Spain**, rather than, **The government imposed export restrictions Tuesday.**

Don't place undue emphasis on minor developments to freshen a story. But do look for a different perspective. For example, on a provincial budget: Were human-interest angles neglected? How will the budget influence the next election? On a disaster, was there an eyewitness who can provide a lively account of what it is like to be caught in such a situation? Could it have been prevented? What are the implications?

The essential details of the news must be covered so it is understandable to readers who may be hearing about it for the first time. If these details are lengthy or complex, they can sometimes be handled in a Quick so they don't burden down a lead that is taking a new approach.

A writing checklist

1. Is the lead right? Does it capture only the most significant angles? Is there secondary information getting in the way of the main points? Is there an appealing human touch or quotation deep in the story that would fit in the first paragraph? Is the time element placed where it falls naturally in speech?

2. Does the writing appeal to a reader's senses? Are there gobs of *officialese*, jargon or abstractions? If so, can they be translated into direct language? The language people use when they're discussing events of the day over dinner?

3. Would a point summary help the reader? With the main news angle covered in the lead, should readers be given a capsule taste of other interesting angles awaiting them lower in the story?

4. Does the story give the reader any sense of where the news happened and how it happened, how people in the immediate area reacted? Did some of the audience start to leave before the speech was over? Did the speaker seem to notice?

5. Is there another side to the story? Is one side buried, throwing the story off balance? If someone whose viewpoint is obviously part of the story was unavailable, does the story say so? When pertinent, does it spell out what efforts were made to reach the unavailable source?

6. Have legally questionable elements in the story been cleared by a lawyer?

7. Is there overattribution? Are all those *he saids* necessary? Does every direct quote need attribution tacked on?

8. How about sentences? Is each sentence limited to one thought or a closely connected range of thoughts? Can a subordinate clause be changed into a sentence to give the reader a clearer path? Are the sentences active? Are inactive verbs adding fat to sentences? Is there an idea that needs explaining? If so, find a way to explain it better. Or could the problem sentence be cut without loss?

9. How about quotes? Could the story be brightened with stronger human voices? In cutting quotes, have the strongest been saved and the weaker sacrificed? Can some quotes be cut because they aren't controversial and don't give any character to the speaker? Is the story sprinkled with fragmented quotes? Is it necessary to say, **He said he was "out of touch"**?

10. Have words been wasted? Can single words replace phrases: **placed under arrest** (arrested), **in the vicinity of** (near), **charged in connection with** (charged), **in the shooting incident** (shooting)?

11. Can shorter or more familiar words be used: **They attempted** (tried) **to expedite** (speed up) **what they perceived** (saw) **as a viable** (workable) **plan?**

12. Has bafflegab been translated? Have **accommodation units** been turned into **houses and apartments; methods of intercity transportation** into **planes, trains, buses and cars; disadvantaged** into **poor; upwardly mobile** into **ambitious?**

13. Does the writing read like normal English? Is any of it unlike anything you would ever say: **the six-foot-eight 290-pound University of Manitoba product; Paramount vice-president of corporate communications Deborah Rosen?**

14. Are there stale expressions? Is the story dulled by cliches: **court was told; 14-hour marathon session; grim-faced delegates?**

15. Do the transitions lead the reader smoothly from one idea to the next? Could a bump between two sentences be removed with an **and, but, meanwhile** or some other transition? Would it help to repeat a key word or phrase from the preceding sentence or paragraph? **This new strategy . . . ?**

16. Is the tone right? Is the writing too formal, slangy or trendy? Has sexist, racist or other tasteless language slipped in?

Editing

Few people grow up longing to edit someone else's writing. It's not glamorous work; it is invisible at best and resented at worst.

But some people who love the written language develop a passion for perfecting its use on the page. The best publications rely on such editors for success. The best editors strive for excellence in every story they handle.

Pride comes from turning around a mediocre or erroneous story. The trick is to do more than just catch mistakes but less than rewrite.

As the last ones to touch copy before it gets into the reader's hands, editors have a vital role. They are the watchdogs over clarity, good taste, balance and accuracy.

Editors should be the reader's best friend. They add background and perspective. They make a story relevant and fun. They don't challenge readers to get through a story — they dare them not to.

Principles

1. When time allows, read a story three times: once for content, once to edit and once to clean up.

2. If you don't understand the story, the reader certainly won't. When something is unclear, either get it explained or chop it.

3. Generalities blur the picture; demand specifics for your readers. Make sure the story is animated by human beings.

4. Suggest improvements to the writer: revealing quotes, touches of colour, specific details, an example or anecdote.

5. Watch for holes and fill them. Ask the writer. Check reference works. Consult a supervisor.

6. Shorten the story — but not at the expense of human interest, significant detail, daubs of colour or meaty quotations.

7. Avoid overediting, which can reduce good writing to mediocrity or headline language.

8. Change copy if you have a good, explainable reason — not just because it's not the way you would have written it yourself. Leave extensive rewriting to the writer whenever possible.

How to do it

Look at the lead. The first sentence is supposed to lead the reader into the story. If it isn't interesting, why would the reader go any further? If readers aren't enticed by the first sentence or two, they're not going to stick around to be informed or educated or provoked.

1. Replace vague or complicated words with simple, specific ones.

2. Brighten the lead with descriptive verbs and the active voice.

Not: Two men are dead following an avalanche Tuesday on a popular ski slope in the Rocky Mountains.

Better: An avalanche thundered down Mount Norquay on Tuesday, crushing two men who had been learning to ski at the Rocky Mountain resort.

3. Take a scalpel to long leads. Aim for fewer than 30 words. Cut unwieldy phrases. Remove secondary information or unnecessary attribution from the lead and place it lower.

Not: International Development Minister Monique Landry announced Monday that after six months of study, the Canadian International Development Agency has approved an operating plan, including a $3-million bailout, to ensure the future of the World University Service of Canada.

Better: It took six months of study and a $3-million government bailout, but World University Service of Canada will soon be back at work helping people in poor countries.

The federal government agency that co-ordinates Canadian aid abroad has approved a plan to ensure the future of the service, International Development Minister Monique Landry announced Monday.

4. Never assume the reader knows the subject as intimately as the writer does.

Not: Joy Medinski was found Thursday in Bienfait, apparently unharmed.

Better: A five-year-old girl who vanished from a family campsite in southeastern Saskatchewan last week was found two kilometres away on Monday, apparently unharmed.

5. Beware of the double-barrelled lead.

Not: Thousands of seniors angry over federal pension changes marched on Parliament Hill on Monday while their national spokesman condemned Prime Minister Brian Mulroney as the worst threat to seniors in Canadian history.

Pick the most interesting or important element, the seniors or the spokesman, and make that the lead. Put the other one in the second paragraph.

Tighten the story

1. Keep paragraphs short, usually no more than two or three sentences for newspaper copy. Don't assault the reader's eyes with massive blocks of grey.

2. Tighten sentences to clarify, inject life and save space. Be ruthless in cutting wordiness and secondary detail.

3. Replace cumbersome words with short, everyday words that

convey the same meaning.

Not: The correctional facility workers voted in favour of a prolonged work stoppage.

But: The jail guards voted to strike.

4.   Cut vague modifiers and qualifiers: **fairly, really, pretty, quite, very.**

5.   Cut overattribution. Are all those *he said*s necessary?

Brighten the story

1.   Prefer one or two interesting angles fully developed to a dull, bare-bones account that touches all bases regardless of merit.

2.   Change passive voice to active where appropriate. **Police took no action** is better than **No action was taken by police.**

3.   Change boring expressions to lively ones. Watch for participles ending in *-ing* or nouns ending in *-ion* — they may signal that a sentence can be punched up. Watch for the weak verb *to be.* Can it be replaced by an active verb?

Not: The government is planning to implement a program aiming for a reduction in the number of alcohol-related deaths this year.

Better: The government aims to cut alcohol-related deaths this year through a new program.

Best: Police will be able to seize the cars of drinking drivers on the spot under a government plan to cut alcohol-related deaths this year.

4.   Translate or cut journalistic hype and jargon, the kind of language you would never use in ordinary speech. Prefer the specific to the general.

Not: Residents of this farming community were reeling in shock Thursday in the wake of the slaying of two respected schoolteachers.

Better: Flags flew at half-mast outside the Shoal Lake elementary school Thursday in tribute to two teachers killed in an apparently unprovoked attack.

Not: A twofold habitat mitigation program is in full swing at the Oldman River dam site.

Better: The provincial government is spending $2 million to preserve the environment for wildlife around the Oldman River dam and create new protected areas to replace those destroyed by the dam.

Best: Ducks will swim in new ponds and deer will munch on their favourite grasses under a $2-million program to preserve wildlife around the Oldman dam.

Check accuracy

1. Check proper names and unusual spellings. Make sure unusual surnames are spelled the same way throughout. Never guess at capitalization. Think of your reader again — few things are as annoying as misspelled names.

2. Check math. Make sure percentages are right. If portions of a total number are used, make sure they add up.

3. Check days and dates for obvious errors.

4. Watch closely for mistakes in the use of *not* in court cases and important judgments: *not guilty, not responsible.*

Check style

1. Strive to retain the writer's tone and choice of phrasing.

2. Fix errors in grammar, style and structure. Watch for mistakes in word order that mislead the reader.

Not: A Winnipeg police officer who shot a man with a toy gun has been cleared of any wrongdoing.

Better: A Winnipeg police officer who shot a man pointing a toy gun has been cleared of any wrongdoing.

3. Check that plural subjects are followed by plural verbs and pronouns, singular by singular. **The government announced its** (not **their) long-awaited social reform package Tuesday.**

4. Does punctuation mislead the reader? Fix it.

Not: She said the company is run by men, who have no ethics.

But: She said the company is run by men who have no ethics.

Make it clear

1. Lighten overloaded sentences by putting some of the facts into another sentence.

Not: The Nova Scotia government made controversial deals involving the purchase of toilet-seat-cover dispensers and marketing dogfish in the Caribbean with two companies connected to Halifax businessman Robert Cranston, the province's New Democratic Party says.

Better: Nova Scotia's New Democrats want to know why the province lent money to a man who sold it high-tech toilet seats that have never been used.

NDP Leader Alexa McDonough called Wednesday for the release of all details of a $40,000 loan to Halifax businessman Robert Cranston. The Department of Small Business made the loan to help Cranston's company market dogfish in the Caribbean.

2.   Answer all pertinent questions. Make sure all unusual and technical terms are explained.

Wealthy Britons often buy private health insurance, just as they send their children to "public" schools, which in Britain means fee-paying, private and elite.

3.   Move sentences or paragraphs to improve flow or strengthen emphasis.

Make it fair

1.   Put both sides of a controversial issue high in the story.

2.   Tone down or play up material wrongly treated by the writer. Guard against partial quotes that may create the wrong impression.

The woman was hired for her "talent," the premier said.

3.   Watch for unintentional editorializing.

Not: The Opposition blamed the government for ruining the economy.

Better: The Opposition accused the government of ruining the economy.

4.   Remove material that is potentially libellous or in bad taste.

Handle with care

1.   When source material is sensitive or confidential, lock it safely away while the reporter works from a copy.

2.   Make sure a supervisor is fully aware of the source material's contents and the source's reliability.

3.   Before an investigative report is published, make every effort to give everyone who may be criticized an opportunity to reply.

4.   Counsel must approve the final wording of any possibly dangerous material.

➤ See **Principles**, page 13.

Writing for broadcast

It's radio — it's the way we speak.

Writing for radio is writing that's meant to be spoken and heard. It requires special style and form.

(CP – Frank Gunn)

1. Write tight opening sentences that grab the listener's attention.

The first sentence should make listeners want to hear more but not confuse them with too many details.

In other words, it serves as a headline.

Never write lead lines on broadcast copy that are over 15 words long. A long lead line can throw an announcer's breathing off for the entire newscast.

2. Write in the present tense or active voice.

It's the way people speak.

Avoid the passive voice: verb forms like **was hit**, **have grabbed**, etc.

Broadcast copy, written in the active voice, should place the verb as close to the subject as possible.

Not: A Hamilton man has been arrested by police.

But: Police arrested a Hamilton man.

3. Limit sentences to a single idea or closely connected range of thoughts.

Not: Alex Hickman, chief justice of the trial division of the Supreme Court of Newfoundland, has been cleared of any wrongdoing by the Canadian Judicial Council after a review of his financial dealings.

But: The chief justice of the Newfoundland Supreme Court has been cleared of any financial wrongdoing. The Canadian Judicial Council cleared Alex Hickman after a review of the judge's financial dealings.

4. Simplify complex and wordy sentences.

Not: The minister of employment, Jasper Brown, has established a study group within his department to conduct a review of the principles and objectives of the unemployment insurance program. He told the Commons today he expects to table the findings this fall for further discussion.

But: Employment Minister Jasper Brown has ordered a review of the unemployment insurance program. Brown told the Commons he expects to table the findings in the fall.

5. Use the subject-verb-object approach to tell the story in as straight a line as possible.

Not: The gunman was shot by the police.

But: Police shot the gunman.

6. Place the time element, if needed, after the verb.

Don't use **yesterday, last night**, etc. in a lead sentence.

Don't use **continues** in a lead sentence.

Don't start a broadcast story with **as expected.**

7. For ease of understanding, put a person's identification ahead of the name.

Former dentist Barney Clark has become the first person to live with an artificial heart implant.

Twenty-five-year-old Beverly Amies of Toronto was killed.

8. Prefer plain words to fancy ones.

Prefer **end** to **terminate, build** to **construct, confuse** to **obfuscate, poor** to **disadvantaged, shops** to **retail outlets.**

9. Use specific words, not general ones.

Write **rain, snow, fog,** not **bad weather.** Write **one million dollars,** not **financial aid.** Write **She smiled,** not **She looked pleased.**

10. Keep sentences lean. Excess words clutter the facts.

Write **failed,** not **was unsuccessful.** Write **won,** not **chalked up a victory.** Write **lives at,** not **makes her home at.** Write **burned,** not **was devoured by flames.** Write **presided,** not **acted as chairman.**

Eliminate unnecessary and long titles. Would **a union spokesman** serve just as well as **Jean Talon, secretary-treasurer of Local 136?**

11. Write incomplete sentences occasionally. Like this. To make an idea easier to absorb. For a change of pace.

12. Put the source at the beginning of the sentence rather than at the end.

Not: A new wave of violence is showing up, the movie critic added.

But: The movie critic says a new wave of violence is showing up.

13. Use contractions occasionally, as the ear dictates.

I don't know whether he'll come has the sound of everyday English. The formal **I do not know whether he will come** would be starchy in shirtsleeve contexts.

Use **she won't, it couldn't** and other common contractions. Avoid forced contractions like **would've, it'd.**

14. To reflect spoken usage, hyphenate abbreviations that the news reader should pronounce letter by letter.

Write **C-B-C, M-P, N-D-P, R-C-M-P, U-N, U-S** but **NATO, MiG, Sidbec, Stelco.**

Note: BN practice is to hyphenate network abbreviations, **C-B-S, C-T-V,** but to write station call letters solid, **CIHI Fredericton, CKLH-FM Hamilton, CJON-TV St. John's.**

15. Guard against a string of *s*'s and other repeated letters.

Sources at city hall say might cause the news reader to stumble or slow down.

16. Round off large numbers to make them digestible and spell out the dollar sign.

The robber got away with more than 13 hundred dollars is easier on the listener — and the news reader — than **$1,335.** For ease of reading, spell out and hyphenate dollars and cents: **The increase will add one-dollar-and-25-cents to the average monthly electricity bill.**

17. For economy and directness, prefer paraphrased speech to direct quotation. But use a quotation if it is unusually forceful.

The judge explained why he had ruled in favour of the 20-year-old cerebral palsy victim. He said: "We have recognized a gentle, trusting, believing spirit who has a part to play in our compassionate, independent society."

18. Repeat key points in major news breaks.

In an airliner crash, for example, give the location a second time for listeners who missed it. Don't hesitate to add a throw-away sentence at the end summarizing the story.

To recap: An airliner has crashed at the Edmonton airport and at least a dozen people are dead.

For a full treatment of writing for broadcasting, see the *BN Style Guide*, also available from The Canadian Press.

Some useful tools (Part I)

Grammar and style

continued over

Some useful tools (Part II)

Some technical guides

Aboriginal Peoples
  Indians, Métis, Inuit
  Languages
  Writing about
    Aboriginal Peoples
  Métis
  Inuit
Aircraft, ships, guns
Metric
  When metric?
  Let logic be your guide
  Sports
  Odds and ends
  Metric conversion tables
  Common metric units
  Different strokes
  Converting
  Recipes
Military
  Bases
  Units
  Ranks
  Titles
  Retired officers
  Courts martial
  Ceremonies
  Miscellaneous
People, places
  Alphabetical list of countries,
    capitals etc.
  Provincial descriptive terms
  U.S. state derivatives
Placelines
  Canadian placelines
  U.S. placelines
  Other foreign placelines

Place names
  Exceptions
  Regions
  People and places
Technical terms
  Scientific names
  Drugs
  Medical
  Condition
  Burns
  AIDS
  Richter scale
Time
  What day is it?
  What time is it?
  What zone is it?
Titles
  Courtesy titles
  Professional titles
  Religious titles
  Honourable, Lady, Lord
Trade names
Weather
  Weather in metric
  Terminology

Access to information
  Some tips
  Limitations
  Keep trying

Words
  Alphabetical listing of tricky
    words

Abbreviations and acronyms

General

1. Use only abbreviations and acronyms (abbreviations pronounced as words) that are familiar to ordinary readers.

CN, CTV, MP; Stelco, NATO, radar

2. An abbreviation is sometimes acceptable to avoid an unwieldy lead: **a PLO rocket attack**. But in general, provide the full name later: **Palestine Liberation Organization**.

3. Abbreviations that have become household terms are acceptable in all references. That is, they need not be spelled out, though the full word or phrase may make for more graceful reading.

CBC, MP, NATO, NDP, PoW, RCMP

Note: As to familiarity, it is impossible to set lasting rules. The once-familiar **RAF** (Royal Air Force), for instance, no longer commands widespread recognition, whereas **BBC** does. When in doubt, spell out.

4. In general, do not put a bracketed abbreviation after the name of an organization: Transportation Safety Board (**TSB**), Liberation Tigers of Tamil Eelam (**LTTE**).

Abbreviations that need this device to be clear should rarely be used.

5. For ease of reading or variety, a general term is often preferable to an abbreviation.

the labour relations board, the arms talks, the union, the autoworkers, the company, the association instead of CLRB, SALT, CAW and the like.

6. Do not spell out common abbreviations if the full term is not in general use or is hard to pronounce: **TNT** (for **trinitrotoluene**), **DNA** (**deoxyribonucleic acid**).

Where necessary, include a brief description to help the reader: **DNA, the carrier of genetic information**.

7. Abbreviations suitable in one context may be unsuitable in another. **MLA**, for instance, might puzzle readers in Newfoundland, Quebec and Ontario, and should be spelled out for general service: **member of the legislative assembly**, or **member of the legislature**.

Similarly: **MHA** — **member of the** (Newfoundland) **house of assembly**; **MNA** — **member of the** (Quebec) **national assembly**; **MPP** — **member of the** (Ontario) **provincial parliament**.

8. Non-English abbreviations that may be unfamiliar to English-speaking readers should be explained at some point.

the terrorist group ETA, the acronym for the Basque name meaning Basque Land and Liberty; the French union federation CGT, short for Confédération générale du travail; the Quebec steel company Sidbec; Soquip, which stands for a French name meaning Quebec Petroleum Development Corp.

9. Text studded with abbreviations is hard to read and unsightly.

Style for abbreviations

1. Omit periods in all-capital abbreviations unless the abbreviation is geographical or refers to a person.

AD, CST, PLC, UBC, UFO, VIP; B.C., P.E.I., N.W.T., U.S., U.S.S.R.; J. R. Ewing, J.R., E.T., good ol' J.B.

Note 1: Some public figures become known by initials without periods.

FDR (Franklin Delano Roosevelt), **JFK** (John Fitzgerald Kennedy), **PET** (Pierre Elliott Trudeau), **GBS** (George Bernard Shaw)

Note 2: Put a *thin space* between a person's initials, **G. K. Chesterton**, except where they stand alone, **G.K.**

Note 3: Compound abbreviations are written without spaces.

M.Sc., P.Eng.

Note 4: Omit periods from currency abbreviations.

$500 US, $800 Cdn

2. Most lowercase and mixed abbreviations take periods.

f.o.b., Jr., lb., Mrs., No., m.p.h., B.Comm.

Note: Metric symbols are not abbreviations and take periods only at the end of a sentence.

m, l, km/h

3. Mixed abbreviations that begin and end with a capital letter do not take periods.

PhD, PoW, MiG, U of T

4. Single-letter abbreviations are followed by a period.

36 King St. E. (for East)

But **brand X, the letter E**

Style for acronyms

1. Acronyms formed from only the first letter of each word are all capitals.

NATO (North Atlantic Treaty Organization), a **CAT** (computerized axial tomography) **scan, AIDS** (acquired immune deficiency syndrome)

2. Acronyms formed from initial and other letters are in caps and lowercase.

Dofasco (Dominion Foundries and Steel Corp.), **Nabisco** (National Biscuit Company)

But **HTML** (accepted style for Hypertext Markup Language)

3. Acronyms that have become common words are not capitalized.

radar (radio detection and ranging), **scuba** (self-contained underwater breathing apparatus), **snafu** (situation normal, all fouled up), **laser** (light amplification by stimulated emission of radiation), **zip** (zoning improvement plan)

Dates and times

1. For months used with a specific date, abbreviate only **Jan., Feb., Aug., Sept., Oct., Nov.** and **Dec.** Spell out standing alone or with a year alone.

Oct. 1, 1995, was a Friday. January 1998 was wet.

Note: Do not abbreviate a month spelled out in the name of an organization: **the November 17 terrorist group.**

2. In tabular matter, use these forms without periods:

Jan, Feb, Mar, Apr, May, Jun, Jul, Aug, Sep, Oct, Nov, Dec

3. Days of the week are abbreviated only in tabular matter and without periods.

Sun, Mon, Tue, Wed, Thu, Fri, Sat

4. **AD** is acceptable in all references for **anno Domini** (Latin for *in the year of the Lord*) and **BC** for **before Christ**. AD precedes the year; BC follows it.

AD 410, 55 BC

But write **12th century AD.**

5. Write **10 a.m., 3:30 p.m., EDT, AST**

➤ See **Time**, page 287.

Measurements

1. In general, spell out such terms as **foot, hundredweight, kilogram, metre** and **minute.**

A five-kilogram packet costs $2.

2. A few common terms — **km/h, mm, m.p.h., c.c.** — are acceptable on second reference when used with figures.

70 km/h, 105-mm cannon, the old 30-m.p.h. limit, 2,000-c.c. engine

3. Terms may be abbreviated in tabular matter.

kg, l, cwt., min.

4. Use this style for imperial abbreviations, both singular and plural, in tabulations:

in., ft., yd., mi.; oz., lb., cwt.; sq. ft.

Similarly: **sec., min., hr.**

5. Use this style for metric symbols, both singular and plural, in tabulations:

mm, cm, m, km, kg, g, t, ml, l, ha, kPa

➤ See **Metric**, page 253; **Numbers**, page 215.

Organizations

1. Use **Bros., Co., Corp., Inc.** and **Ltd.** with corporate names and without commas.

General Motors Acceptance Corp., Canadian Pacific Ltd., Texaco Inc.

Note: Spell out **company**, etc., in the names of entertainment groups unless the group name includes an abbreviation.

Canadian Opera Company, Smothers Brothers

2. Do not abbreviate other terms — **association, department, division, organization** and so on — in corporate and government names.

Reader's Digest Association, Justice Department

3. Spell out **United Nations** as a noun, but the abbreviation **UN** may be used as an adjective with well-known organizations.

The United Nations will meet. The UN Security Council voted no.

Places

1. For Canadian provinces and territories, use these abbreviations after the name of a community:

Alta.	N.B.	N.S.	Que.
B.C.	Nfld.	Ont.	Sask.
Man.	N.W.T.	P.E.I.	

Note 1: After the name of a community, use **Yukon** rather than Y.T. When standing alone, make it **the Yukon**.
Note 2: An abbreviation has not yet been established for Nunavut, so it should be written out in all references.

2. For American states, use these abbreviations after the name of a community.

Ala.	Kan.	Neb.	R.I.
Ariz.	Ky.	Nev.	S.C.
Ark.	La.	N.H.	S.D.
Calif.	Me.	N.J.	Tenn.
Colo.	Md.	N.M.	Tex.
Conn.	Mass.	N.Y.	Vt.
Del.	Mich.	N.C.	Va.
Fla.	Minn.	N.D.	Wash.
Ga.	Miss.	Okla.	W.Va.
Ill.	Mo.	Ore.	Wis.
Ind.	Mont.	Pa.	Wyo.

Note: Do not abbreviate **Alaska, Hawaii, Idaho, Iowa, Ohio, Utah**; or **Puerto Rico, Virgin Islands**.

3. A placeline should refer to the province or territory a community is in. Exceptions are stories from territorial and provincial capitals other than **St. John's, Nfld.**, and these cities: **Montreal, Ottawa, Hamilton, Saskatoon, Calgary** and **Vancouver**.

GLACE BAY, N.S., PRINCE GEORGE, B.C., but YELLOWKNIFE.

➤ See **Placelines**, page 275; **Place names**, page 280; and **People, places**, page 267.

4. Generally do not abbreviate the names of countries, provinces or states when standing alone or used adjectivally.

The United States (not U.S.) declared war. The Nova Scotia (not N.S.) cabinet met. The United Kingdom (not U.K.) consists of Britain and Northern Ireland.

Note: The abbreviations U.K., U.S., B.C. and P.E.I. may be used adjectivally to reflect spoken usage.

the B.C. legislature, a U.K. bank holiday, rival U.S. teams

5. In numbered addresses, write **Ave., Blvd., Cir., Cres., Dr., Hwy., Rd., Rte., Sq., St., Ter.**

36 King St. E., 111 Sutherland Dr., 9 Binkley Ter.

Note 1: Spell out general locations.

on King Street, down Portage Avenue, the Yonge Street subway

Note 2: Spell out these official residences:

24 Sussex Drive, 10 Downing Street.

6. In general, abbreviate Saint and Sainte in place names.

St. John's, Nfld., Sault Ste. Marie

But **Saint John, N.B.**

Note: Use a hyphen instead of a period after **St** and **Ste** in Quebec place names.

Ste-Agathe, St-Eustache

➤ See **French**, page 207.

7. Do not abbreviate **county, fort, mount, point** and **port** as part of a proper name.

Fort McMurray, Mount Everest, Port Stanley, Ont.

Titles

1. Abbreviate **Gov. Gen.** and **Lt.-Gov.** before names on first reference.

Gov. Gen. Pamela King, Lt.-Govs. Joan Pappas and Alan Bucyk.

Note: Lowercase former governor general (not former Gov. Gen.), former governors general Georges Vanier and Jules Leger, the late lieutenant-governor Pat Filippo, the then-president John Redway (but prefer a more graceful construction: John Redway, who was president at the time, or some such).

2. Do not abbreviate **attorney general, auditor general, district attorney, postmaster general, representative, secretary, secretary general, senator** or **treasurer.**

3. Abbreviate **Dr., Msgr., Prof., Rev., Sgt.** and the like before full names on first reference.

Dr. Pamela Gucci, Msgr. Brian Doyle, Profs. Eva Oberast and John Green, Rev. Freda Cernetig

Miscellaneous usages

1. Use this style for bracketed political affiliations in parliamentary and legislature copy:

Tom Arlee (NDP—Edmonton East), Senator Mary Atkins (PC—Man.), Myron Martin (Ref—Snowy River), Representative John Whyte (R—Pa.), Senator Obie Black (Ind—Va.), state Senator Darleen Healey (D—Queens)

Note: In general, prefer a descriptive phrase to the bracketed style.

➤ See **Government**, page 209.

2. Abbreviate degrees, awards, honours and orders after a name.

BA, LLD, MA, OBE, PhD, SJ, VC; Louis Buncak Jr., PhD, P.Eng.

Note: Avoid unfamiliar abbreviations. Use a descriptive phrase instead: **Marie Macdonald, who has a commerce degree.**

3. Abbreviate ship and plane designations.

HMCS Restigouche, USS Johnson, SST (but spell out on first reference: **supersonic transport**)

4. Do not abbreviate books of the Bible.

Genesis, Leviticus

5. In general, spell out serial terms, but **article (Art.), number (No.), page (p.), section (Sec.)** and **volume (Vol.)** may be abbreviated before a number.

Block 1, Chapter 2, page 3, p. 3, Vol. 9

➤ See **Numbers**, page 217.

6. Do not use periods with clipped forms that have become accepted as complete words.

ad, disco, exam, gym, hi-tech, lab, math, polio, porn

7. Do not use periods with shortened forms of first names if they are pronounced as spelled.

Al, Alex, Barb, Ben, Ed, Fred, Marj, Pat, Sam, Will

But **Danl., Geo., Thos.** when such terms appear in textual matter.

8. Do not use periods when letters designate persons or things.

the spy chief Z, exhibit A, the mysterious Madame X

But use a period if the letter is an abbreviation.

Mrs. G., (shortened from **Gamp**), T.O. (Toronto)

9. In general, do not use such shortenings as **Penetang** (for Penetanguishene), **Peterboro** (for **Peterborough**), **Soo** (for **Sault Ste. Marie**) and **Xmas** (for **Christmas**).

Note: Write **Soo Greyhounds**, the official name of the Ontario Hockey League team.

Abbreviations can be used in graphics, where space is at a premium.

Here's how to wrap them:

Whether they be tortillas, naan, lavash, wonton skins, rice papers, leaf and vegetable wrappers, phyllo, nori, grape leaves or pitas, the following spread ideas will work well on all types of wraps.

Apricot-ginger cream cheese: Mix one 225 g (8 oz) container non-fat cream cheese, 60 ml (1/4 cup) apricot preserves and 5 ml (1 tsp) grated, peeled ginger root until blended. Makes 8 servings.

Mexican spread: Mix 3 ml (3/4 tsp) sauce from canned chipotles en adobo with 180 ml (3/4 cup) fat-free mayonnaise until blended. Makes 6 servings.

Peach mustard: Mix 125 ml (1/2 cup) grainy Dijon mustard and 60 ml (1/4 cup) peach preserves until blended. Makes 6 servings.

Sun-dried tomato topping: Puree 6 chopped sun-dried tomatoes packed in water, 125 ml (1/2 cup) fat-free mayonnaise. Makes 8 servings.

Horseradish cream: Mix 60 ml (1/4 cup) non-fat sour cream, 60 ml (1/4 cup) fat-free mayonnaise and 30 ml (2 tbsp) prepared white horseradish until blended. Makes 4 servings.

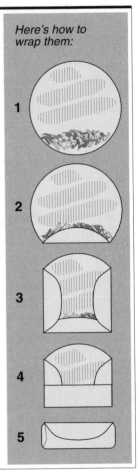

Source: Weight Watchers Wrap-Up Magazine

Tammy Hoy – **CP**

Capitalization

General

1. The Canadian Press follows a modified down style. That is, where a reasonable choice exists, CP uses lowercase. This is the basic rule:

Capitalize all proper names, trade names, government departments and agencies of government, names of associations, companies, clubs, religions, languages, nations, races, places, addresses. Otherwise lowercase is favoured where a reasonable option exists.

Here are some guidelines:

2. Capitalize common nouns — base, drive, ocean — when they are part of a formal name: **Canadian Forces Base Comox, Sussex Drive, Atlantic Ocean.** Lowercase them when standing alone in subsequent references: **the Canadian Forces base, the drive, the ocean.**

Note: In sports references the words **Games** (as in **Olympic** or **Commonwealth Games**), **Plate** (as in **Queen's Plate**), **Series** (as in **World Series**) and so on are capitalized when standing alone in subsequent references. This is to avoid confusion with the generic use of the words (as in **a series of rained-out games**).

3. Lowercase the common-noun elements of names in plural uses: **the Atlantic and Pacific oceans, prime ministers Marie Leclair and James Dunn.** But retain capitalization for the plurals of abbreviations: **Lt.-Govs. Michael O'Hara and Robert Bernard, Drs. (Revs., Profs., Sgts.) Fraser Douglas and Berthe Lucas.**

4. Capitalize formal titles directly preceding a name: **Energy Minister Marc Edmond.** Lowercase them when standing alone or set off from the name with commas: **the energy minister; the energy minister, Marc Edmond; Marc Edmond, the minister of energy.**

5. As a rule of thumb, formal titles are those that could be used with the surname alone: **Bishop Vardy.** These embrace government titles (**Prime Minister Brown, Ald. Chester**), professional titles (**Dr. Masse, Prof. Seguin**), military and paramilitary titles (**Pte. Kirkup, Insp. Low**) and religious titles (**Rabbi Dubuc, Brother Agnew**).

6. Lowercase occupational titles and job descriptions: **GM president Andre Lefort, general manager Sid James, news editor Agathe Simard, author Susan Sontag, nurse Tom Atfield.**

Note: Such descriptions usually read better preceded by *the*.

➤ See **Titles**, page 290.

7. The instruction *capitalize* refers only to the first letter of a word. If other letters are to be capitalized, *all-caps* or other specific instructions are given.

8. In sections dealing with the capitalization of book, film, music and other such titles, the term *principal words* means nouns, pronouns, adjectives, adverbs, verbs, the first and last word of the title, as well as prepositions and conjunctions of four letters or more.

9. In The Canadian Press and many other organizations, internal documents capitalize staff titles (even when standing alone), department names and the like.

the President; Vice-President, Marketing; Head Office; Personnel

Alliances

1. Capitalize alliances and similar groupings.

Confederation, the British Empire, Commonwealth, NATO allies, Warsaw Pact, East and West (ideological groupings), Allies (in world wars), Group of Seven (industrial countries)

2. Write western allies, imperial ambitions, the coalition against Iraq.

Animals and birds

1. Generally lowercase the names of animals, birds, fish and so on.

collie, dachshund, grizzly bear, palomino, pinto, quarter-horse, shorthorn, blue jay, herring gull, mallard, phoebe, robin, snowy owl, eastern cottontail rabbit, brown trout, snapping turtle, western rattlesnake, red admiral, hawk moth, dragonfly

2. Capitalize names derived from proper nouns except where usage has established the lowercase.

angora (cat, goat, rabbit), Angus cattle, Baltimore oriole, Canada goose, Cheviot sheep, Clydesdale horse, Dalmatian, German shepherd, Great Dane, Guernsey cow, Holstein-Friesian, Irish terrier, Kodiak bear, mandarin duck, Newfoundland dog, Percheron, St. Bernard, Shetland pony, Siamese cat, spaniel

Note: Unless the sex has been established, refer to an animal as *it*.

The dog wolfed its dinner. Toby, who was famished, wolfed his dinner. A bull gored his tormentor. The doe licked her leg.

3. In scientific names, capitalize only the first word.

Orcinus orca (killer whale), Ovis canadensis (Rocky Mountain bighorn sheep), Ursus arctos horribilis (grizzly bear), Branta canadensis (Canada goose), Cyanocitta cristata (blue jay), Grus americana (whooping crane)

Awards

1. Capitalize awards, honours and decorations.

Order of Canada, Order of Merit, Knight Commander of the Bath, Governor General's Awards, National Newspaper Awards, Southam Fellowship, Nobel Peace Prize, Nobel Prize for chemistry, a Nobel Prize winner, Pulitzer Prize for international reporting, a Pulitzer Prize-winning writer, Victoria Cross, Bronze Star.

Note: French awards follow French style: Croix de guerre.

2. Lowercase common-noun references standing alone.

the order, the awards, the prize, the cross

Buildings

1. Capitalize the proper names of well-known buildings, bridges, canals, parks, roads, rooms and other manufactured features.

Parliament Buildings, East Block, White House, Oval Office, Buckingham Palace, U.S. Capitol, Archambault Penitentiary, Calgary City Hall, Lions Gate Bridge, St. Lawrence Seaway, Welland Canal, Laurentian Autoroute, Vancouver International Airport, Union Station, War Memorial, CN Tower, Maple Leaf Gardens (the Gardens), Montreal Neurological Institute, Toronto Hospital, Square of Heavenly Peace, Hall of Mirrors, Sistine Chapel, Fundy National Park, French Embassy

2. Lowercase general terms standing alone, in plurals or in descriptive uses.

the palace, the international airport, the capitol, the city hall, the hospital, the Panama and Suez canals, a St. Lawrence bridge, Banff and Jasper national parks

Compositions

1. Capitalize the principal words in the titles of books, broadcast programs, films, plays, poems, songs, speeches, works of art and other compositions.

The Watch That Ends the Night, The Sheep Look Up, CBC's World at Six, Gone With the Wind, The Taming of the Shrew, In Flanders Fields, Gettysburg Address, The Laughing Cavalier

Note: Composition titles are not enclosed in quotation marks.

2. Do not capitalize *the* at the start of names of almanacs, the Bible, dictionaries, directories, encyclopedias, gazetteers, handbooks and the like.

the Canadian Almanac, the Concise Oxford Dictionary, the Encyclopedia Britannica

3. Volume, chapter, section, act, scene, etc., are capitalized when they precede a number. But **page, paragraph, verse** and **line** are lowercase in keeping with widespread practice: **page 20, line 7.**

➤ See **Numbers** below.

4. Use this style for references:

Act 1, Scene 2; 1 Kings 15:5-7 (i.e. **First Book of Kings, Chapter 15, verses 5-7**); Henry IV, Part 2 or 2 Henry IV

5. Capitalize the names of artistic movements, groups and styles, but lowercase terms used in a general sense.

Romanesque, the Renaissance, Gothic, Impressionism, the Impressionists, the Bloomsbury Group, Art Nouveau, Op Art, Art Deco

But a gothic novel, a renaissance of painting, a rococo air

➤ See **Music** below.

Computer terms

1. Capitalize specific proper names.

World Wide Web, Web site, Web master, Web page, Internet, the Net

2. Lowercase descriptive or generic terms.

electronic mail, e-mail, electronic commerce, home page

3. Use all-caps for such acronyms as:

HTML (Hypertext Markup Language); CD-ROM (compact disc read-only memory); RAM (random access memory); URL (universal resource locator)

Courts

1. Capitalize superior courts.

Privy Council, Supreme Court, Federal Court, Court of Queen's Bench, Superior Court (Quebec, Ontario), Appeal Court, International Court of Justice (the World Court), European Court of Justice, High Court of Justice (the High Court)

Lowercase divisions.

the appeal division (or trial division) of the Supreme Court

2.   Lowercase lower courts.

family court, youth court

3.   Capitalize **Crown** when referring to the supreme governing power.

The Crown dropped the charge. The matter was in the hands of the Crown attorney.

CP, PC, AP, AFP, Reuters

1.   Capitalize **The Canadian Press** and **The Associated Press** when the full names are used. On second reference, write **CP** and **AP** or **the AP** (lowercase *the*).

Note: Where the use is possessive, the *The* is capitalized: **The Canadian Press's membership, The Associated Press's reporter.** But where the use is adjectival rather than possessive, the article is lowercased and the apostrophe omitted: **the Canadian Press membership, the Associated Press reporter.**

2.   The name of CP's French-language operation is **La Presse Canadienne.** The abbreviation **PC** is acceptable in second reference.

3.   **Agence France-Presse** is so spelled. **AFP** is acceptable in second reference.

➤   See **Newspapers and magazines** below.

Derivatives

1.   Lowercase proper names that have acquired independent meaning.

arabic numerals, bohemian, brussels sprouts, cardigan, chinese red, draconian, duffel coat, dutch oven, french fries, mackintosh, manhattan, manila paper, morocco leather, oxford cloth, plaster of paris, portland cement, roman type, sandwich, scotch whisky, spartan, venetian blind, watt

2.   Medical terms tend to retain the capital longer than commoner words.

Achilles tendon, Fallopian tube, Pap smear, Freudian slip

But caesarean section, siamese twins

Note: When in doubt, capitalize.

Food and drink

1.   Brand names of foods and drinks are capitalized.

Alphabits   Mars bar
Lee-Perrin sauce   Pepsi-Cola

2. In the names of food, most proper nouns are capitalized.

beef Stroganoff
Bing cherries
Boston baked beans
Cheshire cheese
McIntosh apple

oysters Rockefeller
Parmesan cheese
quiche Lorraine
Smithfield ham
Swiss cheese

3. Names that have acquired independent common meaning are lowercased.

baked alaska
cheddar cheese
caesar salad
danish
french fries
graham crackers

hamburger
melba toast
napoleon
peach melba
russian dressing
spanish omelette

4. The names of drinks are generally lowercased.

brandy
burgundy
champagne
claret
cognac

Madeira
manhattan
Sauterne
scotch
Zinfandel

Note: Follow Oxford's style for capitalizing the names of foods and drinks unless *(CP) Caps and Spelling* shows otherwise.

5. At the start of a recipe list, capitalize the name of the dish being made:

Apple Oatmeal Squares
250 ml (1 cup) all-purpose flour
250 ml (1 cup) quick-cooking rolled oats, etc.

➤ See **Metric**, page 259, for more on recipes.

Foreign personal names

Such particles as **de, des, di, du, le, la, lo, van** and **von** are usually lowercase except when they begin a sentence.

Charles de Gaulle. De Gaulle said no. Manfred von Richthofen was nicknamed the Red Baron. Von Richthofen was a flying ace.

Note 1: Observe personal preferences.

Pierre De Bane, S. S. Van Dine, Martin Van Buren, Jean de La Fontaine

Note 2: Particles are sometimes dropped on second reference.

Ludwig van Beethoven, Beethoven; Guy de Maupassant, Maupassant; Jean de La Fontaine, La Fontaine; Joachim von Ribbentrop, Ribbentrop; Lorenzo de Medici, the Medici

Geography

1. Capitalize geographic and widely recognized descriptive regions.

the North (Canada), **Far North, Northern Canada, High Arctic, Western Canada, Central Canada, East Coast** (region, not shoreline), **Maritime provinces, Prairies, Barrens, the Front, Niagara Peninsula, Nile Delta, Alaska Panhandle, West End** (London), **Upstate New York, Southern California, Far East, Orient, North Atlantic, Central Africa, Central Asia, Western Europe, Western Hemisphere, North Pole, the Pole, Tropic of Cancer**

Note 1: Write **eastern Quebec, southern Ontario, northern Ontario**

Note 2: The **Atlantic provinces** are New Brunswick, Newfoundland, Nova Scotia and Prince Edward Island. The **Maritimes** consist of New Brunswick, Nova Scotia and Prince Edward Island.

Note 3: Write **English Canada** and **French Canada** but **English-Canadian** and **French-Canadian.**

➤ See **Political divisions** below.

2. Capitalize specific natural features.

Canadian Shield, Gulf Stream, Rocky Mountains, Mackenzie River, Yellowhead Pass, Niagara Escarpment, Lake Winnipeg, Great Lakes

3. Capitalize fanciful or imaginative terms.

Rust Belt, Deep South, Down Under, Bible Belt, Ho Chi Minh Trail, Promised Land, Eternal City, Silicon Valley

4. Lowercase points of the compass, mere direction and location, and descriptive regions not widely recognized as such.

north, to the west of Newfoundland, rain sweeping south, **east coast** (shoreline, not region), **southern Saskatchewan, northwestern Ontario, eastern Newfoundland, downtown Calgary, north-end Toronto**

5. Lowercase **northern, southern, eastern** and **western** in terms derived from regions.

a **northern** custom, **southern** hospitality, **southern Californians, an easterner, eastern provinces, a western Canadian, a westerner, western armies, far eastern peoples**

Note: In Western Canada, Ontario people are referred to as **easterners.** In Ontario, Maritimers are referred to as **easterners.**

6. Lowercase **parallel** and the like.

48th parallel, international date line, equator

7. Lowercase generic terms standing alone except when they are conventionally used as a short form of the proper noun.

Lake Erie, the lake; Rocky Mountains, the mountains; Grand Canyon, the canyon

But the Interior (for instance, British Columbia), **the Island** (for instance, Prince Edward Island), **the States** (the United States), **the Continent** (Europe), **the Channel** (English Channel), **the Lakes** (Great Lakes)

8. Lowercase the common-noun element in plurals.

lakes Superior and Erie, Red and Assiniboine rivers, the Northern and Southern hemispheres, King and Front streets

9. Lowercase **province** and **state** used in a geographic sense.

Quebec province, New York state

But capitalize as part of the corporate name.

Province of Quebec bonds, New York State vs. Smith

➤ See **Political divisions** below.

Government departments

1. Capitalize specific international, national, provincial and state government departments, ministries, agencies, boards, etc., including short forms of the proper name.

World Health Organization, United Nations Children's Fund, Department of Agriculture, Agriculture Department, Canada Post Corp., Canada Post, St. Lawrence Seaway Authority, National Parole Service, Library of Parliament, Revenue Canada, Canada Labour Relations Board, Pensions Appeal Board, Census Bureau (U.S.), War Office (Britain), Ukrainian Embassy, Italian Consulate, Secret Service, Office of the Commissioner of Official Languages, Ontario Ministry of Labour, Ontario Labour Ministry, B.C. Highways Ministry, Georgia Department of Human Resources

2. Capitalize cabinet portfolios only as part of a title directly preceding a name: **Finance Minister June Atkins.** But **June Atkins, minister of finance. John Lee is in charge of transport.**

Note: The line between capitalization and lowercase is the line between the actual ministry and its function. The sentence **John Lee is in charge of transport** is intended to suggest he's responsible for policy on rail lines, airports and other elements of national transportation. **John Lee is in charge of Transport Canada** signifies he runs the ministry itself.

3. Capitalize proper-name elements of a department or ministry when they stand alone.

The cuts will affect Justice and Communications. In those 25 years, she worked in the Archives, Housing and Natural Resources.

4. Lowercase common-noun elements standing alone and in plurals.

the department, a ministry spokeswoman, board figures, the authority, the service's record, departments of Justice and Defence

5. Lowercase local government councils, departments, boards, etc.

Peel regional council, Edmonton city council, Saskatoon board of education, Moncton development department

Historical terms

Capitalize the names of historic periods and events.

Stone Age, Dark Ages, Middle Ages, Crusades, Norman Conquest, Reformation, Age of Discovery, Industrial Revolution, the Depression or **the Great Depression, Dirty '30s, Cultural Revolution, Me Decade, Creation, Exodus, the Flood, Civil War** (American), **Battle of the Plains of Abraham, War of 1812, Reign of Terror, Riel Rebellion, First World War, Prohibition, Holocaust, Battle of Britain, Vietnam War, Quiet Revolution**

But medieval, **a reformation, a renaissance in painting, 19th century, ice age** (no single period)

Note: Capitalize **Confederation** in references to Canada: **Fathers of Confederation.**

Holidays

Capitalize holidays, religious feasts and all special times.

New Year's Eve (but **in the new year), Ash Wednesday, April Fool's Day, Mother's Day, Canada Day, St-Jean-Baptiste Day, July Fourth, Fourth of July, Halloween, Christmas Day, Hanukkah, Yom Kippur, Passover, Ramadan, D-Day, Education Week**

Note: Write **election day**.

Laws and documents

1. Capitalize proclaimed laws, treaties, important legal codes and historic documents.

British North America Act, Constitution (Canada), **Charter of Rights, Colombo Plan, UN Charter, Criminal Code, Declaration of Independence, Magna Carta**

Note: Constitution is capitalized in all references when the Canadian Constitution is meant. Otherwise it is capitalized only when preceded by a name: **the U.S. Constitution, the constitution.** Also lowercase **constitutional: the constitutional crisis.**

2. Lowercase proposed and defeated legislation, general references and plurals.

the proposed charter of rights, the Charlottetown accord, a disarmament treaty, the code, the BNA and human rights acts

3. Lowercase **speech from the throne, royal assent, third reading, the president's state of the union message, white paper, green paper.**

Legislative bodies

1. Capitalize international and national legislative bodies and their equivalents, including some short forms.

UN Security Council (Security Council), UN General Assembly (General Assembly), Parliament (national), **House of Commons, the House, the Commons, the Senate, House of Lords (the Lords), House of Representatives (the House), Chamber of Deputies (the Chamber), Bundestag, Cortes, Diet, Knesset, National Assembly** (French)

Note: Generic uses of parliament are lowercase: **the Knesset, Israel's parliament; the Sejm (Polish parliament).**

2. Lowercase general terms, informal terms (except short forms listed above), plurals and derivatives.

the administration, the council, an assembly motion, government, cabinet, lower house, the Canadian and British parliaments, parliamentary, senatorial

But the Commons motion

3. Lowercase provincial, state and regional legislatures and local councils.

Quebec national assembly, Ontario legislature, Ontario provincial parliament (but avoid), Newfoundland house of assembly, New South Wales parliament, the Virginia senate, the Northwest Territories council, Peel regional council, Victoria city council

4. Lowercase committees and subcommittees.

the committee on communications and culture

5. Capitalize the full name of royal commissions.

the Royal Commission on Corporate Concentration, the Royal Commission on Bilingualism and Biculturalism

But the royal commission, the bilingualism commission

➤ See **Laws and documents** above.

Military

1. Capitalize **Canadian Armed Forces, Canadian Forces, Armed Forces** (Canada only).

2. Capitalize **Canadian Army, (Royal) Canadian Navy** and **(Royal) Canadian Air Force** in references to pre-unification forces (before 1968).

3. The general terms **army, navy** and **air force**, written lowercase, may be used of the appropriate branches of the unified Canadian Forces: **a Canadian navy boat.**

4. For foreign forces, lowercase **army, navy** and **air force** when they are preceded by the name of a country.

Lebanese army, U.S. air force, Russian navy

Note: This style is intended for consistency. Many countries do not use **army, navy** or **air force** as the proper name.

5. Otherwise capitalize full, specific names of formations, both military and paramilitary.

Royal Navy, U.S. 8th Air Force, the 27th Army, French Foreign Legion, Royal Marines, Canadian Coast Guard, U.S. National Guard

But the army, the navy, the air force, the legion, the marines, a marine, the coast guard, a coast guard plane, the national guard, a national guardsman

6. Capitalize specific bases, commands, schools and ships.

Canadian Forces Headquarters, Canadian Forces Base Comox, the Citadel (Quebec City), Joint Chiefs of Staff, French General Staff, 6th Fleet, Royal Military College, HMCS Restigouche, HMS Antelope, USS Iowa

But a Canadian Forces base

➤ See **Aircraft, ships, guns**, page 249.

7. Capitalize official names of units.

Royal 22nd Regiment, 3rd Battalion, B Company, 3rd Infantry Division, 126 Squadron

8. Capitalize nicknames of units.

Van Doo, Desert Rats, Green Berets

9. Capitalize major armed conflicts and rebellions.

Battle of Marathon, Wars of the Roses, French Revolution, U.S. Civil War, Boxer Rebellion, Bolshevik Revolution, Battle of Britain, Battle of the Bulge, Six-Day War, Cultural Revolution

10. Capitalize fronts and important positions.

Western Front, Maginot Line

➤ See **Abbreviations**, page 167; **Military**, page 260.

Music

1. In general, capitalize the principal words in the English titles of musical compositions.

Tchaikovsky's Symphony No. 4 in F minor, Tchaikovsky's Fourth Symphony, Light My Fire by the Doors, Michael Jackson's Beat It

Note: The words **major, minor, sharp** and **flat** are written lowercase in keeping with widespread practice.

2. Informal names don't need quotation marks.

Beethoven's Sonata in E flat, Les Adieux (not "Les Adieux"), Mozart's Coronation Mass (not "Coronation")

3. When the opus number is given, set it off with a comma.

Handel's Concerti Grossi Nos. 4-6, op. 6; Mozart's Exultate, Jubilate, K. 165; Bach's St. Matthew Passion, BWV 244

4. Translate a foreign title into English unless the work is commonly known by its foreign name.

La Bohème, L'Après-midi d'un faune, Eine kleine Nachtmusik

5. For non-English titles the style varies.

In French titles, capitalize the first word, and the second word too when the first word is an article, and proper nouns: **Mon rêve, Le Rêve passé.**

In Italian, capitalize the first word and proper nouns: **La donna e mobile, La clemenza di Tito.**

In German, capitalize the first word and every noun: **Du bist mein ganzes Sehnen.**

In Latin, capitalize each word: **Te Deum.**

Names

1. For all-caps corporate and promotional names, capitalize only the first letters of words.

Amtrak (not **AMTRAK**), **Band-Aid** (not **BAND-AID**), **Oxfam** (not **OXFAM**), **Scrabble** (not **SCRABBLE**), **Via Rail** (not **VIA Rail**), **Visa** (not **VISA**)

Note: Initials are capitalized: IBM, CTV, EMI.

2. For names consisting of two or more words written solid, follow the organization's capitalization.

SkyDome, TransCanada PipeLines, PepsiCo, MuchMusic

3. For names of people or performing groups, follow their preference, as long as it doesn't excessively hamper readability.

k.d. lang (not **K.D. Lang**); **bp Nichol** (not **B.P. Nichol**); **hHead** (not **HHead**); **e.e. cummings** (not **E.E. Cummings**)

But for other names, follow normal style:

Adidas (not **adidas**); **Presstime magazine** (not **presstime**); **Sex, Lies and Videotape** (not **sex, lies and videotape**)

Nationalities and race

1. Capitalize the proper names of nationalities, peoples, races, tribes and the like.

Aboriginal Peoples, Arab, Arabic, African, African-American, Asian, Caucasian, Chipewyan, Chinese, English-Canadian, Gypsy, Hispanic, Indian, Inuk, Inuit, Jew, Jewish, Latin, Negro, Nordic, Pygmy

2. Write **aboriginal** (but **Aborigine** for the Australian race), **black, brown, caucasoid, coloured** (but **Cape Coloured**), **red, white, yellow.**

Newspapers and magazines

1. Lowercase **the** in names of newspapers.

the Toronto Star, the Star; the New York Times, the Times

2. For French-language papers, write **Montreal La Presse** rather than **the Montreal La Presse** in first reference. In subsequent references avoid sentence constructions that juxtapose **the** and **le** or **la**: the La Presse editorial. Alternatives include La Presse's editorial, an editorial in La Presse, La Presse said in an editorial.

3. CP includes qualifiers like **daily, evening** and **Sunday** if the paper prefers them: **Halifax Daily News; New York Daily News.**

4. Capitalize **magazine** only when it is part of the title.

Maclean's magazine, Harper's Magazine

➤ See **CP, PC, AP, AFP, Reuters** above.

Nicknames

Capitalize fanciful names and nicknames.

Iron Curtain, Third World, Boat People, Red Power, Little Italy, Golden Horseshoe, Old Guard, Big Three, Grits, Grand Old Party (GOP, but avoid), Tiger Williams, Herman (Babe) Ruth, Mack the Knife, Ethelred the Unready, Coeur de Lion, the Sun King

➤ See also **Names, nicknames, initials**, page 213.

Note: Father, Mother, Mom, Uncle and the like are capitalized when used as a name: **The doctor told Father that Aunt Jane is worse.** After a personal pronoun, they are lowercased: **The doctor told my father that my aunt Jane is worse.**

Numbers

1. In general, capitalize a noun followed by a number denoting place in a numbered series.

Act 1, Article 29, Book 3, Channel 2, Chapter 10, Cloud 9, Cosmos 150, Figure 13, Grade 3, Part 2, Pershing 2, Phase 1, Room 125, Square 1, Volume 12, Ward 7

Note: Avoid roman numerals except in personal sequences and in proper names where specified. **Henry Ford III, Bluenose II, Rocky IV**

2. Lowercase such words in plural use.

acts 3 and 5, chapters 1-3, grades 9 through 11

3. Lowercase **page, paragraph, sentence, size, verse, line.**

page 36, paragraph 2, line 3

Organizations

1. Capitalize the full names of organizations and institutions, but lowercase general references, with the exceptions noted below.

Canadian Airlines International, the Canadian Auto Workers, the B'nai Brith, the National Organization for Women, the airline, the autoworkers, the organization

Note 1: Company, Limited, Incorporated, Brothers and similar words are abbreviated as part of a name, **Inco Ltd.**, except in cultural references: **Canadian Opera Company, Clancy Brothers.**

Note 2: For consistency, lowercase **the** in the names of organizations, except for those noted in *(CP) Caps and Spelling.*

➤ See **The** below.

2. Capitalize the names of major subdivisions of an organization.

the General Council of the United Church of Canada, the Chevrolet Division of General Motors

3. Lowercase ordinary internal elements of an organization.

the United Church's division of mission, the board of directors of General Motors, the fire management centre of the Ministry of Natural Resources

4. Retain capitalization when the short form of a name is a household word. But use lowercase when referring to members of an organization.

Scouts Canada, the Scouts but two boy scouts; International Brotherhood of Teamsters, Chauffeurs, Warehousemen and Helpers of America, Teamsters union, the Teamsters; Ku Klux Klan, the Klan, a klansman; Odd Fellows and an Odd Fellow (capped to avoid ambiguity)

5. Retain capitalization when popular usage has reversed a name and eliminated **of, of the** and the like.

Department of Justice, Justice Department; Ministry of the Interior, Interior Ministry

➤ See **Abbreviations and acronyms**, page 167.

Plants

1. In plant names, capitalize proper nouns and adjectives derived from proper nouns.

Scotch pine, Kentucky blue grass, Douglas fir, white Dutch clover

2. In botanical names, capitalize the first word, lowercase others.

Primula japonica (Japanese primrose), **Taraxacum officinale** (dandelion), **Acer rubrum** (red maple), **Cornus florida** (dogwood)

3. Capitalize the names of fruit and vegetable varieties.

McIntosh, Delicious (apples); **Yukon Gold** (potatoes)

4. Capitalize wheat varieties generally except where usage has established the lowercase.

Selkirk, durum

➤ See **Technical terms**, page 283.

Political divisions

1. Capitalize specific political and administrative divisions.

British Empire, Dominion (Canada), **United Kingdom, French Republic, Greater Vancouver Regional District, Montreal Urban Community, Ward 2, 11th Congressional District, Precinct 2, Muskoka District, McGillivray Township, Niagara Region.**

But **Niagara region, Muskoka district** when referring to the geographical area.

2. Lowercase such words as **city, county, province** and **state** except when they are part of the incorporated name.

in the city of Halifax, the City of Halifax's credit rating; in Quebec province, the Province of Quebec vs. Smithers; the California state capital, the State of California's damage suit

Quebec City, New York City, Kansas City, Greenwich Village

Politics

1. Capitalize the full names of political parties and movements, but lowercase **party** in short forms.

Liberal Party of Canada, Liberal party, Progressive Conservative Party of Canada, Progressive Conservative party, Reform Party of Canada, Reform party, Pacific party, Green party, Christian Heritage party, Communist party, Young Liberals, National Liberation Front, IRA Provisional wing, United Alternative

But **New Democratic Party, Bloc Québécois, Parti Québécois**

2. Capitalize **Communist, Conservative, Democrat, Fascist, Liberal, Nazi, New Democrat, Socialist** and the like when they refer to a specific party or its members.

3. Lowercase these words when they refer to a political philosophy, except when they are derived from a proper name.

communism, democracy, fascism, socialism, separatism, democratic rights, conservative principles, independent nations, republican system, the left, right-wing group, liberals, communists, social democrats

But **Marxism, Marxists, Nazism, Nazis**

4. Capitalize fanciful names and nicknames.

Grits, Tories, Grand Old Party (GOP, but avoid), **Old Guard, Young Turks, Black Power, Reds**

5. Capitalize **Leader, Chairman** or **Secretary** when used with the name of a party and directly preceding a name, but lowercase as the title for others.

Reform (party) **Leader Preston Manning** (but **party leader Preston Manning**); **Communist party General Secretary Do Muoi** (but prefer **Do Muoi, the Communist party general secretary**)

But **Libyan leader Moammar Gadhafi, PLO leader Yasser Arafat, NDP chairman Roy Brown, party secretary Ann Rogers**

6. Capitalize **Politburo** and **Central Committee**, but lowercase other principal political bodies as well as political conventions.

the government, the administration, the cabinet, Liberal leadership convention, Republican platform committee

➤ See **Legislative bodies** above.

Quotations

1. Capitalize the first word of a complete quotation.

Pickets yelling "Scab!" deterred 200 men from entering.

McCabe replied to the lawyer's "Ah, Mr. McCabe" with an "Oh, hello, Mr. Trout."

Poirier asked, "Did you expect to hear shouts of 'Well done' and 'Good luck'?"

2. Do not capitalize a word or phrase that is quoted merely for discussion or because it is controversial or used ironically or oddly.

What does "gating" mean?

One of the words used was "scab."

The "gift" cost $10.

➤ See **Punctuation**, page 239.

Religion

1. Capitalize sacred names.

Adonai
Allah
the Almighty
the Angel Gabriel
the Apostle Paul,
  Paul the Apostle
the Baptist
Blessed Virgin
Buddha
the Child Jesus
Divine Providence
Father
God
the Godhead
the Guru
the Holy Family
the Holy Spirit
Jehovah
King of Kings

Lord of Lords
the Madonna
the Messiah
Mother Mary
the Omnipotent
the One Great Spirit
our Lady
Prince of Peace
the Prophet (Mohammed)
the Saviour
Siva
the Son
the Son of Man
the Twelve Apostles
the Virgin
Vishnu
the Word
Yahweh

Note: Lowercase fatherhood, providence (in a general sense), messianic, a saviour (in a non-religious sense), the angel, an apostle.

2. Capitalize personal pronouns referring to God: He, Him, His, Me, My, Mine, Thou, Thee, Thine and so on. Lowercase relative pronouns: who, whom, whose.

3. Capitalize the proper names and nicknames of the devil.

Satan, Lucifer, Father of Lies, Old Nick, the Antichrist

Note: Lowercase satanic, capitalize Satanism.

4. Lowercase god and goddess in references to pagan gods but capitalize their proper names.

the sun god, the gods of Olympus, the goddess Venus, the god Thor

5. Capitalize the names of religions, faiths, their current heads and their adherents.

the Baha'i faith	Islam	Parsee
Buddhist	Jain	the Pope
Christianity	Jew	Shintoist
the Dalai Lama	Muslim	the Sikh religion
Hinduism	Neo-Confucianism	Zen-Buddhism

Note: Lowercase pagan, atheist, agnostic (in a general sense), gentile, spiritualist, theosophist.

6. Capitalize the names of religious denominations, movements, orders and their adherents.

Catholicism	Oxford Movement
Eastern Orthodoxy	High, Low Church
Protestantism	an Anglican
Sephardism	Baptist
Mormonism	Papists
Christian Science, a Scientist	Reform Jews
Jehovah's Witness, a Witness	Sons of Freedom, a Freedomite
Seventh-day Adventist, an Adventist	Franciscans
Salvation Army, the Army	Grey Nuns
	Essenes
	Pharisees

7. Capitalize sacred writings and their parts.

the Bible	Laws of Manu	the Talmud
Book of Genesis	New, Old Testament	the Upanishads
the Epistles	Romans	the Vedas
the Koran	Scripture	

Note: Lowercase fisherman's bible, biblical, the gospel truth, a parable, an epistle, apocryphal, talmudic, koranic, vedic.

8. Capitalize such familar references as the following.

Garden of Eden	Holy Week	the Shroud of Turin
the Chosen People	Good Friday	Diet of Worms
Tower of Babel	the Crucifixion	the Hegira
Noah's Ark	the Resurrection	(Mohammed's)
Ten Commandments	the Prodigal Son	Ramadan
City of David	Three Wise Men	Festival of Sacrifice
Day of Atonement	Good Samaritan	the Second Coming
Yom Kippur	Council of Trent	the Last Day

Note: Lowercase heaven, hell, paradise, purgatory, nirvana.

9. Lowercase sacraments, rituals and the like.

aqiqa	confession	holy communion
baptism	eucharist	kaddish
bar mitzvah	evensong	mass
christening	high mass	seder

10. Capitalize **church** as part of the name of a building, a congregation or a denomination.

St. Paul's United Church, the Anglican Church

Note: Write an Anglican church, the Roman Catholic and Anglican churches, church and state.

➤ See **Titles**, page 292.

Schools

1. Capitalize universities and colleges but not their departments.

Simon Fraser University, Macdonald College, McGill medical school, department of dentistry, English department, faculty of education

2. In general, lowercase schools.

York collegiate institute, York collegiate, Banff high school, Rolph Road elementary school, St. John's separate school

Note: Write London School of Economics, Harvard Graduate School of Business, University of Toronto Schools.

Slogans and headlines

1. Capitalize the principal words of written slogans and newspaper headlines, but do not use quotation marks.

On one placard was written Restraint — Practise What You Preach. Another sign read Help the Economy.

The editorial appeared under the heading Show Some Leadership.

➤ See **No. 8**, page 176, for a definition of principal words.

2. Capitalize only the first word of rules and mottoes.

Another rule suggests Think before you write.

There's much truth in the saying Too many cooks spoil the broth.

Space

1. Capitalize the proper names of asteroids, comets, constellations, planets, stars and other unique celestial objects, and nouns and adjectives derived from proper names.

Ceres, Andromeda, Great Bear, Ursa Major, Charles's Wain, Big Dipper, Milky Way, Anik E-1, Martian, Jovian, Venusian

2. In general, lowercase the common-noun element of the names of celestial objects.

Ceres asteroids, the constellation of Andromeda, Halley's comet, Crab nebula, Barnard's star

But the North Star (Polaris)

3. Lowercase **earth** except when referred to as an astronomical body. Lowercase **sun** and **moon** in all instances.

down to earth, move heaven and earth, returned to Earth from Mars, Earth's atmosphere, the new moon

4. Lowercase the names of meteorological phenomena.

northern lights, aurora borealis

Sports

1. Capitalize major sports events and trophies.

Olympic Games, Winter Olympics, World Series, World Cup, Canadian Open, Canada Cup, Grey Cup, Queen's Plate, Stanley Cup playoffs, Super Bowl, Vezina Trophy

2. In second references, capitalize **Games, Series, Cup, Open, Plate, Stakes** and the like: **the Series' leading batter, the Plate also-rans.** This is an exception to the rule that common nouns standing alone are lowercased.

➤ See **Sports**, page 78.

The

1. The word **the** (or its non-English equivalent) is capitalized at the start of titles of books, magazines, movies, TV programs, songs, paintings and other compositions.

The Last Spike, The New Yorker, L'Amour masqué, The Journal, The Holly and the Ivy, The Artist and His Model

2. **The** is not capitalized at the start of the names of such works as almanacs, the Bible, directories, encyclopedias, gazetteers and handbooks.

the Canadian Almanac, the Reader's Encyclopedia, the Concise Oxford Dictionary, the Canadian Press Stylebook

3. When **the** is capitalized in a geographical name, retain the capitalization.

The Pas, The Hague, El Salvador

But the Yukon, the Netherlands, the Congo, the City (London financial district), **the** Front (sealing ground off Labrador), **the** Barrens

4. In rare instances, **the** can be capitalized when it is used to give a singular meaning to an ordinary word.

The Change (menopause), **The Show** (baseball's major leagues)

5. For consistency, lowercase **the** in all other names: companies, associations, institutions, newspapers, awards, ships, trains, nicknames, rock groups and so on.

the Bay, the Royal Canadian Legion, the House of Commons, the Foreign Affairs Department, the Anglican Church, the Air Defence Command, the Gazette, the Juno Awards, the Queen Elizabeth, the Transcontinental, the Royal York Hotel, Mack the Knife, the Beatles, the Prince of Wales

Note: Capitalize the definite article in the names of French-language newspapers in accordance with French style: **Le Droit**.

➤ See **Newspapers and magazines** above.

Times and seasons

Lowercase the seasons and spelled-out references to time.

spring, winter
mountain standard time, eastern daylight time,
Atlantic daylight time

But MST, EDT, ADT

Titles

1.   Capitalize formal titles — those that are almost an integral part of a person's identity — when they directly precede the name.

Pope Pius, Queen Elizabeth, Prime Minister John Major, Dr. Hans Selye, Prof. Harold Smith, Sgt. Ann Rutherford, Brother Marcus

Note: With few exceptions, a title more than two words long should be set off from the name with commas: **Arnold Schaur, trade and commerce minister, . . .**

2.   A title set off from a name by commas is lowercased. **The prime minister, Tony Blair, will represent Britain at the talks.**

3.   Lowercase occupational titles and descriptions. Titles of officials of companies, unions, political organizations and the like are also lowercased.

Widget president Barbara Sansom, UAW secretary Margaret Wilson, defenceman Ted Green, general manager Art Simpson, coach Guy Lebrun, contralto Maureen Forrester, astronaut John Young

Note 1: Avoid the inelegant practice of invariably affixing the description to a person's name as a false title: **rock star Bill Glass, bus driver Mary Owens, Niagara Falls businessman Mario Gucci.** Offer occasional relief by using a **the** phrase: **the contralto Maureen Forrester, the English historian Arnold Toynbee.** Or use a comma construction: **Violet Haynes, a Liberal member, disagreed. The spokesman, Tom Jameson, refused to comment. Ford's president, Bobbi Gaunt; a truck driver, Mary Owens.**

Note 2: Avoid such pileups as **public relations director John O'Connor's department; best-selling Canadian mystery writer Eric Wright.**

4.   Capitalize all references to the current Pope, Canada's reigning monarch and the current Canadian Governor General. But lowercase most formal titles standing alone.

the Pope's visit, the Queen's family, wrote to the Governor General

But the king of Denmark, the prime minister, the president, the Communist party chairman

5.   Capitalize **Royal Family** when referring to the British Royal Family. Also **Queen Mother, Her** or **His Majesty** and **Her** or **His Royal Highness,** whether standing alone or with names. For former and future British monarchs, capitalize the title: **the former King.** With foreign royalty, capitalize all current titles used with a proper name and lowercase others: **Queen Astrid, former king Farouk.**

6.   **Royal** — as in **royal visit, royal assent** — is lowercase.

7. **Crown** is capitalized when it refers to the state.

the Crown corporation, the Crown alleged, the Crown jewels; but the Queen's crown

8. Capitalize titles of nobility, religion and such that are commonly used instead of the personal name. Lowercase on subsequent references.

the Prince of Wales, the prince; the Earl of Snowden, the earl; the Archbishop of Canterbury, the archbishop; the Bishop of Toronto, the bishop

9. Capitalize terms of honour, nobility and respect.

His Excellency, His Honour, Your Honour, Hon. John Jones, Her Worship, His Grace, My Lord

Note: Use such terms only when they appear in direct quotations.

10. To avoid ambiguity, all references to legislative **Speakers** are capped.

11. Lowercase titles preceded by **former, acting** and so on.

prime minister-designate Mary Brown, acting prime minister John Burgess, president-elect Tony Leech, the onetime president Gerald Ford, former mayor Joanne Lesniak

But Deputy Prime Minister Oskar Arendt

Note 1: Abbreviated titles are capped: the late Dr. Jean Savard.

Note 2: In references to past events, titles are capped when words like **former** and **the late** are dropped:

The official opening of the St. Lawrence Seaway — on June 26, 1959 — was attended by Prime Minister John Diefenbaker and U.S. President Dwight Eisenhower.

12. Lowercase plural uses of titles.

premiers Jean Martineau and Gerry Germain, popes John Paul II and John XXIII

Note: Capitalize the plural use of abbreviations: **Profs. Giuseppe Gucci and Helen Bruno.**

13. Lowercase derivatives.

presidential, papal, ministerial, senatorial, mayoral

14. Variations on the titles of cabinet ministers are not capitalized.

junior finance minister Robert Jack; acting health minister Kim Shen

Note: Titles of government officials below cabinet rank are lowercased: **deputy minister Eva Swartz, House leader Ian Loy** (federal), **house leader Ian Loy** (provincial).

15. Following titles are in CP style:

Prime Minister Jean Chrétien
Deputy Prime Minister Herb Gray
the prime minister, Jean Chrétien
former prime minister John Turner
junior finance minister Jean Fortin
deputy trade minister Aldo Conti
Conservative Leader Joe Clark
the Speaker
the Governor General
Gov. Gen. Romeo LeBlanc
lieutenant-governor
Lt.-Gov. Hilary Weston
Senator John Buchanan

➤ See **Government**, page 208; **Titles**, page 290. Also, **Government departments**, **Military** and **Religion** above. For composition titles, see **Compositions** and **Music** above.

Trade names

1. Capitalize all trade names but use them only when they give point, colour or impact to a story.

The doctor refused to prescribe Laetrile or Essiac.
She blew the inheritance on a Rolls-Royce.
Jim Jones gave Kool-Aid laced with poison to 900 members of the People's Temple.

2. A generic term can often be used instead.

headache pill (Aspirin); **adhesive bandage** (Band-Aid); **cola drink** (Coca-Cola); **fibreglass** or **glass fibre** (Fiberglas); **jelly dessert** (Jell-O); **tissues** or **paper handkerchiefs** (Kleenex); **hardboard** (Masonite); **heat-resistant glass** (Pyrex); **cotton swabs** (Q-Tips); **sticky tape** (Scotch Tape); **plastic foam** (Styrofoam); **petroleum jelly** (Vaseline); **photocopier** (Xerox)

Note: Trade names subject to protection in Canada are normally listed in the *Canadian Trade Index*. Do not follow the capitalization in the *Canadian Oxford Dictionary*.

➤ See **Trade names**, page 294.

Compounds

General

1. In the absence of widely agreed rules, writers and editors sometimes have to decide whether a compound word should be written open (**knuckle ball**), hyphenated (**knuckle-ball**) or solid (**knuckleball**).

2. In practice, a new compound is normally written at first as two or more words (**on line**), becomes increasingly hyphenated (**on-line**) and is then combined into a single word (**online**).

3. In North America, the tendency is to drop the hyphen as soon as a new compound becomes familiar.

Guidelines

1. Hyphens are used to unravel meaning.

an old-book collector, an old book-collector; a white-slave racket, a white slave-racket; a light-blue coat; a dry-ice machine

2. Compound adjectives are often hyphenated before the noun they modify.

a world-class athlete, up-to-the-minute fashion, a 12-year-old child

3. When the words forming a compound adjective stand alone in a sentence, they are usually not hyphenated.

an athlete of world class, fashion that's up to the minute, the child is 12 years old

Note: In the sentence **The 12-year-old is from Vancouver,** 12-year-old is properly hyphenated as a noun. Similarly: **a race for three-year-olds.**

4. When Oxford and *(CP) Caps and Spelling* offer no help, write a compound noun as separate words or one word rather than with a hyphen.

Note: Compound nouns are not necessarily created from nouns but may be combinations of verbs, adverbs and so on.

teeter-totter, know-how, the down-at-heel, letdown

5. Compound verbs are usually either hyphenated or written as one word.

hand-picked, babysit, dry-clean, whitewash, deep-six

6. Compound verbs ending in an adverb or a preposition are not hyphenated.

break away, hold up, shoot out, run in, lean to, clip on

Note: The same two words used as nouns or adjectives are written solid. But if the solid form would be hard to grasp, use a hyphen.

breakaway, holdup, shootout
But **run-in** (not **runin**), **lean-to** (not **leanto**),
a **clip-on lid** (not **clipon**)

7. Keep in mind the advice of the Oxford University Press stylebook:

"If you take hyphens seriously, you will surely go mad."

➤ See **Punctuation**, page 236.

French

The Canadian Press delivers its news report in English for an audience that is not necessarily bilingual. Stories peppered with French break the flow and make reading difficult. At the same time, it is not always possible to avoid the use of French in the names of organizations or movie and book titles. In that case, a translation that remains as faithful as possible to the French should be provided. If a precise translation is impossible, an explanation or description can be used.

The aim is always ease of understanding without sacrificing the meaning of the French text.

Names of organizations

1. Prefer the English form for the names of organizations.

Quebec Liquor Corp. (not Société des alcools du Québec); University of Montreal (not Université de Montréal); the Montreal campus of the University of Quebec (not Université du Québec à Montréal or University of Quebec in Montreal); Montreal Transit Corp. (not Société de transport de la communauté urbaine de Montréal); Quebec Labour Federation (not Fédération des travailleurs du Québec); Quebec provincial police (not Sûreté du Québec); Museum of Fine Arts (not Musée des beaux-arts); Great Whale hydro project (not the Grande baleine project)

2. The names of some organizations cannot readily be translated. Others become familiar in their French version, or have no official English version. In such cases, the French name should be accompanied by an explanation.

Conseil du patronat, the largest employers group in Quebec; Centrale de l'enseignement du Québec, the teachers federation; Société pour vaincre la pollution, an environmental group; Union des producteurs agricoles, the farmers union; Ecole polytechnique, the engineering school affiliated with the University of Montreal

Note: Be careful with the following agencies set up in conjunction with Quebec's French-language law *(Law 101)*.

Office de la langue française, the agency that administers the provisions of the provincial language law; Conseil de la langue française, a research and advisory body on language issues.

3. For some organizations, known even to English speakers in Quebec by their initials, prefer a substitute rather than the full name or initials.

CEGEP (Collège d'enseignement général et professionel): junior college; CLSC (Centre local de services communautaires): community health centre

4. Some Quebec titles have equivalents in other provinces. Prefer a similar form for the Quebec version even if that means the translation is not identical to the French.

Corporation professionnelle des médecins du Québec: Quebec College of Physicians rather than the Professional Corporation of Quebec Doctors; Directeur général des élections: chief returning officer

5. A few organizations, titles and the like are commonly known by their French names and need not be followed by a translation.

Le Droit, Société St-Jean-Baptiste, Notre Dame

Books, movies, etc.

1. Prefer the English form for the titles of books, movies and the like if the English name is widely known.

Remembrance of Things Past (not A la recherche du temps perdu); Jesus of Montreal (not Jésus de Montréal); The Decline of the American Empire (not Le Declin de l'empire américain)

2. When a French name or title is used in a quotation, a list of awards or a review, it should be followed by the official translation, if available, in parentheses.

Le Malade imaginaire (The Imaginary Invalid); Le Matou (The Alley Cat); Dans l'oeil de l'aigle (In the Eye of the Eagle); Dans le ventre du dragon (In the Belly of the Dragon)

3. When there is no official translation — for example, if the movie or book has not been issued in English — provide a translation in parentheses that accurately conveys the meaning of the French title.

Au revoir, les enfants (Goodbye Children); Les Belles-soeurs (The Sisters-in-Law)

4. When there is no official or simple English title of a novel, TV program, movie or the like, or when the English translation conveys a different meaning from the French, an explanation is in order.

Les Fous de Bassan, the novel by Anne Hebert which was issued in English as In the Shadow of the Wind. Fous de Bassan refers to gannets, a type of seabird.

Bonheur d'occasion by Gabrielle Roy, which translates as Second-Hand Happiness but was issued in English as The Tin Flute

Un Train d'enfer, a movie whose title translates as A Train From Hell, but which also carries the meaning of breakneck speed

René Lévesque's Memoirs, whose original title, Attendez que je me rappelle, had a typically offhand suggestion of Hang On, It'll Come to Me — with a hint of Quebec's official motto

Accents

1. When technically possible, use accents on French proper names, including place names, and on the rare instances when French common words are not translated into English.

Jean Chrétien, Bloc Québécois, L'Actualité, Trois Rivières, Fête nationale, raison d'étre

Note: Accents are not used on **Quebec** and **Montreal**, which have long-established English versions, unless they are part of a proper name: **Le Journal de Montréal**

2. Follow Oxford for English words.

cliché, resumé, café, debut

Capitalization

1. For most names in French, capitalize the first word, the second word too when the first is an article, and proper nouns.

This applies to:

a) Titles of books, songs, movies and the like.

De la terre à la lune, Sur le pont d'Avignon, Les Liaisons dangereuses

b) Names of newspapers and magazines.

Le Journal de Montréal, L'Actualité, Le Courrier du peuple, L'Acadie nouvelle, La Voix de l'Est (l'Est, meaning **the East**, is capitalized as the name of a region)

Note: When referring to a French newspaper, avoid repetition of the article. **La Presse reported today** (not **the La Presse report said today**).

c) A variety of other kinds of names.

Fête nationale (a holiday), **L'Auberge bonne nuit** (a hotel), **La Petite marmite** (a restaurant), **L'Académie canadienne-française** (an association), **Place d'armes** (a city square), **Conseil du patronat** (employers' organization), **Office de la langue française** (government agency)

2. For names of corporate organizations, CP uses the English article preceding the name. Otherwise, capitalize the first word and proper nouns, lowercase other words.

the **Service de perception**, **Emballages St-Laurent ltée**, the **Caisse de dépôt et placement**

3. The main exception to the basic rule is for place names, which follow normal CP capitalization.

La Tuque, Pointe-aux-Trembles, St-Basile-le-Grand

4. **Franco-Albertan** and **Anglo-Quebecer** take capital letters; **francophone** and **anglophone** do not. Generally, prefer **French-speaking** and **English-speaking**. The word **allophone** is also entering the vocabulary to describe someone who is neither French-nor English-speaking, but it should be avoided.

5. **Fleur-de-lis** is capitalized when it refers to Quebec's flag.

Hyphens in place names

In CP copy, French place names follow the French style of punctuation, with hyphens instead of periods (St-Hyacinthe) or spaces (Rivière-du-Loup).

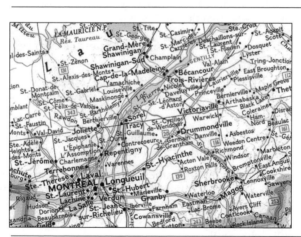

1. Most multiple-word place names in Quebec and other French-speaking areas of the world are hyphenated.

Trois-Rivières, St-Georges-de-Beauce, Stanstead-Est, Que.; Petit-Rocher, N.B.; Val-d'Isère, France

Note: In names preceded by the definite article, do not put a hyphen after the article.

La Malbaie, La Pocatière

2.   Hyphens are omitted from purely English place names.

Stanstead Plain, East Broughton, Otterburn Park

3.   Hyphens are omitted if the first word is not a place name but refers to a natural feature (*lake, river, mountain* etc.).

Lac Barrière, Baie des Chaleurs, Rivière des Prairies

Note: A natural feature can be part of the corporate name of some municipalities. They are hyphenated: **Baie-Comeau, Lac-Beauport, Mont-Laurier.**

4.   Street names take hyphens.

Ste-Catherine Street, 136 René-Lévesque Blvd.

Saint

1.   Family and place names that include *saint* or a variant are tricky, needing the same care in checking as *Mac* and *Mc* names.

2.   In Quebec place names, *saint* and *sainte* are abbreviated to *St* and *Ste* (no periods) and joined to the next word by a hyphen. Elsewhere in Canada, practice varies.

St-Jean-Port-Joli, Que; Ste-Anne-des-Monts, Que.

But **St. Boniface, Man.; Sault Ste. Marie, Ont.; Saint John, N.B.; St. John's, Nfld.; St. Brieux, Sask.; Saint-Antoine, N.B.; St. Jacques, Nfld.**

Note: It is not always obvious that a name is feminine or masculine (e.g. **St-Hyacinthe**); check if in doubt.

3.   Quebec family names may be written either with **saint** and **sainte** spelled out (**Louise Saint-Pierre, Marcel Sainte-Marie**) or in abbreviated form (**Chantal St-Amour** or **Pierre Ste-Croix**). Check with the person for a preferred spelling; if that is not possible, prefer the long form.

4.   For the names of saints, follow normal English practice and use St. for female as well as male saints and do not hyphenate.

St. Jean de Brébeuf, St. Marguerite Bourgeoys

Translation

1. CP avoids double translation. The risk of error is compounded when a quotation moves from one language into another and then back again. Paraphrasing a quotation reduces the risk.

2. When translating from an interview or from a French text, avoid awkward literal translations. Translate to convey the meaning of the quote or French text while remaining as true as possible to the original. If that requires too many contortions, paraphrase.

"Il a réussit à sauver les meubles": not "He managed to save the furniture" but "He was able to salvage the essentials."

3. Be alert to words that look alike in French and English but have different meanings.

amateur (in sports, fan); bulletin d'information (news report); circulation (traffic); commission parlementaire (legislature committee); déception (disappointment), déçu (disappointed); éditeur (publisher), rédacteur-en-chef (editor); exploiter (operate); formation (training, education); ignorer (be unaware of, not know); impliquer (involve); militant (member of a political party); nomination (appointment); populaire (popular, but more often of or for the people); sécurité (safety); sensibiliser (educate), sensible (sensitive to)

4. **Business terminology:** The business world uses some terms that present translation problems.

actif (assets); action (share); administrateur (director); bénéfice net (profit); chef de l'exploitation (chief operating officer); chiffres d'affaires (income); membre de la direction (officer); obligation (bond, debenture); passif (liabilities); président-directeur-général — pdg (president and chief executive officer — CEO); président du conseil (chairman of the board); société (company or corporation); société fermée (private company); société ouverte (public company)

5. **Legal terminology:**

effraction (break and enter); homicide involontaire (manslaughter); mandat de perquisition (search warrant); outrage au tribunal (contempt of court); voies de fait (assault)

Note: In Quebec, the Civil Code based on the French Napoleonic Code is used in civil litigation. The Canadian Criminal Code applies in criminal cases.

As a result, many procedures differ from elsewhere in Canada.

➤ See **Legal** section, page 94.

Government

Introduction

Question period shouting matches and hallway scrums offer only a small glimpse of what government does. Good reporting goes further. It humanizes statistics, puts issues into perspective, illustrates the effects of new regulations and penetrates the silent bureaucracies that shape the lives of Canadians.

Most people connect with government through taxes, schools, police, hospitals, highways, jobs and the price of beer. These are tangible elements. They should appear in stories. That means putting real people looking for jobs in a report on unemployment statistics. It means showing how car owners and trout anglers will be affected by new environmental laws.

Corruption and waste are pursued, where they exist, but reporters must not become another official Opposition, looking only for something — *anything* — to criticize. The best reporting is concerned with more than quick hits from mock-indignant politicians. Time is better spent exploring how little-known regulatory agencies affect everyday concerns like food quality, aircraft safety or personal privacy.

The relationship between issues raised in the political arena and the concerns of the reader at home is often obscure. The reporter works to make that connection clear.

Capitalization

➤ For questions of capitalization on government, parliaments, laws, royalty, etc., see the chapter **Capitalization**, starting page 175.

National and provincial legislatures

1. Ministers with more than one portfolio should be referred to by the title most appropriate to the story. **Sergio Marchi, minister of citizenship and immigration**, becomes **Immigration Minister Sergio Marchi** in stories about immigration levels.

2. The **official Opposition** is the opposition party with most seats: **the Opposition Liberals, the two opposition parties**.

3. **MP** is always acceptable for member of Parliament. Don't use an abbreviation for members of provincial legislatures, since the title varies from province to province.

4. Write **Senate, Senator Nate Nurgitz, a senator, former senator Robert de Cotret**.

5. Make it **Parliament Hill, the Hill, Parliament Buildings, East Block, Peace Tower, lower chamber, upper chamber, lower house, upper house**.

6. The official residence of the Canadian prime minister is **24 Sussex Drive**; that of the Opposition leader is **Stornoway**.

7. Write **prime minister-designate** Jean Chrétien, not **prime minister-elect** Jean Chrétien, because the Canadian electorate does not vote for a prime minister or premier as such. But **president-elect** Bill Clinton is correct in U.S. contexts.

8. The forms **Progressive Conservative** and **Conservative** are equally acceptable in casual reference to the federal party. Some provincial parties prefer the full title. Check.

Political affiliations and designations

1. The political affiliation of elected members and the names of their constituencies are specified when they are relevant. For members of Parliament and provincial legislatures, give the party and constituency; for senators, party and province.

2. Streamlined abbreviations for party designations are fine in routine parliamentary and legislature copy, or in stories where many members are named. They are avoided otherwise, except for **NDP** and **PQ**.

The abbreviations are: **AD** (L'Action democratique), **BQ** (Bloc Québécois), **EP** (Equality Party), **Ind** (Independent), **Lib** (Liberal), **NDP** (New Democratic Party), **PC** (Progressive Conservative), **PQ** (Parti Québécois), **Ref** (Reform), **SP** (Saskatchewan Party), **SC** (Social Credit).

Style is **(Lib—Winnipeg North Centre)**. The abbreviation is separated from the constituency by a dash with no spaces on either side.

Usually, a descriptive phrase reads better than a streamlined style: **George Baker, the longtime Liberal member for Gander-Grand Falls**. Sometimes a fuller description is desirable. For example, in a debate about federal transfer payments to Newfoundland: **George Baker, Liberal member for Gander-Grand Falls, is a politically well-connected Newfoundlander whose brother, Winston, is the province's deputy premier and finance minister**.

3. In the bracketed style, the names of federal constituencies not easily identified are followed by the name of the province: **(Lib—Egmont, P.E.I.)**.

4. The names of cities are given when they have more than one seat: **Toronto Broadview-Greenwood** (city first). Similarly, the name of a subdivided constituency precedes that of the subdivision: **York West**.

First minister

Where the choice is between **prime minister** and **premier**, use **prime minister** for the heads of national governments in general but **premier** for the heads of government in France and its former colonies, Canadian provinces and Australian states. Some West Indies governments also have premiers; follow individual preferences.

Monarchy

The Queen and members of the Royal Family deserve normal respect for their constitutional role in Canada, but coverage of their visits to this country and other activities is governed by basic news standards.

In particular, that means stories should not gush (**looking radiant**). Nor should they pretend the visitor's casual asides are profound or witty, nor quote meaningless exclamations from bystanders ("**It's the most thrilling day of my life**," said 11-year-old Melanie Simpson), nor be littered with royal this's and that's (the **royal breakfast**, the **royal limousine**, etc.).

It is no more acceptable to write condescendingly about ordinary people's responses to a royal tour. The fact that someone puts on hat and gloves to watch royalty pass, or belongs to the Monarchist League, is a matter of personal choice, not an occasion for fun.

The best stories tend to focus on one or two events in the visitor's day, stressing human elements that are genuinely newsworthy and describing them fully and frankly. The organization is also worth a story at times: in Halifax, they once used green paint on a bald stretch of the common as part of their spruce-up.

Such coverage excludes the kind of social-page filler that lists every hand shaken, royal guard inspected, memorial book inscribed and ribbon cut.

1. The Queen is Canada's **head of state**; the prime minister is **head of government**. Officially, the **Governor General** acts as head of state when the Queen isn't in Canada, but avoid referring to the Governor General in such terms.

2. Unless there are problems with identification — for instance, in a story dealing with a number of monarchs — the preferred term for Queen Elizabeth is **the Queen**, rather than **Queen Elizabeth**. **Queen of England** is wrong.

3. Don't refer to the late Princess of Wales as **Princess Diana**, since she wasn't a princess by birth.

Succession

Order of succession to the throne:

1. Prince Charles, Prince of Wales (Queen's eldest son)
2. Prince William (elder son of Charles)
3. Prince Henry (second son of Charles)
4. Prince Andrew (second son of the Queen)
5. Princess Beatrice (elder daughter of Andrew)
6. Princess Eugenie (second daughter of Andrew)
7. Prince Edward (third son of the Queen)
8. Princess Anne (only daughter of the Queen)
9. Peter Phillips (only son of Anne)
10. Zara Phillips (only daughter of Anne)
11. Princess Margaret (only sister of the Queen)

Ceremonies

1. The Queen and other members of the Royal Family receive a **royal salute** — the playing of *God Save the Queen* by a royal guard.

2. The Governor General and lieutenant-governors are accorded a **vice-regal salute** — part *God Save the Queen,* part *O Canada.*

3. The prime minister, visiting heads of state and political leaders, etc., are greeted with a **general salute** — a few bars of music other than *God Save the Queen* or *O Canada.*

➤ See **Military**, page 264.

First Lady

The Americanism **First Lady** refers to the wife of a U.S. president and is capitalized as a fanciful term. Prefer **Hillary Rodham Clinton** and the like. Do not apply the term to the Queen or to the wives of Canadian governors general, lieutenant-governors or prime ministers.

Nationhood

Nation means the people of a country; **country** is the territory of a nation. Hence avoid **nationwide** when used in a geographical sense, **the nation's capital** (for Ottawa), etc.

Canada

1. The national flag is the Maple Leaf.

2. The national anthem is *O Canada;* the royal anthem, *God Save the Queen.* The patriotic song *The Maple Leaf Forever* enjoys semi-anthem status outside Quebec.

3. The national emblem is the maple leaf. The beaver is a semi-official emblem.

4. Canada's coat of arms bears the inscription *A Mari Usque Ad Mare* (From Sea Even Unto Sea).

5. Canada's patron saint is St. Joseph (March 19).

Government jargon

1. Avoid using the jargon that often flows so freely from government news releases or officials' mouths. Jargon fails to convey information to those unfamiliar with the term and can even mislead.

2. Some words or phrases may be used sparingly. For example, **committee** can usually be substituted for **task force**. But **the Task Force on National Unity** may be referred to as **the task force**, because it is part of the official name.

3. Avoid new verbs ending in *ize*, such as **priorize** or **prioritize**.

4. Steer clear of pompous or awkward phrasing. Not **government initiative**. Initiative means **personal drive**. Use **government program** or **plan**. Not **referenced** (use **refer to**), not **impact on** (use **affect**), not **negatively impact on** (use **hurt**).

5. Government budgets are rife with specialized terms. Keep it simple. A **negative growth in revenues** means government took in less money. A **surplus on the ordinary account** should not find its way into copy. Explain it instead: **The government showed a modest $10-million surplus on day-to-day operations, but once money spent on capital projects was taken into account — such as road repairs and a new court building — it ran a deficit of $500 million for the year.**

Many institutional stories, such as annual budget coverage, can be illustrated with graphics that help a reader navigate through numbers and other material that is easier to understand in a visual format.

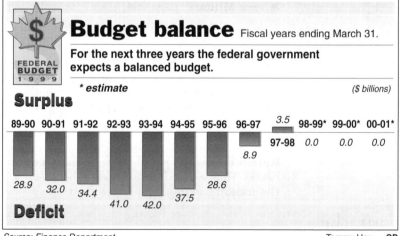

Budget balance Fiscal years ending March 31.

For the next three years the federal government expects a balanced budget.

FEDERAL BUDGET 1·9·9·9

* estimate   ($ billions)

Surplus

| 89-90 | 90-91 | 91-92 | 92-93 | 93-94 | 94-95 | 95-96 | 96-97 | 3.5 | 98-99* | 99-00* | 00-01* |

97-98   0.0   0.0   0.0

28.9   32.0   34.4   41.0   42.0   37.5   28.6   8.9

Deficit

Source: Finance Department   Tammy Hoy — **CP**

Names, nicknames, initials

1. In general, the names of people should be given in the form they normally use: **Ed Schreyer**, not **Edward Schreyer**; **Joe Clark**; **Kenneth Thomson**, not **Lord Thomson** (except when he is in the United Kingdom); **John F. Kennedy** or **J. F. Kennedy**; **P. G. Wodehouse.**

2. Follow personal preference for lowercased names: **k.d. lang** (not **K.D. Lang**), **bp Nichol** (not **B.P. Nichol**).

➤ For the names of organizations, see **Capitalization**, page 189.

3. In obituaries, try to spell out initials at some point but not in the lead where the unfamiliar name might confuse readers: **Pelham Grenville Wodehouse.**

4. A given name reads better than a single initial: **Robin Hood**, not **R. Hood.**

5. First and middle initials are used if that is a person's preference: **W. O. Mitchell**, **Ernest C. Manning**. And they are important in identifying a person charged with a crime and in listing accident victims.

6. Insert a *thin* space between initials — **E. P. Taylor, Sir John J. C. Abbott** — except when a person is referred to by initials only: **J.R., P.G.**

Note: Occasionally a public figure becomes known by initials without periods: **GBS, PET.**

7. Use **Sr.** and **Jr.** only with the full name and do not set them off with commas: **John Smith Jr.** But **John Smith Jr., PhD, B.Comm., was the name on the card.**

Note: In general, reserve **Sr.** and **Jr.** for cases where father and son are alive and known: **Edgar Bronfman Jr.**

8. Retain the designation **II** or **2nd** and the like if it is a person's preference: **Henry Ford III, Eric Van Husen 2nd.**

9. When necessary to distinguish between father and son in second reference, write **the elder** or **the younger Talbot.**

10. If confusion with another person is possible, include clarifying information: **O'Brien is not related to the businessman of the same name.**

11. When common names like **Mary Smith** and **Jean Dupont** get into the news, ages and occupations are needed to ensure proper identification, especially in police stories and if middle initials are not known.

12. People with first names applicable to either sex — **Beverley, Chris, Jean, Lee, Leslie, Terry, Tony** — should be identified as man or woman. Not **the accused, Pat O'Brien**, but **the woman accused, Pat O'Brien.** Often a pronoun introduced quickly — **he** or **she, him** or **her** — suffices.

13. A nickname is essential if it helps identify the subject: **Joseph (Joey) Smallwood**. Use a nickname instead of a given name only when a person is best known by the nickname: **Magic Johnson** (given name Earvin).

➤ See **Sports**, page 77.

14. To enclose nicknames, use parentheses, not quotation marks: **Gen. Norman (the Bear) Schwarzkopf**, not **Gen. Norman "the Bear" Schwarzkopf**.

15. If the relationship of a married couple is unclear, explain: **Joanne Woodward and her husband, Paul Newman.**

16. In non-English names, **de, di, la, ter, van, von** and the like are usually lowercase except at the start of a sentence: **Charles de Gaulle, the de Gaulle era**. But: **She said, "De Gaulle lived to retire."** And respect an individual's preference: **Bill Vander Zalm.**

17. In transliterating a Russian name, use the English phonetic equivalent where one exists: **Alexander Solzhenitsyn**, not **Aleksandr**. Prefer **-ov** and **-ev** endings: **Khrushchev**, not **Khrushchyov**. But with Russian émigré names, follow the individual's preference: **Ignatieff, Rachmaninoff.**

18. In Chinese, Korean and many other Asian names, the family name comes first: **Roh** in **Roh Tae-Woo**. But westernized people often put the given name first: **Morris Lee.**

19. For Spanish and Portuguese names, the only safe guide is the way the individuals use them.

20. After first reference, it is often useful to include in important stories the pronunciation of unfamiliar, difficult names of people and places breaking into the news: **Gennady Yanayev (pronounced ghen-AH-dee yah-NYE-ev)**. Check Broadcast News as a source.

21. First names may be used on second reference for children and youths under 18, except in sports stories; they may also be used for adults for deliberate informality.

22. Plurals of proper names are usually formed by adding *s* or *es:* **Alexes, Burnses, Charleses, Henrys, Joneses, Marys, Perrys, Rubys**. But **Tommies, Johnnies.**

➤ See **Capitalization**, page 187; **Government**, page 208; **Plurals of nouns**, page 220; and **Titles**, page 290.

Numbers

General

1. In general, spell out whole numbers below 10 and use figures for 10 and above.

three batters, the fifth inning, nine minutes, 10 guests, the 16th hole, the 22nd day, the sixth Earl of Hodderston

2. In a series there will often be a mixture.

There are 27 trees: two beeches, 10 chestnuts, three elms and 12 maples. The dealer sold 10 four-cylinder cars, three sixes and 12 eights.

3. For numbers in official names, follow the organization's spelling style even when it is at odds with CP practice.

the TV show Thirtysomething, the film 7 Fathers

Note: Follow CP style on capitalization, however: **Thirtysomething,** (not **thirtysomething**).

4. Use arabic numerals unless roman numerals are specified below.

5. Do not use commas with dimensions, measurements and weights consisting of two or more elements.

a woman five feet 11 inches tall; the baby weighs seven pounds six ounces; a trip of six months three weeks two days; in two hours 21 minutes 45 seconds (but the **six-foot-three, 250-pound tackle**)

6. To avoid ambiguity, write **increased to 15 per cent from 10** (not **increased from 10 to 15 per cent**).

7. To be meaningful, a percentage loss or gain should normally be accompanied by a dollar or some other amount.

Sales fell 10 per cent to $10,000. Sophie Dukakis, a hairdresser, said she now had 10 customers, a 20 per cent increase.

When to use figures

1. In addresses:

2 Newgate St., 3A Western Ave.

Note: Spell out **First** through **Ninth** as street names.

37 Fifth Ave., 23 59th St.

2. In ages standing alone after a name:

Melanie, 2, has two brothers, eight and nine. Tim, two months old, had typhoid.

Note: When the context does not require **years** or **years old**, the reader presumes the number is years: **He was 21. One girl is five.**

3. In dates and years:

3 BC, AD 5; Dec. 8, 8th of December; 1983, '83; the 1920s, the '20s; the Dirty '30s; the mid-1940s, the mid-'40s; he's in his late 50s.

Note: Write **the second century, the 20th century, the fifth century BC**.

4. In decimals, and in numbers larger than 1 with fractions, and in uncommon fractions:

0.25 centimetre, a .30-calibre rifle, pressures of 0.45 and 3.25, 2½ days, 15/16ths, 99 44/100ths

But two-fifths, two-thirds finished

Note 1: Unless precision is essential, keep decimals to two places: **12.25 metres** (not **12.254 metres**).

Note 2: If there is no unit before a decimal point, use a cipher: **0.25.** But write **.30 calibre** and the like in keeping with common practice.

5. In decisions, rulings, scores, votes and odds:

The court ruled 6-3, a 6-3 ruling. Montreal beat Vancouver 3-1 (but a two-goal margin). The bill was passed by a vote of 35-6, with one abstention; or a 35-6 vote. Of the 35 ballots, two were spoiled. It was a majority of nine.

odds of 5-2, a 10-1 longshot

6. In heights expressed informally:

He stands 6-11.

7. In highlights at the start of an item:

— 156 tanks and armoured personnel carriers.

— $1.8 billion for new aircraft engines.

8. In military and paramilitary terms:

2nd Lieut. Esther White (but White is a second lieutenant), U.S. Petty Officer 3rd Class Mike Kenny (but prefer **Mike Kenny, a U.S. petty officer third class**), a 6-pounder, 8 mm, M-16 rifle, 8th Army, 6th Fleet, 1st Canadian Division

9. In monetary units preceded by a symbol:

$2 (not $2.00), two dollars; two francs, 2.5 francs; $1 million (but one million people); $2 billion, the $2-billion project; but the two-million-member federation and the 2.2-million-member CLC

10. In designations of aircraft, ships, spacecraft and vehicles:

Dash 7, A-4 Skyhawk, the liner Queen Elizabeth 2, QE2, the yachts Australia II and Canada 1, Apollo 8, Alouette 2

Note: Use a hyphen before the numeral but not after it: DC-8B.

11. In sequential designations:

Act 1 (but the first act), Article 3, Channel 2, Chapter 9, Grade 7, Highway 6, in No. 2 position, Room 4, RR 2, Section 5, back to Square 1

Note: The common nouns line, page, paragraph and size followed by figures are not capitalized: page 3, line 9, size 8 shoes.

12. In temperatures:

5 C, −6 C (tight dash, not hyphen)

But when Celsius or Fahrenheit is not specified spell out: five degrees.

13. In times:

1 a.m. (not 1:00 a.m.), 9 at night, 2 o'clock, 10:15 p.m., a 2:09 run, 3:20:15 but a time of three hours 20 minutes 15 seconds

When to spell out

1. At the start of a sentence, if you must start with a number:

Twenty to 30 escaped unharmed, as well as 10 horses.

Note 1: Do not spell out the year at the start, but avoid: 1972 was a leap year.

Note 2: Do not spell out a street address at the start: 221 had a discreet sign: Oceano Palms.

Note 3: When numbers from 21 through 99 must be written out, use a hyphen: Thirty-five or 36 may have died.

2. In informal or casual usage:

Letters poured in by hundreds and thousands. Damage was in the millions. a thousand and one delights

3. In figures of speech and the like:

Twelve Apostles, Ten Commandments, Big Ten, wouldn't touch it with a ten-foot pole, a ten-gallon hat

Note: Write the Dirty '30s, the Roaring '20s, the No. 1 or number 1 choice.

4. In common fractions below 1 standing alone:

one-half, one-quarter inch, five-eighths

Note: In casual use, write a half, half a loaf, a quarter share.

Roman numerals

Use roman numerals to indicate sequence for people and animals and in proper names where specified. Otherwise avoid them as hard to grasp.

Queen Elizabeth II (rarely needed); Pope John XXIII; Henry Ford III; Nijinsky II; Bluenose II (but Canada 1); The Godfather, Part II; Superman III

Note 1: For the ship, write Queen Elizabeth 2 or QE2.

Note 2: Write SALT II, Vatican II and the like to conform to widespread practice.

Large numbers

1. Round numbers in the thousands are usually given in figures.

They took 2,000 prisoners. $3,500, 375,000 francs

Note: Spell out for casual usage: There were thousands of mosquitoes.

2. Express large numbers in millions and billions instead of the less familiar trillion, quadrillion and the like.

a million billion (instead of quadrillion), a billion billion (instead of quintillion)

Note: In Canada and the United States, a billion is a thousand million; in the United Kingdom and some other places, it is a million million.

3. Except for monetary units preceded by a symbol, round numbers in the millions and billions generally follow the rule of spelling out below 10.

two million bushels, 2.5 million bushels, 10 billion cubic metres, five billion marks, $1 billion

Note: Spell out for casual usage: What's a billion? I've told you a million times. a billion and a half

4. In expressing a range, repeat **million** or **billion**.

25 million to 30 million

Note: The adjectival form may be written **a $2- to $3-million loss,** but prefer **a loss of $2 million to $3 million.**

5. Hyphenate adjectival forms before nouns.

a two-million-bushel crop, a $10-billion gap, the 2.2-million-member CLC

6. Use commas to set off numbers of four or more figures except house, telephone, page, year and other serial numbers.

2,500; 100,000 billion; 1265 Yonge St.; 1-800-268-9237; p. 1025; 2000 (year)

7. Use figures for numbers up to 999,999. Above that, switch to words if absolute precision is not required.

a loss of $100,000, a $1.2-million project

Plurals of nouns

In general, form the plural of a noun by adding *s* to the singular; add *es* if the singular ends in *s, x, ch, sh* or *z*.

taxis, lenses, complexes, stitches, lashes, topazes

The plurals of the following words often cause problems.

Nouns ending in *f, fe* and *ff*

1. Most nouns in this category have a plural in *s*.

beliefs, briefs, chiefs, griefs, mischiefs, roofs, safes, skiffs, tariffs, tiffs

2. Some have a plural in *ves*.

calves, elves, halves, knives, leaves, loaves, selves, shelves, thieves, wives, wolves

3. A few have two plurals; CP style is shown.

dwarfs, handkerchiefs, hoofs, scarves, still lifes, wharfs

Write **staffs** (poles), **staves** (music).

Nouns ending in *o*

1. Nouns ending with an *o* preceded by another vowel usually have a plural in *s* (not *es*).

cameos, folios, kangaroos, patios, portfolios, radios, ratios, rodeos, studios, tattoos, zoos

2. Nouns ending in *o* preceded by a consonant have a variety of plurals.

a) Some end in *es*.

dominoes, echoes, embargoes, heroes, mementoes, mosquitoes, mottoes, Negroes, noes, potatoes, tomatoes, tornadoes, volcanoes

b) Some end in *s*.

albinos, avocados, cantos, contraltos, dittos, dynamos, Filipinos, gauchos, ghettos, gigolos, octavos, pianos, piccolos, provisos, quartos, silos, solos, tangelos, tobaccos, twos, tyros, zeros

c) Some have two forms; CP style is shown.

banjos, buffaloes, cargoes, concertos, Eskimos, frescoes, innuendoes, lassos, salvoes, sopranos

Nouns ending in *y*

1. Nouns ending in *y* preceded by a vowel have a plural in *s*.

alloys, attorneys, chimneys, days, forays, keys, monkeys, storeys

But soliloquies; prefer moneys to monies.

2. Nouns ending in *y* preceded by a consonant have a plural in *ies*.

armies, authorities, beauties, bodies, caddies, categories, cherries, cities, communities, companies, cries, flies, ladies, parodies, skies

But drys (prohibitionists), standbys

Nouns ending in *ics*

Nouns of this type are singular or plural depending on use. They are singular when denoting the science or a course of study, plural when denoting an activity or quality.

Classics means Latin and Greek. The classics are neglected nowadays. Ethics is defined as a moral philosophy. His ethics are questionable.

➤ See **Singular or plural**, page 243.

Proper nouns

1. Proper nouns usually form the plural by adding *s*.

Drapeaus, Elizabeths, Germanys, Kansas Citys, Kennedys, Little Italys, Marys

Note: Some follow the *ies* rule: Johnnies, Tommies, the Alleghenies (Allegheny Mountains), the Rockies (Rocky Mountains)

2. Proper nouns ending in *ch, s, x* and *z* have a plural in *es*.

Finches, Joneses, Foxes, Heinzes

Compound words

1. Most compounds form the plural by changing the principal word to its plural form.

ambassadors at large, assistant surgeons general, attorneys general, chiefs of staff, commanders-in-chief, consuls general, courts martial, editors-in-chief, fathers-in-law, goings-on, governors general, lieutenant-governors, ministers-designate, ministers without portfolio, notaries public, secretaries general, solicitors general, trade unions

But Trades Union Congress

2. If both nouns are of about equal weight, both take the plural.

men employees, menservants, women writers

3. If no word is significant, the final word usually takes *s* or *es*.

forget-me-nots, hand-me-downs, no man's lands, pick-me-ups, will-o'-the-wisps, Johnny-come-latelies

4. Compounds ending in *ful* add *s*.

armfuls, cupfuls, handfuls, spoonfuls

Foreign nouns

Nouns of this type sometimes have an English as well as a foreign plural. CP style is shown.

addendum, addenda
adieu, adieus
alga, algae
alumna, alumnae (fem.)
alumnus, alumni (masc.)
analysis, analyses
antenna, antennas (aerials),
   antennae (feelers)
apparatus, apparatuses
appendix, appendixes
aquarium, aquariums
automaton, automatons
axis, axes
bacterium, bacteria
basis, bases
beau, beaus
bureau, bureaus
cactus, cactuses
census, censuses
cherub, cherubs
coccus, cocci
crisis, crises
criterion, criteria
curriculum, curricula
datum, data
dilettante, dilettantes
dogma, dogmas
ellipsis, ellipses
erratum, errata
focus, focuses
formula, formulas
fungus, fungi
genius, geniuses
genus, genera
gladiolus, gladioli
helix, helixes
hypothesis, hypotheses
impetus, impetuses
index, indexes

larva, larvae
larynx, larynxes
madam, mesdames
   (madams for
   brothel-keepers)
matrix, matrixes
maximum, maximums
medium, media
   (mediums in
   spiritualism)
memorandum,
      memorandums
minimum, minimums
minutia, minutiae
monsieur, messieurs
nucleus, nuclei
oasis, oases
opus, opuses
parenthesis, parentheses
phenomenon, phenomena
plateau, plateaus
prospectus, prospectuses
radius, radii
referendum, referendums
sanatorium, sanatoriums
seraph, seraphs
sinus, sinuses
stadium, stadiums
stimulus, stimuli
stratum, strata
syllabus, syllabuses
symposium, symposiums
tableau, tableaus
terminus, terminuses
thesis, theses
vertebra, vertebrae
virtuoso, virtuosos

Nouns with the same singular and plural

aircraft, alms, amends, bellows, bison, chassis, corps, counsel, deer, fish, forceps, goods, grouse, head (of cattle, etc.), headquarters, insignia, means, moose, offspring, pains, precis, proceeds, rendezvous, remains, series, salmon, shambles, sheep, species, sweepstakes, swine, trout, United States, wheat, whereabouts

Note: But when more than one kind or species is referred to, a regularly formed plural is sometimes used.

Many fishes, ranging from salmon to eel, are netted. New wheats — crosses of Thatcher and Selkirk — continue to be developed.

Nouns plural in form, singular in meaning

checkers, dominoes, measles, mews, mumps, news, rickets, shingles (disease), **works** (factory)

Dos and don'ts

Such expressions form their plurals normally.

no ifs, ands or buts; yeses and noes; all the ins and outs

But words being discussed as words form the plural by adding 's.

Some writers mistakenly leave out the the's. He filled his speech with like's and you know's.

➤ See **Punctuation**, page 226.

Possessives

1. Singular and plural nouns not ending in *s* take an apostrophe and *s* to form the possessive case.

father's pipe, women's lib, people's food, the kibbutzim's leaders, alumni's donations

Note: It looks careless to err on words like **children's** (not **childrens'**) shoes, **women's** (not **womens'**) issues, **men's** (not **mens'**) salaries.

2. Plural nouns ending in *s* take an apostrophe alone.

teachers' apples, the two peoples' history, the Joneses' daughter

3. Singular nouns ending in *s* (or an *s* sound) normally take an *'s* to indicate a *sis* or *siz* sound. But if adding the extra *s* would make the word hard to say or grate on the ear, use an apostrophe alone.

Chris's sandwich, Burgess's novel, Butz's statement, the press's responsibility, Strauss's opera, the witness's testimony, Zeus's laws

But: **Moses' laws, Euripides' plays, Jesus' followers, Ulysses' wanderings, Silvers' cat, Ann Landers' column**

4. Names ending in a silent *s* or *x* take an apostrophe and *s*.

Duplessis's cabinet, Delibes's Coppelia, Malraux's paintings, Francaix's symphony

Note: A few French names end in an *s* sound and follow normal rules for the possessive.

Saint-Saens' music, de Lesseps' canal

5. For company and institutional names, follow the organization's preference.

Eaton's, Professional Golfers' Association, Canadian Forces Headquarters

Note: The possessive is an English form. In Quebec, corporate names and outdoor signs must follow the French form: **Eaton, Birk**.

6. Where the usage is more descriptive than possessive, omit the apostrophe.

an autoworkers spokesman, a board of directors meeting, the carpenters union, citizens band radio, a Leafs defenceman

7. Use a single apostrophe for joint possession, separate apostrophes for separate possession.

Smith and Cusak's pharmacy, Pierre and Marie's children, Pierre's and Marie's shoes

8. A group of words used to express a single idea takes an apostrophe on the last word only, although many such phrasings can and should be avoided.

the mayor of Calgary's speech; the government of Canada's policy; her mother-in-law's car; Dodd, Mead's latest books

➤ For plurals of compound words, see **Plurals of nouns**, page 220.

9. In general, inanimate objects take an *of* phrase rather than an apostrophe.

the colour of the coat, not **the coat's colour**
the incidence of flu, not **the flu's incidence**

Note 1: But many idioms, particularly expressions of time and measure, take an apostrophe even though there is no actual ownership.

a stone's throw, the law's delay, a couple of dollars' worth

Note 2: To test whether an apostrophe is needed in such expressions as **two weeks(') pay** and **six months(') pregnant**, mentally substitute the singular and the correct answer will appear: **a week's pay, one month pregnant**.

10. Compound nouns with built-in apostrophes are generally singular.

arm's length, baker's dozen, confectioner's sugar, cow's milk, debtor's prison, farmer's market, fool's paradise, fuller's earth, printer's ink, traveller's cheques, writer's cramp

11. Most pronouns are written without an apostrophe.

hers, its, ours, yours, theirs, whose

But **anyone's guess, another's hopes, others' feelings, each other's view, nobody's fool, anyone else's house, no one else's**

Note: Beware the careless confusion of **its** and **it's** (it is), **theirs** and **there's** (there is), **your** and **you're** (you are), **whose** and **who's** (who is).

Punctuation

General

Punctuation brings order to writing. It helps make the message of a sentence immediately clear. But don't overdo it. A sentence littered with clauses set off by commas, dashes and semicolons can look like a word jungle and chase the reader away.

Apostrophe

1. Use an apostrophe to denote possession.

Davis's car, the Davises' house, Marx's Capital, children's toys, the media's problem, Jesus' name

➤ See **Possessives**, page 224.

2. Use an apostrophe to indicate the omission of letters or figures.

she'd, it's (for it is), couldn't, rock 'n' roll, fo'c's'le, Where E'er You Walk, "Give 'em hell!", the early '30s, the class of '80, "We'll 'elp 'im for 'is mother, an' 'e'll 'elp us by-an'-by." — *Rudyard Kipling*

Note: Contractions are acceptable, but avoid such forced contractions as it'd, should've, Tom'll go; use only readily recognized forms: won't, shouldn't, he'd.

3. Use an apostrophe with verbs formed from capitals.

OK's, OK'ing, KO'd, MC'ing, X'd out

4. Use an apostrophe in plurals of lowercase letters.

Mind your p's and q's. Dot your i's and cross your t's.

5. In general, do not use an apostrophe with plurals of capital letters or numbers.

She graduated with straight As, the three Rs, the ABCs, two VIPs, a formation of F-18s, the Dirty '30s

Note 1: Use an apostrophe with plurals of capital letters if necessary to avoid ambiguity.

A's in math and physics are hard to come by.

Note 2: Whether to write a single letter as a capital or lowercase in a particular context depends somewhat on personal taste; logic favours with a capital S and with a small s.

6. Do not use an apostrophe to form the plurals in expressions like the whys and wherefores.

Here are a few dos, don'ts and maybes. I don't want any ifs, ands or buts. Just give us straight yeses or noes.

Note: Use the apostrophe to form the plurals of words being discussed as words.

three as's, too many is's, not enough the's

7. Do not use an apostrophe with shortened forms that have become accepted as complete words.

cello, copter, flu, gym, phone

Brackets (parentheses)

1. In general, try to use brackets sparingly, when other punctuation won't do the job.

Their biggest difficulties were the heat (temperatures were in the high 20s) and clouds of blackflies.

2. Use brackets to insert fuller identification in proper names, direct quotation and such.

the Moose Jaw (Sask.) Times-Herald. Use commas when no proper name is involved: the Moose Jaw, Sask., daily. But prefer the daily in Moose Jaw, Sask., or some such.

"When you ask how (Finance Minister Ellen) McFadden can survive, you are asking the wrong question."

3. Use brackets to enclose a nickname within a name.

William (Bible Bill) Aberhart

➤ See **Names, nicknames, initials**, page 213.

4. Use full brackets in numbering or lettering a series within a sentence.

The union pressed for (a) more pay, (b) a shorter work week and (c) better pensions.

➤ See **Period**, paragraph 6 note, below.

5. Use brackets to enclose political affiliations.

Senator Iva Villman (PC—Man.)

6. Use brackets to enclose equivalents and translations.

"We can expect two more inches (five centimetres) of rain." The measure now goes to the Bundestag (the lower house of parliament).

7.   If a punctuation mark applies to the whole sentence, put the mark after the closing bracket.

Words must be reputable (not socially frowned on). "I tell you this" (turning to the jury): "I am innocent."

8.   If a punctuation mark applies only to the words inside the parenthetical section, put the mark inside the closing bracket.

Most employees learned the new system quickly. (It helped to have supervisors on hand.)

"After I gave the alarm (by shouting 'Fire!'), I slid down the rope."

9.   In general, a parenthetical sentence takes a capital only if it is a direct quotation.

"We couldn't meet today (she had an appointment), but arranged to have lunch tomorrow."

His comment ("Wow, you're not exactly tall") had annoyed her.

Colon

1.   Use a colon, rather than a comma, to introduce a direct quotation longer than a short sentence.

Winston Churchill said in 1942: "This is not the end. It is not even the beginning of the end. But it is, perhaps, the end of the beginning."

2.   Use a colon in lines introducing lists, texts and tables.

VICTORIA (CP) — Highlights of the throne speech:
— The creation of 10,000 jobs . . .

3.   Use a colon to introduce an amplification, an example or a formal question or quotation. It takes the place of **for example, namely, that is.**

It was a mixed cargo: iron ore, wheat and coal. Various solutions were possible: sell the herd, try to renew the loan, take a partner.

4.   Generally do not capitalize the first letter of a sentence that follows a colon; but a capital may be used if emphasis is desirable.

Their learning is like bread in a besieged city: every man gets a little, but no man gets a full meal. — *Samuel Johnson.* This is the rule: Write in easy, conversational English. Verdict: Not guilty.

Note: Capitalize the first word of a quoted sentence: **The prince cried: "Too late! Help came too late."**

5.   Use a colon to mark a strong contrast.

Man proposes: God disposes. Eating isn't just a necessity: it's a pleasure.

6.   Use colons in question-and-answer formats and for interviews. Quotation marks are not used.

Q: When do you expect an agreement?
A: Before Christmas.

Tatje: Why are you a critic?
Papadakos: One must live.

7.   Use a colon to separate hours, minutes and seconds in clock and elapsed times, and periods before fractions of a second.

7:30 p.m.   a record time of 1:25:15.4

Note: Write **8 a.m.**, not **8:00 a.m.**

8.   Use a colon after a formal salutation.

Madam Speaker: Gentlemen: Dear Mrs. Odisho:

Note: Informal salutations may take a comma.

Dear Jack,   My dear Puran,

9.   Use a colon to indicate chapter and verse, act and scene and other citations.

A soft answer turneth away wrath. — *Proverbs 15:1*
There's daggers in men's smiles. — *Macbeth 2:3.147*

10. Use colons to separate titles and subtitles unless the author's or publisher's form differs.

The Chinese: Portrait of a People

11. Put colons outside closing quotation marks.

Paisley said of the charge of "bigot": "It's a lie."

She was referring to "the most serious of all charges": murder.

Comma

1.   Put commas between the elements of a series but not before the final **and, or** or **nor** unless that avoids confusion.

men, women, children and pets

The major decided he must either attack at once, await fresh troops or withdraw.

Breakfast consisted of oatmeal, fried eggs, and bread and butter.

2. Use commas before clauses introduced by the conjunctions **and, but, for, or, nor** or **yet** if the subject changes.

We are all in the gutter, but some of us are looking at the stars. — *Oscar Wilde*

Note: The comma may be omitted when the clauses are short or the subject of both is the same.

The gun boomed and the race was on. The twins shouted and waved and finally managed to attract the driver's attention.

3. Use commas to set off an introductory clause or long phrase that precedes the main clause.

If God did not exist, it would be necessary to invent Him. — *Voltaire*

Note: Even if the introductory clause or phrase is short, a comma may be used for emphasis: **Even so, the vote was close.**

4. Put a comma after the main clause only if the clause that follows is parenthetical.

I'm selling you this gold brick because I like your face. The doctor bought a ticket, though she didn't expect to win.

5. Use commas to separate adjectives before a noun when the commas represent **and**.

a frank, open face; a vigorous, genial, popular man; well-meaning, enthusiastic, immature novices

6. Omit commas if the adjectives could not be separated by **and** and still make sense.

a cold marble floor; Tom's new 10-speed racing bike; her old brown winter coat; an aristocratic French family

Note 1: As another rule of thumb, if the order of the adjectives could not be changed (as in these examples), omit the commas.

Note 2: When in doubt, err on the side of too few commas.

7. Do not put commas around an identifying word, phrase or clause if it is essential to the meaning of the sentence.

Margaret Atwood's novel Lady Oracle won.
But: One of Margaret Atwood's novels, Lady Oracle, won.

The Queen was accompanied by her son Prince Edward.

But: The Queen was accompanied by her youngest son, Prince Edward.

The girl who is singing is my daughter.
But: The girl, who was alone, got into the cab.

They drove to a village where they had seen bandits.
But: They drove to a village, where they bought bread.

8. Use a comma to separate an introductory clause from a short, complete sentence in quotations.

The prime minister replied, "I have nothing to add to what I said in the House."

Note: Do not use a comma if a quotation is extremely short or is an integral part of the clause.

Stop saying "I told you so."

She heard a voice yelling "Baby needs new shoes!" and there was her husband shooting craps.

"A guy comes up to me and says 'Oh, yeah?' and I say 'Oh, yeah?' and slap his face."

9.   Use a comma to set off a paraphrased question or statement.

The question is, How can it be done? She said, No, she hadn't seen the boy.

But: She said no.

10. Use commas to set off parenthetical expressions, direct address and the like.

That's right, isn't it? Come into the garden, Maud.
Madam Speaker, I deny that.

Note: Commas are used with transition words like **besides, meanwhile, indeed, of course, too, in fact, as a result** and **consequently** if the sentence reads better with a pause.

11. Use a comma to separate words and numbers when confusion might otherwise result.

He who can, does. He who cannot, teaches. — *G.B. Shaw.* Ralph waxed the floor, and his sister dusted. All day, workers had been preparing the field. Some time before, the Plateans had surrendered. Instead of 20, 50 came.

12. When words readily understood are omitted for brevity, use commas to mark the omission, unless the sentence reads smoothly without them.

To Rolf he gave $5; to Mohammed, $2; to Darrin, nothing.
One child received $5, another $2 but the third nothing.
Let your yea be yea and your nay, nay.

13. Use commas to separate geographical elements.

The tour bus runs from Basel, Switzerland, to Milan, Italy, with frequent stops.

Note 1: Do not omit the second comma.

The runner left St. John's, Nfld., last week.

Note 2: Do not put a comma before **of**, indicating place.

Tom Stoddard of Mission, B.C., was first.

Note 3: Avoid this clumsy construction: a Prince George, B.C., lawyer.

Prefer: A lawyer in Prince George, B.C.

14. Use commas to set off the year from the month plus day.

March 31, 1949, was the date that Newfoundland joined Confederation.

Note: Do not use commas when the day is not included.

January 1998 was mild in Victoria. Clark died at Easter 1835.

15. In general, use commas to set off thousands but not in years, street addresses or page, phone or serial numbers.

13,250 kilometres $1,450,250
2000 (year)   1530 Rose St.   page 1235
416-364-0321   serial 76543

16. Use commas to set off a person's age, degrees, awards and affiliations.

Jean Tateyama, 48, Brandon, Man.; René Tremblay, PhD, faced Alex Dodd, VC, in the debate.

17. Do not use commas with **Sr.** or **Jr.**, or with numerals that can similarly be regarded as an integral part of a name.

Maurice Leblanc Sr. spoke first. Pope John XXIII was popular. Albatross II finally reached port.

18. Do not use commas with multi-unit dimensions, measures, weights or times.

two feet four inches by three feet 10 inches, 10 pounds 12 ounces,
two hours 30 minutes 25 seconds

But: a four-foot-11, 90-pound youngster

19. Put commas inside closing quotation marks.

Barb said, "I don't want any," but the pedlar only smiled. The clue consisted of four words: "spinner," "blackbird," "watchman" and "maple." "It sounded like 'gorp,'" he said.

Note: Occasionally, such punctuation is not needed. **More than 1,600 protesters chanting "We're anti-violent people" marched along Portage Avenue.**

20. A comma follows a bracket if sentence structure requires it.

The speech was long, hard to hear (people were coughing), uninspired and uninspiring.

21. Use a comma or a dash but not both.

Not: Wilfred was, — like all the Clutterbucks, — a man of striking personal charm.

Dash

1. The dash is an effective tool but can easily be overused. Many times it can be avoided by breaking a long sentence into two shorter ones.

2. Use dashes to set off mid-sentence lists punctuated by commas.

The ministers will discuss common problems — trade, tourism, immigration and defence — before going to the summit talks.

3. Use dashes when commas (generally preferable) would create confusion.

The pies — meat and fruit — were cheap.

4. Use a dash in placelines after the service logo.

HALIFAX (CP) — An oil . . .

5. Use a tight boldface dash to introduce sections of a list.

OTTAWA (CP) — Highlights of the federal budget Tuesday:
—About 12,500 homeowners are expected to qualify for mortgage assistance.
—Employee benefits . . .

6. Use a tight dash for the minus sign in temperatures and with bracketed political affiliations.

—10 degrees, Joan Singh (PC—Man.)

7. Use a dash to mark a sharp break in a word or sentence.

"I've been laughed at, ignored — but I'm boring you."

Note 1: When a sentence breaks off, no period is used after the dash.

"Really, Madam Speaker, I must —"
"Order!" the Speaker shouted.

Note 2: When a quotation simply trails away, use three spaced periods.

"Maybe if I had tried harder . . . "

8.   Use dashes to mark off interpolations.

"Besides" — he tapped me on the knee — "you're wrong."

9.   Use a dash to introduce a phrase or clause that summarizes, emphasizes or contrasts what has gone before.

Quiet, respectful, deferential, even obsequious — those were Mulliner's chief characteristics.

Our army is composed of the scum of the earth — the mere scum of the earth. — *Duke of Wellington*

The English country gentleman galloping after a fox — the unspeakable in full pursuit of the uneatable. — *Oscar Wilde*

10. Use a dash to attribute a quotation.

Pedantry is a misplaced attention to trifles which then prides itself on its poor judgment. — *Jacques Barzun*

11. Do not use dashes with colons, semicolons and commas.

12. Write dashes with spaces before and after but not with agate sports summaries and the exceptions noted above.

Ellipsis (. . .)

1.   Use three spaced periods to indicate an omission from a text or quotation.

The decision . . . rests solely with your elected representatives, not with pollsters or the news media.

Note: Put spaces before, between and after the periods. On news circuits, use a *thin space* between the periods so typesetting computers don't split them on two lines.

2.   In condensing a text, use an ellipsis at the beginning, inside or at the end of a sentence.

The decision . . . rests solely with your elected representatives. . .
.

. . . But the government won't ignore thoughtful suggestions, no matter what their origin.

3.   In news stories, use an ellipsis only inside a sentence, not at the beginning or end.

"The   decision   .   .   .   rests   solely   with   your   elected representatives," the prime minister said.

After a reference to comments of delegates, he added, "But the government won't ignore thoughtful suggestions."

➤   But see **Dash, No. 7**, above for one exception.

4.   When condensing texts, put other required punctuation before the ellipsis. Thus four periods end a sentence.

But the government won't ignore thoughtful suggestions. . . .

Similarly: **What is the answer? . . . We must strive harder, . . . produce more, . . . lower our expectations. . . .**

Note: Guard against distortion that might result from putting together statements that were not together in the original. The solution may be to interrupt the sequence by starting a new paragraph or renewing the attribution.

5.   Ellipses may be used to separate entries in the *Notes* section at the bottom of sports game copy.

Jays Notes — The roof at SkyDome was open to start the game but was closed during the third inning with rain threatening. . . . Pitcher Ken Dayley, sent to Florida on a 30-day rehabilitation stint after overcoming a problem with dizziness, returned Thursday with a sore left forearm. . . . Roberto Alomar extended his consecutive-game hit streak to eight with a seventh-inning single.

Exclamation mark

1.   Do not overuse this strong mark of punctuation. Use it to denote great surprise, a command, deep emotion, emphasis and sarcasm.

We won!   "Take aim! Fire!"   Ouch!   Never!   Oh, sure!

Note: If a one-word exclamation rates heavy emphasis, put it in a separate sentence; otherwise treat it as part of another sentence.

"Oh! She almost fell." "Oh! you frightened me!" or "Oh, you frightened me!"

2.   Use an exclamation mark with questions that are exclamatory in form.

"You mean we won!"

"How could she do that to him!"

3.   Do not use an exclamation mark to end a mildly exclamatory sentence.

Hurry along, please. Have your tickets ready.

4. Do not use a comma or period after an exclamation mark.

"Fire! Fire!" the janitor shouted.

Someone cried "She's drowning!"

5. Put an exclamation mark inside quotation marks when it is part of the quoted material, outside when it is not.

"That's a lie!" a backbencher shouted.

Imagine calling a cabinet minister a "liar"!

Hyphen

1. Compound words may be written solid (**sweatshirt**), open (**oil rig**) or hyphenated (**white-haired**).

➤ See **Compounds**, page 200.

2. Write words as compounds to ease reading, to avoid ambiguity and to join words that when used together form a separate concept.

a once-in-a-lifetime chance, a hit-and-run driver, a big-car lover, a used-car dealer, a small-business tax, an extra-high collar, light-year, first-fruits, man-hour, blackbird, streetcar, airbrush

3. In general, hyphenate compound modifiers preceding a noun, but not if the meaning is instantly clear because of common usage of the term.

the third-period goal, three-under-par 69, a 5-4 vote, multimillion-dollar projects, 40-cent coffee

But **the acid rain threat, the United States dollar, a savings bank deposit, a sales tax increase, the task force landing**

4. Adverbs ending in *-ly* are not followed by a hyphen. The *-ly* alerts readers that the word that follows is modified: **a brightly lit room, an eagerly awaited speech.**

5. Hyphens are seldom needed with proper nouns (**a United Kingdom custom**), established foreign terms (**a 10 per cent drop**) or established compound nouns (**a high school principal**).

6. Certain word combinations are often hyphenated even when standing alone.

noun plus adjective (**fire-resistant, fancy-free**), noun plus participle (**blood-stained, thought-provoking**), adjective plus participle (**sweet-smelling, hard-earned**), adjective plus noun plus *-ed* (**open-handed, red-faced**)

7. Use a hyphen to indicate joint titles and to join conflicting or repetitive elements.

secretary-treasurer, writer-editor, musician-painter, comedy-tragedy, drip-drop, walkie-talkie

8.   Hyphenate most well-known compounds of three or more words.

happy-go-lucky, good-for-nothing, Johnny-come-lately, forget-me-not, mother-in-law, a two-year-old

But coat of arms, next of kin, no man's land

9.   Use a hyphen with certain compounds containing an apostrophe.

bull's-eye, mare's-nest, cat's-paw

10. Use a hyphen to avoid doubling a vowel, tripling a consonant or duplicating a prefix.

co-operate, re-emerge, anti-intellectual, doll-like, brass-smith, re-redesign, sub-subcommittee

But readjust, reaffirm, reinstate, reopen, etc.

11. Use a hyphen to join prefixes to proper names.

anti-Trudeau, pro-Communist, French-Canadian

But transatlantic, transpacific

12. Use a hyphen to join an initial capital with a word.

T-shirt, V-necked, X-ray, S-bend, H-bomb

13. Use a hyphen with fractions standing alone and with the written numbers 21 to 99.

two-thirds, three-quarters, fifty-five, ninety-nine

14. Use hyphens with a successive compound adjective (note spacing).

18th- and 19th-century fashions; 10-, 20- and 30-second intervals

15. Use a hyphen in aircraft identification and such, between the symbols for make or type and model number, but not after the number.

DC-10, DC-8L, MiG-25

But Boeing 767

16. Use a hyphen to connect dates except when preceded by from or between.

the 1982-83 tax year, from January to May (not from January-May), between 1970 and 1976 (not between 1970-76)

17. Use a hyphen to differentiate between words of different meanings but the same or similar spellings.

correspondent (letter writer), **co-respondent** (in divorce); **resign** (quit), **re-sign** (sign again); **recover** (regain health), **re-cover** (cover again)

18. Use a hyphen to avoid awkward combinations of letters.

cave-in, not **cavein**; **co-star**, not **costar**; **de-ice**, not **deice**; **non-native**, not **nonnative**; **re-ink**, not **reink**; **set-to**, not **setto**; **sit-in**, not **sitin**

Parentheses ➤ See **Brackets**

Period

1. Use a period to end a declarative or a mildly imperative sentence.

The wind blew and the ground began to dry. Give me the book. Let them have their say.

Note: For greater emphasis, use an exclamation mark, advisedly.

"Stick 'em up!"

2. Use a period to end an indirect question, a request phrased as a question, or a rhetorical question.

The reporter asked how many were killed. Would someone answer my question. What do I care.

3. Use a period with decimals, including decimal currencies.

3.25 $9.50

4. Use a period after certain abbreviations.

➤ See **Abbreviations and acronyms**, page 167.

5. Put periods inside quotation marks.

The writer said, "This is the end." Her brother said, "I don't know why she said 'This is the end.'"

6. Omit periods after headings, figures, roman numerals, single letters (except initials) and scientific and metric symbols.

Pope, unionist meet; $52; Chapter 2; Albatross II; E flat; Au (for gold); 15 cm; 20 C

Note: But use periods, as an alternative to brackets, after a letter or number denoting a series.

To improve readability: 1. Don't be too formal. 2. Organize before you start to write. 3. Be active, positive, concrete.

7. Omit periods after letters used as names without specific designation.

Suppose A takes B to court for damages.

➤ For the use of periods to indicate omission, see **Ellipsis** above.

Question mark

1. Use a question mark after a direct question, but not after an indirect one.

What day is this? The nurse asked what he wanted.

Note: When a question occurs within a question, both ending at the same time, use only one question mark.

Who asked "Why?"

2. Use question marks to express more than one query in the same sentence.

Reporters must ask themselves, How does it look? sound? feel? taste? smell?

Note: If a question is not complete until the end of the sentence, use a question mark there.

Do you want coffee, tea or milk?

3. Use a question mark to express doubt or uncertainty.

The dates of the English dramatist John Heywood are given as 1497(?)-1580(?).

4. Do not use a question mark if the person addressed is expected to act rather than answer.

Would you mind spelling the second name.

5. Question marks go inside or outside quotation marks, depending on meaning.

The Speaker asked, "What was the question?" Did the prime minister say "fuddle-duddle"? He asked, "Did the prime minister say 'fuddle-duddle'?"

6. A question mark supersedes the comma or period that usually ends a quotation.

"Who goes there?" the sentry shouted.

Quotation marks

1. Use quotation marks to enclose direct quotations.

The lawyer said, "I don't think the police should be paying suspects for information."

2. Use quotation marks to begin and end each part of an interrupted quotation.

"We can't hear you," the girl said. "The radio is on."

Note: Capitalize the first word of the second part of an interrupted quotation only if the second part begins a new sentence.

3. Alternate double and single marks in quotes within quotes.

"I heard her say, 'I only hit him when he sneered and said "Never."'"

4. Capitalize the first word of any mid-sentence quote that constitutes a sentence.

The woman said, "He sneered and said 'Never.'"

This has the same effect as the brush-off used in theatrical circles of "Don't call us. We'll call you."

The trainmaster gave the order to "Get the hell out!"

5. Put each speaker's words in a separate paragraph to make it immediately clear that the speaker has changed.

Vilmik laughed. "Who gave him the quarter?"
"Not me," said his wife. "I'm broke."
"I know," said Vilmik. "Let's ask your mother."

6. When a quote by a single speaker extends more than one paragraph, put quotation marks at the beginning of each paragraph but at the end of only the last.

"As I said earlier, my father was always reasonable about things like that.
"But when it came to money, he could be totally unreasonable. An out-and-out miser.
"Still, on the whole, he was fair-minded."

However, if the quote in the first paragraph is a partial one, use quotation marks at the beginning and end of the partial quote.

He said the argument was "remarkably bitter."
"I didn't know two people could hate each other so much."

7. Provide the speaker's identity quickly if a quotation is unusually long. It should either precede the quotation, follow the first sentence

(or the second if it is short and closely linked to the first), or be interpolated.

"This is the best time to call an election," Lumie said. "There is a tremendous momentum going to us. Waiting can only cost us votes. It's now or never."

"We've lost. We've lost," wailed another bystander. "The British have won. Our army has been lying to us."

"The Puritan hated bear-baiting," Macaulay adds, "not because it gave pain to the bear, but because it gave pleasure to the spectators."

8. Use quotation marks to set off a pungent or significant word or phrase but not around routine words or phrases.

His first ship was an old "rustbucket."

Not: The minister replied that the economy is "improving."

Note: Fragmented quotes are justifiable only when the words are controversial, add colour or give the flavour of an event or the style of a speaker.

9. Use quotation marks around unfamiliar terms on first reference.

The fluid was named "protoplasm" by a Czechoslovak.

10. Put quotation marks around words used ironically.

The "friendly" soccer game ended with two players booked.

11. In partial quotes, do not put quotation marks around words the speaker could not have used.

Not: Ali boasted "he was rarin' to go."

12. Do not use quotation marks to enclose titles of compositions.

➤ See **Capitalization**, sections **Compositions**, page 177, **Music**, page 186, **Quotations**, page 191.

13. Do not use quotation marks to enclose slogans and headlines.

The pickets carried signs that read Cut Taxes, Not Jobs and Cut Government Spending. The article was headed Drug Squad Flouts Gun Rules.

14. Do not use quotation marks in question-and-answer formats.

Q: Do you recognize this man?
A: Yes.

15. Do not use quotation marks on texts or editorial excerpts in symposiums.

OTTAWA (CP) — Text of Gov. Gen. Rhoda Mann's New Year's message:
The mood at the dawn of a new year . . .

St. John's (Nfld.) Telegram: The real needs of Canadians . . .

Note: In editorial symposiums, the name of the paper is in boldface, followed by a colon, not a dash.

16. Periods and commas always go inside closing quote marks; colons and semicolons outside. The question mark and exclamation mark go inside the quote marks when they apply to the quoted matter only; outside when they apply to the entire sentence.

17. When a sentence ends with single and double quotation marks, separate them by a thin space.

Semicolon

1.   Use a semicolon to separate statements too closely related to stand as separate sentences.

"I never read a book before reviewing it; it prejudices a man so." — *Sidney Smith*

2.   Use a semicolon to separate phrases that contain commas.

Best actor, Robert De Niro, Raging Bull; best actress, Sissy Spacek, Coal Miner's Daughter; best film, Ordinary People.

3.   Use a semicolon to precede explanatory phrases introduced by **for example, namely, that is** and the like when a comma seems too weak.

Some pleasures cost next to nothing; for example, reading.

4.   Semicolons go outside quotation marks.

Police finally cornered the "bear"; it was a poodle.

Slash

1.   Use a slash mark to separate alternatives.

and/or, either/or

But use a hyphen for joint titles and to join conflicting elements.

secretary-treasurer, comedy-tragedy

2.   Use a slash mark to replace **per** in measurements.

80 km/h (80 kilometres per hour)

3.   A slash is also used to separate the numerator and denominator of a fraction.

3 5/8, 1 7/8, 17 2/3

Singular or plural?

1. In general, a subject singular in form takes a singular verb; a subject plural in form takes a plural verb.

An outbreak of bombing and shelling was heard. On each side of the road were drifts of trilliums.

2. Collective nouns (groups of people and things) take a singular verb unless the individuals are to be emphasized.

The audience was silent. The audience were stamping their feet. Her family is sending money. Her family are all ill.

3. When two parts of a compound subject are separated by **with, together with, including, besides, no less than, in addition to, plus, as well as** or **likewise**, the verb agrees with the first part.

The ship with all its crew was lost. Gray as well as his wife and son was in the car. The meat plus packaging weighs about a kilogram.

4. **All, a lot, any, half, majority, more, most, per cent, remainder, rest** and **some** take either a singular or plural verb depending on whether the noun is singular or plural.

Is all the money accounted for? All the cars are new. The government's majority makes it safe from defeat. A majority of Canadians favour wage control.

5. **Anybody, anyone, another, anything, each, either, every, everybody, everyone, many a, neither, no one, nobody, somebody** and **someone** take a singular verb.

Everyone wants his money back. No one knows the future. Neither of the teams stands a chance. Each of the three students comes from a different country.

6. When a sentence contains **not only . . . but also, either . . . or** or **neither . . . nor**, the verb agrees with the nearer subject.

Either the sergeant or the troops are out of step. Either the troops or the sergeant is out of step. Not only the children but also the babysitter was asleep.

7. **None** takes a plural verb when it stands for *not any;* it takes a singular verb when it is followed by a singular noun or when the idea of *not one* is to be emphasized.

None of the passengers were Canadian. None of the furniture was dusted. Ten climbers have tried but none (preferably **not one**) has succeeded.

8. In general, **acoustics, economics, gymnastics, politics, mathematics** and other words ending in *-ics* are singular when they are referred to as a science or course of study and plural when referred to as a practical activity or a quality.

The acoustics are bad. Acoustics is on the curriculum. Her politics are left wing. Politics is a dirty business. My mathematics are weak. Mathematics, rightly viewed, possesses not only truth, but also supreme beauty. — *Bertrand Russell*

Note: When in doubt, use the singular.

9. When **number, total** and **variety** are preceded by *the*, they take a singular verb. Preceded by *a*, they take a plural verb.

The number of unemployed rises monthly. A number of unemployed have found jobs. The total stolen has topped $1 million. A total of 21 people were involved.

10. When **couple** is used in the sense of two persons, it almost always takes a plural verb and plural pronouns.

The couple were hurt when their car crashed.

Note: Couple in this sense is singular on the rare occasion when it is treated as a unit.

A couple pays $5 a ticket.

11. A numerical statement may be singular or plural depending on whether the number is thought of as a unit or as a collection of items.

Three weeks is a long time. Six feet of earth is enough for any man. There was two minutes left in the game. Two days of spring make winter seem almost worthwhile.

12. Subjects plural in form but singular in effect take a singular verb.

Great Expectations has been made into a movie. Jarndyce and Jarndyce is literature's most famous lawsuit.

13. When two subjects form one idea, the verb is singular.

Bread and butter is included. The tumult and the shouting dies. — *Rudyard Kipling*

14. **Data** and **media** are plural. Treat **agenda** as singular.

The media were blamed. The data support this theory. The agenda was short.

Note: Data is sometimes treated as a collective noun: **This is vital data**, a use disliked by conservative writers, who prefer **These are vital data**.

15. When a sentence begins with an introductory **there**, the number of the verb is determined by the delayed subject.

There is much to be seen. There are many beautiful sights.

16. **One of those** takes a plural verb when the phrase introduces a clause.

The clerk is one of those people who are always right. It must be one of the longest sentences that have ever been written.

Note: To confirm that the verb must be plural, reverse the sentence: **Of the longest sentences that have (not has) ever been written, it must be one.**

Spelling

1. CP's authority for spelling is the *Canadian Oxford Dictionary,* with exceptions listed in *(CP) Caps and Spelling.*

2. Where Oxford gives alternative spellings — **amok/amuck, judgement/judgment** — CP style is the first, unless shown otherwise in *Caps and Spelling:* **judgment.**

3. When the spelling of the common-noun element of a proper name differs from CP style — **U.S. Labor Department, Primary Colors** (book), **Lincoln Center** — use the spelling favoured by the subject.

4. Unless Oxford shows otherwise, the plural of a noun is formed normally, by adding *-s* or *-es:* **shaman/shamans, box/boxes.** If the plural is irregular, it is given in parentheses: **man (men).** Where there is a choice — **mango (-es** or **-s), virtuoso (-i** or **-os)** — CP uses the first spelling: **mangoes,** except when *Caps and Spelling* says otherwise: **virtuosos.**

5. When a verb has two forms for the past tense — **kneeled/knelt, leaped/leapt** — CP uses either one without preference.

6. CP prefers the *sh-* spelling for Yiddish words: **shlemiel, shlock, shmatte.** This is a departure from Oxford's *sch-.*

➤ See **Plurals of nouns**, page 220; see also *(CP) Caps and Spelling.*

Aboriginal Peoples

Indians, Métis, Inuit

Canada's Aboriginal Peoples comprise three distinct groups: Indians, Inuit and Métis. Their numbers are estimated at about one million.

About 600,000 of these are status Indians registered with the federal government. The term means they qualify as Indians under the Indian Act and can take advantage of certain rights reserved for them, such as tax breaks and special hunting and fishing rights.

By agreeing to treaties most Canadian Indians exchanged some interests in their ancestral lands in return for various payments and promises from Crown officials. About 60 per cent of registered Indians live on reserves. They do not pay income tax and qualify for education, housing and other grants.

There are 608 Indian bands and about 2,400 reserves across Canada, comprising over 2.8 million hectares of land – an area almost as large as Belgium. The largest band is the Six Nations group of about 19,000 near Brantford, Ont.

The remaining registered Indians, as well as most non-status Indians, live off reserves. A larger proportion of the overall Indian population now live in urban centres than anywhere else.

Languages

The most common aboriginal language in Canada is **Cree**, with about 76,000 speakers. **Inuktitut,** spoken by about 27,000 Inuit, places a distant second, followed by **Ojibwa**, with 22,000 speakers. There are dozens of other aboriginal languages, which fall into 10 broader language families. In most cases, the speakers of these languages number well under 10,000 — often only 2,000 or so.

The most prevalent language family is **Algonquian**, which includes the Prairie Cree, the Ojibwa and Algonquin of Central Canada, Micmacs of the Maritimes and Montagnais and Naskapi of northeastern Quebec and Labrador.

(Note the difference in spelling: **Algonquian** is the overall term for the language group. **Algonquin** is classified as an Ojibwa dialect, one of the languages of the Algonquian family. The Algonquin live along the Ottawa River in Quebec and Ontario.)

Iroquois languages are spoken by such groups as the Six Nations, including the Mohawk and Oneidas.

Northern aboriginal people speak **Athapaskan** languages, while those in British Columbia speak languages from several families, the most common being **Salishan**.

Writing about Aboriginal Peoples

Canada's First Nations are not a homogeneous group with a standard set of interests and grievances. An effort should be made to reflect their diversity in stories specifically dealing with aboriginal groups.

Saying someone is **an Alberta native** is unhelpful. Try to identify the tribal affiliation or the reserve.

Milton Born With a Tooth, an Alberta Peigan; Cameron Kerley, a former resident of Sioux Valley reserve in Manitoba; Neil Sterritt, hereditary chief of the Gitxsan-Wet'suwet'en Nation in British Columbia; Mike Mitchell, chief of the Mohawk council at Akwesasne reserve near Cornwall, Ont.

If a language other than English or French is spoken, include it in the body of the story: **Ellen Gabriel, who addressed the forum in Mohawk.**

In general, CP prefers the terms **aboriginal** and **First Nations** to **Indian** and **native**. The preference of the group or individual should be followed if it is known.

Use the spelling preferred by aboriginals for the names of their communities. For instance, some Micmac communities in Eastern Canada prefer the spelling **Mi'kmaq**.

Métis

The meaning of the word **Métis** is elusive and subject to argument.

Originally, the word was applied to descendants of French traders and trappers and Indian women in the Canadian northwest. Now it is usually taken to mean anyone of mixed Indian and European blood, although there are Métis communities on the Prairies where French is spoken.

There were 210,000 Métis in the 1996 census. However, many status Indians are in fact Métis and many whites have Indian blood but do not consider themselves Métis.

Inuit

There are about 41,000 Inuit (never Eskimo) in Canada, strung out in small settlements from Labrador to Alaska. Their language is Inuktitut.

The Inuit of the western Arctic call themselves Inuvialuit.

The singular of Inuit is Inuk.

Aircraft, ships, guns

Style for names

1. For the names of aircraft, guns, tanks, rockets, satellites and the like, use a hyphen when a figure follows a letter.

a DC-10 jetliner, a CF-18 fighter, an M-16 rifle, an M-60 tank, a Russian SSN-8 rocket

2. Do not use a hyphen when a letter follows a figure.

an FA-18A fighter, a 727-100C cargo plane, the JT-15D fan-jet engine

3. Do not put a hyphen between a spelled-out name and a number.

a Dash 8-300, an F-4 Phantom 2 fighter, a Leopard 2 tank, a Polaris A-3 rocket, a Cosmos 650 satellite

4. Form plurals by adding *s* without an apostrophe.

two Dash 7s, a shipment of AK-47s, 15 M-60s

Aircraft

1. Refer to an aircraft with or without the name of the maker or designer.

Lockheed L-1011 TriStar, Lockheed L-1011, L-1011, TriStar

2. North American military aircraft carry a prefixed letter to indicate the basic function: *A* for *attack*, *B* for *bomber*, *C* for *cargo* or transport, *F* for *fighter*, *H* for *helicopter*, *S* for *anti-submarine*, *T* for *trainer*.

Note: Do not confuse the prefix *C* for *Canadian* (a CF-18 fighter) with the *C* for *cargo* (a CC-130 Hercules).

3. Russian aircraft carry a prefix that is an abbreviation of the maker's or designer's name: *Il* for *Ilyushin*, *M* for *Myasishchev*, *MiG* for *Mikoyan and Gurevich*, *Su* for *Sukhoi*, *Tu* for *Tupolev*, *Yak* for *Yakovlev*.

4. The NATO name for a Russian plane may be used or omitted as desired.

Tu-144 Charger, MiG-25 Foxbat, M-4 Bison, Il-76 Candid

5. A jumbo jet is any very large jet aircraft, such as a *DC-10, Boeing 747, L-1011* or *Airbus*.

Ships

1.   The terms **ship** and **boat** are less than precise. A good general rule is to use **boat** for smaller inshore or lake craft, **ship** for larger ocean-going craft. **Vessel** is a handy catch-all for anything bigger than a rowboat. Deepsea freighters, tankers, bulk carriers, container ships, ocean-going passenger liners and most naval ships should never be called boats. (Naval exceptions: motor torpedo boats and submarines.)

2.   Words to describe boats and ships vary from region to region. **Laker** is a common term for Great Lakes vessels but may be unfamiliar to readers in some areas of the country. **Fish boat** is an everyday term on the West Coast but unheard of on the East Coast, where such craft are called **fishing boats**.

3.   Avoid *nauticalese* that is indecipherable to the average reader — or be prepared to translate it: **fo'c's'le** (forward part of a ship where crew live); **bottom** (a freighter or tanker); **hawser** (cable or heavy rope used to secure a ship to a wharf); **dead-reckoning** (fixing a ship's position by instruments when observation of stars is not possible); **"She's going down by the head."** (A ship is sinking bow-first.)

4.   For numbers in ships' names, use the vessel's own style: **Queen Elizabeth 2, Bluenose II**.

5.   The familiar abbreviations **HMCS, USS** or **HMS** may be used before the name of a military ship: **HMCS Terra Nova, USS Coral Sea**, etc.

Note: Do not put *the* in front of HMCS or HMS for reasons that are obvious when the abbreviation is written out: *(the)* **Her Majesty's Canadian Ship Halifax**, etc. Naval tradition also drops *the* on second reference to military ships: **The damaged tanker was escorted by Terra Nova into port at Vancouver.** But use the article *the* before names of non-military ships: **The Titanic sank off Cape Race, Nfld.**

6.   Avoid or spell out less familiar, cumbersome or archaic abbreviations: **MV** (for motor vessel) **Lollipop**; **CCGS** (for Canadian Coast Guard Ship) **Louis S. St. Laurent**; **RMS** (for Royal Mail Ship) **Titanic**, etc.

7.   Avoid terms like **seamen** and **fishermen** unless the sex is important and known to be male. **Crew members** and **crew** are always serviceable.

8.   Ships have been referred to in the feminine form — **she** and **her** — for generations. But some readers find it objectionable, especially if the statement being made is sexist (**she's temperamental**). Use **it**, except in direct quotes.

9.   Ships' tonnage is measured and expressed in several ways, all of them complex and rarely in need of explanation in news stories. If tonnage must be noted, use the **gross register tonnage** as listed in large boldface type in column No. 3 of each ship's entry in *Lloyd's Register of Shipping*. Never write that a ship **weighs** such-and-such. The tonnage figures relate to the capacity of a ship, which means little to the non-nautical reader. Better to check Lloyd's for such dimensions as length and try to express these in everyday terms to provide a sense of size: **The tanker is about as long as 40 typical transit buses parked bumper to bumper.**

10. A ship's country and port of registration may have nothing to do with the vessel's ownership or the nationality of its crew. Many ships sail under what is known as a **flag of convenience**, meaning they are registered in countries with lower registry charges and wage rates than the owners would pay in their home countries. Hence, a ship identified as **Panamanian-registered** may in fact be owned in a country halfway around the world from Panama. Check Lloyd's for the name and nationality of the ship's owners. Shipping agents may be able to help with such details as the nationality of the crew, the nature of the cargo, last port of call, etc.

11. Some marine measures:

nautical mile 1.853 kilometres (6,080 feet)
knot one nautical mile an hour
fathom six feet (slightly under two metres)

Graphics can be particularly useful in presenting technical details to the reader.

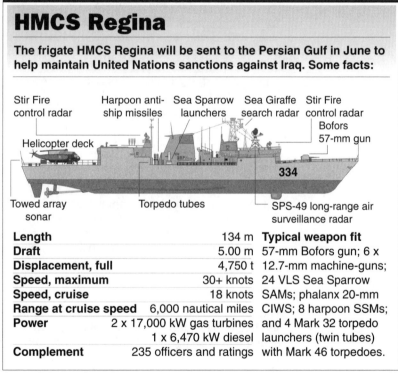

HMCS Regina

The frigate HMCS Regina will be sent to the Persian Gulf in June to help maintain United Nations sanctions against Iraq. Some facts:

Stir Fire control radar — Harpoon anti-ship missiles — Sea Sparrow launchers — Sea Giraffe search radar — Stir Fire control radar — Bofors 57-mm gun

Helicopter deck

334

Towed array sonar — Torpedo tubes — SPS-49 long-range air surveillance radar

		Typical weapon fit
Length	134 m	57-mm Bofors gun; 6 x
Draft	5.00 m	12.7-mm machine-guns;
Displacement, full	4,750 t	24 VLS Sea Sparrow
Speed, maximum	30+ knots	SAMs; phalanx 20-mm
Speed, cruise	18 knots	CIWS; 8 harpoon SSMs;
Range at cruise speed	6,000 nautical miles	and 4 Mark 32 torpedo
Power	2 x 17,000 kW gas turbines	launchers (twin tubes)
	1 x 6,470 kW diesel	with Mark 46 torpedoes.
Complement	235 officers and ratings	

Source: Saint John Shipbuilding   - CP

Guns

1. A **rifle** has a grooved bore and fires bullets from cartridges. A **shotgun** has a smooth bore, may be double-barrelled and fires shot from shells. A **pistol** may be a revolver, which holds cartridges in a revolving cylinder, or an automatic, which holds cartridges in a magazine. A **cartridge** is a case consisting of an explosive charge and

a bullet or shot. Shotgun **shells** are filled with powder and shot made of lead or steel.

2. When reporting crime stories, avoid the casual use of the term **hunting rifle**, which wildlife and hunting organizations argue is accurate only when used in context with a hunter legally pursuing game. Try to get a precise description of weapons from police and other authorities.

3. Rifles, pistols, revolvers and other small arms are usually described in **calibre**, which is a measurement of the diameter of the inside of the barrel and is expressed in decimal fractions of an inch or in metric. The word calibre is not used in metric measurements. Write **a .22-calibre rifle, a 9-mm pistol.**

4. More precise description of calibre is expressed by an added set of figures (after a hyphen) to designate load, speed of bullet or year of adoption: **.30-30, .250-3000, .30-06.** Often such precision is necessary to differentiate among .30-calibre guns.

5. Shotguns are measured in **gauge.** Gauge refers to the number of balls, with a diameter the size of the inside of the barrel, that can be made from a pound of lead. For a shotgun with a barrel 0.729 inches in diameter, for instance, a pound of lead yields 12 balls, so the gun is called a **12 gauge.** The .410 is a calibre but is commonly called a gauge. Other gauges have no decimal point.

6. **Gun** is an acceptable term for any firearm; it may also be used to describe larger weapons, such as artillery pieces.

7. Large naval and artillery guns fire **shells**; mortars fire **bombs.** A **round** is one shot, whether from a handgun, a rifle or a cannon.

8. The **magazine** of a firearm simply refers to the reservoir or device holding extra rounds of ammunition to be fed into the chamber through spring, bolt or some other action. The magazine can take various forms, such as the **rotary** (as found on the Thompson machine-gun or **tommy-gun**), **tubular** (in some bolt action, semi-automatic, lever and pump-action rifles), **belt** (which feeds ammunition into rapid-fire automatic weapons) or **box** (either a fixed or detachable compartment).

The term **clip** describes a detachable magazine used with bolt-action, semi-automatic and automatic rifles, as well as some shotguns and handguns (usually semi-automatic or fully automatic) holding a varying number of cartridges, from two up. Note that a magazine is not always a clip.

➤ See **Military**, page 260.

Metric

General

Metric, eh?

It was a typical Canadian compromise: the country would join most of the rest of the world in using metric measurements — but gradually.

That was in the 1970s. Since then Canadians of all ages have become accustomed to charting winter freezes in Celsius, family drives in kilometres and milk in litres.

But it will be a long time before imperial measures disappear. Old habits die hard, especially among Canadians educated in the imperial system. Then there is the daily bombardment of feet and Fahrenheit, pounds and miles-an-hour from the United States.

In Canada, the media have largely adopted metric, with a dwindling number of exceptions.

CP's position from the beginning has been: **Metric, yes,** but even more important, **Be clear.** Specific descriptions are often needed, but comparative examples from everyday life can be even more helpful: **big as a truck, small as a thimble, knee-deep snow** and the like.

When metric?

1. In general, report measurements in metric. Among the lingering exceptions are cases where some other measurement remains conventional — personal weights and heights, sections of land on the Prairies, precious metals in troy ounces, two-by-fours, quarter-inch screws and the like.

2. The number of exceptions is limited. Many farmers in Canada may still think in acres and grocery shoppers in pounds, but CP uses metric when figures are needed and descriptions when they're not (**a dusty patch of Saskatchewan grain field, a bag full of turnips**).

3. Metric measurements are not put into the mouths of those who speak in the inch-pound system, either in direct quotes or in indirect speech. Rephrasing can be used to limit such occasions.

4. In most other cases when imperial must be used, it should be accompanied by a metric equivalent. For example, Canada's 200-nautical-mile (**370-kilometre**) fishing limit, or the number of litres in a 35-gallon barrel of oil (**about 159**).

5. But when repeated use of bracketed equivalents may slow down or annoy the reader, consider a separate line or paragraph giving the metric equivalent. Thereafter let the specialists speak in their own tongue.

6.   Speed and distances are expressed in metric, including very great distances such as the number of kilometres between planets in the solar system. Certain astronomical distances, such as those between stars or galaxies, are often measured in light-years — the distance light travels in one year moving at almost 300,000 kilometres a second, or about 9.46 trillion kilometres.

7.   The altitude of airplanes and the height of mountains are expressed in metres, not feet, and distances at sea are expressed in kilometres, not miles or nautical miles. Measure speeds in kilometres an hour, not knots.

8.   The size of animals is expressed in kilograms and metres (centimetres and the like for extremely small animals). Meat on the store shelf is in kilograms.

Let logic be your guide

1.   In handling material from U.S. sources, it is usually possible to make a straight conversion from imperial. **The plane crashed about 90 metres from a home for the elderly.** (The source material reads **100 yards.**)

2.   But tend to use round figures. Most of the world uses metric and material routed through the United States from abroad has possibly gone through one conversion already.

3.   In converting to metric, do not use figures that imply greater accuracy than justified by the original data. For instance, using 2.54 centimetres to the inch, convert 35 inches to 89 or even 90 centimetres, not 88.9.

4.   Don't needlessly mix imperial and metric in comparisons in the same sentence. Make it **the 60-pound boy was attacked by a dog almost twice his weight.** Save the exact weight of the dog (50 kilograms in this case) for another sentence.

5.   And, of course, it's axiomatic that a writer doesn't meddle with the idiomatic: **The crowd inched forward.**

Sports

1.   Most Olympic and many non-Olympic sports are contested and reported in metric. But others, such as golf, horse racing and North American football, continue to use imperial.

2.   Where figures are appropriate in descriptions of imperial-measure sports, CP increasingly uses metric: **a 10-metre slapshot, a 120-metre homer to left field.** And use of imperial is kept to essentials in stories and results. Often a descriptive phrase will do instead: **won by three car lengths.**

3.   Different types of motor racing use different measures. Grand Prix racing is in metric, but motorcycle, U.S. stock car and Indy-type racing are in imperial.

4.   A race for 12-metre yachts should be described as such. But include an explanatory note that the vessels themselves are about 20 metres

long and that the classification of 12 metres is determined through a complicated formula involving length, sail area and displacement.

➤ For details, see **Sports**, page 77.

Odds and ends

1. The names of metric units are usually spelled out: **a 20-kilogram sack**, not **a 20-kg sack**; covering **50 hectares**, not **covering 50 ha**; ran **10 kilometres**, not **ran 10 km**.

2. There are no abbreviations in metric, only symbols. These symbols take periods only at the end of a sentence, never take *s* in the plural and are separated from a number by a space. In adjectival uses, the space is replaced by a hyphen.

3. *C* (for Celsius) can be used on first reference. Other common symbols such as **km/h** and **mm** may be used on second reference when preceded by a number: **at 70 km/h, a 105-mm cannon**.

4. A number less than one has a zero before the decimal: **0.25 ha**, not **.25 ha**; but prefer **a quarter hectare** and the like when common fractions are involved.

5. Treat the names of metric units as singular when the number preceding them is less than one: **0.25 litre** but **2.5 litres**.

6. For temperatures less than 0 C do not write **below zero**; use a minus sign as in **−5 C**. The minus sign is a dash preceding a number with no space between.

7. The clipped form **kilo** is not acceptable for **kilogram** or **kilometre** since kilo simply means a thousand and is not a specific unit.

8. Superior numbers are not available on many keyboards for the preferred symbols for square metres (m^2), cubic centimetres (cm^3) and such. Instead write **sq. m, cu. cm**, etc. The symbol for degree (°) is unavailable; for **15°C** write **15 C**, or **15 degrees C**.

9. Symbols may be used in tabular matter and certain sports and financial routine.

10. Metric units named after people have capitalized symbols (**A** for Andrew Marie **A**mpere, **C** for Anders **C**elsius, **Pa** for Blaise **Pa**scal and **W** for James **W**att); but when the name of a unit is written in full, only Celsius is capitalized. Otherwise write ampere, pascal, watt, etc.

11. A few symbols for metric prefixes are capped, including **M** for **mega** (one million) and **G** for **giga** (one billion); for example, **MPa** (megapascal), **GJ** (gigajoule). But avoid prefixes denoting extremely large multiples and such small fractions as **pico** (one-trillionth), **nano** (one-billionth), **micro** (one-millionth).

➤ See **Abbreviations and acronyms,** page 167.

Metric conversion table

Into metric

If you know	multiply by	to get
Length		
inches	25.4	millimetres
inches	2.54	centimetres
inches	.0254	metres
feet	0.3	metres
yards	0.91	metres
miles	1.61	kilometres
Area		
sq. inches	6.45	sq. centimetres
sq. feet	0.09	sq. metres
sq. yards	0.84	sq. metres
sq. miles	2.59	sq. kilometres
acres	0.4	hectares
Mass (weight)		
ounces	28.35	grams
pounds	0.45	kilograms
tons (short)	0.907	tonnes/metric tons
Volume		
Imp. — not U.S.		
fluid ounces	28.41	millilitres (cu. cm)
pints	0.57	litres
quarts	1.13	litres
gallons	4.54	litres
cubic inches	16.39	cubic centimetres
cubic feet	0.03	cubic metres
cubic yards	0.76	cubic metres
Temperature		
Fahrenheit	Subtract 32, then multiply by 5/9ths	Celsius
Temperature variations		
Fahrenheit	.555	Celsius

Out of metric

If you know	multiply by	to get
Length		
millimetres	0.04	inches
centimetres	0.39	inches
metres	3.28	feet
metres	1.09	yards
kilometres	0.62	miles
Area		
sq. centimetres	0.15	sq. inches
sq. metres	10.76	sq. feet
sq. metres	1.19	sq. yards
sq. kilometres	0.4	sq. miles
hectares	2.47	acres
Mass (weight)		
grams	0.035	ounces
kilograms	2.2	pounds
tonnes/metric tons	1.1	tons (short)
Volume		*Imp. — not U.S.*
millilitres (cu. cm)	0.03	fluid ounces
litres	1.76	pints
litres	0.88	quarts
litres	0.22	gallons
cubic centimetres	0.06	cubic inches
cubic metres	35.31	cubic feet
cubic metres	1.31	cubic yards
Temperature		
Celsius	Multiply by 9/5ths, then add 32	Fahrenheit
Temperature variations		
Celsius	1.8	Fahrenheit

Common metric units

	CP style for symbol		CP style for symbol
Length			
millimetre	mm	metre	m
centimetre	cm	kilometre	km
Area			
square millimetre	sq. mm	hectare (10,000 sq. m)	ha
square centimetre	sq. cm	square kilometre	sq. km
square metre	sq. m		
Volume			
millilitre	ml		
litre	l		
cubic centimetre	cu. cm		
cubic metre	cu. m		
Mass (weight)			
milligram	mg	kilogram	kg
gram	g	tonne/metric ton (1,000 kg)	t
Electricity			
volt	V	ohm	ohm
ampere	A	hertz	Hz
Energy		**Power**	
joule	J	watt	W
kilojoule	kJ	kilowatt	kW
megajoule	MJ	megawatt	MW
kilowatt hour	kW-h		
Pressure		**Temperature**	
pascal	Pa	Celsius	C
kilopascal	kPa		
megapascal	MPa		
Speed			
metres a second	m/s		
kilometres an hour	km/h		

Different strokes

1.   In much of the world, spaces are used to separate long numbers into blocks of three digits (**25 353 425**) and a comma is used as a decimal mark (**245,3**). CP style is to separate figures with commas rather than spaces (**25,353,425**) and to use a period rather than a comma in decimals (**245.3**).

2.   In Quebec, French-language media have adopted the international style: a space instead of a comma in long numbers, a comma instead of a decimal point and a currency symbol after an amount instead of before. Thus **12,24$** is used for **$12.24**.

Converting

1.   Fuel consumption of automobiles is given in number of litres per hundred kilometres, written **l per 100 km**. The lower the figure, the lower the rate of consumption. To convert miles per U.S. gallon into litres per 100 kilometres, divide 234.2146 by the number of miles. To convert miles per Canadian gallon into litres per 100 kilometres, divide 282.48 by the number of miles.

2.   To change Fahrenheit to Celsius, subtract 32, then multiply by five and divide by nine. To convert Celsius to Fahrenheit, multiply by nine, divide by five, then add 32.

3.   Convert large numbers of hectares into square kilometres. To do so, divide the number of hectares by 100.

Recipes

Follow this style for recipes, where imperial continues to be in wide use:

Apple Oatmeal Squares

250 ml (1 cup) all-purpose flour
250 ml (1 cup) quick-cooking rolled oats
125 ml (1/2 cup) firmly packed brown sugar
5 ml (1 tsp) nutmeg
2 ml (1/2 tsp) salt
175 ml (3/4 cup) butter
6 medium cooking apples
50 ml (1/4 cup) sunflower seeds

Combine flour, oats, sugar, nutmeg and salt. Cut in butter until mixture is crumbly. Measure out 125 ml (1/2 cup) and set aside for topping. Press remaining oatmeal mixture evenly in bottom of greased 23-cm-square (9-inch-square) pan.

Peel and core apples, cut in halves lengthwise. Place cut side down on oatmeal base. Add sunflower seeds to reserved crumb mixture and sprinkle over top. Bake at 190 C (375 F) for 40 to 45 minutes. Cut into squares and serve warm or cooled. Makes 12 squares.

Note: To save space, punctuation in abbreviations (tsp, tbsp) can be eliminated and numbers below 10 don't need to be written out.

Military

General

1. All Canadian servicemen and servicewomen are members of the **Canadian Armed Forces**, often shortened to the **Canadian Forces**, the **Armed Forces** or simply **the Forces**.

Note: Uppercase **Armed Forces** applies only to Canadian forces; all others are down.

2. The Canadian Forces are headed by the **chief of the defence staff**, responsible to the minister of defence.

3. There are five commands: **Maritime**, **Mobile**, **Air**, **Communications** and **Canadian Forces Europe**.

4. Units making up land, sea and air formations go by a variety of names. The main field units are **division, brigade, regiment, battalion, squadron, company, troop** and **platoon**; naval units are **fleet, squadron** and **ship**; air units are **division, group, wing, squadron** and **flight**.

5. One rank structure, based on army grades, is used for army and air force personnel, another for navy personnel.

➤ See **Ranks**, page 261.

6. The terms **army, navy** and **air force** are acceptable, and personnel may be referred to as **soldiers, sailors** and **airmen** or **airwomen**.

Bases

1. National Defence Headquarters in Ottawa is the headquarters of the Canadian Forces and the Defence Department.

2. Major service establishments include **Canadian Forces bases: Canadian Forces Base Comox, B.C.**, or **CFB Comox** in second reference. There are smaller establishments called **Canadian Forces stations** and specialist installations such as **Canadian Forces ammunition depots**.

3. Canada's four **rescue co-ordination centres** — at Halifax, Trenton, Ont., Edmonton and Victoria — are controlled and staffed by the Canadian Forces. In addition, a Canadian Coast Guard officer is on duty at each of the rescue centres in Halifax, Trenton and Victoria.

4. Avoid the abbreviations **CFS, CFAD** and **RCC** as being unfamiliar to readers.

Units

1. To help readers evaluate a military action, put the numbers and types of troops and their support high in the story. Because **battalion, brigade, army** and other formations vary in size and makeup from country to country, the terms mean little unless qualified.

2. These are some Canadian land units and their approximate sizes: **section**, 10 soldiers; **platoon**, three sections totalling 35; **company**, three platoons totalling 125-150; **battalion**, three or four companies totalling 375-600. A **brigade** consists of three battalions, but a **brigade group** — an infantry brigade supported by armour and artillery — numbers about 4,500 troops.

Note: The figures do not add up because, in addition to fighting personnel, each unit includes a varying number of commanders, signallers, etc.

3. A **regiment** is a unit with a proper name — **the Grey and Simcoe Foresters**, for example — and usually consists of three battalions. It remains a regiment whether it has 20 or 2,000 members.

Capitalization

> See chapter **Capitalization**, page 185.

Ranks

1. The Canadian Forces modify British tradition in the use of ranks and appointment titles, particularly for land forces. In an artillery regiment, for example, a private is a gunner, and a corporal is a bombardier. In an engineer regiment, a private is a sapper; in an armoured unit, a trooper; in a communications unit, a signalman; in a guards regiment, a guardsman; in a rifle regiment, a rifleman.

2. Plurals of military ranks and appointments add *s* to the principal rank category, not to the qualifying word: **major-generals, lieutenant-colonels, sergeants major**.

3. Since ranks were reorganized at the time of Armed Forces unification, the rank of **corporal** has signified a person with four years of service who has achieved certain technical qualifications. In effect, it is equivalent to a senior private rather than a rank indicating leadership responsibility. The first level requiring leadership and special qualifications is the rank of **master corporal**.

Titles

The Canadian Forces use such titles as guardsman and master seaman for both males and females. Following are listed by descending order of rank.

Use these titles for army and air force personnel:

Rank	Before a name
general	Gen.
lieutenant-general	Lt.-Gen.
major-general	Maj.-Gen.
brigadier-general	Brig.-Gen.
colonel	Col.
lieutenant-colonel	Lt.-Col.
major	Maj.
captain	Capt.
lieutenant	Lieut.
second lieutenant	2nd Lieut.
officer cadet	Officer Cadet
chief warrant officer	Chief Warrant Officer
master warrant officer	Master Warrant Officer
warrant officer	Warrant Officer
sergeant	Sgt.
master corporal	Master Cpl.
corporal	Cpl.
bombardier	Bombardier
private	Pte.
guardsman	Guardsman
gunner	Gunner
rifleman	Rifleman
sapper	Sapper
signalman	Signalman
trooper	Trooper

Use these titles for navy personnel:

Rank	Before a name
admiral	Admiral
vice-admiral	Vice-Admiral
rear admiral	Rear Admiral
commodore	Commodore
captain	Capt.
commander	Cmdr.
lieutenant-commander	Lt.-Cmdr.
lieutenant	Lieut.
sub-lieutenant	Sub-Lieut.
acting sub-lieutenant	Acting Sub-Lieut.
chief petty officer first class, second class	Chief Petty Officer 1st Class, 2nd Class
master seaman	Master Seaman
leading seaman	Leading Seaman
able seaman	Able Seaman
ordinary seaman	Ordinary Seaman

Usage for some foreign ranks and old Canadian ranks that may appear in copy periodically. They are listed alphabetically, not by descending order of rank:

Rank	Before a name
air commodore	Air Commodore
aircraftman first class	Aircraftman 1st Class
airman	Airman
airman first class	Airman 1st Class
air marshal	Air Marshal
air vice-marshal	Air Vice-Marshal
chief master sergeant	Chief Master Sgt.
commissioned warrant officer	Commissioned Warrant Officer
craftman	Craftman
ensign	Ensign
field marshal	Field Marshal
first lieutenant	1st Lieut.
first sergeant	1st Sgt.
flying officer	Flying Officer
fusilier	Fusilier
group captain	Group Capt.
gunnery sergeant	Gunnery Sgt.
lance-corporal	Lance-Cpl.
leading aircraftman	Leading Aircraftman
master chief petty officer	Master Chief Petty Officer
master gunnery sergeant	Master Gunnery Sgt.
master sergeant	Master Sgt.
midshipman	Midshipman
pilot officer	Pilot Officer
platoon sergeant	Platoon Sgt.
private first class	Pte. 1st Class
regimental sergeant major	Regimental Sgt. Maj.
seaman apprentice	Seaman Apprentice
seaman recruit	Seaman Recruit
senior chief petty officer	Senior Chief Petty Officer
sergeant first class	Sgt. 1st Class
sergeant major of the army	Army Sgt. Maj.
technical sergeant	Tech. Sgt.
wing commander	Wing Cmdr.

Retired officers

1. In certain circumstances, a military rank may be used in first reference before the name of an officer who has retired. Do not use the abbreviation **Ret.** but put **retired** before the lowercase rank: **retired brigadier Pat Turner.**

2. In stories involving military activities, former majors, lieutenant-commanders, squadron leaders and other high officers may be referred to by their old rank.

3. Even in stories involving purely civilian matters, brigadiers and higher may be referred to by rank, if the officers prefer.

4. When rank is used, decorations may at times be added. In civilian stories, decorations need not be mentioned except for the Victoria Cross, Cross of Valour or other outstanding awards normally pertinent to the story.

Courts martial

1. Military courts martial are properly open to the media, though in many instances the media are not advised they are in progress. Their decisions are privileged.

2. Keep in mind that a court martial's decision must be reviewed by the commander of the unit that convened it and by other military authorities. The decision may be overruled by the federal cabinet or the court martial appeal board upon the person aggrieved presenting a petition. In either case the further ruling merits equal prominence.

Ceremonies

1. **Guards**

a) A **royal guard** is paraded for visiting royalty, governors general and lieutenant-governors. It consists of 100 men and women with arms, a band and colours (regimental flags). A **guard of honour** is turned out for any other dignitary: 50 troops with arms and usually a band. A **mounted escort** accompanies the dignitary's vehicle, the riders armed, often with lances, and drawn from the RCMP or a regiment.

b) In Canada, a dignitary **inspects** the guard by walking up and down the ranks. In the United States, a dignitary **reviews** it.

2. **Colours**

a) In Canada, the colours are carried by a **colour party**, an officer bearer escorted by non-commissioned officers. The American equivalent is called a **colour guard**.

b) Regimental colours are dipped only to the sovereign or a member of the Royal Family. In the ceremony of **trooping the colour** — carrying the regimental flag along ranks of soldiers — only one colour is trooped, hence the name.

c) Flags are always raised to the top of the mast or pole. Then, if required, they are **lowered to half-mast**. If tangled with the rope, they are **fouled**.

3. **Military funerals**

a) A **gun carriage** consists of a towed gun, with a platform fixed above the barrel, on which the coffin is fastened. The six who carry the coffin are the **bearer party**; the 12 who fire volleys at the graveside are the **firing party**.

b) Wreaths are **laid** or **placed**, trumpets **sounded** and bugles **blown** or **sounded**.

Miscellaneous

1. Write **promoted major-general**, not **promoted to major-general**. But **promoted to the rank of major-general** is correct.

2. Distinguish between **rank** (position within the military hierarchy) and **appointment** (specific duty). A person with the **rank** of master warrant officer may be given the **duties** of regimental quartermaster sergeant, a non-commissioned officer in charge of a regiment's quarters, supplies, etc.

Master Warrant Officer Pat Smith has been named regimental quartermaster sergeant.

Regimental Quartermaster Sergeant John Smith holds the rank of master warrant officer.

3. When locating a Canadian regiment, be sure to use the *official* home town or towns.

4. Do not refer to the Princess Patricia's Canadian Light Infantry as **the Pats**, a term disliked by its members. But **the Patricias** (no apostrophe) is acceptable for the unit or a group of individuals.

5. The nickname of Quebec's Royal 22nd Regiment is **the Van Doo** (from vingt-deux). Personnel of the regiment may be referred to as **the Van Doos** and one of them as **a Van Doo**.

6. Write **Mobile Command**; avoid the bilingual designation **Force Mobile Command** except in direct quotation.

7. The term **Snowbirds** is officially used to designate the Canadian Forces aerobatic team. The full complement including support personnel is designated 431 Air Demonstration Squadron.

8. The **Skyhawks** parachuting performers are formally known as the Canadian Forces Parachute Team.

9. **CF-18** is the designation for the Canadian version of the U.S. fighter aircraft F-18.

10. Avoid Americanisms. Canadian usage is **Last Post, guard of honour** and **AWL** (absent without leave). American usage is **Taps, honour guard** and **AWOL**. And Canadians take **basic military training**; they do not attend **boot camp**.

11. Do not refer to the Royal Military College at Kingston, Ont., as the **West Point of Canada** or **Canada's Sandhurst** in stories for Canadian consumption.

12. A **volley** is one shot from each of several weapons fired simultaneously; a **fusillade** is several shots fired from one weapon sequentially. One gunman can fire a fusillade but not a volley. Artillery fires in **salvos**.

13. A **sniper** fires shots from hiding, usually at long range, into the enemy's camp or at individuals.

14. In flying, a **sortie** is one mission by one plane.

15. While the term **troops** can be used to refer to a body of soldiers — **100 troops advanced** — it should not be used in the singular as a substitute for **soldier**. A troop is a military unit.

➤ See **Aircraft, ships, guns**, page 249.

People, places

(Numbers refer to notes at end, page 273.)

Country/ Region	Noun	Adjective	Capital	Currency
Afghanistan	Afghan(s)	Afghani	Kabul	afghani
Albania	Albanian(s)	Albanian	Tirana	lek
Algeria	Algerian(s)	Algerian	Algiers	dinar
American Samoa	American Samoan(s)	American Samoan	Pago Pago	dollar
Andorra	Andorran(s)	Andorran	Andorra La Vella	franc/ peseta
Angola	Angolan(s)	Angolan	Luanda	kwanza
Antigua	Antiguan(s)	Antiguan	St. John's	dollar
Argentina	Argentine(s)	Argentine	Buenos Aires	peso
Armenia	Armenian(s)	Armenian	Yerevan	dram
Aruba	Aruban(s)	Aruban	Oranjestad	guilder
Australia	Australian(s)	Australian	Canberra	dollar
Austria	Austrian(s)	Austrian	Vienna	schilling
Azerbaijan	Azerbaijani(s)	Azerbaijani	Baku	manat
Azores	Azorean(s)	Azorean	Ponta Delgada	escudo
Bahamas	Bahamian(s)	Bahamian	Nassau	dollar
Bahrain	Bahraini(s)	Bahraini	Manama	dinar
Bangladesh	Bangladeshi(s)	Bangladesh	Dhaka	taka
Barbados	Barbadian(s)	Barbadian	Bridgetown	dollar
Belarus	Belarussian(s)	Belarus	Minsk	ruble
Belgium	Belgian(s)	Belgian	Brussels	franc
Belize	Belizean(s)	Belizean	Belmopan	dollar
Benin	Beninese (sing. and pl.)	Beninese	Porto-Novo	franc
Bermuda	Bermudian(s)	Bermudian	Hamilton	dollar
Bhutan	Bhutanese (sing., pl.)	Bhutanese	Thimphu	ngultrum/ rupee
Bolivia	Bolivian(s)	Bolivian	La Paz	boliviano
Bosnia-Herzegovina	Bosnian(s)	Bosnian	Sarajevo	dinar
Botswana	Motswana (sing.) Batswana (pl.)	Botswana	Gaborone	pula
Brazil	Brazilian(s)	Brazilian	Brasilia	real
Brunei	Bruneian(s)	Bruneian	Bandar Seri Begawan	dollar
Bulgaria	Bulgarian(s)	Bulgarian	Sofia	lev
Burkina Faso	Burkina Fasan(s)	Burkina Fasan	Ouagadougou	franc

Country/ Region	Noun	Adjective	Capital	Currency
Burundi	Burundian(s)	Burundi	Bujumbura	franc
Cambodia	Cambodian(s)	Cambodian	Phnom Penh	riel
Cameroon	Cameroonian(s)	Cameroonian	Yaounde	franc
Canary Islands	Canary Islander(s)	Canary Island	Las Palmas	peseta
Cape Verde	Cape Verdean(s)	Cape Verdean	Praia	escudo
Cayman Islands	Cayman Islander(s)	Cayman	Georgetown	dollar
Central African Republic	Central African(s)	Central African	Bangui	franc
Chad	Chadian(s)	Chadian	N'djamena	franc
Chile	Chilean(s)	Chilean	Santiago	peso
China	Chinese (sing., pl.)	Chinese	Beijing	renminbi/ yuan
Colombia	Colombian(s)	Colombian	Bogota	peso
Comoros	Comoran(s)	Comoran	Moroni	franc
Congo (formerly Zaire)	Congolese (sing., pl.)	Congolese	Kinshasa	franc
Congo-Brazzaville	Congolese (sing., pl.)	Congolese	Brazzaville	franc
Cook Islands	Cook Islander(s)	Cook Islands	Avarua	dollar
Costa Rica	Costa Rican(s)	Costa Rican	San Jose	colon
Croatia	Croat(s)	Croatian	Zagreb	runa
Cuba	Cuban(s)	Cuban	Havana	peso
Cyprus	Cypriot(s)	Cypriot	Nicosia	pound
Czech Republic	Czech(s)	Czech	Prague	koruna
Denmark	Dane(s)	Danish	Copenhagen	krone
Djibouti	Afar(s), Issa(s)	Afar, Issa	Djibouti	franc
Dominica	Dominican(s)	Dominican	Roseau	dollar
Dominican Republic	Dominican(s)	Dominican	Santo Domingo	peso
Ecuador	Ecuadoran(s)	Ecuadoran	Quito	sucre
Egypt	Egyptian(s)	Egyptian	Cairo	pound
El Salvador	Salvadoran(s)	Salvadoran	San Salvador	colon
Equatorial Guinea	Equatorial Guinean(s)	Equatorial Guinean	Malabo	franc
Eritrea	Eritrean(s)	Eritrean	Asmara	birr
Estonia	Estonian(s)	Estonian	Tallinn	kroon
Ethiopia	Ethiopian(s)	Ethiopian	Addis Ababa	birr
Falkland Islands	Falkland Islander(s)	Falkland Island	Stanley	pound
Faroe Islands	Faroe Islander(s)	Faroe Islands	Thorshavn	krone
Fiji	Fijian(s)	Fijian	Suva	dollar
Finland	Finn(s)	Finnish	Helsinki	markka
France	French(wo)man	French	Paris	franc
French Guiana (sing., pl.)	French Guianese Guianese	French	Cayenne	franc
French Polynesia	French Polynesian(s)	French Polynesian	Papeete	franc

Country/ Region	Noun	Adjective	Capital	Currency
Gabon (sing., pl.)	Gabonese	Gabonese	Libreville	franc
Gambia	Gambian(s)	Gambian	Banjul	dalasi
Georgia	Georgian(s)	Georgian	Tbilisi	lavi
Germany	German(s)	German	Bonn❶	mark
Ghana	Ghanaian(s)	Ghanaian	Accra	cedi
Gibraltar	Gibraltan(s)	Gibraltan	Gibraltar	pound
Greece	Greek(s)	Greek	Athens	drachma
Greenland	Greenlander(s)	Greenlandic	Godthab	krone
Grenada	Grenadian(s)	Grenadian	St. George's	dollar
Guadeloupe	Guadeloupian(s)	Guadeloupe	Basse-Terre	franc
Guam	Guamanian(s)	Guamanian	Agana	dollar
Guatemala	Guatemalan(s)	Guatemalan	Guatemala City	quetzal
Guinea	Guinean(s)	Guinea	Conakry	franc
Guinea-Bissau	Guinean(s)	Guinean	Bissau	peso
Guyana	Guyanese (sing., pl.)	Guyanese	Georgetown	dollar
Haiti	Haitian(s)	Haitian	Port-au-Prince	gourde
Honduras	Honduran(s)	Honduran	Tegucigalpa	lempira
Hong Kong		Hong Kong	(part of China)	dollar
Hungary	Hungarian(s)	Hungarian	Budapest	forint
Iceland	Icelander(s)	Icelandic	Reykjavik	krona
India	Indian(s)	Indian	New Delhi	rupee
Indonesia	Indonesian(s)	Indonesian	Jakarta	rupiah
Iran	Iranian(s)	Iranian	Tehran	rial
Iraq	Iraqi(s)	Iraqi	Baghdad	dinar
Ireland	Irish(wo)man	Irish	Dublin	pound
Israel	Israeli(s)	Israeli	Jerusalem❷	shekel
Italy	Italian(s)	Italian	Rome	lira
Ivory Coast	Ivorian(s)	Ivorian	Abidjan	franc
Jamaica	Jamaican(s)	Jamaican	Kingston	dollar
Japan	Japanese (sing., pl.)	Japanese	Tokyo	yen
Jordan	Jordanian(s)	Jordanian	Amman	dinar
Kazakhstan	Kazakh(s)	Kazakh	Alma-Ata	tenge
Kenya	Kenyan(s)	Kenyan	Nairobi	shilling
Kiribati	Kiribatan(s)	Kiribatan	Bairiki❸	dollar
Kuwait	Kuwaiti(s)	Kuwaiti	Kuwait	dinar
Kyrgyzstan	Kyrgyz	Kyrgyz	Bishkek	som
Laos	Laotian(s)	Laotian	Vientiane	kip
Latvia	Latvian(s)	Latvian	Riga	lat
Lebanon	Lebanese (sing., pl.)	Lebanese	Beirut	pound
Lesotho	Masotho (sing.) Basotho (pl.)	Basotho	Maseru	maloti
Liberia	Liberian(s)	Liberian	Monrovia	dollar
Libya	Libyan(s)	Libyan	Tripoli	dinar
Liechtenstein	Liechtensteiner(s)	Liechtenstein	Vaduz	franc
Lithuania	Lithuanian(s)	Lithuanian	Vilnius	litas
Luxembourg	Luxembourger(s)	Luxembourg	Luxembourg	franc

Country/ Region	Noun	Adjective	Capital	Currency
Macedonia	Macedonian(s)	Macedonian	Skopje	dinar
Madagascar	Malagasy (sing., pl.)	Malagasy	Antananarivo	franc
Malawi	Malawian(s)	Malawian	Lilongwe	kwacha
Malaysia	Malaysian(s)	Malaysian	Kuala Lumpur	dollar/ ringgit
Maldives	Maldivian(s)	Maldivian	Male	rufiyaa
Mali	Malian(s)	Malian	Bamako	franc
Malta	Maltese (sing., pl.)	Maltese	Valletta	lira
Martinique	Martinican(s)	Martinican	Fort-de-France	franc
Mauritania	Mauritanian(s)	Mauritanian	Nouakchott	ouguiya
Mauritius	Mauritian(s)	Mauritian	Port Louis	rupee
Mexico	Mexican(s)	Mexican	Mexico City	peso
Micronesia, Federated States of	Micronesian(s)	Micronesian	Palikiv	dollar
Moldova	Moldovan(s)	Moldovan	Chisinau	leu
Monaco	Monacan(s)	Monacan	Monaco	franc
Mongolia	Mongolian(s)	Mongolian	Ulan Bator	tugrik
Montserrat	Montserratan(s)	Montserratan	Plymouth	dollar
Morocco	Moroccan(s)	Moroccan	Rabat	dirham
Mozambique	Mozambican(s)	Mozambican	Maputo	metical
Myanmar	Myanmar	Myanmar	Yangon	kyat
Namibia	Namibian(s)	Namibian	Windhoek	rand
Nauru	Nauruan(s)	Nauruan	Yaren	dollar
Nepal	Nepalese (sing., pl.)	Nepalese	Kathmandu	rupee
Netherlands❹	Netherlander(s)/ Dutch(wo)man	Netherlander/ Dutch	Amsterdam❺	guilder
Netherlands Antilles	Netherlands Antillean(s)	Netherlands Antillean	Willemstad	guilder
New Caledonia	New Caledonian(s)	New Caledonian	Noumea	franc
New Zealand	New Zealander(s)	New Zealand	Wellington	dollar
Nicaragua	Nicaraguan(s)	Nicaraguan	Managua	cordoba
Niger	Nigerois (sing., pl.)	Niger	Niamey	franc
Nigeria	Nigerian(s)	Nigerian	Abuja	naira
Niue	Niuean(s)	Niuean	Alofi	dollar
Norfolk Island	Norfolk Islander(s)	Norfolk Island	Kingston	dollar
North Korea	North Korean(s)	North Korean	Pyongyang	won
Norway	Norwegian(s)	Norwegian	Oslo	krone

Country/ Region	Noun	Adjective	Capital	Currency
Oman	Omani(s)	Omani	Muscat	rial
Pakistan	Pakistani(s)	Pakistani	Islamabad	rupee
Panama	Panamanian(s)	Panamanian	Panama City	balboa
Papua New Guinea	Papua New Guinean(s)	Papua New Guinean	Port Moresby	kina
Paraguay	Paraguayan(s)	Paraguayan	Asuncion	guarani
Peru	Peruvian(s)	Peruvian	Lima	inti
Philippines	Filipino(s), Filipina(s)	Philippine	Manila	peso
Pitcairn Island	Pitcairn Islander(s)	Pitcairn Island	Adamstown	dollar
Poland	Pole(s)	Polish	Warsaw	zloty
Portugal	Portuguese (sing., pl.)	Portuguese	Lisbon	escudo
Puerto Rico	Puerto Rican(s)	Puerto Rican	San Juan	dollar
Qatar	Qatari(s)	Qatari	Doha	riyal
Reunion	Reunionese (sing., pl.)	Reunionese	Saint-Denis	franc
Romania	Romanian(s)	Romanian	Bucharest	leu
Russia	Russian(s)	Russian	Moscow	ruble
Rwanda	Rwandan(s)	Rwandan	Kigali	franc
St. Helena	St. Helenan(s)	St. Helenan	Jamestown	pound
St. Kitts-Nevis	Kittsian(s), Nevisian(s)	Kittsian, Nevisian	Basseterre	dollar
St. Lucia	St. Lucian(s)	St. Lucian	Castries	dollar
St-Pierre-Miquelon	St-Pierrais (sing., pl.)	St-Pierrais	St-Pierre	franc
St. Vincent, Grenadines	St. Vincentian(s), Grenadinian(s)	St. Vincentian, Grenadinian	Kingstown	dollar
Samoa	Samoan(s)	Samoan	Apia	tala
San Marino	San Marinese (sing., pl.)	San Marinese	San Marino	lira
Sao Tome, Principe	Sao Tomean(s), Principian(s)	Sao Tomean, Principian	Sao Tome	dobra
Saudi Arabia	Saudi(s)	Saudi Arabian, Saudi	Riyadh	riyal
Senegal	Senegalese (sing., pl.)	Senegalese	Dakar	franc
Seychelles	Seychellois (sing., pl.)	Seychellois	Victoria	rupee
Sierra Leone	Sierra Leonean(s)	Sierra Leonean	Freetown	leone
Sikkim	Sikkimese (sing., pl.)	Sikkimese	Gangtok	rupee
Singapore	Singaporean(s)	Singaporean	Singapore	dollar
Slovakia	Slovak(s)	Slovak	Bratislava	koruna
Slovenia	Slovene(s)	Slovenian	Ljubljana	dinar
Solomon Islands	Solomon Islander(s)	Solomon Island	Honiara	dollar
Somalia	Somali(s)	Somalian	Mogadishu	shilling

Country/ Region	Noun	Adjective	Capital	Currency
South Africa	South African(s)	South African	Pretoria❻	rand
South Korea	South Korean(s)	South Korean	Seoul	won
Spain	Spaniard(s)	Spanish	Madrid	peseta
Sri Lanka	Sri Lankan(s)	Sri Lankan	Colombo	rupee
Sudan	Sudanese (sing., pl.)	Sudanese	Khartoum	pound
Suriname	Surinamer(s)	Surinamese	Paramaribo	guilder
Swaziland	Swazi (sing., pl.)	Swazi	Mbabane	lilageni (emalan-geni, pl.)
Sweden	Swede(s)	Swedish	Stockholm	krona
Switzerland	Swiss (sing., pl.)	Swiss	Bern	franc
Syria	Syrian(s)	Syrian	Damascus	pound
Taiwan	Taiwanese (sing., pl.)	Taiwanese	Taipei	dollar
Tajikistan	Tajik(s)	Tajik	Dushanbe	ruble
Tanzania	Tanzanian(s)	Tanzanian	Dar es Salaam	shilling
Thailand	Thai(s)	Thai	Bangkok	baht
Togo	Togolese (sing., pl.)	Togolese	Lome	franc
Tokelau Islands	Tokelau Islander(s)	Tokelau Islands	Fakaofo	dollar
Tonga	Tongan(s)	Tongan	Nuku'alofa	pa'anga
Trinidad and Tobago	Trinidadian(s), Tobagan(s)	Trinidadian, Tobagan	Port-of-Spain	dollar
Tunisia	Tunisian(s)	Tunisian	Tunis	dinar
Turkey	Turk(s)	Turkish	Ankara	lira
Turkmenistan	Turkmen (sing., pl.)	Turkmen	Ashkhabad	manat
Turks and Caicos Is.	Turks/Caicos Islander(s)	Turks/Caicos Islands	Grand Turk	dollar
Tuvalu	Tuvaluan(s)	Tuvaluan	Fongafale❼	dollar
Uganda	Ugandan(s)	Ugandan	Kampala	shilling
Ukraine (not the)	Ukrainian(s)	Ukrainian	Kyiv	hryvnya
United Arab Emirates	Emirian(s)	Emirian	Abu Dhabi	dirham
United Kingdom	Briton(s)	British	London	pound
United States	American(s)	American/U.S.	Washington	dollar
Uruguay	Uruguayan(s)	Uruguayan	Montevideo	peso
Uzbekistan	Uzbek(s)	Uzbek	Tashkent	som
Vanuatu	Vanuatuan(s)	Vanuatuan	Port Vila	vatu
Vatican City		Vatican	Vatican City	lira
Venezuela	Venezuelan(s)	Venezuelan	Caracas	bolivar
Vietnam	Vietnamese (sing., pl.)	Vietnamese	Hanoi	dong
Virgin Islands (Br.)	Virgin Islander(s)	Virgin Island	Road Town	dollar

Country/ Region	Noun	Adjective	Capital	Currency
Virgin Islands (U.S.)	Virgin Islander(s)	Virgin Island	Charlotte Amalie	dollar
Western Sahara	Western Saharan(s)	Western Saharan	Laayoune	dirham
Yemen	Yemeni(s)	Yemeni	Sanaa	riyal
Yugoslavia	Yugoslav(s)	Yugoslav	Belgrade	dinar
Zambia	Zambian(s)	Zambian	Lusaka	kwacha
Zimbabwe	Zimbabwean(s)	Zimbabwean	Harare	dollar

❶ Bonn is the capital of unified Germany but legislators decided in June 1991 to return the capital to Berlin. The Bundestag, the decision-making lower house of parliament, and most of the ministries will move to Berlin by early in the next decade. The Bundesrat, or upper house, will remain in Bonn.

❷ Recognition withheld by many countries over the Palestinian question. Tel Aviv is the administrative capital.

❸ Bairiki on Tarawa Atoll.

❹ Holland may be used in casual contexts.

❺ The seat of government is The Hague.

❻ Pretoria is the executive capital, site of the president's office and of foreign embassies. The legislature sits in Cape Town.

❼ Fongafale on Funafuti Atoll.

Provincial descriptive terms

Albertan
British Columbian
Manitoban
New Brunswicker
Newfoundlander

Nova Scotian
Ontarian
Prince Edward Islander, Islander
Quebecer
Saskatchewanian (rare; prefer *a resident of Saskatchewan*)

U.S. state descriptive terms

Alabamian
Alaskan
Arizonan
Arkansan
Californian
Coloradan
Connecticuter
Delawarean
Floridian
Georgian
Hawaiian
Idahoan
Illinoisan
Indianian
Iowan
Kansan
Kentuckian

Louisianian
Mainer
Marylander
Massachusettsan
Michiganite
Minnesotan
Mississippian
Missourian
Montanan
Nebraskan
Nevadan
New Hampshirite
New Jerseyite
New Mexican
New Yorker
North Carolinian
North Dakotan

Ohioan
Oklahoman
Oregonian
Pennsylvanian
Rhode Islander
South Carolinian
South Dakotan
Tennessean
Texan
Utahn (Utahan, adj.)
Vermonter
Virginian
Washingtonian
West Virginian
Wisconsinite
Wyomingite

Placelines

General

1. Most stories carry a placeline as their first piece of information. The placeline tells a reader where most of the story took place. Whenever possible, place stories where the main event occurred. The community is written in lightface capitals and any other designation (country, province, state) is in upper and lower. On news agency copy, the agency logo and a heavy dash follow.

Avoid **here** in copy, since it may force the reader to check the placeline a second time. Do the reader a favour by repeating the name of the community at appropriate times in the story (**the mayor of Ste. Agathe, south of Winnipeg**).

2. Although the placeline normally tells the reader where the event occurred, there are exceptions. On an exclusive picked up from a newspaper, the placeline is usually the city where the paper is based, even if the event took place elsewhere. Such pickups are usually under 300 words and the fact that the exclusive is being reported is as much a part of the story as the news itself.

> WINNIPEG (CP) — The Conservatives plan a leadership convention in March, the Winnipeg Free Press said today in a report from Ottawa.

But use the placeline given by a newspaper to a story when the material is not exclusive or is readily available, and the newspaper has granted permission for it to be used.

> MONTREAL (CP) — As much as 20 per cent of Canada's 10 million tonnes of annual newsprint capacity could disappear over the next two years as producers close aging and unproductive mills.
> "It's a disaster out there," consultant Jim Rowland told the Globe and Mail in an interview.

Note: It is often necessary to obtain permission from the newspaper to pick up a story from outside the paper's Return News district. If the story is voluntarily filed to CP, that implies permission for it to be picked up.

3. A story that rounds up events or developments in several centres does not have a placeline, but instead is slugged **Roundup**.

> **AM-Budget-Rxn-Rdp, Bgt**
> code:3
> **Roundup Budget**
> **Taxpayers angered by increases**
>
>   **By Bruce Cheadle**
>   **The Canadian Press**

Note: Many member papers prefer a placeline on all stories, so use one whenever possible. The **Roundup** slug should be reserved for those stories that are true roundups, not stories with most of the elements from one centre and a couple of elements from another. In that case, placeline the story in the first centre and specify in the body of the story where the secondary material came from.

4. Other items that don't carry a placeline include stories and Quicks that don't have or need a geographic focus, and columns for sports, entertainment or other inside sections. These types of stories do not need an UNDATED slug.

AM-Video-Views
code:3
Six Christmas movies re-released

By John McKay
The Canadian Press

Use an UNDATED slug on an exceptional story from a specific community where the reporter deserves a byline, but was not in the community. This will alert editors not to put a placeline on the story if they are using the byline.

5. A byline is used on a placelined story only when the reporter has been in the community to collect information. In a story obtained by phone but carrying the placeline of the event, it is sometimes worth explaining how the information was gathered.

The masked gunman disrupted the meeting just as city council was to vote on the Sunday shopping proposal, Mayor Shirley Millson said in a phone interview.

➤ See **Bylines**, page 376.

6. Stories based on news releases in Canada reporting incidents abroad should be placelined where the release is issued.

7. Avoid contrived novelty placelines, for example: IN THE CAB OF A SEMI-TRAILER TRUCK SOMEWHERE ON HIGHWAY 97. Unconventional placelines are occasionally legitimate when copy is written and filed from that point, for example: HMCS ATHABASKAN (not ON BOARD HMCS ATHABASKAN). Ensure the approximate position of the ship is described early in the text.

8. Stories that take place on Armed Forces bases can carry the short form CFB – for example, CFB TRENTON. Or they can be placelined in a nearby civilian community – for example, HALIFAX – with an explanation in the body of the story that the event took place on an Armed Forces base.

9. Prefer placelines that would fit in one line of body type in a newspaper column. Most domestic and foreign news is reported from capitals or major cities; those listed in this chapter under Canadian, U.S. and foreign placelines require no other identification in the placeline.

10. It saves readers the trouble of guessing if stories from lesser-known placelines outside Canada and the United States name the country in the placeline or the first paragraph.

Canadian placelines

1. The community is followed by the province or territory with the exceptions of these well-known cities:

CALGARY	MONTREAL	VANCOUVER
CHARLOTTETOWN	OTTAWA	VICTORIA
EDMONTON	QUEBEC	WHITEHORSE
FREDERICTON	REGINA	WINNIPEG
HALIFAX	SASKATOON	YELLOWKNIFE
HAMILTON	TORONTO	

Note 1: WHITEHORSE and YELLOWKNIFE stand alone as placelines, but *the Northwest Territories* or *the Yukon* should be mentioned in the opening paragraph.

Note 2: QUEBEC stands alone as a placeline; use *Quebec City* in the body of a story.

Note 3: Write ST. JOHN'S, Nfld., and SAINT JOHN, N.B., to avoid confusion.

2. A short form for the new territory of Nunavut has not yet been established so the name should be written out in all placelines, including stories from its capital: IQALUIT, Nunavut.

3. Most multiple-word place names in Quebec are hyphenated: **Trois-Rivieres, Notre-Dame-de-la-Merci.** Names preceded by the definite article do not need a hyphen after the article: **La Malbaie, La Pocatiere.** Hyphens are omitted from purely English place names: **Otterburn Park, Stanstead Plain.**

➤ See **French**, page 202.

4. The former municipalities of *Scarborough, Etobicoke, York, East York* and *North York* are all part of Toronto and carry a Toronto placeline. All other Greater Toronto Area communities carry their own placelines.

The 28 municipalities on the Island of Montreal are part of the Montreal Urban Community and carry a MONTREAL placeline. Communities off the island carry their own placelines.

Vancouver does not have a regional government, so communities such as *West Vancouver* and *North Vancouver* carry their own placelines.

U.S. placelines

1. The community is followed by the state abbreviation with these exceptions:

ATLANTA	HOUSTON	OKLAHOMA CITY
BALTIMORE	INDIANAPOLIS	PHILADELPHIA
BOSTON	LAS VEGAS	PITTSBURGH
CHICAGO	LOS ANGELES	ST. LOUIS
CINCINNATI	MIAMI	SALT LAKE CITY
CLEVELAND	MILWAUKEE	SAN DIEGO
DALLAS	MINNEAPOLIS	SAN FRANCISCO
DENVER	NASHVILLE	WASHINGTON
DETROIT	NEW ORLEANS	SEATTLE
HONOLULU	NEW YORK	

➤ For state abbreviations, see **Abbreviations**, page 171.

2. Use the commonly accepted **United States**, not United States of America.

Other foreign placelines

1. The community is followed by the country in the placeline with these exceptions:

ADDIS ABABA	DUBLIN	MOSCOW
ALGIERS	EDINBURGH	MUNICH
AMSTERDAM	FRANKFURT	NAIROBI
ATHENS	GENEVA	NAPLES
AUCKLAND	GIBRALTAR	NEW DELHI
BAGHDAD	GLASGOW	PANAMA
BANGKOK	GUATEMALA CITY	PARIS
BARCELONA	HAGUE, THE	PRAGUE
BEIJING	HAMBURG	RIO DE JANEIRO
BEIRUT	HANOI	ROME
BELFAST	HAVANA	ST. PETERSBURG
BERLIN	HELSINKI	SAN SALVADOR
BOGOTA	HO CHI MINH CITY	SEOUL
BOMBAY	HONG KONG	SHANGHAI
BONN	ISTANBUL	SINGAPORE
BRASILIA	JERUSALEM	STOCKHOLM
BRUSSELS	JOHANNESBURG	TEHRAN
BUCHAREST	KUWAIT	TEL AVIV
BUDAPEST	LIMA	TOKYO
BUENOS AIRES	LISBON	TUNIS
CAIRO	LONDON	VATICAN CITY
CALCUTTA	LUXEMBOURG	VENICE
CANBERRA	MADRID	WARSAW
CAPE TOWN	MARSEILLE	WELLINGTON
CARACAS	MEXICO CITY	ZURICH
COPENHAGEN	MONACO	
DAMASCUS	MONTE CARLO	

Note: Write HAMILTON, Bermuda and SYDNEY, Australia to avoid confusion with the Canadian cities. MONTE CARLO is used for racing stories; MONACO for all others.

2. Use the commonly accepted short version of a country's or region's name.

Argentina, not Republic of Argentina
Bahamas, not Commonwealth of the Bahamas
China, not People's Republic of China
Congo, not People's Republic of Congo (formerly Zaire)
Congo-Brazzaville, not Republic of Congo
Hong Kong, not Special Administrative Region of Hong Kong
Kuwait, not State of Kuwait
Sikkim, not Kingdom of Sikkim
Taiwan, not Republic of China

3. Do not use *The* with the name of a country in placelines.

Bahamas	Gambia	Philippines
Congo	Netherlands	Ukraine

Note: Do use El Salvador.

4. Use UNITED NATIONS alone in placelines.

Place names

General

1. The style authority for Canadian place names is the *Canadian Oxford Dictionary*, with some exceptions. Those exceptions are listed in *Caps and Spelling*. If the place name is not in Oxford, editors should turn to the Secretariat of the Canadian Permanent Committee on Geographical Names (http://geonames.nrcan.gc.ca/). So check Caps first, then Oxford, then the Web site.

2. In Quebec place names, retain hyphens and shorten *saint* and *sainte* to *St* and *Ste* (no periods): **Ste-Anne-des-Monts.** When technically possible, retain accents except in the case of **Montreal** and **Quebec**, which have long-standing English versions of their names. Do not hyphenate English place names in Quebec: **East Broughton, Otterburn Park.**

➤ See **French**, page 202.

3. *The National Geographic Atlas of the World* is CP's authority for place names outside Canada with exceptions listed below.

4. The umlaut in German names is indicated by placing the letter *e* after the vowel affected. *Düsseldorf* becomes *Duesseldorf*.

5. Use the Ukrainian, not the Russian, transliteration for Ukrainian place names. This means it is **Kyiv** (not Kiev) and **Chornobyl** (not Chernobyl). Other Ukrainian transliterations: **Kharkiv, Lviv, Odesa** (cities); **Crimea** (southern region of Ukraine); and **Carpathy** and **Zacarpatia** (mountains).

Exceptions

The following are exceptions to National Geographic Society spellings:

Algiers	Corinth	Lisbon
Antwerp	Damascus	Lucerne
Archangel	Dardanelles	Marcus Island
Athens	Devil's Island	Milan
Bangkok	Doha, Qatar	Moscow
Belgrade	Dubai	Mukden
Benares	Dunkirk	Munich
Blue Nile River	Florence	Nansei Island
Brest Litovsk	Geneva	Naples
Brunswick	Genoa	New Siberian Islands
Brussels	Hague, The	North Cape
Bucharest	Hamelin	Nuremberg
Canton	Havana	Olympus
Coblenz	Hook of Holland	Ostend
Cologne	Ithaca	Padua
Copenhagen	Kingstown (Ireland)	Pescadores Island
Corfu	Lions, Gulf of	Port Arthur

Prague
Rhodes
Rome
Sinai, Mount
Sofia
Sparta
Tadzhikistan
Taipei

Tiber River
Tibet
Tiflis
Turin
Tyre
Venice
Vesuvius, Mount

Vienna
Vistula (Wislo)
Warsaw
Wenchow
White Sea
Wrangel Island
Zuider Zee

Regions

1. In the broadest sense, *America* refers to North and South America, and *American* to any resident of the continents. But the narrower meanings of the words — the United States and its citizens — are acceptable in informal and unambiguous contexts.

2. **North America**: Canada, the United States, Mexico, Greenland, Central America, the tiny French islands of St-Pierre-Miquelon and, in broad contexts, the islands of the Caribbean.

Central America: Belize, Costa Rica, El Salvador, Guatemala, Honduras, Nicaragua and Panama.

3. **South America**: Argentina, Bolivia, Brazil, Chile, Colombia, Ecuador, Paraguay, Peru, Uruguay, Venezuela, plus French Guiana, Guyana and Suriname on the northeastern coast which regard themselves as Caribbean countries.

4. **Latin America**: the parts of Central and South America where Spanish or Portuguese is the dominant language. Most countries south of the United States are included. Exceptions are French Guiana, Suriname and areas with a British background: the Bahamas, Barbados, Belize, Grenada, Guyana, Jamaica, Trinidad and Tobago and the smaller islands in the West Indies.

5. **British Isles**: Britain and all Ireland and the islands near their coasts.

United Kingdom: England, Scotland, Wales and Northern Ireland.

Britain: England, Scotland and Wales, but *British* encompasses the United Kingdom.

Ireland: The island is divided into Northern Ireland (part of the United Kingdom) and the independent republic of Ireland.

6. **Middle East** or, less desirably, **Mideast**: usually taken to include Afghanistan, Bahrain, Egypt, Iran, Iraq, Israel, Jordan, Kuwait, Lebanon, Oman, Qatar, Sudan, Saudi Arabia, Syria, Turkey, the United Arab Emirates and Yemen. Do not use *Near East*.

7. **Far East**: China, Japan, North and South Korea, Taiwan and the eastern Soviet Union. **Note:** Hong Kong and Macau are now part of China.

8. **Southeast Asia**: Cambodia, Indonesia, Laos, Malaysia, Myanmar, New Guinea, the Philippines, Singapore, Thailand and Vietnam.

People and places

1.   Shorten *Great Britain* to *Britain* in news stories. Write *Briton*, not *Britisher*.

2.   Refer to the British capital, both in placelines and the body of a story, simply as *London*. Use *London, England,* only if ambiguity would otherwise result; for example, if two Londons appear in the same story.

3.   For the people, prefer *Scot, Scots(wo)man,* not *Scotch(wo)man.* Use *Scottish* as the usual adjective, meaning pertaining to Scotland: **Scottish Highlands, Scottish thrift.** Use *Scotch* of food, drink, plants, animals and things originating in Scotland: **Scotch broth, Scotch tweed, Scotch thistle, Scotch terrier.** But **scotch** (whisky).

4.   Where necessary, specify *the republic of Ireland* or *Northern Ireland.*

5.   *Ulster* is acceptable as an informal name for Northern Ireland, though the original Ulster comprised the present Northern Ireland and the counties of Cavan, Donegal and Monaghan, now part of the republic of Ireland.

6.   *Eire* is the former name of the republic of Ireland.

7.   Israel declared Jerusalem its capital in 1950 despite Arab protest. Many countries, including Canada, do not recognize it as such. They maintain their ambassadors in Tel Aviv, which may be referred to as the administrative capital.

➤   See **Placelines**, page 275; **People, places**, page 267.

Technical terms

General

1. Avoid unfamiliar scientific, medical and technical terms. When they must be used, give a simple, accurate explanation.

She acted oddly because she had Tourette's syndrome, a nervous disorder characterized by involuntary movements and vocal sounds.

2. Explain the unfamiliar in terms of the familiar.

A centrifuge acts like a cake mixer or merry-go-round, forcing objects outward from the centre.

Keratin is the main protein in fingernails, tiger claws, alligator scales, rhinoceros horns and feather quills.

3. Technical language can be less intimidating if the explanation is given first.

The medical team said a study of the mammoths' white blood cells, called leucocytes, shows them to be perfectly preserved.

4. An everyday term is generally preferable to a scientific one. For example, use **evergreen** instead of **coniferous**, **marijuana** instead of **cannabis**.

Scientific names

1. The name of a family or genus is capitalized: **Branta**. Use lower case for the species, even when derived from a proper name like Canada: **Branta canadensis** (Canada goose).

2. The genus may be shortened on second reference:

Brucella abortus (aborts cows, causes undulant fever in people)	Br. abortus
Escherichia coli (intestinal bacterium)	E. coli
Staphylococcus aureus (causes boils)	S. aureus

Drugs

1. In general, refer to a drug by its generic name, not its brand name: **a tranquillizer, diazepam; a pain reliever, ASA**.

2. If an unfamiliar brand name has to be used, follow it with the generic name and a description: **Antabuse, a brand of disulfiram used to discourage the drinking of alcohol**.

When allied news agencies use the term **aspirin**, change it to **ASA** in most cases. In Canada, Aspirin is a trademark and it must be capitalized.

➤ See **Capitalization**, page 199; **Trade names**, page 294; **Business terms**, page 45.

Medical

1. Prefer a common term to a medical one:

bleed to hemorrhage	chickenpox to varicella
broke to fractured	whooping cough to pertussis
clot to embolism	German measles to rubella
indigestion to dyspepsia	bad breath to halitosis
cut to laceration	scarlet fever to scarlatina
scrape to abrasion	shingles to herpes zoster
injury to lesion	stitch to suture

2. In general, don't capitalize diseases, conditions, symptoms, tests and treatments:

legionnaires' disease, scarlet fever, infarction, barium X-ray, cobalt therapy.

But capitalize proper names that are part of the term:

Alzheimer's disease, German measles, Parkinson's disease, Down's syndrome, Lassa fever, Pap smear, Heimlich manoeuvre.

3. Unless there's a compelling reason to give the precise cause of death, it's usually enough to say a person died, say, of **a stroke, a heart attack** or **in childbirth**, rather than of **cerebral hemorrhage, coronary thrombosis** or **puerperal fever**.

4. Similarly, say **Gruber sprained his right thumb**, instead of **Stress X-rays taken on Gruber, under local anesthetic, showed a tear of the ulnar collateral ligament of the metacarpal-phalangeal joint of the right thumb.**

5. Widespread interest justifies giving more details in reporting the illness or death of a prime minister, president, pope, movie star or other major figure.

➤ See **Obituaries**, page 68.

Condition

1. Descriptions used by hospitals to report a patient's condition are often vague. It helps if a story explains that a patient is **conscious, allowed to sit up** or **receive visitors, is being fed intravenously,** and so on.

2. Here are four common descriptions of conditions, with the meanings some hospitals attach to them:

Good: The pulse, breathing and other vital signs are normal and stable. The patient is comfortable and conscious, and the outlook for recovery is good.

Fair: The pulse, breathing and other vital signs are near normal and the patient is conscious, but he or she is uncomfortable or may have minor complications. The outlook for recovery is favourable.

Serious: The patient is acutely ill and the chance of recovery is uncertain. The pulse, breathing and other vital signs may be abnormal or unstable.

Critical: Death may be imminent. The pulse, breathing and other vital signs are abnormal and unstable and there are major complications.

Burns

There are four degrees of burns, but most hospitals refer to only three: *first, second* and *third* — the third being the most severe.

First degree means the skin is red; *second*, it's blistering; *third*, skin has been destroyed along with underlying tissue and won't heal without grafting.

In a *fourth*-degree burn, muscle and bone have also been damaged.

Hospitals may also refer to partial and full burns. Ask specifically about the extent of tissue damage and the need for skin grafts and other measures.

AIDS

Acquired immune deficiency syndrome (or acquired immunodeficiency syndrome) is a breakdown of a person's immunological system, the body's natural defences against disease.

Someone is said to have AIDS if a life-threatening infection or cancer results from failure of the defence system.

It's inaccurate to say someone has died of AIDS. Give the actual cause of death — pneumonia, perhaps — and add that it was complicated by AIDS or was AIDS-related.

AIDS is believed to be spread through the exchange of blood, semen and vaginal secretions in the following ways: through sexual activity; use of HIV-infected syringes; transfusion of HIV-infected blood; and from an infected mother to her fetus.

AIDS was first diagnosed in the early 1980s and most of the early victims were homosexual males. The disease has since spread among male and female heterosexuals, intravenous drug users and hemophiliacs who received tainted blood before a proper screening system for donations was set up.

Although much research is still being conducted into the onset of AIDS, researchers generally agree that HIV, the human immunodeficiency virus, must be present. Therefore, it is permissible to say that **HIV causes AIDS**.

Remember, however, that HIV can cause several infections or diseases, not just AIDS. In some contexts, it may be better to use the more inclusive **HIV**, rather than **the AIDS virus**.

The onset of AIDS has understandably led to a public tolerance of much greater frankness in discussing risky sexual behaviour. CP stories must not shy away from plain language, where warranted, to inform readers.

➤ See **Obituaries**, page 68; **Disabilities**, page 20.

Richter scale

The Richter scale is an open-ended gauge of ground motion recorded on a seismograph during an earthquake. Every increase of one number means that the ground motion is 10 times greater.

However, science has refined the art of comparing earthquakes since 1935 when Charles Richter helped develop a scale that measured quakes in southern California. Modern seismology equipment is more sensitive and can measure a wider range of quakes than the original Richter scale, although newer scales have been designed to meld with Richter's model. Don't automatically use the phrase **on the Richter scale** when writing about earthquake magnitudes. General references, such as **a quake of 5.2 magnitude**, are usually sufficient.

A quake with a magnitude of 2 is the smallest normally felt by humans. One of magnitude 4 can cause moderate damage in a populated area, one of 5 considerable damage, one of 6 severe damage, and one of 7 widespread heavy damage. A quake of magnitude 8, a "great" earthquake, is capable of tremendous damage.

Time

Introduction

The Canadian Press divides its day into two news cycles.

The **PMs** cycle runs from 2 a.m. to 2 p.m. for papers that publish in the afternoon-evening. Copy carries a **PM** slug.

The **AMs** cycle runs from 2 p.m. to 2 a.m. for morning papers. Copy carries an **AM** slug.

The goal is to provide fresh stories for papers in each cycle.

Sometimes copy will carry a **BC (both cycles)** slug to identify stories that might straddle the cycles or that stand up in either cycle.

What day is it?

1. In copy for afternoon papers, write **today** to mean the current day. A lead sent after 2 p.m. for PMs papers will sometimes still say **today** for the current day.

2. In copy for morning papers, write **today** and **tonight** to mean the date of publication. If it's very early in the cycle (say 3 p.m.) consider a note to editors to clarify: **EDs: Today in para 2 is Thursday.**

3. CP doesn't use **yesterday** or **tomorrow**. To avoid confusion, the day is named.

4. Name the day if it falls within seven days of the current date: **on Tuesday** or **next Sunday** or **last Friday.**

5. For more distant dates, use the date: **May 5**.

6. For significant events and in sports schedules, give the day and the date: **The budget will be presented Friday, Nov. 4**; or **Dec. 22 (Sat.) Edmonton at Calgary.**

7. Place the day in a sentence where it would fall normally in conversation: not **The premier Thursday announced** but **The premier announced Thursday.**

8. Use **on** when it helps readability or to break up a series of capitalized words:

The measure passed in the House of Commons on Monday. The Quebec Nordiques defeated the Vancouver Canucks on Friday.

9. Don't wrench a lead out of shape trying for a weak or phoney **today** angle. Bury the time element if necessary, and get the news in the lead.

10. For afternoon-evening papers, especially, avoid putting an obsolescent angle in a lead: **The vote was expected today**. The event will have occurred by the time the newspaper is read. Instead, concentrate on getting the latest information in the lead and bury the time element so it can be dumped if necessary. Get a new lead out as soon as possible after events overtake the story.

11. Don't write that an event has taken place if the story is written beforehand in anticipation of the event.

➤ See **Advances,** page 372.

What time is it?

1. The exact time of an event is usually unnecessary. Instead, give the reader a sense of the time by describing the scene.

Not: A spectacular collision between two commuter trains occurred at 9 a.m. today.

But: A spectacular collision between two commuter trains caused chaos in downtown Montreal during the morning rush hour.

2. But give a specific time for important announcements, key votes, space launches, ransom deadlines or other events in which the time is a vital component. Give the time in the placelined community, with the equivalent in eastern time in brackets if necessary: **The volcano erupted at 8 a.m. local time (4 p.m. EDT).**

3. Specify the time zone in undated stories.

4. Specify time zones in stories involving the time of live radio and TV programs broadcast nationally. In cases of recorded or delayed broadcasts, provide the eastern time. Each newspaper can provide information on local broadcasts if need be.

5. Time is written in figures. However, write **noon** or **midnight**, not **12 noon** or **12 midnight.**

6. Write **5 a.m.,** not **5:00 a.m.**

7. A colon separates hours, minutes and seconds when figures are used. A period separates seconds from tenths of seconds: **7:32 p.m.** or **Her time was 3:45:20.6.** When written out it would be: **Her time was three hours 45 minutes 20.6 seconds.**

What zone is it?

1. Use abbreviations for time zones with a clock reading: **11 a.m. MST** or **midnight Sunday night PST.** Spell out time zones when they are not accompanied by a clock reading: **Newfoundland daylight time.**

2. Capitalize Newfoundland, Atlantic and Pacific time zones when spelled out. Other time zones — eastern, mountain and central — are lowercase: **Atlantic daylight time,** but **eastern standard time.**

3. Write **daylight time**, not **daylight saving time**.

4. Greenwich mean time is five hours ahead of eastern standard time and four hours ahead of eastern daylight time. From April through October, when Britain is on **summer time** — their equivalent of **daylight time** — London is one hour ahead of GMT.

➤ See **Abbreviations and acronyms,** page 169.

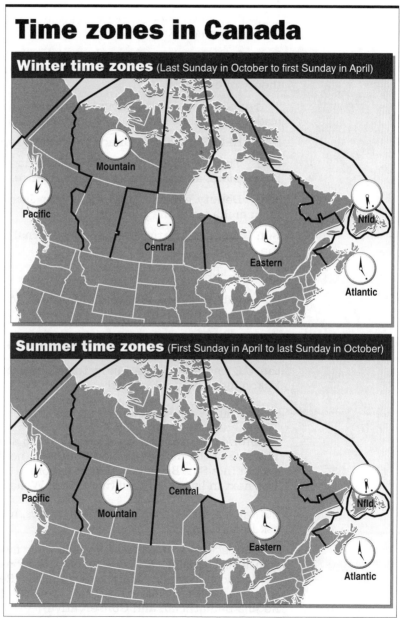

Time zones in Canada

Winter time zones (Last Sunday in October to first Sunday in April)

Mountain

Pacific

Central

Eastern

Nfld.

Atlantic

Summer time zones (First Sunday in April to last Sunday in October)

Pacific

Mountain

Central

Eastern

Nfld.

Atlantic

Source: National Research Council Canada   Sean Vokey **- CP**

Titles

General

1. For rules on capitalization of titles, ➤ see **Capitalization**, page 197.

2. With few exceptions, a person's given name is used with surname on first reference.

Note: Famous authors, composers and the like may be referred to by surname only: **Dickens's Bleak House, Beethoven's Fifth, Darwin's theory of evolution.**

3. Front-loading — piling nouns in front of a name — is hard on the reader. Instead, use *of*, *the* and *a*, and set off long titles with commas.

Not: RPM Records of Canada president Gerry Lacoursiere . . .

But: The president of RPM Records of Canada, Gerry Lacoursiere, attended the news conference.

Not: Deputy external affairs minister Jacques Martin was the main architect of the program.

But: Jacques Martin, the deputy external affairs minister, was the main architect of the program.

4. False titles are best avoided.

U.S. modern dance innovator Margaret Mason, retired Yukon judge Roger Kimmerly

A phrase in apposition, preceded by *the*, is proper English.

the U.S. modern dance innovator Margaret Mason, the retired Yukon judge Roger Kimmerly

5. Use titles on first reference but seldom after that.

Ambrozic (not Archbishop Ambrozic) also attended the mass. The size of the deficit startled Bourassa (not Premier Bourassa). Berger (not Sgt. Berger) was first ashore. The next in line is William (not Prince William).

But when a story is long or filled with names, repeat a title rather than risk losing a reader.

6. Use such titles as **Dr.** and **Rev.** only when those named are dealing with their speciality. A doctor in the Commons speaking about the environment is simply **Martha Singer, the Regina Conservative.** Speaking about medicare, she becomes **Dr. Martha Singer, the Regina pediatrician and Conservative.**

7. Use **chairman** or **chairwoman, spokesman** or **spokeswoman** as appropriate. **Chairperson** and **spokesperson** are increasingly in use, and can be used if the sex of the person is not known. But use substitutes for awkward constructions (**councillor** instead of **alderperson**) whenever possible.

Courtesy titles

1. In general, do not use the courtesy titles **Mr., Mrs., Miss** or **Ms.**

Justice (not **Mr. Justice**) **John Sopinka wrote the ruling. Murray said she enjoys singing. Campbell said abortion should be illegal.**

When it is necessary to use **Mrs., Miss** or **Ms.**, follow the woman's preference.

2. When possible, refer to a couple on first reference by their first names and their common last name: **William and Jane Levinski.** If their relationship is not that of husband and wife, explain: **Wayne Gretzky and his sister, Kim.**

3. When married people do not use a common surname, an explanation is needed.

Joanne Woodward and her husband, Paul Newman

4. To distinguish between persons of the same last name on second reference, repeat first names.

Professional titles

1. In general, use **Dr.** for licensed health care professionals. Where pertinent specify.

Dr. John Lucyk; Lucyk, an orthodontist. Dr. Sonya Chong; Chong, a chiropractor. Dr. Bert Clifford; Clifford, a veterinarian

Note: Each province decides which of its health care practitioners may use **Dr.** If in doubt, check.

2. Do not use **Dr.** for people with doctorates outside the health-care field. If pertinent, say a person has an earned or an honorary degree and give the discipline.

Lynch, a doctor of divinity. Callaghan received an honorary doctorate of letters from the University of Moncton

Religious titles

1. Use a religious title before a person's name on first reference. Subsequently use either the surname alone (in most instances), the title preceded by *the*, or a general description.

Archbishop Adam Exner; Exner, the archbishop. Rabbi David Silverstein; Silverstein, the rabbi. Rev. Keith Wallace; Wallace, the priest

Note: Write **Rev.**, not **the Rev.** Never write **Rev. Wallace**.

2. All popes and some Eastern Orthodox archbishops and bishops, as well as some Roman Catholic and Anglican nuns and brothers, are known by a title and given name only. In such instances, the title is usually retained in subsequent use of the name.

Pope John Paul, Metropolitan Andrew, Archbishop Volodymyr, Mother Mary, Sister Agatha, Brother Jude

Note: The convention of referring to **Pope John Paul** in subsequent references as **John Paul** is acceptable.

3. The name of the office (**Bishop, Canon, Deacon**, etc.) is preferred as the title before the name: **Archbishop T.D. Somerville.** But such forms as **Most Rev. T.D. Somerville, Archbishop of New Westminster, B.C.**, are acceptable on occasion.

4. Write **John Cardinal Brown**, not **Cardinal John Brown**.

5. Some of the more common identifying titles that apply to various levels of Christian religious office include:

Roman Catholic:
The Pope - **His Holiness**
Cardinal - **His Eminence**
Archbishop - **Most Rev.**
Bishop - **Most Rev.**
Monsignor - **Right Rev.** (but usually **Msgr.**)

Anglican:
Primate - **Most Rev.**
Archbishop - **Most Rev.**
Bishop - **Right Rev.**
Dean - **Very Rev.**
Canon - **Rev.** (**Rev. Terry Scott** or **Canon Scott**)

United Church:
Moderator - **Right Rev.**
Ex-moderator - **Very Rev.**

Presbyterian:
Moderator - **Rev.**

6. Some religions lack a formal hierarchy, with leaders chosen by the congregation or community. In such cases use descriptive terms such as **holy man** or **priest**, as in **Hindu priest Sharad Rao** or **Sikh priest Satinder Singh**.

7. Forms of address familiar to the clergy but not to others should be avoided except when in direct quotation:

His Holiness, His Eminence, His Grace, Lord Bishop, His Lordship, His Excellency

8. Unfamiliar titles should be explained.

Primate Michael Peers, the head of the Anglican Church of Canada; Imam Mohammad Nasim, minister of the Jami Mosque; Kazi Mohammad Abdul, a Muslim religious judge.

9. **Rev.** precedes the full name of most ministers and priests, including Buddhists. It is not used by Christian Scientists, Mormons, Jehovah's Witnesses or Seventh-day Adventists, among others. Muslims use the title **Imam** for leaders of their mosques.

Note: Do not use **Rev.** as a noun meaning clergyman: **The reverend reads murder mysteries**.

10. Unless it is immediately obvious from the context, do not use **Catholic Church** on first mention for the **Roman Catholic Church**. Several other communions maintain the Catholic tradition in varying degrees while rejecting papal infallibility and other dogmas. These include Eastern Orthodox, Anglican, Old Catholic, Polish National Catholic, Lusitanian (Portugal), Spanish Reformed Episcopal and Philippine Independent Catholic.

Honourable, Lady, Lord

1. The honorary titles **right honourable** and **honourable** are used only when they appear in direct quotation.

2. **Right Hon.** applies for life to the Governor General, prime minister, chief justice of Canada, and members of the British Privy Council.

3. **Hon.** is applied for life to members of the Canadian Privy Council and lieutenant-governors. With royal assent, it may be used **for life** by retired judges of superior courts and some others. It is applied **during office** to senators, Speakers of the Commons and legislatures, judges of the Supreme and Federal courts of Canada and corresponding courts in the provinces, and members of provincial cabinets. Also applied to most peers' children.

4. **Lady**, as in **Lady Anne** or **Lady Jane**, is applied only to the daughters of dukes, marquesses and earls. Wives of baronets or knights are simply **Lady Simpson**. Life peeresses select a title. The wife of the British wartime prime minister became **Baroness Spencer-Churchill of Chartwell**, addressed as **Lady Spencer-Churchill**.

5. **Lord** is a conventional term for any nobleman from baron to marquess (whose wife is marchioness). Life peers are barons; but some baronies are hereditary.

Trade names

1. Capitalize trademarks: names (and symbols) used by organizations and protected by law.

Frigidaire, Hostess potato chips, Baggies

Note: Brand name is a non-legal term for **trademark** or **service mark**.

2. Variety names and names of market grades are capitalized.

Golden Delicious apples, Choice lamb

3. Common-noun elements of trademarks are generally lowercased.

Pears soap, Harris tweed, White Owl cigars, Spancore spandex yarn, Spic and Span cleaner

4. In general, follow an organization's capitalization. But for readability, capitalize all-lowercase names.

TelePrompTer, SkyDome, Toys "R" Us, Adidas (not adidas) sportswear, the American movie Sex, Lies and Videotape (not sex, lies and videotape)

5. For all-caps promotional names, capitalize only the first letters.

Scrabble (not SCRABBLE), Via Rail (not VIA Rail), Oxfam (not OXFAM)

6. The use of a trademark is easily avoided by substituting a general term.

soft drink/pop for Coke, adhesive bandage for Band-Aid, flying disc for Frisbee

7. Use a brand name when it gives point, colour or impact to a story.

She wore an Yves Saint Laurent gown that had seen better days.

The children were playing a board game using Smarties as counters.

The robbers escaped in a red Cadillac convertible.

➤ See **Capitalization**, page 199.

8. **Aspirin** is a trademark in Canada. Generic alternatives include acetylsalicylic acid, ASA pills and a painkiller.

9. Trademarks not guarded by their owners from being used as generics may lose the protection of the law.

cellophane	kerosene	raisin bran
corn flakes	lanolin	shredded wheat
cube steak	linoleum	trampoline
dry ice	milk of magnesia	yo-yo
escalator	nylon	

10. Sources of information about trademarks include the *Canadian Trade Index* and reference books on drugs. Do not follow the capitalization in the *Canadian Oxford Dictionary*.

11. Here are trademarks often encountered in news stories, with generic alternatives.

Baggies plastic bags
Band-Aid adhesive bandage
Benzedrine pep pill
Bic ballpoint pen
Brillo soap pads
Caterpillar tractor
Celanese acetate, nylon
    polyester, rayon
Chiclets chewing gum
Coca-Cola, Coke cola drink
Cream of Wheat cereal
Crisco shortening
Dacron polyester fibre
Dictaphone dictating machine
Diet Coke, Diet Pepsi low-
    calorie soft drink
Dramamine travel-sickness
    medicine
Fiberglas glass fibre, fibreglass
Fig Newton cookies
Formica laminated plastic
Frigidaire appliances
Frisbee flying disc
Fritos corn chips
Fudgsicle ice cream on a stick
Hamburger Helper dinner
Hawaiian Punch fruit drink
Hush Puppies casual shoes
Jacuzzi whirlpool tub
Javex bleach
Jeep vehicles, but **jeep** for the
    military vehicle
Jell-O gelatin dessert
Kleenex tissues
Laundromat laundry
Levi's jeans

Lycra spandex fibre
Lysol disinfectant
Mace tear gas
Masonite hardboard
Minute rice rice
Mixmaster food mixer
Muzak background music
Novocain anesthetic, but
    novocaine
Orange Crush soft drink
Orlon acrylic fibre
Pablum baby cereal, but
    pabulum
Pampers disposable diapers
Pepsi-Cola, Pepsi cola drink
Plexiglas acrylic plastic
Polaroid camera, sunglasses
Popsicle flavoured ice on a stick
Pyrex oven glassware
Q-Tips cotton swabs
Realtor (a member of the
    National Association of
    Realtors, prefer **real estate
    agent**)
Scotch tape adhesive tape
Seven-Up or **7Up** soft drink
Stetson hat
Styrofoam plastic foam
Tabasco pepper sauce
Technicolor coloured movies
Teflon non-stick coating
TelePrompTer cueing device
Terramycin antibiotic
Touch-Tone push-button
    dialling
TV Dinner frozen dinner

Valium tranquillizer
Vaseline petroleum jelly
Velcro tape fasteners

Walkman headset stereo
Xerox photocopier

Weather

Introduction

Weather affects everyone. It's almost impossible to write too much about the weather. But write about it in human terms.

The heavy snowfall that is commonplace in northern Ontario during the winter months — closing schools, stranding motorists, generally disrupting life — is news to Vancouver residents basking in 20 degree C sunshine. It is certainly news to anyone planning to travel through the region.

Endless rainfall on the Prairies while farmers are trying to bring in their fall harvest not only causes the farmers major concern but affects the commodity markets as well.

Write about weather in terms of its effects on people. Numbers help but prefer descriptions: **ankle-deep puddles, knee-deep snow, winds turning umbrellas inside out and bending small trees, a downpour causing wading pools to overflow and soaking through clothing.**

Weather knows no boundaries. A storm in Halifax affects those in Truro to the northeast and fishermen off the Atlantic coast. Did the storm originate in Maine and sweep through New Brunswick? Are Prince Edward Island and Newfoundland in the storm's path?

Add Canadian content to any story about weather problems in the northern United States.

Where warranted, use comparisons of other recent storms or those that caused major damage.

Consider a regional weather roundup to provide a proper perspective of what the weather pattern has done.

National weather stories should be considered whenever there is a thread to tie everything together.

Weather in metric

Temperatures are expressed in degrees Celsius, with **0 C** the freezing point of water and **100 C** the boiling point. Do not use **below zero**; use **–5 C** (minus five degrees C). **Degrees C** is commonplace; it is not necessary to write out Celsius each time.

For everyday comparison: **30 C** is swimming weather, **20 C** room temperature, **–10 C** skating weather.

Wind speed is measured in kilometres an hour: **light**, up to 20 km/h; **moderate**, 21-40 km/h; **strong**, 41-60 km/h; **gale**, 61-90 km/h; **whole gale**, 91-116 km/h; **hurricane**, over 117 km/h.

Rainfall is given in millimetres and **snowfall** in centimetres. A centimetre of snow equals a millimetre of rain.

Light shower   2.5 mm/h rainfall.

Heavy downpour   25 mm/h rainfall.

Good base for skiing 100 cm of snow

Atmospheric (barometric) pressure is measured in kilopascals. Normal pressure ranges from 98 to 103 kPa.

Terminology

Following are terms that may appear in weather forecasts from Environment Canada. Temperatures are Celsius.

acid rain: Rain mixed with sulphur dioxide, nitrogen oxide and other industrial and automobile pollutants to form acids, at times as strong as lemon juice or vinegar.

air mass: A large body of air with uniform temperature and moisture in a horizontal plane. The transition zone between different air masses is called a **front**. In a **cold front**, cold air is replacing warm; in a **warm front**, warm air is replacing cold.

atmospheric (or **barometric**) **pressure:** The pressure exerted by the atmosphere as a result of gravity. A rapidly falling barometer generally heralds a storm; when the barometer is rising, fair weather can usually be expected.

blizzard: A fierce storm with winds of more than 40 kilometres an hour, temperatures of less than –10, visibility less than half a kilometre.

chinook: A warm, dry wind which mainly affects the foothills of the Rockies. Can raise temperatures 20 degrees within minutes.

cyclone: A wind system rotating counterclockwise around a calm central area. In North America the term is sometimes used for a tornado or storm, in the Indian Ocean region for a hurricane.

flash flood: A sudden flood caused by heavy rain or the rapid melting of snow. A **flood crest** is the highest level reached before the water recedes.

freezing rain, freezing drizzle, ice storm: Rain or drizzle that freezes on impact with objects.

gale warning: Issued when winds are expected to be 34 to 48 knots (about 63 to 89 km/h) over water.

heavy snow: The definition varies from region to region. Heavy snow in Vancouver may be five centimetres, in Montreal 15.

high: An area of high pressure with winds moving clockwise, which often brings fine weather. Used interchangeably with anticyclone (a term not widely understood, however).

humidex: An index that combines the effects of summer temperatures and humidities:

Humidex	Degree of comfort
20-29	Comfortable
30-39	Varying degrees of discomfort
40-45	Most people uncomfortable
46 and over	Some outdoor work must be restricted

humidity, relative: The amount of water vapour in the air expressed as a percentage of the maximum amount the air can hold at that temperature and pressure.

hurricane or **typhoon:** A tropical storm with wind speeds of over 117 kilometres an hour. The hurricane eye is the relatively calm centre. Hurricanes develop east of the international date line. Typhoons develop west of the line; in the Indian Ocean they are called cyclones.

inversion: Instead of decreasing with height as is normal, the temperature remains constant or increases.

knot: A unit of speed: one nautical mile (6,080 feet) an hour is about 1.85 km/h.

low: An area of low atmospheric pressure that has an air circulation counter-clockwise in the Northern Hemisphere.

marine warning: Alerts mariners and shoreline residents of dangerous winds or freezing spray.

nearshore waters, coastal waters: Within five to 10 kilometres of shore.

offshore waters: Up to 400 kilometres from shore.

probability of precipitation: The chance of rain, snow and so on for a specified period, expressed in increments of 10 per cent, from zero (none expected) to 100 (a certainty).

ridge: An elongated area of relatively high pressure extending from the centre of a high-pressure region.

severe thunderstorm: Damaging winds usually with gusts to more than 60-80 kilometres an hour, heavy rain and possibly hailstones, frequent lightning and occasionally a tornado.

small craft warning: A warning issued for pleasure boaters when winds are expected to maintain speeds of 20-35 knots (37-63 km/h).

snow pellets: Tiny balls of snow that rebound on striking hard ground.

thundershower: Rain lasting 10-15 minutes, associated with a thunderstorm.

tornado: A destructive rotating column of air with a funnel shape touching the ground and accompanied by a loud roar. Sometimes called a twister.

tropical storm: A weather system one step below a hurricane; winds from 62 to 117 km/h.

trough: An elongated area of relatively low pressure extending from the centre of a low-pressure region.

typhoon: ➤ See **hurricane**.

UV index: A measure of the intensity of ultraviolet rays. The index ranges from 9.0 or higher, which is considered extreme (takes less than 15 minutes to get sunburn), to less than 4.0 (takes an hour or more).

weather advisory: Alerts the public that weather conditions, though not dangerous, may cause general inconvenience.

weather warning: Alerts the public to conditions that may endanger life, property and the public welfare.

whiteout: Dense blizzard and total obscurity of physical features. Commonest in the Arctic and on the Prairies.

wind chill factor: An index of the effects of wind velocity and low temperature.

Factor	Degree of discomfort
700	Comfortable when dressed for skiing
1200	Conditions unpleasant on overcast days
1400	Conditions unpleasant on sunny days
1600	Exposed skin may freeze depending on the degree of activity and amount of sunshine
2300	Outdoor travel such as walking is dangerous; the exposed face may freeze in less than a minute
2700	Exposed flesh freezes within half a minute

Note: While Environment Canada uses a factor expressed in watts per square metre, especially in Western Canada, the wind chill factor is often expressed using a temperature equivalency.

wind direction: The direction from which the wind blows: an east wind blows toward the west.

wind shear: A swirling current of air produced at the junction of two horizontal air streams of greatly differing speed or direction. A possible hazard to aircraft landing or taking off.

Access to information

The federal government and all provinces but one currently have laws that give Canadian citizens, corporations and others the right to acquire government-controlled information. Prince Edward Island is the exception.

The federal law, in effect since 1983, is called the Access to Information Act. Provinces generally use the phrase "freedom of information" in their statutes. The laws are intended to foster open, transparent government and are used primarily by businesses and individual citizens.

Freedom of information laws can be effective tools for journalists seeking the story behind the headlines. The process can also be lengthy and frustrating, depending on the jurisdiction and the nature of the request.

Delays are common. Media-related requests for sensitive material normally take far longer than the 30-day deadline imposed by the federal law, for example, which also gives departments the right to claim time extensions. Even so, dated material can shed new light on key issues and developments and provide an opportunity to revisit important stories. Other information on issues never before in the public arena can still play as news, even though the audit, report or study may be months or years old. Typically, the released material has the added attraction of being exclusive to a reporter or newsroom.

Freedom of information requests are a supplement to, not a substitute for, informal requests for government information. A formal request has the advantage of clear rules and, in most cases, a system of appeals. But a reporter working a source effectively can often get more timely information. Consider using both approaches simultaneously when chasing a story.

The laws are generally inexpensive to use, despite horror stories about million-dollar fees for searching and photocopying. Most jurisdictions charge a fee for making an application, $5 under the federal law. A certain amount of free search time and photocopying is usually available, but costs can rise steeply after these thresholds are crossed.

Some tips

- A well-focused request can avoid additional charges. Limit the time period covered; exclude newspaper clippings; ask for executive summaries only; break down large requests into smaller individual requests; ask for title pages or lists of documents, then file second requests for specific documents. Photocopy charges can be avoided by asking to view the records in a local office of the government department.

- Some categories of records are relatively fruitful sources of information: briefing notes, audits, program reviews, polls, expense claims, contracts, minutes, and accident investigation reports.

- Requests for information can usually be sent by letter, though pre-printed forms are faster. Use the word "record" when asking for material, as this term includes a broad range of formats, from photographs, audio tapes, videotapes and computer disks to printed reports, letters and memorandums. Governments are not required to create records in response to a request, only to release existing records. Requests are sent directly to the person designated by a department, agency or ministry to handle freedom of information inquiries. This person can often be a good source of confidential advice about how to narrow requests.

Limitations

The statutes give governments the right to refuse disclosure of certain kinds of information. Cabinet confidences, police investigation records, material related to inter-government relations, legal advice, national security records, records impinging on the privacy of a person or business, can all be withheld legally. Crown corporations, such as the CBC, are usually exempt altogether. The laws are also typically restricted to governments rather than Parliament or legislative assemblies. The federal auditor general, for example, is not covered by the Access to Information Act because his office answers to Parliament rather than to the federal government.

Complaints about delays or exemptions can be made to public officials whose job is to investigate alleged breaches of the law. (The notable exception is Newfoundland, which eliminated its information ombudsman to save money.) At the federal level, the office of the Information Commissioner of Canada can take complaints to court at taxpayer's expense on behalf of a requestor if moral suasion does not resolve disputes. Requestors can themselves take matters directly to court. Such cases can further delay release of material but may also heighten public interest.

Keep trying

Freedom of information laws can be an exercise in frustration, but for tenacious reporters they can also unlock vital information about government operations and public policy. Despite their weaknesses, the laws remain effective tools for enterprising journalists.

Words

This chapter is designed to demonstrate some tricky distinctions in the meanings of words and some rulings on correct or preferred usage in the CP news report.

according to	Avoid in attributions if it seems to cast doubt on the source's credibility.
adventuresome **adventurous**	ready to take risks fond of adventure
adverse **averse**	unfavourable opposed
affect (verb) **effect** (noun or verb)	influence, have an effect on a result; bring about, accomplish
aggravate **irritate**	make worse annoy, exasperate
allude to **refer to**	suggest without naming name
allusion **illusion**	a casual or indirect reference a false impression
altercation	a noisy dispute or quarrel (not a fistfight)
alternate, an	a person who substitutes
alternate(ly) **alternative(ly)**	in turns, first one and then the other: The raiders lay alternately watching and sleeping. providing a choice (usually the word wanted): an alternative route.
ambiguous **ambivalent**	having two or more meanings: The large lady's hat is ambiguous. having mixed feelings: He was ambivalent about arms spending, recognizing the need for defence but wishing the money better spent.
amiable **amicable**	friendly, of people friendly, of situations and agreements
amount **number**	How much? (weight and money) How many? (individual items)
antagonist	➤ See protagonist.

apparent	Write He died apparently of a heart attack, not He died of an apparent heart attack.
apparently **obviously**	seemingly, presumably plainly, unmistakably

apt
  liable
  likely
	customarily inclined; naturally fit
	open to something unpleasant
	probable, expected

arbitrate **mediate**	render a binding decision in a dispute help settle a dispute
as	meaning *since* or *because* should be used with care. It can sometimes be mistaken for *while* or *during the time that*: **As he was going out, she asked him to buy a paper.**
as **like**	introduces clauses: **It tastes good as a cigarette should.** introduces a noun or pronoun not directly followed by a verb: **He smokes like a chimney.**
as if, as though	may be used interchangeably to connect clauses.
assume **presume**	accept for the sake of argument take for granted
assure	➤ See **ensure.**
at present	➤ See **presently.**
audience **spectators**	watches or listens. watch.
avenge **revenge**	retaliate for another retaliate for oneself
averse	➤ See **adverse.**
avocation **vocation**	a hobby, diversion a career, occupation
awhile	➤ See **while.**
bait **bate**	lure (a baited hook); torment hold in (bated breath)
barely	➤ See **hardly.**

beg the question	assume the truth, usually unjustifiably, of the thing to be proved: **The worthless Senate should be abolished.** Beg the question doesn't mean evade a straight answer.

begin
   commence
   start
	is the general word.
	 sounds formal.
	 usually applies to physical motion.

beside **besides**	at the side of in addition to
bi-	is ambiguous in **biweekly, bimonthly, biennial,** etc. Prefer **twice a week, every two weeks, semi-weekly, semi-annual, half-yearly,** etc.
blatant **flagrant**	offensively noisy, obtrusive shameless, brazen
bloc **block**	a combination of people, countries or organizations to foster a shared interest a group of things: shares, seats, tickets
blond (adjective) **blond** (noun)	She has blond hair. a male or female

boat
 	
   ship
   vessel
	a small craft propelled by oars, sails or motor; also a submarine, motor torpedo boat, ferry
	 a large craft with sails or engine
	 a ship or a boat bigger than a rowboat

born **borne**	come into being by birth carried, endured
breach **broach**	break a contract or a wall open a barrel or a topic
breech birth	baby born buttocks first
bring **take**	carry here carry there
can (could) **may (might)**	denotes ability or power to do something. suggests doubt; also expresses permission to do something.
cannon **canon**	a gun a church decree; a clergyman
canvas **canvass**	coarse cloth solicit

careen	heel over, lean, sway
career	move at high speed
catch-22	a dilemma from which there is no escape. Note the lowercase.
celebrator	one who celebrates, a partygoer
celebrant	an officiating priest
cement	powder used in making concrete
concrete	rocklike material for roads, buildings, etc.
centre (verb)	is followed by **on** or **in**.
revolve (verb)	is followed by **round** or **around**.
childish	silly, puerile
childlike	innocent, confiding
chord	used in musical and mathematical senses: **The name struck a chord.**
cord	used in anatomical senses: **spinal cord, vocal cord, umbilical cord**; also: **nylon cord, cord of wood.**
client	uses the services of a professional person other than a doctor, or of a business.
customer	buys goods from a shop or a business.
climactic	of a climax
climatic	of climate
climax	➤ See **crescendo**.
collide	strike a moving object
commence	➤ See **begin**.
communique	Use for official communications, not for terrorists' threatening notes and the like.
compare to	liken to: **The staff compared (likened) him to Hitler.**
compare with	show similarities and differences (the term usually wanted): **He cannot compare with Ruth Rendell as a writer of mysteries.**
contrast with	show differences
complementary	completing; supplying needs
complimentary	praising; free
comprise (no of)	contain all the parts
include	contain some of the parts

concrete	➤ See cement.
connotation	➤ See denotation.
consensus	agreement, majority view (**general consensus of opinion** is redundant)
contagious **infectious**	passed on by contact passed on by contact or some other means
contemptible **contemptuous**	despicable scornful, insolent
continual **continuous**	frequently repeated (a dripping tap) uninterrupted (Niagara Falls)
controversial	is not needed when it is clear from the context that the subject is contentious: **The Opposition let the legislature bells ring for three hours Monday in its fight against a (controversial) housing bill.**
convict	➤ See inmate.
convince **persuade**	is followed by **of** or **that**, but not **to**. is followed by **of, that** or **to**.
cord	➤ See chord.
council (noun) **counsel** (n. or v.)	an assembly advice, a legal adviser; to advise
country	➤ See nation.
couple	almost invariably plural in reference to people: **The couple were hurt when their plane crashed.** But **A couple pays $5.**
credible **creditable** **credulous**	believable praiseworthy gullible
crescendo **climax**	increasing in strength or loudness highest point, top of a crescendo
customer	➤ See client.
debate	Write debate **something**, not **someone**.
defective **deficient**	faulty lacking, incomplete

definite	firm, clear
definitive	final, absolute
defuse (verb)	to render harmless
diffuse (adjective)	scattered
demolish, destroy	**completely** is redundant. (Avoid as synonym for **defeat** in sports stories.)
denotation	what a word specifically means: **Pig denotes a swine.**
connotation	what a word suggests: **Pig connotes dirt, greed, the little pig who went to market and other storybook characters.**
deny	➤ See **rebut, refute.**
dependant (noun)	one who depends on another
dependent (adj.)	depending on
deprecate	express disapproval of
depreciate	lose in value; belittle
desert	barren; something deserved; to abandon
dessert	a sweet
different from	is used with a noun or pronoun.
different than	introduces a clause.
dilemma	a choice between two equally pleasant or unpleasant things (not a synonym for **difficulty**)
disc	in such references as **a compact disc, a disc jockey, a slipped disc**
disk	of computers only: **disk drive, a floppy disk**
discomfort	make uncomfortable, uneasy
discomfit	embarrass, thwart
disinterested	impartial
uninterested	not interested
dissatisfied	➤ See **unsatisfied.**
dove	Make it **dived.**
draft	current of air, sum of money, rough plan, military service, hauling, beer drawn from a barrel (never **draught**)

due to	Use only if *caused by* or *ascribed to* could be substituted: **The crash was due to ice.** Not: **Due to ice, the plane crashed.** Try **because of, owing to.**
each other **one another**	refers to two. refers to three or more.
eatable **edible**	can be eaten because not revolting can be safely eaten
economic **economical**	relating to economics thrifty
-ee, -er	In general, *-ee* denotes the recipient of an action: **employee, examinee, trainee;** *-er* denotes the doer of the action: **employer, examiner, trainer.** But *-ee* sometimes applies to a person who behaves in a certain way: **absentee, debauchee, escapee, refugee.**
effect	➤ See **affect.**
effective **effectual**	having an effect; coming into operation answering its purpose
elder, eldest	used to denote seniority in a family
elicit (verb) **illicit** (adjective)	to draw out, evoke not legal

emigrant
  immigrant
  migrant
	leaves the country.
	enters the country.
	moves from one place to another.

eminent **imminent**	prominent near at hand
ended **ending**	Use of past: **week ended (last) Jan. 1.** Use of future: **week ending (next) May 1.**
enormity **enormousness**	monstrous wickedness, serious error great size

ensure
  insure
  assure
	to make sure
	to provide insurance
	to remove worry or uncertainty

especially	➤ See **specially.**
execute	describes judicial or politically motivated killings, not gangland murders.

exhausting	causing exhaustion
exhaustive	complete
expedient	suitable for a particular purpose; advantageous
expeditious	quick
extradite	hand person to another country; obtain such person for trial
extricate	disentangle, release
farther	denotes physical distance: **farther down the road.**
further	everything else: **to slip further into debt.**
female	refers to sex of human beings, animals or plants: **female servants.**
feminine	applies to qualities said to be characteristic of girls and women: **feminine charm.** ➤ See **gender.**
fewer	Use with plurals: **fewer bills.**
less	Use with singulars: **less sugar, a man less.**
figuratively	means in an allied but not exact sense: **She (figuratively) broke his heart.**
literally	means exactly as stated. Wrong: **She literally broke his heart.**
find	➤ See **locate.**
first, firstly	Write either **first, second, third** or **firstly, secondly, thirdly,** but not a mixture.
flagrant	➤ See **blatant.**
flair	aptitude, knack
flare	a flame; a widening
flaunt	show off
flout	mock, scoff at
flounder	move clumsily
founder	fill with water and sink; fail
following	Prefer **after** as a preposition.
foot, feet	In compounds before a noun, use **foot: a six-foot pass.** In more formal and precise contexts, use **feet: six feet three inches.** In informal usage, **inches** is omitted and **foot** is usual: **six foot three.**

forbid	is followed by to: The captain forbade them to go ashore.
prohibit	is followed by from: Government workers were prohibited from striking.
forego **forgo**	precede abstain from
fortuitous **fortunate**	by chance lucky
fulsome	disgusting, loathsome, excessive
gambit	a chess opening in which a player sacrifices a piece to secure an advantage; any opening move
gamut	a whole series or scope of anything
gas	may be used for **gasoline** if there is no confusion with manufactured or natural gas.
gender	refers to words: **A noun or pronoun that denotes a male is in the masculine gender: boy, brother, he, him.** ➤ See **Popular usage,** page 7.
sex	refers to humans, plants and animals: **athletes of both sexes** (not **genders**).
generation	about 30 years
genius	➤ See talent.
gibe	➤ See jibe.
Gothic **gothic**	of architecture: **a Gothic cathedral** all other uses: **a gothic novel**
gourmand **gourmet**	a heavy eater a connoisseur of food
greeted by **greeted with**	used with people used with things
grill **grille**	a metal frame for cooking; question closely grating, screen
grisly **grizzly**	gruesome, horrible greyish, of bears and beards
hail **hale**	greet, call to take forcibly (as to court). But avoid.

hanged **hung**	killed by hanging suspended
happen	➤ See transpire.
hardly, barely, **scarcely**	1. These are used without a negative: I can (not can't) hardly read the small print. 2. They are followed by when, not than: Scarcely had they got home when (not than) the phone rang.
healthful **healthy**	promoting good health in good health
historic **historical**	important or famous in history about or based on history
hoard **horde**	a store a crowd
homosexual **lesbian**	either male or female a female homosexual (lowercase *l*)
human (adjective) **humane** **humans**	used for both good and bad traits of humanity merciful, kind used in contrast to animals. In other cases, **human beings** is more appropriate.
hurting	normally requires object. **Poor sales hurt the** **company** (not **The company was hurting**); **Guy Carbonneau has been playing with** **knee problems** (not **Guy Carbonneau has** **been hurting**).
if and when	Use one, not both.
if, whether	are interchangeable when they make sense and are not ambiguous.
illusion	➤ See allusion.
immigrant	➤ See emigrant.
imminent	➤ See eminent.
imply **infer**	suggest or hint at; speakers or writers imply. deduce or conclude; hearers or readers infer.
inapt **inept**	unsuitable clumsy

individual   used of a person when contrasted with a society or a group

infectious   ➤ See contagious.

inflammable,
  flammable   Used interchangeably to mean capable of being set on fire. Prefer **flammable**.

inmate   occupant of a hospital, home, prison or other institution
  prisoner, convict   occupant of a prison

insure   ➤ See ensure.

irritate   ➤ See aggravate.

it's   abbreviation for it is (or it has)
  its   belonging to it (**held its own**)

jibe   agree or be in accord with
  gibe   jeer, mock

judicial   of a judge or law court
  judicious   sound of judgment

jurist   a person versed in law (not necessarily a lawyer or a judge)

laden   a truck **laden** with melons implies it is weighed down.
  loaded   a truck **loaded** with melons is simply carrying melons.

lay (laying, laid, laid)   to lay something down (takes a direct object): The boy laid the towel on the sand.
  lie (lying, lay, lain)   to recline (does not take a direct object): Then he lay on the towel.

lead (noun and verb)   metal; present tense of **to lead**
  led (verb)   past tense of **to lead**

leading question   a question so worded that it prompts a person to give the desired answer: "You weren't in the house at the time of the murder, were you?"

lectern   ➤ See podium.

lend (lent,
  not **loaned)**   Use as the verb: Lend me your ears. Lend me $10.
  loan   Use as the noun: a $100 loan

lesbian	➤ See homosexual.
less	➤ See fewer.
lighted, lit	Used interchangeably in the past tense, though lit is more common: **The lamps were lighted/ lit.** As an adjective before a noun, **lighted** is preferable: **a lighted cigarette**; except when the adjective is preceded by an adverb: **a brightly lit room.**
like	Normal usage for examples is **Mother Teresa helped rescue people like the poor, the sick and the abandoned.**
such as	is often used to introduce examples set off with commas: **Several famous composers, such as Mozart and Schubert, died young.**
like - as	➤ See as - like.
likely, liable	➤ See apt.
linage 　**lineage**	number of lines ancestry, descent
lit	➤ See lighted.
literally	➤ See figuratively.
loaded	➤ See laden.
loath 　**loathe**	reluctant to detest
locate 　**find**	fix the position of (a downed aircraft) discover without reference to a particular setting (a missing child)
luxuriant 　**luxurious**	lush costly, rich
madam	a polite form of address: "**No, madam**"; a brothel-keeper
madame	a French title of respect: **Madame Jules Benoit**
male	refers to sex of humans, animals or plants: **a male lion.**
masculine	applies to qualities said to be characteristic of boys and men: **masculine vigour.** ➤ See gender.
masterful 　**masterly**	domineering expert, skilful

may (might)	➤ See can (could).
me, I	To, with, from and other prepositions are followed by me, him, her, us and them, not I, he, she, we or they: Mother gave it to Jack and me (not I). Put your trust in him (not he) who knows best. Many of us (not we) voters are tired of promises.
media	takes a plural verb: The media are blamed.
mediate	➤ See arbitrate.
meter **metre**	a measuring machine a measure of distance; a verse rhythm
meticulous **scrupulous**	careful about small details conscientious, thorough
migrant	➤ See emigrant.
momentarily	➤ See presently.
momentary **momentous**	short-lived, for a moment important
moral **morale**	virtuous; a lesson from a story mental attitude
more than	is followed by a singular verb when the noun is singular: More than one tank was hit. ➤ See over.
myself	is properly used to intensify: I myself wouldn't have gone. Do not use it instead of I or me: Gord and myself (I) weren't invited. The bride didn't invite Gord or myself (me).
naked **nude**	the general word meaning without clothing or covering often a synonym for **naked**; otherwise usually restricted to artistic or pornographic contexts
nation **country**	the people of a country a nation's territory
nauseous **noxious**	causing nausea, feeling nausea, nauseated harmful, unpleasant
negligent **negligible**	careless small, unimportant

noisome	harmful, foul-smelling
no sooner	is followed by **than**, not **when**.
notable **noticeable**	worth noting easy to see, prominent
nude	➤ See **naked**.
number	➤ See **amount**.
O **oh**	is usually restricted to invocations: **O God, help me**. It is always capitalized and is written without a comma. is an exclamation: **Oh God, he's back. Oh, did he?** It is capitalized only at the start of a sentence. Write **oh-oh**, not **oh, oh**.
observance **observation**	obeying, paying heed to noting, looking at
obsolete **obsolescent**	no longer in use becoming obsolete
obviously	➤ See **apparently**.
official **officious**	connected with an office; authorized meddlesome, bossy
oh	➤ See **O**.
one another	➤ See **each other**.
one of those who	is followed by a plural verb.
oral **verbal**	spoken spoken or written
over	In the sense of *in excess of,* used interchangeably with **more than**: **Creasey and Simenon have each published over (more than) 500 books**.
overall **overalls**	total, all-inclusive protective clothing
pair	generally plural: **The pair were seen with their son**. But **A pair receives a smaller pension**.
paramount **tantamount**	supreme equal to

parliamentarian	an expert in parliamentary procedure; a skilled debater; not a synonym for **MP**
peddle	sell; a **pedlar** sells.
pedal	cycle; a **pedaller** pushes pedals; to **softpedal** is to play music with the soft pedal down.
people	In general, use **people**, even if the number is small or precise: **Two people died.** Better: **A man and a woman died.**
persons	Use for formality or occasional variety: **Persons over 21 are eligible.**
perquisite	special privilege, advantage (a perk)
prerequisite	a necessary condition
persuade	➤ See **convince.**
podium	the platform a speaker stands on
lectern	the reading desk a speaker stands behind
pompon	ornamental tuft
pompom	rapid-firing gun
practicable	able to be done
practical	useful, sensible, functional
precede	to go before
proceed	to go along, continue
prerequisite	➤ See **perquisite.**
presently	soon, in a moment (**avoid:** usually misunderstood)
at present	now
momentarily	for a moment
presume	➤ See **assume.**
principal	chief, most important; capital sum; school head
principle	basic truth or rule; code of conduct
prior to	Use **before.**
prisoner	➤ See **inmate.**
prohibit	➤ See **forbid.**
prone	➤ See **supine.**
protagonist	chief actor, champion of a cause
antagonist	opponent

punctilious	attentive to detail
punctual	prompt

quartet	➤ See trio.

rack (noun)	framework: **hat-rack**
rack (verb)	to trouble, torture, destroy: **nerve-racking**
wrack (noun)	wreckage, seaweed

rampage	➤ See spree.

rankle	A thing **rankles**; it does not **rankle someone**. Right: **The insult rankled.** Wrong: **The insult rankled Joe.**

ravage	damage badly, devastate
ravish	delight, enrapture; rape

reason	is followed by **that** or **why**, not **because**: **The reason for the loss was that taxes rose.**

rebut, refute	prove to be false: **She refuted the charge of theft by producing a sales receipt.**
deny	declare to be false: **He denied the charge but had no alibi.**

regretful	full of regret
regrettable	the cause of regret

reign	monarch's rule
rein	harness

reluctant	unwilling, grudging
reticent	sparing of words, reserved

repetitive	characterized by repetition: **a repetitive beat**
repetitious	characterized by unnecessary or tedious repetition: **repetitious arguments**

revenge	➤ See avenge.

revolve	➤ See centre.

rob	A person or place is robbed, not the thing stolen: **A company was robbed of a payroll.** Not: **A company's payroll was robbed.**

rush	Do not use when the idea of speed is implicit, as in stories involving ambulances, fire trucks and police cruisers. Not: **She was rushed to hospital.** Write **taken** or some such.

scarce	of things normally available
rare	of things seldom found at any time
scarcely	➤ See hardly.
scrupulous	➤ See meticulous.
seasonable	suitable to the occasion or season
seasonal	occurring at a particular season
sensual	arousing or satisfying bodily appetites or sexual desire: the sensual pleasures of eating; a sensual striptease
sensuous	appealing to the senses, sometimes the mind: a ballet dancer's sensuous movements; a sensuous passage of Mozart
sex	➤ See gender.
ship	➤ See boat.
shot	Use the specific shot and wounded or shot and killed as appropriate.
situation	Avoid the practice of putting other nouns or phrases before situation: a crisis situation, a classroom situation, a bad-debt situation.
some	meaning *about* is proper: some 20 years later, some 500 troops.
spare	scanty, frugal; thin: a spare diet, a spare style of writing; a spare man
sparse	thinly scattered, not thick: a sparse population, a sparse beard
specially	for a particular purpose
especially	to a great degree, outstanding
spectators	➤ See audience.
spree	a frolic; a drinking or shopping bout; not violent behaviour
rampage	violent behaviour, a bout of violence
start	➤ See begin.
stationary	unmoving
stationery	writing material
stimulant	drug, etc. (not alcohol, a depressant)
stimulus	incentive, spur

strait	narrow, confined (**straitjacket**, **Davis Strait**)
straight	unbent, direct
strategy	refers to the overall campaign.
tactics	the art of moving forces; adroit management
such as	➤ See **like**.
supine	face upward (but **avoid**)
prone	face downward
tack	course of action or policy
tact	ability to deal sensitively with others; sensitivity
tactics	➤ See **strategy**.
talent	special ability
genius	exceptionally great talent
tantamount	➤ See **paramount**.
that	As a conjunction, *that* may be omitted if no confusion results: **King said** (that) **she would go**. It is often needed after such verbs as **assert, declare, estimate, make clear, point out, propose, state, warn: She warned** that **the committee would oppose the plan**. It may be needed with time elements (**White said** that **in 1950 he was destitute**) and before such conjunctions as **after, although, as, because, before, in addition to, when: Green said** that **when she heard the shot, she was asleep.**
that	often introduces an essential clause — one that defines the noun it is attached to and cannot be omitted: **The house that is painted white is mine.**
which	introduces a non-essential or parenthetical clause — one that adds information that could be omitted without changing meaning: **The house, which was built in 1940, is white.**
that-who	➤ See **which-who-that**.
the	Do not drop *the* from the beginning of sentences or wherever idiom or grammar demands it. Not: **Terms of the contract were secret; Police would not reveal names of the injured.**

then	Avoid putting *then* as an adjective before a noun if it sounds equally well or better in its normal position. Not: **the then prime minister, Lester Pearson.** But: **the prime minister then, Lester Pearson.**
transpire **happen**	become known occur
trio, quartet	Use only in the musical sense, not of any casual grouping of three or four.
troops	In general, **troops** describes a body of soldiers: **The troops were flown in by helicopter.** It is not used of small numbers of individuals: **30 troops.** But idiom permits its use with large numbers, say in the hundreds: **Some 250 troops surrounded the prison.**
try to	**try to** (not **and**) **understand**
uninterested	➤ See **disinterested.**
unsatisfied **dissatisfied**	falling short of satisfaction discontented
upcoming	Write **coming, approaching** or **forthcoming** if an adjective is needed.
urban **urbane**	of a town or city well-bred, suave
usage	a manner of use established by custom
verbal	➤ See **oral.**
vessel	➤ See **boat.**
veteran	one who served in the military; person of long experience. Avoid such descriptions as **five-year police veteran** and **a veteran of four NHL seasons.**
vocation	➤ See **avocation.**
waive **waver**	give up, forgo falter, move to and fro
-ward, -wards	Americans prefer the **-ward** form: **toward, backward, afterward;** Britons prefer **-wards: towards, backwards, afterwards;** Canadians use both forms.

was	simple past tense
were	Use **were** when expressing a wish or a condition contrary to fact, and after **as if** and **as though**: I wish I were you. She spoke to him as if he were a fool.
whether, if	➤ See if, whether.
whether or not	Retain the *or not* when an alternative is emphasized: I will go whether you like it or not.
which-that	➤ See that-which.
which	normally refers to things but may be used of people in a body: She spoke to the crowd, which grew silent.
who	usually refers to people but sometimes to animals, especially those with names: Snip, who is 14, is a toy poodle.
that	refers to people or things: It was the pilot that (or who) spoke.
while (noun) **awhile** (adverb)	They had to wait for a while (note the for). They had to wait awhile (no preposition).
who-whom	Who stands for **he-she-they**, whom for **him-her-them**. When in doubt, break the sentence in two: She met a man who she thought was her brother. (She thought he was her brother, so **who** is correct.) She met a man whom she took for her brother. (She took **him** for her brother, so **whom** is correct.)
wove	the normal past tense of **weave**: His daughter wove him a scarf.
weaved	the past tense of **weave** means to avoid hitting something: The forward weaved through the defence; or to tell an involved story: The old man weaved a chilling plot.
wrack	➤ See rack.
yoke	wooden crosspiece
yolk	yellow of an egg

Illustrating the news

Pictures

Pictures sell stories.

A strong photo gives the layout editor a chance to promote a story that might otherwise be passed over. This compelling photo shows England's Robert Denmark (left) winning the men's 5,000 metres at the Commonwealth Games in 1994.

(CP – Frank Gunn)

A good picture can carry a story onto page 1; lack of a picture can take a good story off the front page – and right out of the paper. CP aims to illustrate every worthwhile story with photos, maps or graphics.

Having that happen depends on awareness. All editors, writers and photographers need to be alert to illustrating the story, whether it is a rewrite or the germ of an idea for a staff-written series. The story without pictures and graphics won't get the play it deserves.

Good CP work involves developing an understanding of what makes a good illustration and the mechanics of getting it from the photographer or artist to the network of receiving newspapers.

Canadian Melanie Turgeon blasts out of the start gate during a training run at a World Cup ski race in Lake Louise. Unique lighting – a combination of natural and flash – makes this photo unusually dramatic.

(CP – Frank Gunn)

CP Picture Service began in 1948 as an exchange of mailed photos. The first Wirephoto network based on an analogue or sound signal transmitted over telephone wires began in Ontario and Quebec in 1954 and 10 years later was coast-to-coast. Wirephoto became LaserPhoto in 1978, when new transmission equipment using a laser beam was introduced. The network name was changed to PhotoNet in 1991 after digital transmission by satellite began.

PhotoNet delivers an average of 220 photos a day, 98 per cent in colour, to Canadian daily newspapers. Half the photos originate in Canada, with about half of these coming from newspaper photographers. CP staff photographers and freelances hired by CP provide the rest. The Associated Press and its photographers around the world provide the international content, about 110 photos a day.

Every newspaper subscribing to the photo network – three-quarters of the CP membership – is obligated to provide its local photos from news events to CP. Each newspaper subscriber has the capacity to transmit pictures directly to CP over the Internet or by dialling into the CP bulletin board.

A separate network called **GraphicsNet** sends CP and Associated Press graphics directly to Macintosh computers in newsrooms, using the same delivery system that handles CP pictures.

Good illustrations

Good photos have similarities to good stories. They:

1. Are new and in some way unusual.

2. Show action the instant it happens.

3. Portray people and appeal to the emotions.

4. Relate to some important person, event or place.

5. Wrap up a story or provide an overall view of it.

6. Tie in with a current story, the season, the weather, a fad.

A good illustration will be marked by attention to **quality, content** and **composition.**

Quality

A pair of firefighters are illuminated by the lights of a search-and-rescue helicopter as it scours the rocky shore of Peggy's Cove, looking for survivors and bodies from the downed Swissair Flight 111 in September 1998. The unusual, dramatic lighting reinforces the tragic drama of the story.

(Halifax Chronicle-Herald – Tim Krochak)

1. The main subject has clear, sharp details.

2. There are bright, natural colours or a gradual range of grey tones between black and white.

3. Skin tones for light-skinned people are a natural colour or light grey against a white shirt. There must be definition in the facial shading of people with darker skins.

A poor-quality picture might be slightly out of focus – look at the eyes. It might have heavy blacks and brilliant whites, or have an overall grey cast with no blacks and whites. Colours may be washed out or too dark.

The sole exception to these demands for quality is a shot of such outstanding news value that it will get into print despite poor quality.

Follow these basic rules when scanning negatives or acquiring and enhancing digital camera images to ensure maximum quality:

1. Start with an acknowledgment that "less is more" when enhancing images.

2. Do as many enhancements as possible in the pre-scan or when

acquiring a digital image.

3. Keep enhancements in PhotoShop to a minimum. Often an unsharp mask is added in the pre-press handling of the image, making excessive use at the scanning stage unnecessary.

When toning, use levels or curves to adjust colour and tone rather than colour balance or brightness/contrast.

Content

Former prime minister Pierre Trudeau, his son Sacha, former wife Margaret Kemper and son Justin leave a memorial service for their son and brother Michel in 1998. Their grief-stricken faces evocatively capture the tragedy of the story.

(CP – Ryan Remiorz)

1. Does the photo tell a story?

2. Is its subject important?

3. Is it appealing, well-composed and striking?

4. Is there outstanding human interest or some other quality that overrides minor news value?

Any newsbreak that is visually important or interesting makes the good-quality photo worth distributing. A window cleaner suspended in mid-air by his braces makes a good shot; a minor auto wreck usually doesn't because all wrecks tend to look much the same. A 20-car pileup, multiple deaths or trapped passengers can give an accident photo the news value needed to get it on the network.

Picture judgment is partly personal and partly a matter of experience. A photo is almost certainly worthwhile if an editor experienced in handling news finds it eye-catching. A newspaper photo editor's recommendation is always a valid reason for selecting a picture.

Composition

1. Are the main subject and its surroundings arranged so as to be attractive and cohesive? The right camera angle often allows

information such as signs, buildings and other people to line up with the main subject, making the photograph informative and interesting.

2. Does the entire frame contain relevant content? Large empty areas that add little useful information limit the impact of the photograph.

3. Is the picture cropped to make the subject stand out clearly?

Standup group shots are not wanted, although sometimes the personalities involved create exceptions. The Queen with Commonwealth prime ministers or a new cabinet is usually newsworthy. In the best such photos, the group's attention is not centred on the camera and are compressed using a side angle "to stack up" the subjects.

Be careful that the "arranged" photo does not turn into a picture that is contrived or set up by the photographer. There is no objection to cleaning up a cluttered background or moving the company president from behind his desk to stand in front of his widget-stamping machine.

The photo becomes contrived when elements or interpretations are added or subtracted to make a point that would not normally have been there. Spot news pictures should not be arranged.

A team from Belarus celebrates after a gold-medal win at the world canoe championships. This photo is an excellent example of how clever composition – in this case the placement of the canoeists' arms – can create a memorable image.

(CP – Andrew Vaughan)

Photo manipulation

CP does not alter the content of photos. Pictures must always tell the truth – tell what the photographer saw happen. Nothing can damage our credibility more quickly than deliberate untruthfulness. The integrity of our photo report is our highest priority.

PhotoShop is a sophisticated editing tool that allows photographic images to be manipulated easily. It's technically possible to change their content and impact on the reader, whether by accident or design.

Use of this tool must follow the long-established chemical darkroom standards of photo printing. Simple *burning* (making light portions of a print darker), *dodging* (making dark portions lighter), *colour balancing, toning* and *cropping* are acceptable. Exaggerated use of these features to add, remove or give prominence to details in the photo is not acceptable.

Retouching is limited to removal of dust spots, film scratches or abnormal marks and patterns.

Colour adjustment is to be minimal. Adjustments can be made to ensure honest reproduction of the original when the scanning and transmission processes alter colours.

Consult the Picture Editor first on any question of photo manipulation.

PhotoNet

CP PhotoNet facilities can get a picture across Canada in time to illustrate any breaking story in the same publishing cycle if newspapers and CP bureaus move fast.

Pictures that don't move in the same cycle with the story they illustrate will likely not be used, unless the content is exceptional or they illustrate a continuing story.

When a story breaks CP immediately co-ordinates coverage plans with its staff photographers, its member newspapers and AP. The most important consideration while setting up coverage is that a photographer must be at an event when it happens. Coverage must be lined up quickly.

Every paper uses photos to accompany local stories that could have wider interest. To get these on the network in the same cycle for use by others, papers should send their best pictures to the CP Picture desk as soon as they are available.

But what pictures should be sent?

1. Ask yourself whether you would be interested in printing it if you were the editor of a newspaper 100 kilometres away. If the answer is yes, transmit it.

2. Send it if there is a story to go with it.

3. Does it pique your interest in any way?

The most frequent request from newspaper editors is for more news photos that can be used on their inside national pages. On a slow day for spot-news photos, even pictorially interesting weather and feature photos will help fill this demand. Watch for them.

Sending photos

Pictures sent to the Toronto Picture Desk for transmission must be of the highest possible quality. Full captions and relevant International Press Technical Committee (IPTC) field information – used to find and sort archived pictures – must be written and saved with the JPEG file before being transmitted.

Scanning:

CP photographers and newspapers use a scanner that takes negatives or digital pictures and imports them into PhotoShop software for conversion to JPEG files. These are transmitted on PhotoNet.

Images should be scanned/acquired at 200 dpi. The longest dimension should not exceed 25 centimetres. Keep the photograph in the RGB mode.

Pictures should be compressed in standard JPEG format, at a ratio of about 15:1, to achieve an average 500-kilobyte file. When the file dips below 500 kilobytes it is clear they have been compressed too much.

Images downloaded from the CP Picture Archive (*http://cparchive.cp.org*) must be checked for size before they are transmitted on the network. Historical material is scanned at a much higher resolution. These must be resized if they exceed the above guidelines.

IPTC fields

Take care when filling out IPTC fields, especially the caption field, which is publishable. CP member newspapers are able to read all IPTC information fields by using their picture browsers or opening the image *File Info* viewable in PhotoShop.

CP now writes captions in the same style used by most newspapers under the published picture. They should no longer include information from other IPTC fields.

These are the descriptions of the IPTC fields, and the information that should be placed in them:

Object name field: This lists the story slug associated with the photo. For photos without stories, or when a slug is not available, photographers and editors should use a slug that would be a logical search criterion for a story that moves later. Use either the subject's last name, the name of the event, or a word that generally describes the photo.

Original transmission reference field: This field lists a call letter-number combination associated with the photo. It includes an originating point's call letters and a picture number; for example, CPT105.

Caption field: A standard CP caption would look like this:

Prime Minister Jean Chrétien gestures during a speech to the Canadian Club in Toronto Tuesday, Dec. 15, 1998. Chrétien said that health-care funding would be increased in the next federal budget. (CP PHOTO/Fred Chartrand)

Regular captions have no **overlines** – all-caps descriptions detailing the type of picture. But instructive overlines should be used on file photos and specials as in these examples:

FILE – Roger Clemens of the Toronto Blue Jays clenches his fist in victory in this Aug. 15, 1998 file photo during a game against the New York Yankees. (CP PICTURE ARCHIVE/Frank Gunn)

SPECIAL FOR THE VANCOUVER SUN – Roger Clemens of the Toronto Blue Jays clenches his fist in victory in this Aug. 15, 1998, file photo during a game against the New York Yankees. (CP PICTURE ARCHIVE/Frank Gunn)

The full date – day of the week, date and year – should appear in the body of all captions. If only the month and year are known, use that. In file photos use the date the photo was originally shot. If the date is not known, use the year. If there is no known date, state "date of photo unknown" in the body of the caption and in the *special instructions file* of the IPTC header.

The sign-off for a CP staffer or freelancer is in parentheses: **(CP PHOTO/Kevin Frayer)**. If the name of the photographer is not known or needs to be withheld, the sign-off is **(CP PHOTO)**.

Include the name of the newspaper for a member photo sign-off: **(CP PHOTO/Toronto Star-Boris Spremo)**.

For a handout, use **(CP PHOTO/General Motors)**. If the photographer is known, add the name: **(CP PHOTO/General Motors-John Smith)**. **Note:** Handout photos should also use the code **HO** in the *byline title field* of the IPTC header, but do not put it in the sign-off.

For a pool photo sign-off, use **(CP PHOTO/Peter Jones-Pool)**. Do not name the newspaper or agency that shot for the pool in the caption sign-off. Note: The name of the organization that shot the pool and the word **POOL** should be included in the source field and the word **POOL** should be in the *byline title field*.

For a Specials photo sign-off for a photo made by CP, use **(CP PHOTO/Tom Hanson)**. If it was made by a member's own photographer the sign-off is **(Montreal Gazette/Pierre Obendrauf)**.

A file photo sign-off is **(CP PICTURE ARCHIVE/Doug Ball)**. If the name of the photographer is not known, the sign-off is: **(CP PICTURE ARCHIVE)**.

For a CP Graphic sign-off: **(CP GRAPHIC/Tammy Hoy)**.

A TV frame grab photo sign-off is **(CP PHOTO/CBC-TV)**. **Note:** TV frame grab photos use the byline title code **TEL** in the byline title field, but do not put it in the caption sign-off. Also, a mandatory credit is often required when using a frame grab. This instruction should be included in the special instructions field: **MANDATORY CREDIT REQUIRED WITH THE USE OF THIS PHOTO.**

Date field: Date the photo was taken.

Filename field: Name originally given to the file when it was saved.

Caption writer field: This lists the initials of all the people who wrote or edited the caption, header fields or image file. This includes any toning of the photo file.

Headline field: Lists keywords to aid in a more detailed search for a photo. It typically lists who is in the photo.

Special instructions field: Lists any special notations that apply uniquely to a photo such as CP Picture Archive, correction, outs, or mandatory credits.

Byline field: Lists the name of the person who made the photo.

Byline title: Lists the title of the person who made the photo. Pick one of these categories:

STF – CP photographs by staff photographers, including Associated Press photographers.

FRL – CP photographs by freelance photographers.

MBR – Photographs from member photographers.

SUB – Photographs picked up by foreign subscribers.

MAG – Photographs provided by magazines.

TEL – Frame grabs from television.

POOL – Photographs by pool photographers.

HO – Handout photographs.

Credit: The name of the service transmitting the photo; almost always CP or AP.

Source: Lists the copyright holder or the original provider of a photo, such as CP, AP, a CP member, pool photo provider, or handout provider.

Category: Lists codes that aid in a more detailed search. Categories are:

A – U.S. news or features

C – Canadian news and features

F – Financial

I – International

S – Sports

V – Advisories

Supplemental categories: Lists codes that aid in a more detailed search for a photo. For example: **HKN** will show all NHL hockey photos. A list of categories is in the AP guide.

City, province, country: Lists the city, province or state and country where the photo was made. For file photos, do not use the transmitting point's city, province or country.

Keywords: Used by CP Picture Archive staff.

Writing captions

Captions are always written in the present tense. They tell the reader, briefly and clearly, the basic details of the picture and tie it to the story it illustrates. Remember that photos attract even the most casual reader, so captions are probably the best-read words in the paper, after headlines. Like headlines, captions must be crisp. Like stories, they must be readable and informative, interesting and lively.

Some reminders to make caption-writing easier:

1. Does the caption say when and where?

2. Does it identify, fully and clearly?

3. Are the names in the right order? List people in a group shot from the left, and specify position (left or front row, second from right).

4. Use at least two short, snappy sentences. One long, involved sentence is boring.

5. Stick primarily to explaining the action in the picture, but don't speculate. The prime minister's "grin" may be teeth-gritting anger. The "dozing" legislator may be reading a paper on his desk. Be sure or leave it out.

6. Watch attribution and don't let libel creep in.

7. Read what you've written. Are all the questions answered? Count the people in the picture and the number of names. Are the left-to-right designations correct? Is the action mentioned in the caption really shown?

Credit the photographer in the body of the caption if the picture has exceptional merit or the circumstances in which it was shot were very unusual. Say so when abnormal techniques such as multiple exposures or time exposures were used.

A police officer is hit by a Molotov cocktail outside the Turkish embassy in Ottawa during a protest by Kurds in 1999. Cutlines should be basic background about the news event – in this case, that the Kurdish demonstrators were upset about the arrest of their leader, Abdullah Ocalan, in Kenya.

(CP – Tom Hanson)

Kills and corrections

All picture kills and corrections are handled by the Toronto Picture Desk, which knows the exact distribution of a picture.

If you see an error in a caption or a graphic, phone the Picture Desk immediately.

Kills and corrections are transmitted on the same photo networks that carried the original. The style differs slightly from the style on news circuits.

CORRECTION: A CP caption correction is moved when a simple and non-libellous error occurs in a caption. Examples would be a misspelled name, or wrong home town, sports score or slug. The procedure CP uses to file a caption correction form on PhotoNet is to point out the information that is being corrected in the *instructions field* of the IPTC header and write a corrected caption in publishable form. The word CORRECTION and the original photo's number are added to the object name field of the IPTC header. The photo follows the form with a corrected publishable caption noting so in the *instructions field* of the IPTC header.

ADDITIONS: A CP caption addition is moved when the original caption is incomplete, but otherwise accurate. It may add the name of someone in the photo or other important background information. The procedure for a CP caption addition is the same as that for a correction.

ELIMINATIONS: A CP caption elimination is moved when an acceptable photo has a caption that misrepresents the photo or is in bad taste. When this occurs a CP caption elimination form is moved alerting members. Then the photo is retransmitted using the same procedure as a correction.

KILLS: A CP photo KILL is moved on PhotoNet for a photo that is objectionable and presents the possibility of legal action, libel or copyright infringement. Photo kills move in consultation with the Toronto photo supervisor and senior management.

Pictures and the law

The **Legal** section of the stylebook applies equally to the Picture Service. Ensure that neither the caption nor the contents of a photo violate the law or individual rights.

A Supreme Court of Canada ruling in April 1998 added a new wrinkle to the publication of news photos. The court ruled that an individual's right to privacy under the Quebec Charter of Human Rights and Freedoms includes the ability to control use of his or her image.

Although the ruling dealt with Quebec alone, its effect has been to change the way photos are handled in several provinces with privacy statutes: Quebec, British Columbia, Manitoba, Saskatchewan and Newfoundland. It means care must be taken with some photos that feature identifiable people in them. Consent must be obtained from the subjects of such photos unless one of the following applies:

a) The people are incidental to the photo.

b) The identifiable person is not the subject of the photo but is one of a group in a public place – a crowd scene, for example.

c) The photo is part of coverage of a legitimate news event that the subject has a role in – a trial, for example.

d) The subject is a public figure.

e) The subject's success in her profession depends upon public opinion.

Otherwise, consent for use of the picture should be obtained and the subject's name and age must be included in the caption transmitted with the photograph.

In all jurisdictions, a picture of a person accused of a crime could prejudice the outcome of the court hearing if there is a question of identity. And there usually is. If in doubt, consult the editor before transmitting a picture.

Withhold immediately any picture questioned after transmission by sending a news-circuit advisory and a note on all photo networks that received the original. Send a followup advisory and note killing or releasing the picture as soon as the question is resolved.

Copyright photos

CP owns the copyright of photos made by its staff and freelance photographers working on direct assignment from CP. A freelance photographer who shoots a picture before selling it to CP retains the copyright. CP can use it only for the purpose agreed to when it was bought – usually unlimited editorial use by CP and AP member newspapers and magazines.

Any unusual restrictions that the freelance demands must be noted in the *special instructions field* to avoid inadvertent violation of a copyright picture. These restrictions could include:

1. **One-time use only.** The photo can be used once with the current news story.

2. **Magazines out.** The photographer hopes to sell the picture separately to that market.

3. **Copyright photo, credit mandatory.** The newspaper must credit the photographer.

Photos provided by public relations firms or businesses may not be legally available for CP transmission other than at the time they illustrated a specific story. Always check with the photographer or the source before reissuing a picture of this type.

The CP Picture Service contract requires newspaper subscribers to include CP in copyright release of photos by their staff and regular freelances. Be especially careful of occasional freelance photos picked up from newspapers or borrowed later from their libraries. The libraries file every picture used, no matter what the source. Rights may not have been obtained for CP use and must be checked. Do not use a photo if the source is not indicated or cannot be determined from the newspaper's own publication.

Picturing money

It is generally against the law to picture in print any Canadian banknote or a recognizable portion of one. Such photos cannot be carried on PhotoNet. It's prohibited by Section 457 of the Criminal Code.

This does not apply to the printed likeness of a banknote if the length or width is less than three-quarters or greater than 1.5 times the length or width of the real one. Neither does it apply if the likeness is in black and white only or features just one side of the banknote. This gives photographers a fair amount of leeway in illustrating stories about money without breaking the law.

Occasionally the Bank of Canada will provide a replica of a banknote and agree to waive prosecution, usually to promote a newly issued note. These replicas may be transmitted.

Cartoons

CP picks up cartoons for use with news stories in special circumstances, – for example, when a cartoon becomes the subject of political controversy, or to illustrate a story about a cartoonist.

Cartoons may also make good illustrations for a situational or analysis if they offer fair comment. Where there is controversy, more than one cartoon may be needed to reflect opposing views.

Newspapers are not obligated to provide CP with their cartoons, and most editorial cartoonists retain and syndicate the rights to their work. Permission for the use of each cartoon must be arranged in advance with the newspaper or the cartoonist.

The use of any cartoon must be approved in advance by the Chief of Picture Service. Requests for such approval should include the name of the newspaper editor or cartoonist authorizing use.

Graphics

Readers have changed. Busy lives, lightning-fast telecommunications and 20-second TV news items are only a few factors shaping the demands being made upon newspapers. Alert editors and designers have responded with dynamic changes in newspaper presentation.

Some of the changes have been bold and sudden; others have involved the gradual introduction of a new look. In all successful cases, readers' needs are being met with a design and editing approach that is both practical and esthetically pleasing.

For many papers the move has been toward shorter stories, supported by stronger illustrations that may include a sophisticated information-intensive graphic.

Graphics can help readers see the story, especially in cases where a photo would be impossible. The success of this type of graphic depends on good detail.

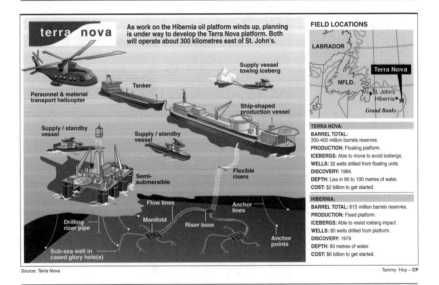

Source: Terra Nova

Tammy Hoy – CP

Graphics artists are working in newsrooms researching, designing and constructing graphics that show readers the HOW of a story.

The artist can manipulate drawings, take graphs apart and store bits of them in computer memory for later use in another graphic, vary text styles and sizes, and apply colour electronically. The slow mechanical work done in typesetting shops or separation labs is a thing of the past.

CP has met the changing needs of newspapers in Canada with **GraphicsNet**, a service of graphics created by CP and Associated Press artists and delivered by satellite into a newspaper's computer. There they can be further manipulated to change typestyles, colour or size.

CP's graphics service is not limited to single graphics, but includes full pages organized around one topic, such as a major news story or trend, and containing both words and pictures. These pages allow CP writers and graphics artists to work closely together to present a story in the most illuminating way possible.

Staffers everywhere should suggest ideas for graphics. They are often the best way to locate an event, explain a complicated statistical trend or compare products. A good graphic, like a good photo, can help editors squeeze a story into today's tight news holes.

The average news day is full of material that can be made into a graphic. The letterhead on an accreditation application might make a good standing logo for continuing stories on a coming sports tournament. The diagram in the back of the press release that helps reporters understand a new product might be just as helpful for readers. Pass these along to the graphics department.

Information, please

Graphics can be used to highlight sidebar material and aid understanding with diagrams.

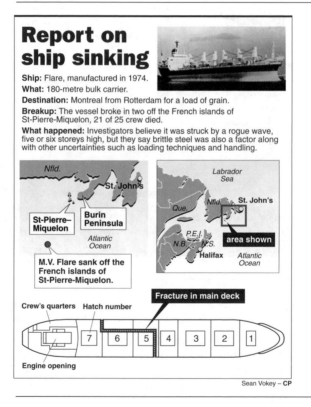

Report on ship sinking

Ship: Flare, manufactured in 1974.
What: 180-metre bulk carrier.
Destination: Montreal from Rotterdam for a load of grain.
Breakup: The vessel broke in two off the French islands of St-Pierre-Miquelon, 21 of 25 crew died.
What happened: Investigators believe it was struck by a rogue wave, five or six storeys high, but they say brittle steel was also a factor along with other uncertainties such as loading techniques and handling.

Nfld.
St. John's
St-Pierre–Miquelon
Burin Peninsula
Atlantic Ocean
M.V. Flare sank off the French islands of St-Pierre-Miquelon.

Labrador Sea
Que.
Nfld.   St. John's
P.E.I.
N.B.   N.S.
Halifax   Atlantic Ocean
area shown

Fracture in main deck
Crew's quarters   Hatch number
7 6 5 4 3 2 1
Engine opening

Sean Vokey – **CP**

The first element in producing any news graphic is always the same: information. Reporters need to gather this detail in their contacts with news sources.

If a plane crashed on takeoff, find out what runway it was using. How are the runways configured? How far did it go past the runway? Did it crash in trees or a field? What buildings are in the area? Reporters can get this information on the phone. Often, those on the scene – reporters or sources – can sketch a rough drawing for the graphics artist. It's the kind of detail the artist needs, and it's the kind of detail readers are demanding.

From the Montreal massacre, a reporter learns that the gunman used a Ruger Mini-14 rifle. A graphics artist in Toronto, using that information, borrows a catalogue and buys a few bullets from a nearby sporting goods store. The result is a graphic that brings the details of the rifle and size of the bullets home to the reader.

A business reporter who hears that a company's sales have been climbing steadily since 1996 can get a graphic going if the annual sales figures can be obtained. Specific numbers are required to produce a graphic, obliging sources to back up their statements with precise facts. The numbers might show that sales are up from 1996, but there have been a number of ups and downs in the period. The fact-digging needed for a graphic is often important in getting an accurate understanding of the story.

Press kits, catalogues, guidebooks, instruction manuals and program books are often the source of overlooked material that can be turned into a news graphic.

The artist needs reference images. A graphic about the new offshore oil project requires a depiction of the rig as seen by the planners. The artist can't just dream something up. Details are important and are known by somebody familiar with the story. Find the person. That detail included in the graphic ensures accuracy and conveys a sense of heightened realism for readers.

If the jackknifed tractor-trailer has four axles, the graphic is wrong if it shows only three. Sometimes a photographer's pictures will help with detail, but many times graphics portray action that can't be seen by photographers, like the inside of a mine that's collapsed. Get it from an expert.

Fax machines get information to artists quickly. A scientist at the other end of the country can sketch something fast, fax it to the artist and discuss the graphic as it develops.

Packaging information makes a page more interesting and also helps readers digest some of the facts and figures that give weight to a story. This page is from CP's What's Up service, which is designed for high-school readers.

What's Up?

Let's talk about SEX

Do the media reflect reality when it comes to teenage sex?

BY LORRAYNE ANTHONY
THE CANADIAN PRESS

Marsha Brady had plenty of dates that never seemed to worry about getting pregnant.

It didn't cross Wally Cleaver's mind that he might catch herpes from Mary Ellen – and AIDS didn't even crash back them.

Today, television presents a far different image from the days of the Brady Bunch and Leave It to Beaver.

Current shows give the impression that teens have sex constantly. School, homework, sports, hobbies, parents and siblings – they're all mere backdrops to teens' sex lives.

Parents who inadvertently tune in to Dawson's Creek may end up thinking, "Boy, things have changed since I was a teenager."

Things have changed, but perhaps not the way parents think.

"I think today's television does reflect what's going on today," says safe sex guru Sue Johanson. "I'm sorry, I know parents don't want to hear that."

That might scare parents, but it makes some teens scoff.

"Those shows aren't realistic," says Jared Sahr, a 16-year-old Grade 10 student at Thornlea secondary school on Toronto's northern outskirts.

"Those kids on Dawson's Creek have sex all the time. They just have sex, it never shows the emotional side or the consequences. It doesn't show if Dawson uses protection. Dawson doesn't have an STD (sexually transmitted disease), so maybe some kids watching it will think they won't get an STD."

Johanson, who hosts WTN's Sunday Night Sex Show, says Canadian schools teach kids about "the plumbing of sex."

"Kids today are much more knowledgeable about their bodies, ejaculation and things like that," she says. "But they don't know a thing about being horny or when to get birth control."

But so all Canadian kids got the basic plumbing of sex education.

In Fredericton, the school system does very little sex education, says Helen Kahlke, executive director of Planned Parenthood Fredericton.

"The high school (up until last year Fredericton had just one) has 3,500 students, no public health nurses and the students don't get proper sex education," said Kahlke. "But they run a day care so students with kids can finish school.

"It is quite possible that kids can graduate from school here with no sex education... and there is absolutely no information on gay and lesbian issues."

There are no recent statistics on how many teens are having sex. Stats from 1994 highlight one aspect: teen pregnancy.

The rates of teen pregnancy vary widely across Canada. The highest is in the Northwest Territories, with 136.7 pregnancies for every 1,000 women aged 15-19. The lowest is in Prince Edward Island, where the comparable figure is 31.3 pregnancies.

It's interesting to note, however, that teen pregnancy rates for 1994 are lower than they were in 1974 in every province and territory with the exception of Quebec and the Northwest Territories.

In fact, the overall teen pregnancy rate in Canada dropped steadily from 1974 to 1987. Since the late '80s, however, it has been rising.

Another disturbing fact is that young women aged 15 to 24 have the highest rate of sexually transmitted infections. The most common, chlamydia, often has no symptoms, so those infected are unaware of their condition and do not get treatment.

Kahlke says the teens she deals with at Planned Parenthood in Fredericton are reacting to a situation: The condom broke, what do I do?

In a perfect world, Kahlke says parents would be teaching their kids about sex, but her experience shows that isn't happening. She says young women have told her they need sex education – not in Grade 11 but as children.

"The first year we put sex education was in Grade 9 and all we were told was 'Don't have it,'" recalls 16-year-old Sahr.

"The next year we were told about STDs, but mostly one teacher told us about his sexual experiences and we thought it was funny, but some of the girls got embarrassed."

Abby Khalil, a 15-year-old Toronto high school student, says she picked up most of her sex education from her sister, who's three years older than her.

"I never had the luxury of running to mommy and daddy and getting the speech about the birds and the bees, but I just picked things up as I grew older," says Khalil.

"My sister taught me a lot. She probably never noticed, but I'd overhear a conversation between her and one of her friends, and I'd learn something new."

As for whether TV presents an accurate image of teen sexuality, Kahlke has her doubts.

"The kids on TV are very sexually active and so are the kids I see, but I'm not sure how representative they are of Canadian teens," says Kahlke.

"But one look at the stats and it's obvious someone is having sex."

CP Illustration – Tammy Hoy

Teen pregnancies
in Canada

(in thousands)
65
60   1995
55   48,771
50
45   1987
40   39,340
35

1974 — 1995

By province, 1994
(Pregnancies per 1,000 teens)

Province	Rate
NFLD.	32.1
P.E.I.	31.3
N.S.	44.1
N.B.	40.3
QUE.	33.1
ONT.	39.6
MAN.	64.4
SASK.	63.0
ALTA.	54.2
B.C.	40.7
YUKON	98.0
N.W.T.	136.7

Source: Statistics Canada   Tammy Hoy – CP

"We aren't all hormone-driven teens"

Diana Tseng is a student at Thornlea secondary school in Thornhill, Ont., on the verge of her 16th birthday. Here are some of her thoughts on teen sex.

"I'm really against the fact that all teenagers have problems with sex, because as far as I can see it's not all true.

"Within my circle of friends, I can guarantee that not one person has problems with sex or even had sex. Sure, the odd kiss or the odd hormone excitement is bound to happen, but it's nothing serious.

"I feel that we are still too young to be worrying about having sex and expressing our love for the person we are having a relationship with. What's the point of having sex?... All it does is tie you down with unwanted problems of a child or a disease.

"It is true that some teens have problems with sex, but I think the issue has been made bigger by the media. Practically every teen show or teen movie has to do with sex. It makes it seem that sex is inevitable in a relationship, but is that true? No. In teen shows teenagers are portrayed to hunger sex due to these hormones, and that is not true at all.

"Since all teen TV shows or movies have to do with sex, parents now find it harder to trust their children because they might be out having sex with their girl or guy friend. Parents should know that TV isn't reality, and they shouldn't assume that teen kids' behaviour will be like those shows."

What's online

**Want to learn more?
Check out these Web sites:**

Kids Help Phone Line. Includes moderated discussions on such topics as birth control and sexually transmitted infections. (Or call 1-800-668-6868, a toll-free line staffed by counsellors 24 hours a day.)
.http://kidshelp.sympatico.ca

Planned Parenthood Federation of Canada
.http://www.ppfc.ca

Sexuality Education Resource Centre Manitoba Inc.
.http://www.serc.mb.ca

Send comments or suggestions to: whatsup 8 cp.org

(CP – Tammy Hoy)

The CP news report

Main Desk and bureaus
Keeping editors advised
  Advisories
  Spot breaks
  Planned events
  Publishable and non-
    publishable notes
  Page 1 advisories
  Long-range advisories
  Other advisories
  Calendar and Look-Ahead
  Fronts advisories
  News Budgets

Slugs and coding
  Priority coding
  Departmental designators
  Keyword slug line
  Version field
  Specific slugs
  Catchlines
Sports news and statistics
  Slugs
  Agate
  Results formats
  Alphabetical list of sports

Packaging the news
  At-a-Glance, Highlights, Quicks
  Editorial symposiums
  Headlines
  Newspage copy

The way we do things
Advances
  Speeches
  Broken embargoes
  Advance slugs
  Advance advisories
Bylines
  Basic guidelines
  Style
Completes
  Examples
Corrections
  Withhold, kill, sub
Correctives
  General guidelines
  Style
  Clarifications

Writing news for online and cable services

News releases
  Content
  Format
  Pictures
  Who gets it?

Main Desk and bureaus

Main Desk in Toronto is the minute-by-minute guardian of the overall quality of the CP news report. Quality originates in the skills of the editors at department desks and regional bureaus countrywide.

Main Desk

Main Desk is staffed by senior editors who co-ordinate coverage and ensure that copy meets CP standards.

Main Deskers:

• See that CP moves quickly and effectively on major breaking stories, tip deadlining members to important developments, consult with Broadcast News and CP Pictures and alert the Editor-in-Chief or the President as warranted.

• Guard against, and act fast to remove, libel or other legal concerns in copy, usually by dealing personally with legal counsel and the bureau involved.

• Approve the content and format of Correctives and Clarifications before they are transmitted and later fill out a relay report confirming they have moved to all outlets that received the erroneous original.

• Ensure that copy is complete, interesting, well-written and properly edited.

• Suggest significant improvements in stories, perhaps asking a bureau to sharpen a lead by bringing key facts or interesting details higher.

• Watch for regional stories that can be developed for a national audience by a change of approach or addition of background detail — noting similar legislation in another province, for example.

• Consult bureaus by message or phone with a view to building the next-cycle News Budget (➤ See **Advisories**, page 357), suggesting story angles if necessary. Prepare and relay the News Budget advisories.

• Field requests, queries and problems from newspapers or the public, or direct them to the appropriate person or department.

• Proofread CRAFT stories — concerning the newspaper and broadcast industries — for style and content before they are transmitted at times when department or bureau supervisors are not available to OK them.

• Mark and relay nightly synopses of the CBC and CTV newscasts, indicating the status of CP coverage of each story.

• Prepare the twice-daily Page 1 advisory, in consultation with senior editors, and update as necessary with developing stories. (➤ See **Advisories**, page 352)

- Oversee marking of the Toronto newspapers, chasing matchers to stories from outside their coverage areas. Scan the front-page advisories sent by bureaus, looking for prominently played stories that rate pickup or chasing.

- At change of shift, prepare and distribute to bureaus and departments via the message wire a Developing Sked, which details the status of major stories during the last cycle and plans for such stories in the cycle ahead.

- Assemble and relay the twice-daily Calendar and weekly Look-Ahead List from bureau contributions (➤ See **Advisories**, page 354).

Bureaus

The deskers at each bureau are charged with the overall goal of explaining their region to the rest of Canada.

Among other things, this demands that bureaus be alert to the kind of context, background information, local colour or other news elements that make a regional story of interest to a broader audience.

The mark of a good bureau is development of its regional news.

Anticipating and planning for news is critical. This starts with a carefully kept datebook of future events; with thorough checks of regional newspapers for news and background information; and with intelligent guidance of newspaper and string correspondents on story development.

Each bureau is responsible for the copy it files, whether written by staff or by travelling staffers assigned to special events. Bureau deskers working alone, or inexperienced deskers, may call upon Main Desk or the National Desk in Toronto to proof important stories before relay.

Bureau staff are familiar with — and are collectively responsible for updating — the Desk Book. This is a loose-leaf record of news-handling tips and style directives, newspaper deadlines, return-news districts, staff and newspaper phone lists, etc.

Cultivating co-operation with the papers is a constant preoccupation. Politeness and helpfulness on the phone are where this starts, and it extends to notifying them promptly on major breaks, especially on Canadian stories that may merit staffing or picture orders.

Stories provided to meet a regional paper's request are pointed out in a bureau phone call to the person who asked.

Duties

Bureau duties include efficient dispatch of certain routine designed to keep members, fellow staffers and other bureaus abreast of coverage:

- Front-page advisories on major papers in the region (➤ See **Advisories**, page 356).

- Marking papers: At the end of each cycle, desk editors leave over for their reliever the latest editions of local papers with stories and pictures marked to indicate handling.

At the same time, staffers watch for major play of CP copy and pictures and follow bureau routine to make sure clips and tearsheets are exchanged.

These are the usual markings:

NO — Not carried by CP, with the reason briefly noted (e.g., LOCAL on stories of strictly local interest). Reasons for not carrying prominently played or controversial stories and pictures should be detailed on the Developing Sked. Rejected stories likely to attract other papers' interest may warrant an advisory to spell out the reasons after consulting Main Desk.

NO ASKED — Not carried, CP checking (with arrangements made for matching spelled out in the Developing Sked).

OLD — Fully covered previously.

NCP — Not CP copy but covered by CP; ensure CP copy covers all significant and interesting points in the newspaper's version.

PU — Picked up for CP use.

PU for PMs (AMs) — Picked up for next-cycle use.

• Developing Sked: Essentially a memo from a desker going off shift at the end of a cycle to the desker who follows, although schedules are also sent on the message wire for the reference of Toronto Main Desk and other supervisors.

Format varies to reflect bureau needs but a DevSked's purpose remains the same: an essential at-a-glance guide to incoming deskers on the status of major stories in the past cycle and in the cycle ahead, on outstanding requests, and on staff assignments and coverage plans, with reminders of new standing orders and changes in routine.

A properly assembled DevSked will be the first thing a seasoned desker consults at the start of a shift and the last thing left at the end of a cycle. If the DevSked is just a time-consuming chore to all concerned, it's not being done properly.

Events in the region for the next day are listed at the bottom of each DevSked under the heading Calendar (➤ see **Advisories** for format). Each bureau's Calendar contribution is assembled by Main Desk into a national list for transmission to newspapers.

Keeping editors advised

"**Extra! Extra! Triple murder!**" Like an old-time newsboy hawking papers on the corner, CP knows that to move news, you have to get the paying customers' attention.

Newspaper editors want to know:

• About the news that's coming 10 minutes from now, and in the cycle ahead.

• What's happening tomorrow? Next week? Next month?

• Will there be pictures and graphics?

• Anything special in the CP report that will be worth saving space for?

• How did other papers play the news?

These questions and others are answered by means of *advisories* — notes to editors transmitted along with the news copy.

Some are improvised, pounded out as a hot story breaks and develops. Some are routine — **Fronts**, the twice-daily **News Budgets**, **Calendar** items and **Page 1** advisories, the weekly **Look-Ahead List**. Others are issued in advance of major events such as elections to detail CP coverage plans. Still others commend editors' attention to special projects that CP has undertaken.

All are driven by the same rationale: customers expect information from an information company.

Advisories

"Keep us posted." — Front-page editor to a CP desker as a major story breaks.

Newspapers say the most helpful thing CP can do is keep them fully and quickly informed. Not only when big news breaks but as it develops, situations change and deadlines approach.

If a story expected at 9:30 a.m. is going to be delayed, send an advisory. Explain the delay if possible.

Don't be shy with **Top Copy** notes. These give editors an early tip that major unbudgeted stories are coming.

But papers also need to know about CP's plans beyond the day's top news. They want advisories as early as possible on major long-range plans for enterprise series, foreign assignments, advance stories leading up to a political leadership convention and the like.

And make no mistake: These advisories translate directly into play.

Note: Most advisories, including all routine ones, move with message — or **M**-type — designators. The exception is when the advisory concerns copy already sent. It takes the same designator as that on the story: **G** for General, **W** for World, **S** for Sports, etc. This ensures the advisory is routed to the same newspaper desk that is handling the story.

Spot breaks

1.   The phone rings. A major break seems to be in the making. But there is no immediate official confirmation. Remember: Newspapers somewhere are on deadline. They want a message like this:

PM-Tornado-Advisory
code:2
   Eds: CP is checking a report that a major tornado has touched down near Olds, Alta., about a 40-minute drive north of Calgary. Official word is expected from police shortly. There are no confirmed reports of injuries or damage at the moment.
   CP EDMONTON

Once the information has been confirmed and a story moved, send a follow-up advisory:

PM-Tornado-Advisory
code:2
   Eds: The town clerk at Olds, Alta., has confirmed a tornado has caused severe damage in the town north of Calgary. See PM-Tornado 1st Writethru at 9:59 MDT. CP-BN reporters Sylvia Strojek and Bill Graveland and a photographer are en route to the scene and are expected to arrive at about 10:45 a.m. A 2nd Writethru will move within 10 minutes.
   CP EDMONTON

---

2.   Keep editors up to the minute as coverage plans take shape. Don't wait until an eyewitness account or other strong sidebar is fully written before sending a tip. Send fast word on the timing of a news conference or official police statement. Move an immediate advisory if a scheduled briefing is delayed or cancelled. Advisories take seconds to write and send. One advisory may save a dozen phone calls, crucial during a major breaking story.

PM-Tornado-Advisory
code:2
   Eds: The town clerk of Olds, Alta., will brief reporters on the tornado that struck today, killing at least seven people and causing severe damage throughout the area north of Calgary. The briefing will be held in the town office at 4911 51st Avenue at 11:45 a.m. CP is staffing.
   CP EDMONTON

---

3. Give editors as full a rundown as possible on plans for copy, CP Graphics and CP Photos in the next cycle. This can be done in either the AMs or PMs Budget message or with a separate advisory:

> Eds: Besides the budgeted stories **AM-Tornado, NL, AM-Tornado-Victims** and **AM-Tornado-Rebuild**, there will be separates on past tornadoes in the West (**Undated—AM-Tornado-Past**) and how tornadoes are formed (**Undated—AM-Tornado-Profile**), a first-person account by a man who saw the tornado strike (**AM-Tornado-Eyewitness**), a QuickSketch, QuickQuotes, CP Graphics and CP Photos.
> **CP EDMONTON**

Co-ordinate advisory handling with Head Office or another bureau when appropriate:

> Eds: An UNDATED list of major Canadian disasters this century will move shortly.
> **CP TORONTO**

> Eds: The prime minister is expected to comment on today's tornado in southern Alberta at 3:45 p.m. EDT. CP's Dennis Bueckert is covering.
> **CP OTTAWA**

Planned events

1. Expected timing of copy on staged events is vitally important as well. Editors want to know whether copy will move in time for final deadlines. Tell them:

> **PM-Theriault-Advisory**
> Eds: Premier Camile Theriault is to hold a media briefing on New Brunswick's new labour laws at the legislature in Fredericton at about 10:40 a.m. ADT. CP reporter Chris Morris is covering. First copy is expected by 11:05. Adds will move in short takes, followed by a 1st Writethru for PMs and a QuickFacts and CP Graphic on the major changes in the law. There will a budgeted Night Lead, incorporating reaction.
> **CP HALIFAX**

2. Give advance notice on major announcements whenever possible, even if details are sketchy:

PM-Chrétien-Economy
code:3
Eds: Expected shortly — in advance for release by advisory — is an announcement by the prime minister on the economy. He is expected to start speaking in the Commons at 2:40 p.m. EDT but other business may cause a delay. An urgent release note will move as soon as he starts to speak. Guard against premature use.
CP OTTAWA

Publishable and non-publishable notes

Advisories carried on the top of stories fall into two general categories: publishable and non-publishable. The former are aimed at the reader. The latter are for editors' information.

Publishable:

BC-NHL-Preview-Red-Wings, Bgt
code:2
See CP Photo CPT11, CP Graphics
Budget

The following story is one in a series by Canadian Press sports writers previewing the new National Hockey League season. Neil Stevens of Toronto reports on the "new-look" Detroit Red Wings and their chances of improving their strong finish in the Central Division last season.
By Neil Stevens
DETROIT (CP) — Gordie Howe may have put it best . . .

And at the end of the story:

. . . nowhere to go but up."
Next: Reg Curren of Calgary looks at the Dallas Stars.

Non-publishable:

Eds: Petr (not Peter) in the following is correct. Macdonald is lowercase "d". Tonight refers to Tuesday.

Page 1 advisories

The CP Main Desk moves an advisory listing possible Page 1 story choices for AMs papers at 5 p.m. and at 4 a.m. for PMs papers. It includes a top photo, three top news stories and a "buzz" story – something that may be the topic of conversation at the coffee shop or water cooler.

Follow this style:

AM-Page-1-Advisory
code:3
WIRE EDITORS:
    At this hour, CP suggests the following stories for front-page consideration:
    TOP PHOTO
    UNDATED WXS133 (horizontal) – Flight deck crew loads a Sidewinder missile aboard an F-14 Tomcat fighter on the USS Enterprise.
— — —

    WASHINGTON – Congressional Republicans are moving ahead with the first presidential impeachment debate in 130 years, even as U.S. bombs rain down on Iraq. 600 words. See AP Photos. PM-Clinton-Impeachment. Moved 04:02 EST.
— — —

    BAGHDAD – Deafening explosions rock Baghdad in the latest wave of U.S. and British air raids that Iraq says have killed at least 25 people in the last two days. The bombardment covered the Iraqi capital with a pall of smoke. 750 words. See AP Photos. PM-Iraq. Moved 02:59 EST.
— — —

    OTTAWA – The Canadian Red Cross has sued the federal, provincial and territorial governments to obtain coverage of legal liabilities of about $8 billion in the tainted blood scandal. Red Cross officials still hope the issue can be resolved through negotiations but the statement of claim filed in court ensures the agency can sue the governments if negotiations fail. 550 words. By Dennis Bueckert. AM-Red-Cross-Lawsuit. Moved 17:17 EST.

    The buzz ...

    TORONTO – Senior Liberals, including top officials in the Prime Minister's Office, are cautiously toying with the idea of ending the Queen's role as Canada's head of state to mark the millennium. 375 words. PM-Monarchy-Axe, 1st Writethru. Moved 03:47 EST.

Long-range advisories

1.   Advance billing on special projects, foreign travel and other major assignments means better play for CP stories. Editors will look for the copy and use the advance notice to block out space in editions days ahead of time. A CP advance advisory also gives papers a chance to plan local follows, often a key selling point.

An example:

BC-VE-Day-Advisory
code:5
MANAGING EDITORS
NEWS EDITORS
FEATURE EDITORS
SPECIAL SUPPLEMENT EDITORS
The Canadian Press will mark the 50th anniversary of the Nazi surrender with a two-part package of stories. The main package will move April 5 and will feature stories focused on Canada's role in the end of the war and how the war changed the country.
An added package of mostly international stories will move in mid-April.
The April 5 package will be suitable for use as a special edition supplement. The stories will also be written so that each main feature can stand on its own and be run on daily newspages in the days leading to the anniversary. A graphic logo will be provided to run with stories used this way.
The packages will be illustrated by graphics and photos.
The lineup for the mid-April package will include items on Hitler, liberation of the concentration camps, and the liberation of the Netherlands by Canadian troops.
If you have any questions or wish to offer any items for the package, call series co-ordinator Malcolm McNeil at 416-507-2150.
CP TORONTO

Other advisories

The range of potential advisories is unbounded.

There is a simple test: If you as an editor were coming up to today's deadline or were in the early planning stages for open pages in next Wednesday's edition, would a CP advisory help?

By no means complete, here is a selection of other advisories:

AM-Copy-Advisory
code:3
Eds: Top copy from Ottawa today includes: OTTAWA — A former Iraqi minister, Jawad Hashim, says he, Mohamed Al-Mashat and one other prominent defector have been sentenced to death in absentia by the Saddam Hussein regime. 400. By Gord McIntosh. AM-Mashat-Death-Sentences.
CP OTTAWA

AM-Chrétien-Advisory
code:2
Eds: Please note 1st Writethru on Tokyo Chrétien on Gary Filmon's reaction should have been slugged WINNIPEG OUT. Winnipeg papers: Please make no use of the material in the insert.
CP WINNIPEG

AM-Budget-Advisory
code:2
   Eds: The sports story slugged AM-Expos-Wallach on tonight's news budget is delayed by technical problems at Olympic Stadium. It is not known immediately how long the problems will last. We will keep you informed.
   CP MONTREAL

AM-Brownwich-Advisory
code:2
   Eds: The trial of former P.E.I. cabinet minister Ethel Brownwich resumes this morning with testimony from her secretary. CP's Derrick Toth is staffing and expects to file a PMs story by noon AST, depending on the testimony.
   CP HALIFAX

AM-Budget-Advisory
code:2
   Eds: The Kamloops, B.C., budget item AM-Loons will move Lifestyles and not Entertainment as listed.
   CP VANCOUVER

AM-Peigan-Advisory
code:2
   Eds: The Maycroft, Alta., budget item AM-Peigan will not be available. A news conference scheduled for 2 p.m. MDT was cancelled. An unbudgeted 250-word night lead will move by 5 p.m. MDT, and if there are further developments later in the day an advisory will be sent outlining coverage plans.
   CP EDMONTON

Calendar and Look-Ahead

Few features of journalism can match the exhilaration of covering a sudden, fast-breaking story. Few frustrations can match trying to catch up with a major story that could have been foreseen and planned for if it hadn't been for neglected datebooking.

Every CP bureau and department seeks out hints of news to come in the reams of news releases, newsletters, press kits and other material that are directed its way.

CP keeps track of coming events for its own coverage planning and to inform its newspaper and broadcast customers. There are two public advisories, the weekly **Look-Ahead List** and the twice-daily **Calendar**.

The Look-Ahead is assembled by Toronto Main Desk from bureau messages, usually prepared by News Editors or their designates and messaged by noon, Thursdays. It moves each Friday morning at about 5 a.m. eastern time.

Each Look-Ahead covers events, by date, from east to west, from the Sunday of the coming weekend through to the Saturday one full month ahead. The Calendar, also prepared by Main Desk, lists events for the following day and is transmitted at 3:30 p.m. eastern time with updated versions at 6 p.m. and 4:30 a.m. The Calendar sent Fridays covers events through Monday.

The format for contributions to both these lists is the same: a brief description of the event, time, place and any other information useful to regional newspapers or broadcasters who may plan to cover. An **x**- in front of the placeline denotes that CP is staffing the event.

Examples:

HALIFAX — Corrections Canada news conference on lack of prison facilities for women in the Atlantic region; offenders now serve sentences in Ontario. 3 p.m., Sheraton Hotel (EDS: Note news conference was rescheduled from Monday to today).

x-MONTREAL — Canadian Medical Association executive meets to draft policy on physicians with AIDS, through Thursday. McGill Medical School (most sessions closed to media; CP staffing open symposiums 2 p.m. Tuesday and 9 a.m. Wednesday).

FORT SMITH, N.W.T. — Dene National Assembly begins, registration only, business sessions begin 9 a.m. Tuesday, continue through Sunday. Bell Rock Campsite.

- Specify when times, places are unavailable. But such detail, or an explanation for its absence, is essential when the event carries an **x-**. Newspapers and broadcasters find such information helpful and the stories they get are shared with CP.

- Description of the event should be brief but still spell out its news interest.

Not: Joe Saxon appears in court.

But: Joe Saxon, accused of attacking a neighbour with an electric weed trimmer, stands trial for first-degree murder.

- Include only events that are likely to produce copy. Routine court dates for secondary crimes are not needed. Include the nature of a court appearance — bail hearing, preliminary hearing, trial, appeal, etc.

- Placelines are capped but not boldfaced. Entries are in full — no in-house abvns. Follow format with care. Reworking entries to conform is time-wasting.

Fronts advisories

Editors are naturally interested in what other newspapers are doing with the major national and international stories of the day. And they like to know what local or regional stories are getting big play in papers elsewhere.

A routine item called a **Fronts Advisory** is CP's method of letting editors across the country know about the front-page picture and news choices of newspapers in most major cities. Each bureau is responsible for preparing and sending these advisories as soon as local papers are available.

As well, the advisories include brief notes on major play for CP's work — especially section fronts and op-ed pages — as a form of instant feedback on how staff's work is received.

Advisories follow these formats:

For a broadsheet:

BC-Advisory-Fronts-Ott-Cit
Ottawa Citizen Fronts, Wednesday, July 29
Above Fold:
    TORONTO (CP, Wendy McCann byline) — Striking teachers may be ordered back to work.
    EDMONTON (Staff) — City proposes rotating schedule for garbage pickup. LOCAL, NOT MATCHING.
    OTTAWA (Southam) — Restless Tories show disenchantment with Clark amid rumours he will step down before next election. Backgrounder. SOME ELEMENTS CVD PREVIOUSLY; NOT IMMEDIATELY MATCHING SPECULATIVE ANGLES.
Below Fold:
    WASHINGTON (News Services) — U.S. may lift trade embargo to allow food sales to Iraq. MAIN ELEMENTS CVD.
    OTTAWA (Staff) — Unnamed Alberta MPs hint at federal aid for troubled oil-drilling sector. PICKED UP WITH CREDIT and CHECKING.
    VANCOUVER (Staff) — Reform party Leader Manning suggests alliance between his party and Tories. MAIN ELEMENTS CVD MONDAY.
    NEW SAREPTA, Alta. (Staff) — Switch to organically grown ginseng brings bonanza to former beet farmer. Feature. PICKING UP FOR PMS BUDGET.
    Pictures: Ontario premier meets teachers (CP, Frank Gunn); goat farmer poses with his stock (staff), PICKING UP.
    CP Major Play: Op-ed analysis on government cost-cutting by Gord McIntosh, Ottawa; lifestyles section-page feature on Alzheimer's disease by Sylvia Strojek, Edmonton; entertainment-page profile of Codco comedy troupe by Michelle MacAfee, St. John's, Nfld.
    CP Edmonton

For a tabloid:

BC-Advisory-Fronts-Ott-Sun
Ottawa Sun Fronts, Wednesday, July 29
   MAIN HEADLINE: TORONTO (Staff) — Parliament Hill janitors to split $13-million lottery jackpot. (CP STORY UPCOMING).
   MAIN PHOTO: OTTAWA (Staff) — Nine-year-old girl points to toilet where she found two-metre-long python; inset pic of herpetologist with snake (STORY AND PHOTOS PICKED UP).
TEASERS:
   OTTAWA (Staff) — Drought threatens trees. LOCAL, NOT MATCHING. HOLLYWOOD — Record sales for Teletubbies video (Reuters).
   CP Major Play: Winnipeg lawyer reaped most government work, access-to-info records show, by Bruce Cheadle, Ottawa; sports section photo feature at Toronto Argo practice, by Frank Gunn, Toronto; business-page Money Monitor by Allan Swift.
   CP Ottawa

• A scan of story queues in the computer usually reveals whether national or international stories are covered. If in doubt, consult Toronto Main Desk.

• Notations such as **CVD** are not needed on stories credited to CP, AP or Reuters.

• Some variation of **CVD PREVIOUSLY** is acceptable for backgrounders and features. But consult archives and include a day or date for hard-news stories that CP has covered before.

• Fronts advisories are sent with **M**-type message headers.

• Credits of syndicates or supplementary services are not abbreviated (e.g. **Knight-Ridder**, not **K-R**).

• Placelines are not boldfaced.

News Budgets

Putting together a newspaper without a clue of what will be available to fill the pages would be like ordering dinner without a menu. Surprises are certain but so is a sense of queasy uncertainty.

CP tells its editors what's cooking with a twice-daily advisory called the **News Budget**. It details the top stories in sight for the next publishing cycle listed by order of domestic, world, business, lifestyles, entertainment, travel and sports news.

The budget is considered essential reading as papers across the country convene news meetings to plan the next edition. Each budget entry provides:

• A summary of the story's content and approach, phrased attractively.

• Expected wordage to help plot a paper's space needs.

• Writer's byline, if applicable.

• What developments are expected that could change the story.

- What illustrations and Quicks will be provided.

- Whether sidebars are planned, whether other current stories are related.

- Whether the story might interest other newspaper departments.

- The keyword slug under which the story can be found in computer queues.

Putting together the budget starts with bureau desk staff, news editors and department editors, who consider the top stories of the day in their regions and specialties and how they can be presented to qualify for the budget.

Staff-written spot stories, analyses, backgrounders and features almost always rate a place. So do the best pickups from newspapers.

Breadth of interest and the quality of the copy are the major criteria. Good writing, background information and local colour can elevate a story from strictly regional interest to a place on the News Budget.

Descriptive lines are messaged to Toronto Main Desk, grouped by category. Lines for the **Night Budget**, which moves each afternoon for morning papers (AMs) of the following day, should be received by 1:30 p.m. eastern time. Contributions for the **Day Budget**, transmitted early each morning for evening papers (PMs) of that day, are needed by 1:30 a.m. In addition to new contributions, the PMs budget includes a listing of AMs budget stories that will stand for afternoon-paper publication.

Main Desk should be notified by message or phone if late budget notes — commonly known as *skedlines* or *budget lines* in CP lingo — are expected. Those received after the main list is transmitted can be sent as an add, but this practice is generally reserved for hard news. If in doubt, consult Main on whether a top-copy advisory is in order.

The targets for transmission of budgeted stories is 6 p.m. for AMs and 3:30 a.m. for PMs. Updating advisories to editors are needed if copy is significantly delayed.

A typical budget line, with a description of its components:

WASHINGTON – While the United States seeks to depose Saddam Hussein in Iraq, Republican legislators will resume their effort to drive Bill Clinton from office. The Republicans are still pressing for a vote that will almost certainly see the president impeached. 650. Developing. By Robert Russo. See AP Photos, Graphic. With AM-Clinton-Iraq. AM-Clinton-Impeachment.

- Placeline is capped, boldface.

- Descriptive line requires as much care as the lead sentence of the story – both are intended to attract interest and convey information. Simply using the lead paragraph as a budget line doesn't always work.

- Wordage of the story or the best possible estimate.

- **Developing** indicates the story is still unfolding. This description would only be used if the developments are hard to anticipate. (A speech planned for later in the day is not a developing story, for instance.) **CP Backgrounder, CP News Analysis, Newsmaker** or **Roundup** can also be used here to signify the nature of the story.

- Byline.

- AP Photos and Graphic are to be sent. Include the number (e.g. **CPT102**) if available.

- Related stories, or sidebars, QuickFacts or QuickQuotes are pointed out.

- Keyword slugline, which newspaper editors will look for when seeking the copy. It must be identical on the story.

More examples:

> **MONTREAL** – Expos president and part-owner Claude Brochu met with the media Friday to announce a corporate-sponsorship agreement, the first time he has publicly commented on his cash-strapped team's busy week on the trade market. 500. By Bill Beacon. Business interest. AM-BBL-Expos.

- The absence of what Brochu had to say hints that this budget line was submitted before the meeting. But it takes care to include context on why the news conference is expected to be newsworthy. Something lame – **Expos owner holds news conference** – does nothing to encourage use of the story.

- The possible interest of this story to another newspaper department – business in this case – is noted. Variations include **Lifestyles interest, Entertainment interest, Sports interest.** Or **Newspage interest** for stories budgeted under any of those categories.

> **OTTAWA** – Parliament concludes a passionate debate about the death penalty with a vote. 500. By Stephen Thorne. Will be 1st Writethru after vote expected at 10 a.m. EST. See CP Photos. With Vars PM-Death-Penalty. PM-Death-Penalty-Vote.

- Developments at a specific time that will result in an update to a budgeted story are noted, especially if copy is likely to be late or the developments fall when key newspaper deadlines are approaching.

> **TORONTO** – The Ontario government has reached a deal that will allow thousands of teachers to retire at an earlier age, clearing the way for the hiring of younger – and cheaper – replacements. 450. With QuickFacts and AM-Teachers-Pensions. TOR OUT. Moves Regional (C). AM-Teachers.

- Pickups from newspapers that are subject to **locals OUT** codes – protection from a competitor's use of the story – are noted.
- Stories that will move with a regional designator are also noted.

Stories that are not worth budgeting but accompany other budgeted stories, as well as routine items such as basketball roundups, can be included in the budget lines under a **See also**: slug.

See also:
– AM-Budget-Seniors
– AM-Budget-Agriculture
– AM-Budget-QuickFacts

See also:
– PM-NBA-Rdp.

A particularly important news event can produce a number of related stories for the budget. They should be grouped under an appropriate subhead: Federal Budget, Stanley Cup Final, Winnipeg Floods.

Sometimes stories just don't pan out as expected. When this happens, or copy for some reason is not available, an advisory is issued to delete the story from the budget.

For example:

AM-Budget-Advisory
code:2
   Eds: Please delete Edmonton-placelined AM-Klein from the Night News Budget. Speech cancelled due to minor illness.
   CP Edmonton

At-a-Glance, Highlights, Quicks

Newspaper market surveys often agree: many readers feel pressed for time. Modern life leaves less time than in the past to devote to their daily paper. Non-subscribers frequently give lack of time as the main reason for not getting a paper regularly.

The response of many newspapers has been to add news summaries, capsules and other digests of information — often along with eye-catching graphics — that can be absorbed quickly. In many cases, these new features have been added without sacrificing the additional detail that devoted readers look for.

CP helps by offering three types of specialized editorial packaging: **At-a-Glance, Highlights** and **Quicks**. Each has a different look but each offers the same thing: fast access to information that is important, helpful or just plain interesting. Illustrations from the Graphics service of CP Photos round out the displays.

Information contained in a Quick can be transferred into an attractive graphic that gives editors visual content for their news pages.

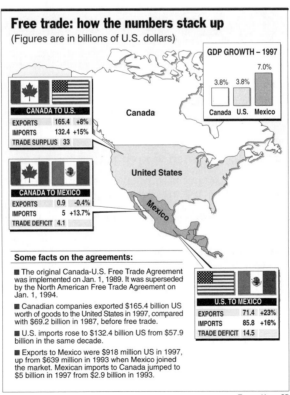

Free trade: how the numbers stack up
(Figures are in billions of U.S. dollars)

GDP GROWTH – 1997

| | 3.8% | 3.8% | 7.0% |
| Canada | U.S. | Mexico |

CANADA TO U.S.

EXPORTS	165.4	+8%
IMPORTS	132.4	+15%
TRADE SURPLUS	33	

Canada

United States

Mexico

CANADA TO MEXICO

EXPORTS	0.9	-0.4%
IMPORTS	5	+13.7%
TRADE DEFICIT	4.1	

U.S. TO MEXICO

EXPORTS	71.4	+23%
IMPORTS	85.8	+16%
TRADE DEFICIT	14.5	

Some facts on the agreements:

■ The original Canada-U.S. Free Trade Agreement was implemented on Jan. 1, 1989. It was superseded by the North American Free Trade Agreement on Jan. 1, 1994.

■ Canadian companies exported $165.4 billion US worth of goods to the United States in 1997, compared with $69.2 billion in 1987, before free trade.

■ U.S. imports rose to $132.4 billion US from $57.9 billion in the same decade.

■ Exports to Mexico were $918 million US in 1997, up from $639 million in 1993 when Mexico joined the market. Mexican imports to Canada jumped to $5 billion in 1997 from $2.9 billion in 1993.

Tammy Hoy – **CP**

At-a-Glance

When a major story is breaking here, there and everywhere, the occasion calls for an At-a-Glance:

AM-Cda-Fish-Glance ❶
code:5
EU-Fish-Dispute-at-a-Glance
                By The Canadian Press ❷
  The feud over fishing rights in the northwest Atlantic took an ugly turn Thursday as the European Union and Canada traded accusations. The major developments: ❸
  – ❹ The captain of one Spanish trawler says Canadian patrol boats tried to cut his nets and board his ship. A captain on another trawler says his nets were destroyed.
                — — — ❺
  – Canada denies the charges, saying three patrol boats had sailed near six Spanish vessels to identify them and see if they were fishing with illegal nets for turbot.
                — — —
  – In Dallas, Prime Minister **Jean Chrétien ❻** strongly defends Canada's position. "We had to do something."
                — — —
  – The French EU presidency condemns ❼ Canada for what it calls continuing harassment of EU trawlers. ❽
                — — —
  – In Madrid ❾ , several thousand angry Spanish fishermen ❿ . . .

---

❶ **Keyword** slug is variation of the slug on the main story the Glance accompanies **(Cda-Fish)**.

❷ Not bylined except for the **CP credit**, boldface, centred.

❸ Glances accompany rapidly developing stories. They are frequently **updated** to keep pace with events.

❹ Each paragraph is indented and preceded by a boldface **em dash** and a **space**. It ends with a period, not a semicolon.

❺ Each paragraph is separated by a **three-em dash**, boldface, centred.

❻ **Names** are boldfaced.

❼ Entries are written in the **present tense** whenever possible to lend immediacy. Avoid headline writing that drops articles and auxiliary verbs. Each paragraph should be constructed in the same pattern for ease of reading.

❽ Paragraphs should not exceed **30 words**. Sentences are kept concise but not to the point where reader understanding or significant detail is sacrificed.

❾ **Location** is noted where the entry concerns a development away from the centre of the action.

❿ An At-a-Glance includes material that is dealt with at least briefly in the **main story**. But a Glance of more than eight entries likely includes secondary material that should be trimmed.

Highlights

When complex elements of a story need summarizing, use Highlights.

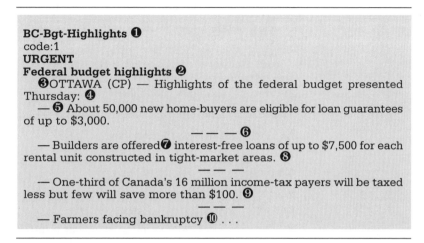

BC-Bgt-Highlights ❶
code:1
URGENT
Federal budget highlights ❷
　❸OTTAWA (CP) — Highlights of the federal budget presented Thursday: ❹
　— ❺ About 50,000 new home-buyers are eligible for loan guarantees of up to $3,000.
　　　　　　— — — ❻
　— Builders are offered❼ interest-free loans of up to $7,500 for each rental unit constructed in tight-market areas. ❽
　　　　　— — —
　— One-third of Canada's 16 million income-tax payers will be taxed less but few will save more than $100. ❾
　　　　　— — —
　— Farmers facing bankruptcy ❿ . . .

❶ **Keyword** slug is a variation of the slug on the main story the Highlights accompany **(Bgt)**.

❷ Carries **headline** but no **byline**.

❸ Usually **placelined** because it pulls together the key points of a major story focused in a single centre.

❹ Usually accompanies fully developed stories. **Rarely requires updating.**

❺ Each paragraph is indented and preceded by a boldface **em dash** and a **space**. It ends with a **period**, not a semicolon.

❻ Each paragraph is separated by a **three-em dash**, boldface, centred.

Note: Short sections of Highlights included in the text of a story — often referred to as **bullets** — are not separated by dashes.

❼ Entries are written in the **present tense** whenever possible to lend immediacy. Avoid headline writing that drops articles and auxiliary verbs. Each paragraph should be constructed in the same pattern for ease of reading.
— Sales tax rises to eight per cent Sept. 1.
— Single parents get child-care deduction up to $2,000.

❽ Paragraphs should not exceed 25 words. Sentences are kept concise but not to the point where reader understanding or significant detail is sacrificed.

❾ Highlights emphasize the key points of a story most closely affecting readers' lives, give specific examples and avoid jargon.

Not: Benefit eligibility for involuntary job-seekers reduced by one week.

But: Laid-off workers get unemployment pay after two weeks instead of three.

❿ Highlights include material that is dealt with at least briefly in the main story. Secondary items are not included. There should be no more than six entries.

Quicks

Almost every good story presents an opportunity for a **QuickFacts**, **QuickSketch** or **QuickQuotes**, whether hard news or feature.

Quickly defined, Quicks are short, sharp collections of information — facts, figures, trivia, biographical snapshots, memorable quotations.

These features are boxed for display or brightened by an accompanying CP Graphic to break up fields of grey type and offer interesting highlights, sidelights or insights into the news.

There is no real limit on what can go into a Quick.

Among other things, Quicks can:

• Provide a tight summary of main points from a high-profile meeting.

• Explain technical language from any kind of specialized get-together.

• Provide a calendar of main events at a multiple-day conference.

• Recite a selection of worthwhile jokes from a comedy festival or one-liners from an entertainer's news conference.

And especially, never neglect a Quick when it can give readers news they can use:

• What a new innovation means to you.

• How to tell if you've got the problem.

• What you can do about it.

• How the program works.

• Where to go for information.

• Pitfalls to watch for.

A Quick should rarely consist only of information already reported in the main news story. It may blend elements of the story with supplementary material from reference works or other sources. Or it may be a collection of related snippets not found anywhere else.

Formats are highly adaptable. Informative, interesting and amusing are the main criteria. Question-and-answer formats are especially useful for complicated subjects.

Some guidelines:

• Quicks can be either placelined or undated. They are not bylined apart from CP credit.

• Quicks should be snappy. Bare-bones, not story form. Unlike At-a-Glances and Highlights, complete sentences not required. Nor detailed tie-ins to main story. **Here are** not a mandatory introduction.

Not: Here are some facts and figures about Yugoslavia, where civil war has claimed hundreds of lives in recent days:

But: Facts and figures on Yugoslavia, embroiled in civil war:

Not: Early career: Born in 1920 to vaudeville entertainers, Rooney made his first stage appearance at 15 months. He made his film debut in silent-era short subjects at six and went on to star as perpetual juvenile Andy Hardy in a popular MGM series that ran from 1936 to 1946.

But: Early career: Born 1920 to vaudevillians. Stage debut at 15 months, on screen from age six. Top box-office draw in Andy Hardy series 1936-46.

• Quicks should be brief; 100 to 250 words is ideal. Anything longer should be packaged as something else. On rare occasions — such as separate QuickSketches prepared in advance on four new Senate appointees — they can be transmitted as a group for ease of handling.

• As in regular news copy, prefer the specific to the general. In some circumstances, Quicks can be used to provide detail that would clutter up the main story, such as province-by-province comparisons or statistical data.

Not: Showed interest in politics from early age.

But: At nine, insisted on joining father at Mackenzie King campaign rally.

Not: Union seeks 11 per cent pay increase over two years.

But: Union wants 76 cents hourly in first year and 67 cents in second half of two-year contract, net rise of 11 per cent over average hourly wage of $12.79.

• Try to include something offbeat in each Quick. A funny or shocking statement is a good lead-in to a collection of otherwise sober QuickQuotes or a good kicker to close a straightforward QuickSketch. An oddball statistic can enliven a businesslike QuickFacts (e.g. **stacked in a pile, copies of the committee's reports would reach higher than the 100-metre Parliament Building Peace Tower**). Don't overlook colourful personal traits in QuickSketches (e.g. **Jean Chrétien's deliberately folksy English, George Burns's trademark cigar**).

• QuickQuotes can expand on statements that appear in the main story. They can offer more direct quotes on statements that are treated briefly, or actual words for paraphrased material, or new quotes that weren't essential to the story. Quotes are separated by **three-em dashes**, boldfaced, centred. Limit the selection to four or five, whether from a single person or several principals in an event. Where essential quotes run too long for the Quick format, adopt a different slug (**BC-Meech-Quotes**).

• QuickTips can offer practical information for readers: five steps to healthier meals, seven ways to organize cupboards, etc.

• Avoid all-caps for headings.

Some examples:

BC-Keep-Fit-QuickFacts
code:3
With BC-Keep-Fit, Bgt

By The Canadian Press

Fitness trainer Bob Delmonteque dispels some myths about aging and fitness:

Myth: You can't turn back the clock.

Fact: The average person can lead a longer, healthier and more productive life by exercising. Keeping active can slow down and reverse the signs typically associated with aging.

Myth: Older people can't build muscle and strength.

Fact: People past middle age can gain muscle and increase strength by as much as 200 per cent. Older exercisers increase their strength at about the same rate as younger people.

BC-TV-Gemini-QuickQuotes
code:8
With Hamilton AM-TV-Gemini

By The Canadian Press

Some of what was said at Sunday night's Gemini awards for Canadian television:

"I have to thank Paul Haggis for being clinically insane." – Paul Gross thanking Due South's producer after winning his best actor award.

—

"No matter how much time I'm forced to live in exile I'm always first, last and foremost a Canadian. This land is your land, this land is my land, from the big snowy part to the other big snowy part." – Stephen McHattie, who won a best actor award for Life With Billy.

—

"I was on an airplane today ...

Note: Prefer the quote, then the attribution and context, if appropriate.

BC-MUSIC-Lightfoot-QuickSketch
code:3
With Toronto AM-MUSIC-Lightfoot

By The Canadian Press

A sketch of Gordon Lightfoot's career:

Beginnings: Piano lessons. Sings in church choir at age eight.

First group: Swinging Singing Eight, on CBC-TV's Country Hoedown.

First album: Joined Terry Whelan in 1962 as the Two Tones on Chateau Records.

Life's work: Eighteen original albums; about 180 songs.

Breakthrough: If You Could Read My Mind, a smash hit in U.S. and Canada.

Greatest Hits: You Are What I Am (1973), Sundown (1974), The Wreck of the Edmund Fitzgerald (1976).

Quote: "If they (the songs) have stood the test of time, it makes me happy."

(Source: Encyclopedia of Canadian Rock, Pop and Folk Music.)

Editorial symposiums

Some cynic once defined editorial writers as bandits who descend from the hills when a battle is over to shoot the wounded.

But at their best, newspaper editorial pages are in the thick of the fray, armed with argument, reason, wit and not-so-common common sense.

A selection of excerpts from well-turned editorials can reflect the depth of debate and range of opinion at play on important national and world issues — federal elections, key developments in the constitutional arena and the like.

Such selections are provided by CP in an **Editorial Symposium**, a sampling of what newspapers countrywide have to say.

Symposiums are most often started by Head Office, via Toronto Main Desk, but bureaus and departments are welcome to suggest appropriate topics. Requests for symposiums from member newspapers should always be referred to Toronto.

Providing a truly national, representative selection is essential. Metropolitan newspapers aren't alone in having opinions worth reading; a small-town view of events can be equally provocative.

Bureaus should actively solicit contributions from newspapers in their region, delivered electronically or by fax. The timeliness of a symposium effectively ends about 24 hours after it starts, so waiting for mailed copies of papers is not practical.

Here's what the first selection looks like:

BC-Bgt-Symposium
code:4
Editorial Symposium
                              By The Canadian Press
   Selections from newspaper editorials and columnists, with headlines, following Monday's federal budget:
New budget misses mark
   Timmins Press: Finance Minister Paul Martin wanted to unite ...

For subsequent contributions:

BC-Bgt-Symposium, add
code:4
Add Editorial Symposium

Martin performs fiscal exorcism
   Toronto Star: Call it a budget of penance for 20 years ...

• Keep excerpts brief. They should rarely exceed 100 words. Choose sentences that fairly summarize the editorial position.

• Use *ellipses* (three periods, separated by *en* spaces) to indicate material omitted. But give preference to blocks of comment that can be run without ellipses, since too many of them can create a poor typographical effect.

• Any citations must be exactly as printed. Paraphrasing isn't allowed.

• Newspaper names are boldface, uppercase and lowercase and followed by a colon.

• Contributions take a G-type designator and are sent on the same circuits normally used for general news copy.

Headlines

General

Strong CP headlines can grab the attention of newspaper editors and win play for stories. A good headline – specific, lively and short – can also be a time saver for newspaper copy editors. If the headline is strong, editors may be able to use it as is or modified slightly to fit space needs.

Headlines are publishable so they must be right. If they aren't, they must be fixed the same way a story would be fixed had it carried the mistake. Typographical, spelling and grammatical errors that would be fixed in the body of a story must also be fixed in a headline. An inaccurate or sloppy headline gives editors the wrong impression and could lead them to compound or repeat the mistake. An erroneous headline that is published could require a Corrective, and a headline damaging to someone's reputation could prompt a lawsuit.

Headlines must face the same tests of accuracy and fairness as all other publishable copy. The headline can't say **Five Dead in Prison Riot** if this is based on radio reports quoting unnamed sources. Such information must be qualified in a headline the same way it would be in the body of the story. Headline style allows statements to be condensed but not by sacrificing accuracy on crucial points.

Headline writing is strongly influenced by the amount of space an editor has to work with. For a newspaper editor, this can vary greatly depending on layout. For a news agency editor, the space is usually the same no matter what the story: under a line on the average computer screen. Copy editors of Internet news usually have more latitude and headlines can often be more detailed. In the case of cable TV news, a headline might be three words or less. No matter what the length, a good headline should use short, punchy words that accurately and vigorously sell the story to a reader.

Some tips

• Use plain, conversational words. Active verbs are the lifeblood of headlines.

• Write in the present tense. Use **Pilots OK Airline Merger,** not **Pilots Have OKed Airline Merger.**

• Use specific information. Headlines attract readers by giving them a reason to read on to the lead of the story. This normally means the headline should make a clear statement using a subject and verb. The active voice is preferred and specifics are wanted. Vague headlines – **Judge Criticizes Government** – tend to say nothing. And the specific **Headless Torso Found in Topless Bar** is much more attractive than the generic **Body Found in Bar.**

• Watch for times when a description or title is better than a name.

While it is OK to refer to the prime minister only as "Chrétien" in a headline, don't use a name-only reference with people who are not well-known. Try to judge how immediately recognizable the names are across Canada.

• Freshness is important. A big story that breaks early in the afternoon presents a challenge to editors writing headlines for the next day's papers. Most readers will already know something about the story from radio and TV by the time the newspaper arrives. Something creative or the promise of fresh information is needed. When Gen. Jean Boyle, head of Canada's Armed Forces, resigned after weeks of speculation about his fate, a headline stating that – such as **Boyle Finally Resigns** – would have been stale. The CP headline for next-day morning newspapers was **Gen. Boyle Leaves Chaos in Wake After Resigning**. This introduces new information and pushes the story ahead, giving the reader a reason to read on. The headline on a next-cycle analysis took it further: **Chrétien Government Relieved To Be Rid of Boyle.**

• Don't be boring. The goal is to make the reader want to read more than the headline. Instead of **Kurds Protest Outside Israeli Consulate**, try **Protesters Hit Cops With Iron Bars**. On a story about the untimely death of Wiarton Willie of Groundhog Day fame, one headline read: **Dead Willie? Cynics Smell a Rat.**

• There's room for inspiration and playfulness in headline writing, although this has to be kept under control. **Polly Vous Francaise?** (Edmonton Journal) worked well over a story about a unilingual Anglo parrot in Quebec ruffling some feathers. It doesn't meet all of the headline tests, but it passes the big one – it invites a reader into the story.

• Avoid long phrases that can't be easily split – newspaper headlines usually run two or three lines.

• Avoid headlines that can be read two different ways – **Iraqi Head Seeks Arms.**

• On CP copy, headlines should be flush left and in boldface. They should never run a full line and only rarely make it to the three-quarter mark. Forty-five characters or less is a good length.

• Only the first letter in the first word of the headline is uppercase. All other words in the headline follow normal CP style for capitalization. However, the principal words of headlines are capped when they are quoted within the body of a story (as they are in this chapter).

➤ See **Capitalization**, page 194.

Newspage copy

1. Newspage copy or *the newspager* is most often tied to a major break in Sports or Business news. These stories fall into two main categories:

a) Short items that capture the key elements of the event and their impact. These items are written to whet the appetite for fuller coverage on sectional pages: for example, a story on the Ottawa Senators winning the Stanley Cup. The top of the newspage story should be complete enough to flag fuller treatment inside.

b) Longer stories that take a non-specialist approach to a specialist event: how Edmonton celebrates a Grey Cup win; how employees in a small town react to a big-city decision by their only employer to go out of business after 80 years; how consumers will be affected by the merger of two meat-packing plants that have long been competitors. Strong human elements are essential in looking behind the game score, job-loss statistics and other hard-news angles.

2. In either case, plain English and the absence of jargon are essential. Sports-page copy on the Senators winning the Cup can talk about goals-against average and assume the reader knows all about Alexei Yashin and Wade Redden, but newspage stories must go back to basics. Technical terms should be explained, issues presented in terms of their impact on the public or readers and leading figures in the story seen in human terms.

3. Advisories tipping editors that newspage copy is planned are essential and should be carried as early as possible. But even short notice about a newspager on a late-breaking development can help editors planning front and section pages.

Advances

General

Texts of speeches, reports and other material are routinely provided to the media in advance of their delivery to the public. That allows reporters to treat the material more carefully and organize background or explanations as needed.

Some of this material can be distributed early by a news agency, embargoed for release when the speech or whatever is delivered. There's no reason to mislead readers in such cases into believing the stories were prepared in haste, on the spot. The stories should be candid about the fact material was prepared in advance.

Once such stories have been distributed with embargoes — or with internal phrasing that suggests the copy was prepared in advance — editors must be kept informed. Was the speech delivered or the report presented? Send advisories. If the stories need to be modified for any reason, do it promptly.

Speeches

1. Stories about speeches distributed before the speech is made need a phrase such as **in a speech prepared for delivery to**. A separate paragraph can say **A text of the governor's address was provided to the news media before delivery**. The paragraph can be easily deleted if a newspaper wishes; it should not include material essential to the story.

2. Divergences from the prepared speech, audience reaction and circumstances surrounding the event can give life to the bare text.

3. Corrections or additions to update a story moved in advance must be transmitted promptly. An important addition by the speaker is indicated by saying **Madhani digressed from her prepared speech and . . .** On occasion, the divergence may rate a new lead. If there is an important omission, say so and indicate in the story the wording of the original text.

4. When a speech has been checked and the advance stands, advise editors with a note.

AM-Madhani, Advisory
   EDS: See Ottawa Madhani. A check shows Madhani did not depart from the text released in advance.
   CP Ottawa

The paragraph referring to an advance text may be deleted and the reference to **prepared for delivery** changed to **in a speech to . . .**

5. When a text contains controversial or spectacular statements, every effort should be made to confirm the statements were indeed made. If CP cannot staff the speech, arrangements should be made for a fast check with an assigned newspaper or broadcast reporter.

6. When a speaker drops a controversial statement from a speech, this is sometimes more important than the speech itself if it indicates a change in policy or a moderation of tone. The speaker must always be questioned about the reason for the omission. As warranted, CP should also seek reaction from others involved in the issue.

Broken embargoes

1. CP editors should tell the source of embargoed material that we will abide by the release time only as long as others do. We will release the material immediately if someone else is found to have broken the embargo.

2. CP will take no account of the size or importance of the newspaper or broadcaster that broke the embargo.

PM-Royal, Release Advisory
   EDs: Toronto PM-Royal-Bank on the Royal Bank of Canada's annual report, moved in advance for release at 10 a.m. EDT, is now available for publication. The embargo has been broken by other media.
   CP Toronto

Advance slugs

1. The tops and bottoms of all advance items and their adds carry cautionary slugs. Style examples follow.

2. In copy relayed by Toronto deskers, embargo times are converted to eastern time. Specific times in the body of a story, however, are not changed to their eastern equivalent.

3. To avoid misunderstanding, sources issuing important releases should be encouraged to provide specific release times. If a source specifies release in morning papers or evening papers, the item should be slugged **for use at 6:30 p.m.** or **6:30 a.m.**, respectively.

Style for slugs

Follow these styles for advances. In examples 1-4, the ADVANCE slugline is the same at the top and bottom of each item.

1. On copy for a specific time today:

PM-Prisons, Advance
ADVANCE — 12:30 p.m. EDT TODAY, June 11

2. On copy for a specific time the following day:

PM-Prisons, Advance
ADVANCE — 10 a.m. EST THU Feb. 12

3. On copy moved more than 24 hours in advance:

AM-Awards, Advance
ADVANCE — 9 p.m. EDT THU Oct. 12
NOTE FUTURE DATE

4. On copy intended for a specific publishing cycle:

AM-Brothers, Advance
ADVANCE — 6:30 p.m. (or a.m.) EDT

Or

BC-Glover, Advance
ADVANCE — SAT June 15
NOTE FUTURE DATE

5. On copy to be held for release by an advisory:

BC-Throne-General, Advance
ADVANCE — NOT TO BE USED UNTIL RELEASED BY
ADVISORY, POSSIBLY ABOUT 2:15 P.M. EDT TODAY JUNE
12. GUARD AGAINST PREMATURE USE

At end:

ADVANCE — NOT TO BE USED UNTIL RELEASED BY
ADVISORY

Use this form to release copy moved in advance for indefinite-time release:

BC-Advisory, Release
URGENT
    OTTAWA — Release all advance copy on federal budget.
    CP Ottawa

6. On copy broken into takes; at end of each take:

MORE — ADVANCE or **MORE LATER — ADVANCE**

Adds are slugged:

PM-Prisons, Advance 1st add
ADVANCE
OTTAWA — 1st add . . . again."

Advance advisories

1. On major announcements to be released in advance, an advisory should be sent where possible.

BC-Economy, Advisory
   EDS: We expect to move shortly in advance for release by advisory an important announcement by the prime minister on the economy. He is expected to start speaking at 2:40 p.m. EDT but other Commons business may cause delay. An urgent release note will be sent immediately when he starts to speak. Guard against premature use.
   CP Ottawa

---

2. Newspaper editors must be kept informed of changes in the prospects for release by advisory. If we have said a release is possible at 2:40 p.m. and it does not develop, a cautionary note slugged Urgent and accompanied by five unspaced bells must be carried at 2:40 p.m. or earlier.

BC-Economy, Advisory
URGENT
   EDS: The prime minister's statement about the economy, originally expected to be released about 2:40 p.m. EDT, is delayed by a procedural wrangle in the Commons. Meanwhile, the embargo on Ottawa Economy continues until the prime minister begins his announcement. Release will be by an urgent advisory.
   CP Ottawa.

---

3. Use this form for the release:

BC-Economy, Release advisory
URGENT
   OTTAWA — Release the prime minister's statement about the economy.
   CP Ottawa

Bylines

General

Bylines recognize a reporter's original contribution and diligence on a story. When a CP byline is preserved by a newspaper, it sends a public signal of a job well done.

Bylines shouldn't be misused. They aren't normally warranted for a rewrite of someone's news release, the monitoring of a telecast or other task involving minimal imagination and enterprise. Solid original reporting and bright writing can rate a byline.

CP staff with full-time specialist beats should let editors and readers know about their expertise. Such identifications are used whenever department heads or specialist writers are reporting about their areas of speciality.

Newspapers are loath to credit more than two people for a single story. Multiple bylines can look awkward. Consult Toronto Main Desk before sending a story with more than two bylines.

Newspaper editors sometimes eliminate bylines when stripping sluglines from a story in their computer. A blank line inserted after the headline and just before the byline helps highlight the writer's name.

Basic guidelines

1. Bylines are used on top stories, outstanding features and stories by specialist writers.

2. A byline may be removed at the request of a writer if extensive changes are made to the story. In the case of Analyses or first-person material, which should not be distributed without a byline, the writer may request that the story be ditched if a dispute over editing changes cannot be resolved.

3. Desk editors may remove the byline when a story requires exceptionally heavy editing and the writer's approval is not available for the changes.

4. Bylines are not used from placelines where the writer has not been to collect the information reported. Where a reporter's diligence with the phone and other resources has helped produce a story that deserves recognition, consider moving the story without a placeline.

5. Department heads and specialist writers drop their titles when their position or speciality is irrelevant; for instance, if the CP Business Editor covers an axe murder next door.

6. Aside from columns, first-person writing is normally reserved for a vivid, dramatic experience involving the writer: **As I watched, the avalanche roared down on the village, flinging trees and rocks aside.** The first person is also justified when a staffer is an expert on the subject in the news: as a former Olympic sculler commenting on a world record in the event, for instance.

7. Always obtain consent (written consent on major events) before using any non-staffer's byline on a first-person descriptive story.

8. Bylines are set uppercase and lowercase, boldface and centred. No other slug intervenes between them and the story.

Style

For staff of CP, AP and Reuters:

1. For most stories with a placeline:

> **By Sarah Binder**
>
> **By Bob Weber**
> **and**
> **Gwen Dambrofsky**

2. For most stories without a placeline:

> **By Rob Russo**
> **The Canadian Press**
>
> **The Associated Press**
> **Reuters**

3. For department heads and specialist writers with job titles:

> **By Anne-Marie Tobin**
> **CP Life-Entertainment Editor**

4. For reviews by staffers without job titles but with special knowledge of a particular field, use the byline and add a boldface note at the end of the review under a boldface three-em dash centred:

> — — —
>
> **CP reporter Arlene Forbes studies opera and is a former freelance opera critic.**

5. For Notes packages and other collections of material from a variety of sources, put together with originality, add a boldface note at the end under a boldface three-em dash centred: **Compiled by Judy Creighton.**

For non-staffers:

1. For string correspondents, use only the byline on stories with a placeline:

By Dennis Passa

But on stories without a placeline, add the service:

By Dennis Passa
Canadian Press Correspondent

---

2. For stories picked up with few if any changes from member newspapers and used with the byline:

By Walter Smith
Hamilton Spectator

Note: On the rare occasion when a story from a member newspaper carrying a byline and newspaper credit must be Undated, use the boldface credit line **Distributed by CP** at the end of the story, on a separate line.

3. For experts writing about their speciality, use the byline alone and add the credentials in a boldface note, usually at the end of the story under a boldface three-em dash centred.

— — —
Eleanor Shu is a professor of economics at the University of British Columbia.

Note: If further detail is needed, the expanded note may go above the byline in boldface and above a boldface three-em dash centred.

4. For arts reviews from papers or freelance writers, use the byline alone and add the identification in a boldface note at the end of the review under a boldface three-em dash centred:

— — —

Michael Walsh is a theatre critic for the Calgary Herald.

Barbara Dumont, a graduate of the National Ballet School, is a freelance dance critic.

---

5. Similarly for travel stories and other material by freelances:

— — —

Joan Hanright is a freelance writer based in Darmouth, N.S.

---

6. For unplacelined copy by freelances, experts and so on, follow this style:

By Rosemary O'Connor
For The Canadian Press

Add the identification, if necessary, in a boldface note at the end under a boldface three-em dash centred:

— — —

Rosemary O'Connor is a freelance writer based in Vancouver.

---

7. For stories written especially for CP, such as a first-person account by an eyewitness, always preceded by a publishable editors note:

Jim Anderson was working in the fields of his 100-hectare farm Friday when a twin-engine jet crashed less than a kilometre away, killing 10 people. Here is his eyewitness account.
Written for CP
By Jim Anderson
BRADFORD, Ont. (CP) — It was the high-pitched whine of the engine that first caught my attention . . .

For unbylined stories:

1. For stories without placelines:

   a) From a single service:

By The Canadian Press
By The Associated Press
By Reuters

---

b) From two or more services:

> **From AP-Reuters**
> **From CP-Reuters-AP**

Note: It is *From,* not *By.*

2. For stories with placelines:

a) From a single service, use an agency credit in the placeline:

> HALIFAX (CP) — Six . . .

b) From two or more services, use a combined credit line above a CP-credit placeline:

> **From AP-Reuters**
> PARIS (CP) — Oil ministers . . .

c) The placeline credit CP-AP or CP-Reuters indicates CP has extensively rewritten an ally's story.

> TOKYO (CP-Reuters) — Canada will gain . . .

Member newspaper credit

All stories picked up from member newspapers should carry a bracketed credit at the bottom of the story:

> (Thunder Bay Chronicle-Journal)

If the story was combined from items from more than one member:

> (Toronto Star, Toronto Sun)

Completes

General

1. A Complete combines the top of a story with any adds. It is done when there are two or more adds to a story.

2. Completes move as soon as possible and are sent only on the full CP Datafile service.

3. A Complete carries the same log number as the Writethru that made it necessary – but with a Z header instead of an originating bureau header.

4. When a Complete includes Bulletin or Urgent material, with five bells, delete the bell characters. Unnecessary alarm signals at the newspapers diminish the overall value of the alarms.

Examples

For the first Complete on a developing story that was filed in takes:

AM-Explosion, Complete
code:8
COMPLETE (combines takes)
   HALIFAX (CP) – A deafening explosion ripped through the Halifax waterfront ...

If a Writethru on the story moves in takes, then another Complete is needed. The slugging this time would be:

AM-Explosion, Complete 2
code:8
COMPLETE (combines takes in 1st Writethru updating with six dead)
   HALIFAX (CP) – A deafening explosion ripped through the Halifax waterfront, killing at least six people...

Note: Completes do not need to be done if the Writethru moves in one take.

➤ See **Writethrus**, page 393.

Corrections

CP uses the following forms to make important changes to stories:

WRITETHRU — makes a change in fact or wording, including any error in the lead.

WITHHOLD — puts a hold on publication of questionable or erroneous material.

KILL — eliminates a story that is wrong, legally dangerous or damaging.

SUB — replaces an earlier story in its entirety; particularly used for a story that has been killed.

1. Explanations or information provided to justify the **WRITETHRU, WITHHOLD, KILL** or **SUB** slugs must be clear and easily understood.

2. All stories carrying any of these slugs get top priority on news circuits where the erroneous or suspect copy was previously transmitted. The slugs are all-caps and boldface, except the Writethru slug.

➤ See **Slugs and coding**, page 393.

3. WRITETHRU — Used to alter an erroneous, unnecessary or superseded statement. Often used to update material. The word CORRECTS, all caps, must be in the Editors' Note. Be specific.

Not: fixes name.

But: CORRECTS Eve to Eva in para 3.

➤ For an example see **Slugs and coding**, page 393.

Writethrus containing important corrections, such as those which substantially change the lead of a story, are flagged with five unspaced bells. The slug !!!!URGENT CORRECTION or !!!!BULLETIN CORRECTION is sometimes used.

PM-Truck-Crash, URGENT 1st Writethru
!!!!URGENT CORRECTION
Eds: CORRECTS criminal charges in para 1.
  REGINA (CP) — A Saskatoon driver was charged with dangerous driving and leaving the scene of an accident today after his pickup truck jumped a curb and demolished the fronts of two downtown stores.

Note: The five bell characters, inserted directly after !!!!URGENT CORRECTION or !!!!BULLETIN CORRECTION and on the same line, must be unspaced to trigger alarms at some papers.

4. WITHHOLD — Used to warn editors that a story may be erroneous, dangerous or premature and that it must not be published pending a check.

Withhold notes are sent as bulletins. They identify the story by placeline and slug, and detail the reason for the Withhold.

> **AM-Truck-Crash, BULLETIN WITHHOLD**
> **BULLETIN WITHHOLD**
>   EDITORS: Withhold from publication Regina Truck-Crash. The identity of the driver charged has been questioned.
>   **CP Edmonton**

5. RELEASE WITHHOLD — Used to notify editors that a story previously withheld has been cleared for publication. Notes releasing a withheld story are sent as bulletins.

> **AM-Truck-Crash, BULLETIN RELEASE**
> **BULLETIN RELEASE**
>   EDITORS: Release Regina Truck-Crash previously withheld because identity of the driver was questioned. Police have confirmed the identity of the driver.
>   **CP Edmonton**

6. KILL — Used to eliminate an erroneous or unnecessary story, whether or not it has been previously withheld. Kills are sent as bulletins. They identify the story by placeline and slug, specify the reason and say whether a substitute story is planned.

> **AM-Truck-Crash, BULLETIN KILL**
> **BULLETIN KILL**
>   EDITORS: KILL Regina Truck-Crash previously withheld, which identified the driver of the pickup truck. Legal counsel confirms it is possibly dangerous. Will be sub.
>   **CP Edmonton**

7. SUB — Used on a story that supersedes an erroneous item. It rates an urgent slug.

A sub repeats the story but with the erroneous material corrected. It is flagged at the top with an explanatory note to editors.

> **AM-Truck-Crash, URGENT SUB**
> **URGENT SUB Regina Truck-Crash**
> **EDITORS: Subs for Regina Truck-Crash previously killed. It eliminates the possibly dangerous identification of the driver.**
>   REGINA (CP) — A Saskatoon driver . . .

8. The bureau originating any Writethru, sub or kill that removes possibly dangerous matter from the CP report must send a note to editors at the start of the next publishing cycle, drawing attention to the elimination.

PM-Truck-Crash, Advisory
  EDITORS: Note the important SUB eliminating possibly dangerous identification of the driver from Regina Truck-Crash.
  CP Edmonton

Correctives

Mistakes happen. Misinformation gets reported. When it does, the first priority is always to get it fixed, quickly and properly.

The CP **Corrective** is used to catch up with an error that has probably already been published. It is specifically designed to face the error head on and set the record straight frankly.

It deals *only* with information shown to be in error, when enough time has passed for the mistake to get into print. If the error is caught in the same news cycle in which it is made — within a few hours, in other words — move a **Writethru** (see page 386).

Always go back to the original story when writing a Corrective. Focus on the precise words that are wrong and deal only with the erroneous information. But deal with it fully and openly. Never try to *interpret* the original. If it is wrong, it is wrong.

Here is a sample Corrective when the mistake is CP's alone:

BC-Bay-Simpsons, CCTV
code: 3
CORRECTIVE
   TORONTO (CP) — The Canadian Press erroneously reported Wednesday that Simpsons was once owned by Sears, Roebuck and Co. of Chicago.
   In fact, Simpsons and Sears, Roebuck and Co. were partners in the formation of Simpsons-Sears stores in Canada in the early 1950s.

When the mistake originates with a newspaper story, the Corrective should say that CP *distributed* an erroneous report. In all but extreme cases (see No. 8 in the *General guidelines* below), consult the newspaper before carrying a Corrective based on a pickup. Put out a **Withhold** (see page 390) if the paper cannot be reached immediately. Advise a CP supervisor so that further steps may be taken to reach newspaper staff.

CP believes that readers should be given both the correct version and the erroneous version together, to make clear what was wrong. It is not enough to present the correct information while acknowledging only that *erroneous information was reported previously*.

When an error originates with a government announcement, a company news release or some other official source, a Corrective is not used.

Rather, the followup story should aim for a legitimate news angle.

For example, a followup to a story based on erroneous mortgage rates released by a bank might be tied to the angle that bank branches were flooded with calls. Failing that, the story simply quotes the bank as saying it gave the wrong information.

The **Clarification** (see page 391) is **not** a substitute for a Corrective. The Clarification deals with a story that is not so much wrong as it is incomplete or capable of leaving a wrong impression.

General guidelines

1. When a mistake is discovered, send a proposed Corrective to Main Desk immediately, with a full explanation of how the error was made and who made it. Make sure it fully corrects what was wrong in the original. The Corrective *always* includes a reference to The Canadian Press erring or distributing an erroneous report. It also includes the date of the error. It carries a boldface **Corrective** slug.

2. Once approved, move the Corrective immediately. Repeat Correctives or point them out by advisory in the next cycle:

PM-Ship-Corrective, Advisory
code:2
   Eds: Note the important corrective item BC-Ship, CCTV, moved in the previous cycle and intended for papers that published the Halifax ship-sinking story of Saturday, May 25.
   CP HALIFAX

---

3. When facts and figures are involved, simply admit the error and give the correct information.

4. Consult counsel if there is a chance libel or contempt may be involved. Seek advice also if a Corrective might hurt CP's legal position or aggravate the damage caused to a potential complainant.

5. Add regrets or an apology where there has been obvious damage to the reputation of a person or corporation. Such a story should be approved by counsel. It must be headed by a boldface note asking newspapers that published the original error to give equal prominence to the Corrective. (See page 387.)

6. Never try to fudge a mistake in a developing story by overtaking it with a Writethru that includes a clarifying statement or skates around the original error completely. A note at the top should specify that the Writethru corrects a previous mistake. If there was time for the error to be published, a Corrective is called for.

7. If a member of the public with a vested interest disputes a story, and if CP itself or an originating newspaper stands by it, carry the person's denial along with a statement that CP or the paper stands by its report. Main Desk may need to check counsel on the appropriate wording.

8. Consider an immediate Corrective if the weight of evidence suggests the original was wrong, even when the originating newspaper cannot be reached. But keep pushing to reach newspaper staff. Consult Main Desk.

9. Correctives carry a placeline, almost invariably that of the original story.

10. Correctives must go on all news circuits on which the original was sent. Main Desk compiles a relay report to make sure the Corrective reaches every newspaper and client that received the original. Specific checks must be made with CP Montreal to establish whether the original story was relayed by the French-language services.

Style

The following forms are for the guidance of editors preparing Correctives for Main Desk approval:

1. Specific reference:

OTTAWA (CP) — The Canadian Press erroneously reported Nov. 28 that oil exports during the first eight months of 1991 declined by 17 per cent. In fact, oil exports fell by 27 per cent.

2. Correcting serious or legally dangerous errors:

Eds: Papers that published the St. John's, Nfld., Elwood Hatcher slaying story of Sunday, June 1, dealing with the arrest of two suspects, are asked to give equal prominence to the following CORRECTIVE.

3. Apology for serious error:

The Canadian Press regrets its error and apologizes for any embarrassment or inconvenience caused John Doe or Margaret Roe.

Clarifications

1. A Clarification is carried when a story is not essentially wrong but is incomplete or may have left room for a possible misunderstanding. It is a brief placelined item with the boldface slug **CLARIFICATION** and follows the handling steps set out for Correctives.

2. A Clarification should make clear that the original CP story — or in the case of a pickup, the story distributed by CP — left out important information or could be misinterpreted. The Clarification would then provide a fuller version or straighten out the possible misunderstanding.

3. A Clarification would be appropriate, for example, if a CP story gave only one side of an issue, or if the wording could be read two ways, or if someone felt unfairly treated, even though there were no errors of fact.

An example:

BC-Suspensions, Clarification
CLARIFICATION

WINNIPEG (CP) — The Canadian Press reported July 15 that Winnipeg city council had ordered two municipal employees suspended from their jobs for going fishing when they should have been inspecting sewage lines.

The story may have left the impression that the suspended workers had not disputed council's action. In fact, both workers have been supported by their union and are contesting the suspensions.

They maintain they were on accumulated leave when they were spotted with fishing equipment on the banks of the Red River just outside Winnipeg.

Slugs and coding

Slugs are labelling lines that help editors figure out at a glance what the story is about. They indicate whether the story is for news or sports pages, what the topic is, whether this is a new story or a variation of an old one, whether there are illustrations to accompany the story, and other information editors should have.

Coding tells computers what material to send where. It can be used to shorten stories automatically or prevent some stories from going to specific receiving points.

Consistency in slugging and coding is important since, in many cases, computers are auto-sorting stories into specific queues based on an exact code.

CP has an elaborate coding system that can change quite often, given software developments. This section provides only an overview of slugging and coding. Practices can vary from bureau to bureau and desk to desk. For details and updates, consult desk books.

Priority coding

One set of codes that has contributed to the folklore of news agencies, not to mention the vernacular of "newspeak", is based on how editors in the old days used to rank stories for transmission based on their urgency. This was necessary because slow technology meant it could take 15 or 20 minutes to transmit one long story. A way was needed to ensure an urgent story could "jump the queue." Today, with high-speed data transmission, stories are transmitted so quickly that priority codes are seldom necessary. But it is still a time-honoured tradition at news agencies to put a bulletin code on the prime minister's resignation and a regular code on the hog sales report.

These priority codes, which go on the first line of a story, include:

f — Flash. The highest priority, only for news of overwhelming urgency. Breaks into news flow and into any other story being transmitted.

b — Bulletin. For one-paragraph items of hot news, Kill advisories or NewsAlerts. Supersedes all but a flash in the computer queue.

u — Urgent. Used on high-priority copy of more than one paragraph.

r — Regular priority. Used on the longer stories that are the backbone of the CP news report.

d — Deferred priority. Used for copy that can be delayed while more important material is transmitted.

c — Cycle priority. These stories are transmitted continuously. Used only for cable television news service.

Departmental designators

Departmental designators help sort copy into categories and into different queues in computer systems.

The file name created at the originating point in the CP news network contains two (uppercase) letters and three or four numbers.

The first letter refers to the bureau or department of origin and is invisible to papers receiving the material.

The second letter is the departmental designator, based on the type of story: Canadian general news, world news, sports and so on.

These are the departmental designators:

A — Atlantic regional general news
B — Business
C — Quebec-Ontario regional general news
D — Western regional general news
E — Entertainment
F — Financial routine
G — National **general** news
H — Quebec-Ontario regional **sport**
I — Atlantic regional **sport**
J — Travel
K — Agriculture
L — Lifestyles
M — Service **messages** and advisories
Q — Photo service captions
R — Sport scores, summaries and other tabular sports copy
S — Sports in general
V — Western regional **sport**
W — World general news
X — Spare category for **sport**, such as Olympics
Y — Spare category for **news**, such as elections
Z — Spare category

Slugs

In order of appearance, the opening slugs say whether the story is for morning (AM) or evening (PM) newspapers or both (BC), what the story is about, whether it's a core story or an update, and whether it is urgent or not.

A one-word or multiple-word keyword slug describing the contents identifies each story. The exact same keyword should be used any time the story is changed by later developments, or when other stories are related to the same topic: **PM-Avalanche; PM-Avalanche, 1st Writethru; PM-Avalanche-Survivors.**

Uniqueness in slugging is important to avoid confusing two or more stories: **Obit-Brian-Moore,** not **Died.** Intriguing or snappy slugs can also go a long way to selling a story to an editor: **AM-Pigs-Escape,** not **AM-Accident.**

Slugs go boldface and most are in uppercase and lowercase.

Keyword slug line

The first line under the coding instructions to the computer is the keyword slug line, consisting of the cycle designator, a keyword or keywords, and the version field:

PM-Toxic-Ban   **AM-IOC-Bribes**

PM-IOC-Bribes, 1st add   **BC-Food-Dollar**

The cycle designators used on CP copy:

AM — Used on stories intended primarily for morning papers.

PM — Primarily for evening papers.

BC (both cycles) — Stories that may be used in either cycle. An example would be a story delivered early in the night news cycle for next-day morning papers that is available for publication in late editions of evening papers in the West, or for use any time on the day of publication if the story has been delivered in advance. It is also used on routine items, such as entertainment lists of best-sellers, concert dates and the like.

Keep slugs tight, yet descriptive. One-word slugs are preferred when possible.

Version field

The version field provides more detailed information for editors using directory displays to search for copy. This information helps editors link the various components of a story.

The version field is separated from the keyword field by a comma and a space. Some examples:

PM-Canadian-Lords, DL Bgt
AM-NAC-Yashin, Urgent 1st Writethru
PM-Canadian-Lords, BULLETIN KILL
AM-NAC-Yashin, 2nd Writethru
PM-Canadian-Lords, 1st add
BC-Clandestine, Advance
PM-Canadian-Lords, Complete
BC-FILM-Sundance, Rpt

Material in the version field is listed in the following order:

— Flash, Bulletin, Kill, Advisory, Withhold, Urgent, Rpt
— Lead status: DL, NL, 1st Writethru, Complete, etc.
— 1st add, Advance, etc.
— Bgt

Note that **Bgt** is not repeated in the version field when Writethrus are filed.

In the version field, **Budget, Day Lead** and **Night Lead** may be abbreviated to **Bgt, DL** and **NL.** However, they should be written out in other slug lines.

Words within the version field are separated by spaces, not by commas or hyphens.

The combined keyword-version field should be kept to a maximum of 45 characters, including punctuation, to allow for proper display in newspaper computer systems.

Specific slugs

This section outlines the main story slugs and the forms in which they are written by CP editors and writers. The code:# line is not included to save space.

FLASH — An emergency signal to editors that outstanding news is breaking. Limited to one sentence, a flash has transmission priority and can break into any other story being transmitted before it. It is extremely rare and must be followed immediately by a Bulletin.

The word **FLASH** is sent all caps, centred and flagged with five unspaced bells. The text is indented and boldface. The item has a placeline but no service logo.

> **BC-Plane-Crash, Flash**
> > **FLASH**
> BLANDFORD, N.S. — A jet with 227 people aboard has crashed in the Atlantic Ocean.

NEWSALERT — Used for more run-of-the-mill newsbreaks — important government announcements, court decisions and the like. It is not intended to be publishable. It provides a one-sentence update to alert editors that a Bulletin or an Urgent is on its way within five minutes.

It is always slugged **ALERT**, all-caps, and is flagged with five unspaced bells. The item has a placeline but no service logo. It moves on an urgent priority

> **BC-ALERT**
> **CP NewsAlert**
> PITTSBURGH — Mike Milbury steps down as coach of New York Islanders, remains as GM.

BULLETIN — Used on the first publishable paragraph — usually not more than 50 words — of important breaks. It should be followed almost immediately by an **URGENT** add. The word **BULLETIN** is sent all caps, centred and carries five unspaced bells. It is publishable and, except for a byline, immediately precedes the story.

> **AM-Plane-Crash, Bulletin**
> > **BULLETIN**
> > **By Steve MacLeod**
> BLANDFORD, N.S. (CP) — A Swissair jetliner carrying 227 passengers and crew has crashed in the Atlantic Ocean near this tiny fishing village.
> > **MORE**

URGENT — Used on the first add to a Bulletin and on stories of Bulletin or near-Bulletin character running more than 50 words or so. Adds to bulletins are kept short for fast relay.

The word **URGENT** is sent all caps, flush left, and carries five unspaced bells. It is not intended for publication and comes immediately after the keyword slug line.

AM-Plane-Crash, Urgent 1st add
URGENT
PEGGY'S COVE, N.S. — 1st add . . . village.
  The MD-11 jet, en route from New York to Zurich, was attempting an emergency landing in Halifax but did not make it that far, said Andrew Ereau of search and rescue in Halifax.
  There was no word on survivors.

                                                               MORE

An urgent lead would be slugged like this:

AM-Clinton, Urgent
URGENT
Clinton to convene peace talks in Middle East
  WASHINGTON (AP) — U.S. President Bill Clinton ...

1st Writethru — Used on a story superseding a previous story in the same cycle. When warranted, it is followed by **2nd Writethru, 3rd Writethru** and so on.

A Writethru repeats the story in its entirety, with any changes incorporated and described in a detailed Editors' Note at the top of the item. Editors' Notes should mention every change that is being made to a story. Include paragraph numbers so editors do not have to read through the story looking for the changes.

Changes fall into four broad categories: corrections, inserts, precedes and leads.

If the story is being corrected, the word **CORRECTS**, all caps, must be in the Editors' Note:

AM-Plane-Crash, 1st Writethru
Eds: CORRECTS number aboard to 229 from 227; fixes destination to Geneva in para 2.
See CP Photos, Graphics
Jet crashes, sinks into ocean
                        By Steve MacLeod
  BLANDFORD, N.S. (CP) — Ships and aircraft were searching the ocean early today for a Swissair jet carrying 229 passengers and crew that crashed near this tiny fishing village.
  The MD-11 jet, en route from New York to Geneva, was attempting an emergency landing at Halifax airport, said Andrew Ereau of search and rescue in Halifax.

Note: Writethrus containing important corrections must also be slugged URGENT CORRECTION or BULLETIN CORRECTION.

➤ See **Corrections**, page 382.

If the placeline of the story is changing, the word PRECEDES, all caps, should appear:

AM-Plane-Crash, 2nd Writethru
Eds: PRECEDES BLANDFORD, N.S. with exact location of Peggy's Cove; adds comments from search and rescue; edits throughout.
See CP Photos, Graphics
Jet crashes, sinks into ocean
                    By Steve MacLeod
     PEGGY'S COVE, N.S. (CP) — Debris, lights and an oil slick were spotted in the Atlantic Ocean early today where a Swissair jet carrying 229 passengers and crew is believed to have crashed just off the southwest coast of Nova Scotia.
     Search and rescue spokesman Dan Bedell said the MD-11 jet, en route from New York to Geneva, had been attempting an emergency landing at Halifax airport when it disappeared from radar screens.

When new material is being incorporated, the word UPDATES, all caps, is used. Use an urgent slug if the material significantly changes the story.

AM-Plane-Crash, Urgent 3rd Writethru
URGENT
Eds: UPDATES with confirmation of no survivors and discovery of wreck of jet.
See CP Photos, Graphics
Jetliner crashes off coast of Nova Scotia; 229 aboard
                    By Steve MacLeod
     PEGGY'S COVE, N.S. (CP) — The wreckage of a Swissair jet that crashed with 229 people aboard has been located in the dark ocean waters off the coast of Nova Scotia.
     "We have no survivors," said Lt.-Cmdr. Glenn Chamberlain at the search-and-rescue centre in Halifax. "The debris field is about one or two miles big."

When an insert is needed, the word INSERTS, all caps, appears:

AM-Plane-Crash, 4th Writethru
Eds: INSERTS after para 14 toll-free numbers for victims' relatives.
See CP Photos, Graphics
Jetliner crashes off coast of Nova Scotia; 229 aboard
                    By Steve MacLeod
     PEGGY'S COVE, N.S. (CP) — The wreckage of a Swissair jet that crashed with 229 people aboard has been located in the dark ocean waters off the coast of Nova Scotia.
     "We have no survivors," said Lt.-Cmdr. Glenn Chamberlain at the search-and-rescue centre in Halifax. "The debris field is about one or two miles big."

Night Lead and Day Lead — Used when a story in the previous cycle is being updated. The slugs are upper and lowercase, flush left.

> **PM-Plane-Crash, DL Bgt**
> **Day Lead**
> **See CP Photo CPT112, CP Graphic CPT12**
> **Swissair jetliner crashes in waters off Nova Scotia**
> **By Steve MacLeod**
>   PEGGY'S COVE, N.S. — A crippled Swissair jet, desperately trying to make it to Halifax to attempt an emergency landing, crashed into the ocean near this tiny village late Wednesday.
>   A massive search-and-rescue effort . . .

See — Used on a story that follows in the next cycle but with a different placeline. The slug is upper and lowercase. The story has the same keyword slugging as the earlier version in the previous cycle.

> **PM-Plane-Crash, DL**
> **Day Lead**
> **See Peggy's Cove night**
>   HALIFAX (CP) — Air traffic controllers who talked to a pilot minutes before his jet crashed into the Atlantic Ocean, killing all aboard, say he was preparing for an emergency landing at Halifax airport before they lost contact with him.

With — Used on a sidebar from another point in either news cycle. The slug is upper and lower.

> **PM-Plane-MD-11**
> **With Peggy's Cove Plane-Crash**
> **Plane model being phased out**
> **By Kevin McGran**
>   TORONTO (CP) — The Swissair MD-11 that crashed off Nova Scotia on Wednesday night is a highly sophisticated wide-body jetliner model that is being phased out by Boeing, putting 600 Canadians out of work.
>   The jetliner, which first flew in January 1990, was the first jet with three engines to be introduced since the Douglas DC-10 and Lockheed L-1011 lifted off in the 1970s.

MORE — Indicates that additional information will move within 10 minutes. The slug **MORE** is sent all caps, flush right at the bottom of copy.

MORE LATER — Indicates that an add will move within 20 minutes. The slug **MORE LATER** goes all caps, flush right.

If information is expected beyond 20 minutes, no slug is used on the bottom. Instead, an advisory is sent specifying when additional copy is expected.

Delays in the 10- or 20-minute relays must also be explained in a quick advisory to editors.

Espy — Used on a story aimed at a particular community or region. The slug is upper and lower, flush left. **Espy Mtl, Espy West.**

Note — Used to draw a bureau's attention to a story. The slug is upper and lower, flush left. **Ottawa note.**

Asked — Used on a story delivered to meet a request. The slug is upper and lower, flush left. **Truro asked, CTV asked, AP asked.** The slug should not be used when it will signal a paper's or subscriber's interest to its competition. Instead, send a message to the nearest CP bureau for relay to the asker. **Wpg Art-Theft is Tor Star asked.**

OUT — Used on a story based on a pickup from a newspaper in a city with more than one paper. The slug includes a three-letter code that prevents the story from entering the computer of the competing paper. It is boldfaced, flush left, with codes in all upper or all lower. It appears before the other sluglines noted above.

TOR OUT
YYY

HFX OUT
hqq

Catchlines

Catchlines are links to previous stories or portions of stories, used at the top of adds. They are in boldface and flush left. Included are the placeline and the last word or two of the previous copy to help confirm where the add goes.

AM-Mayor, 1st add
Calgary — 1st add . . . lost poodle.

Sports news and statistics

For general information on covering sports issues, see Sports, page 77.

Slugs

1. Slugs must be informative. A well-chosen slug can whet the appetite of an editor and also simplify the search for a specific story.

2. All slugs begin with a *cycle designator*. Stories earmarked for morning papers are designated **AM** and for afternoon editions, **PM**. Secondary items that will stand for both cycles, and most agate, are slugged **BC**.

3. The second element of the slug — all caps and no longer than five characters — identifies major sports. Secondary sports are grouped under the generic **MISC** slug, with the specific sport identified in subsequent slug words. For game copy involving established leagues, the league abbreviation substitutes for the sport designator. Here are the major sports and leagues and their keyword slugs:

Sports

AUTO	auto racing
BBL	baseball
BKBL	basketball
BOX	boxing
CANOE	canoeing
CRKT	cricket
CURL	curling
CYCLE	cycling
DIVE	diving
EQUE	equestrian
FTBL	football
GOLF	golf
GYM	gymnastics
HARN	harness racing
HKY	hockey
LACR	lacrosse
RODEO	rodeo
ROW	rowing
RUGBY	rugby
SAIL	sailing
SKTG	skating (figure and speed skating)
SKI	skiing
SOC	soccer
SWIM	swimming
TEN	tennis
THBRD	thoroughbred racing
TRACK	track and field (athletics)
VLBL	volleyball
MISC	all other sports

Leagues

AHL	American Hockey League
AMN	American League (baseball)
NPSL	National Professional Soccer League
CFL	Canadian Football League
CIAU	Canadian Interuniversity Athletic Union
CSL	Canadian Soccer League
IHL	International Hockey League
MLS	Major League Soccer
NAT	National League (baseball)
NBA	National Basketball Association
NBL	National Basketball League
NFL	National Football League
NHL	National Hockey League
NLL	National Lacrosse League
WNBA	Women's National Basketball Association

Multi-sport events

OLY   Olympics

GAMES   Other multi-sport events such as the Pan Am, Commonwealth or Canada Games

4.   The next elements of the slug identify specific subject matter. For example, a story aimed at morning papers and dealing with a world-record swim by Canadian Nancy Sweetnam might be slugged: **AM-SWIM-Sweetnam-Record**. Or, a feature on Canadian table tennis champion Gideon Joe Ng might carry a **PM-MISC-Table-Tennis-Ng** slug.

In game stories, the second element of the slug identifies the league and the third and fourth elements the two competing teams (the visiting team listed first). For example, an NHL game with the Vancouver Canucks visiting the Winnipeg Jets would be slugged: **AM-NHL-Vcr-Wpg.**

Agate

As the design and focus of sports sections continue to evolve, the demand for agate increases.

Agate, or scoreboard, pages allow newspapers to present the essential aspects of a game or competition concisely. In many instances, they provide the option of not carrying a story on the event. These pages also satisfy the appetite among sports readers for more background statistics and comparison tables.

Reporters and editors should think constantly of ways to supplement stories with agate tables, fact boxes and graphics.

All CP-tabulated material carries a **Tab** identifier in the slugline immediately following the cycle designator. Unedited AP tabular copy does not take the Tab slug.

Consult desk books for details on tabulating material.

Results formats

Most results are presented in one of three formats: **bare score**, **field result** or **head-to-head result**. An example of each is given here for fast reference. Individual sports sections will specify which format is appropriate.

Canadian results in international competitions are boldfaced. Home towns for Canadians are provided; others are listed by country.

Bare score

The winning team is listed first, with the exception of European soccer results where the home team is listed first, regardless of the outcome.

BC-Tab-HKY-Rslts
Wednesday's list

By The Canadian Press
NHL

Toronto 3 Montreal 3

Adds go as follows:

BC-Tab-HKY-Rslts, add
Add Wednesday's list
Add NHL

Calgary 6 Vancouver 4

Field result

BC-Tab-TRACK-World-Cup-Rslts
BRUSSELS (CP) — Results Wednesday from a World Cup track and field meet:

MEN

100 metres: 1. Donovan Bailey, Oakville, Ont., 9.87; 2. Maurice Greene, U.S., 9.99; 3. Ato Boldon, Trinidad and Tobago, 10.01.

Note: Where the field is particularly large, such as in a marathon or an auto race, results are broken into paragraphs, approximately of equal length. For example, a 20-member field would be broken into two paragraphs of 10 competitors each. The first paragraph would end with a period, not the semicolon used within each paragraph to separate competitors.

Head-to-head result

BC-Tab-TEN-Wimbledon-Rslts
    LONDON (CP) — Results Wednesday from the Wimbledon tennis championships (seedings in parentheses):
WOMEN
Singles
Third Round
    Martina Hingis (1), Switzerland, def. Monica Seles (6), U.S., 7-6 (7-3) 6-3. Amanda Coetzer, South Africa, def. **Jana Nejedly, Oakville, Ont.,** 6-4, 3-6, 6-2.

Athletics   ➤ See **Track and field.**

Auto racing

1. Report Grand Prix racing in kilometres, but stock-car, Indy-car and drag racing in miles.

2. Results use the field format.

BC-Tab-AUTO-Cdn-GP-Rslts
    MONTREAL (CP) — Results Sunday of the Canadian Grand Prix auto race, 69 laps of the 4.43-kilometre Circuit Gilles-Villeneuve, with lapsed time of drivers finishing race, laps completed by non-finishers and winner's average speed:
    1. **Jacques Villeneuve, Iberville, Que., Williams-Mecachrome, one hour 38 minutes 51.490 seconds (185.520 km/h);** 2. Michael Schumacher (Germany), Ferrari, 1:39:23.322; 3. Mika Hakkinen (Finland), McLaren-Mercedes, 1:39:33.707; 4. Eddie Irvine (Britain), Ferrari, 1:40:11.700; 5. David Coulthard (Britain), McLaren-Mercedes, 1:40:13.841; . . .

Baseball

1. Write **American League, National League, American League East**, etc.

2. In sluglines on game stories, use **AMN** (all caps) for the American League and **NAT** for the National League, followed by the abbreviations of the teams involved, visiting team first.

AM-NAT-NY-Mtl
    MONTREAL (CP) — A ninth-inning homer . . .

For non-game stories, use the generic **BBL** as the keyword in the slug.

3. Use these team abbreviations:

American League: **Bal** (Baltimore), **Bos** (Boston), **Cal** (California), **Chi** (Chicago), **Cle** (Cleveland), **Det** (Detroit), **KC** (Kansas City), **Min**

(Minnesota), **NY** (New York), **Oak** (Oakland), **Sea** (Seattle), **TB** (Tampa Bay), **Tex** (Texas) and **Tor** (Toronto).

National League: **Ariz** (Arizona), **Atl** (Atlanta), **Chi** (Chicago), **Cin** (Cincinnati), **Col** (Colorado), **Hou** (Houston), **LA** (Los Angeles), **Fla** (Florida), **Mil** (Milwaukee), **Mtl** (Montreal), **NY** (New York), **Pha** (Philadelphia), **Pgh** (Pittsburgh), **StL** (St. Louis), **SD** (San Diego) and **SF** (San Francisco).

4.   Scores are normally carried as part of standings. In instances where stand-alone scores are warranted, use the bare scores format.

5.   The first linescore of the day follows this style:

BC-Tab-BBL-Linescores
Thursday's list
                              By The Canadian Press
                                 AMERICAN LEAGUE
Toronto   004 221 020—11 15   2
Cleveland   110 000 213— 8 11   1
     Clemens (W,9-2), Quantrill (8), Persons (S,12) (9) and Fletcher;
Nagy (L,3-3) and S. Alomar (6). **HRs:** Tor — Delgado (5),
Green 2 (13); Cle — Ramirez (15).

Note 1: A *thin space* is inserted after every three innings to break up the figures and make them more readable.

Note 2: There is no spacing around the dash in the team lines, but there is when listing the home runs.

Note 3: Team abbreviations may be necessary for extra-inning games to avoid team lines spilling over.

Subsequent linescores do not carry specific add numbers, such as **1st add**, **2nd add**, and do not carry catchwords.

BC-Tab-BBL-Linescores, add
Add Thursday's list
Add AL etc.

6.   In boxscores, the visiting team is on the left. Each player is shown in the last position he played. Figures in parentheses are the player's total in that category for the season.

Note: CP relays AP boxscores in unedited form.

BC-AMN-Box-Tor-Bal
  BLUE JAYS 8, ORIOLES 2

TORONTO	ab	r	h	bi	BALTIMORE	ab	r	h	bi
Stewart cf	4	2	1	1	Surhoff lf	5	1	2	1
Grebeck 2b	5	1	2	2	Davis dh	4	0	1	1
Canseco dh	4	1	2	0	Bordick ss	5	0	3	0
Green rf	4	0	2	3	Mouton rf	1	0	0	0
Delgado 1b	2	0	2	1	Ripkin 3b	4	0	1	0
Fernandez 3b	4	1	0	0	Hoiles c	3	0	0	0
Fletcher c	5	1	1	0	Palmeiro 1b	1	0	0	0
Cruz Jr. lf	3	0	0	0	Alomar 2b	4	0	1	0
Gonzalez ss	5	1	3	1	Anderson cf	3	1	2	0
Totals	36	7	13	8	Totals	30	2	10	2

Toronto	001 000 060—7
Baltimore	002 000 000—2

E—Grebeck (1), Fernandez (6). DP—Toronto 2, Baltimore 1. LOB—Toronto 10, Baltimore 9. 2B—Delgado (5), Green (7), Canseco (7), Ripken (4). 3B—Surhoff (2). HR—Palmeiro (9). SB—Stewart (11), Alomar 4 (18). CS—Gonzalez (2).

	IP		H	R	ER	BB	SO
Toronto							
Clemens W,9-2	7		9	1	2	2	3
Quantrill	1		0	0	0	0	1
Persons	1		2	1	2	1	0
Baltimore							
Mussina	7	2-3	8	2	2	4	4
Rhodes		1-3	0	0	0	0	0
Coppinger L,0-1		1-3	2	4	4	2	0
Mills		2-3	2	2	2	2	0

Umpires — Home, Ford; First, Clark; Second, Barnett; Third, Kosc. T—3:21. A—25,569.

Note: For weekend games, the day of the week is included in the slugging to assist editors in differentiating between the Saturday and Sunday games.

BC-Tab-AMN-Box-Tor-Bal-SAT

7.   Standings for major league baseball are transmitted throughout the night — after eastern games for early morning editions and   at the conclusion of play — and are slugged accordingly (**Early** and **Final**).

Standings follow this style:

BC-Tab-BBL-AMN-Stdgs-Final
Sunday's standings

By The Canadian Press
(All times EDT)
AMERICAN LEAGUE
East Division

	W	L	Pct.	GBL
Toronto	92	63	.594	—
Boston	90	65	.581	2
Detroit	81	73	.526	10½

etc.

Sunday Results
Toronto 7 Cleveland 6 (11 innings)
Boston 4 Detroit 1

Saturday Results
Toronto 4 Cleveland 0
Detroit 5-4 Boston 3-6

Note: In doubleheaders, combine the two scores for each club, listing the opening game score first.

Monday Games
No games scheduled.

Tuesday Games
Toronto at Baltimore, 7:35 p.m.
Boston at New York, 8:35 p.m. . . .

---

8. **Top 10**

At the conclusion of play each day, the Top 10 feature, listing the hitting and pitching leaders in each league, is carried. This item lists the top 10 hitters graded by average, in tabular form, plus the top five players in 10 separate categories, listed in paragraph form.

BC-Tab-BBL-Top-10
Top 10

By The Canadian Press
AMERICAN LEAGUE

	G	AB	R	H	Pct
LWalker, Cal	68	270	46	95	.352
Olerud, NYM	61	214	37	72	.336
Bichette, Col	64	267	51	88	.330
Piazza, NYM	68	275	46	90	.327

. . .

Runs — Sosa, Chicago, 134; McGwire, St. Louis, 130; . . .
RBIs — Sosa, Chicago, 158; McGwire, St. Louis, 147; . . .
Hits — Bichette, Colorado, 219; Biggio, Houston, 210; . . .
Doubles — Biggio, Houston, 51; DYoung, Cincinnati, 48; . . .
Triples — Dellucci, Arizona, 12; BLarkin, Cincinnati, 10; . . .
Home runs — McGwire, St. Louis, 70; Sosa, Chicago, 66; . . .
Stolen bases — Womack, Pittsburgh, 58; Biggio, Houston, 50; . . .
Pitching (18 decisions) — Smoltz, Atlanta, 17-3, .850, 2.90; Glavine, Atlanta, 20-6, .769, 2.47; . . .
Strikeouts — Schilling, Philadelphia, 300; KBrown, San Diego, 257; . . .
Saves — Hoffman, San Diego, 53; Beck, Chicago, 51; . . .

9. **Probable Pitchers**

This feature, moved for AMs editions, lists the pitchers expected to start and the times of major league games. It is carried one day in advance.

AM-Tab-BBL-Pitchers
Monday's probable pitchers
                By The Canadian Press
   Probable pitchers, with won-lost records, for major league baseball games today (all times EDT):
                AMERICAN LEAGUE
   Cleveland (Nagy 3-3 and Colon 4-6) at Boston (Martinez 8-1 and Saberhagen 4-3), 1 p.m.
   Toronto (Clemens 6-1) at Detroit (Thompson 4-5), 1:30 p.m.
   Texas (Helling 7-1) at Baltimore (Mussina 4-3), 1:30 p.m.
   Anaheim (Dickson 4-6) at Oakland (Rogers 6-3), 4 p.m.
   New York (Wells 8-4) at Seattle (Fassero 4-4), 4 p.m.

---

10. Roundups are written for PMs papers on both the American and National leagues. When play in one league consists of only one or two games, a combined major league roundup may be considered. If such a roundup is contemplated, inform members by advisory as soon as possible.

Basketball

1. Write **National Basketball Association (NBA** also acceptable on sports pages), the **Pacific Division of the Western Conference**, the **Central Division of the Eastern Conference**, etc. On subsequent references: **the NBA West**, etc.

2. Use these NBA team abbreviations in slug lines and the like: **Atl** (Atlanta), **Bos** (Boston), **Cha** (Charlotte), **Chi** (Chicago), **Cle** (Cleveland), **Dal** (Dallas), **Den** (Denver), **Det** (Detroit), **GS** (Golden State), **Hou** (Houston), **Ind** (Indiana), **LAC** (Los Angeles Clippers), **LAL** (Los Angeles Lakers), **Mia** (Miami), **Mil** (Milwaukee), **Min** (Minnesota), **NJ** (New Jersey), **NY** (New York), **Orl** (Orlando), **Pha** (Philadelphia), **Pho** (Phoenix), **Por** (Portland), **Sac** (Sacramento), **SA** (San Antonio), **Sea** (Seattle), **Tor** (Toronto), **Utah** (Utah), **Vcr** (Vancouver), **Wash** (Washington).

3. For results, follow the bare score format.

4. Standings follow this style:

BC-Tab-BKBL-Stdgs
Friday's standings

By The Canadian Press
NBA
(All Times EDT)
Eastern Conference
Atlantic Division

	W	L	Pct.	GBL	
Miami	51	9	.850	—	
New York	44	17	.721	7½,	etc.

Central Division

	W	L	Pct.	GBL	
Chicago	41	21	.661	—	
Indiana	32	31	.508	9½,	etc.

Western Conference
Midwest Division

	W	L	Pct.	GBL	
Utah	39	25	.609	—	
San Antonio	34	30	.531	5,	etc.

Pacific Division

	W	L	Pct.	GBL	
Seattle	45	16	.738	—	
Phoenix	37	26	.587	9,	etc.

Friday Results
New York 107 Seattle 98
Atlanta 110 Vancouver 93, etc.

Tonight's Games
Portland at New York, 7:30 p.m.
Cleveland at Milwaukee, 8:30 p.m.

Sunday Games
New York at Boston, 7:30 p.m.
Cleveland at Milwaukee, 8:30 p.m.

Note: Some leagues use a format that includes a games column and award two points for a win and one for a tie. For such leagues, follow the format for hockey standings.

Bobsled, luge

Use a field results format.

Two-man: 1. Pierre Lueders, Edmonton, and Ken LeBlanc, Beaverton, Ont., four minutes 26.15 seconds; 2. Dave MacEachern, Charlottetown, and Jack Pye, Calgary, 4:27.32; etc.

Boxing

1. These are the Olympic weight categories: *light flyweight* (to 48 kg), *flyweight* (48-51 kg), *bantamweight* (51-54 kg), *featherweight* (54-57 kg), *lightweight* (57-60 kg), *light welterweight* (60-63.5 kg), *welterweight* (63.5-67 kg), *light middleweight* (67-71 kg), *middleweight* (71-75 kg), *light heavyweight* (75-81 kg), *heavyweight* (81-91 kg), *super heavyweight* (more than 91 kg).

2. These are the major pro weight categories: *flyweight* (to 112 lb.), *bantamweight* (113-118 lb.), *featherweight* (119-126 lb.), *lightweight* (127-135 lb.), *welterweight* (136-147 lb.), *middleweight* (148-160 lb.), *light heavyweight* (161-175 lb.), *cruiserweight* (176-195 lb.), *heavyweight* (196 lb. or more).

3. Use a revised head-to-head results format, stating whether the victory was by **decision, knockout (KO)** or **referee stopped bout.**

Note: In pro bouts, the **technical knockout (TKO)** is used instead of **referee stopped bout.**

Light flyweight (48 kg): Ivalio Hristov, Bulgaria, def. Michael Carbajal, U.S., 4-1; **Scott Olson, Edmonton,** etc.
Welterweight (67 kg): Robert Wangita, Kenya, def. Laurent Boudouani, France, bout stopped, 0:44 second; etc.
Heavyweight (91 kg): Ray Mercer, U.S., def. Baik Hyun-man, South Korea, KO, 2:16 first; etc.

Canoeing

Use a field result format. Categories are listed as *C-1* (canoe singles), *K-2* (kayak pairs), etc.

BC-Tab-CANOE-Rslts
NOTTINGHAM, England (CP) — Results Tuesday at the world canoeing championships:
WOMEN
K-1 500 metres (Heat 1): 1. Sharon Smith, Britain, two minutes 7.35 seconds; 2. **Margaret Langford, Lions Bay, B.C., 2:08.55**; 3. etc.

Cricket

Coverage of cricket is generally restricted to Test matches (between national teams) and one-day international matches. Test cricket consists of five six-hour playing days.

Cricket is played by two 11-member teams.

An explanation of some common cricket terminology:

Innings — An innings (singular) is completed when: (1) 10 of a team's batsmen have been dismissed; (2) the batting captain "declares" (voluntarily ends the innings); or (3) a specified number of overs have been bowled.

Overs — consisting of six or eight balls, delivered from alternate wickets.

Wickets — three stumps topped by crosspieces (called *bails*) situated at either end of the pitch (field) and from which the ball is bowled.

Curling

1. Rinks are named in this order: *lead, second, third* (or *vice-skip*), *skip.*

2. Do not write *curling bonspiel.*

3. Abbreviations when necessary in linescores are: **Alta, B.C., Man, N.B., Nfld, N. Ont, N.S., Ont, P.E.I., Que, Sask** and **Terr** (Territories).

4. Linescores follow this style:

BC-Tab-CURL-Women-Rslts
 MOOSE JAW, Sask. (CP) — Linescores Tuesday at the Canadian women's curling championship:

	Round 10
P.E.I.	001 010 201 1 — 6
Manitoba	200 101 010 0 — 5

Adds go as follows:

BC-Tab-CURL-Women-Rslts, add
MOOSE JAW, Sask.— add linescores

	Round 11
Nova Scotia	103 021 010 x — 8
Newfoundland	020 200 101 x — 6

 Bye: Territories.

---

5. Standings follow this style:

BC-Tab-CURL-Women-Stdgs
 MOOSE JAW, Sask. (CP) — Standings after the 11th round at the Canadian women's curling championship Wednesday:

	W	**L**	
Alberta	7	0	
B.C.	7	1	
Ontario	7	1	
Nova Scotia	6	2	
N. Ontario	5	3	etc.

Cycling

Use a field result format.

BC-Tab-CYCLE-Tour-Que
QUEBEC (CP) — Results Sunday from the Tour de Quebec men's cycling series:
220-kilometre third stage: 1. Czeslaw Lukaszewicz, Chateauguay, Que., three hours 32 minutes 10 seconds; 2. Gord Fraser, Nepean, Ont., same time; 3. Mark Walters, Toronto, five seconds behind; 4. John Harris, New Zealand, 0:17 behind; . . .
Overall standing: 1. Fraser, 5:51:05; 2. Walters, 5:51:10; 3. Mark Anand, Calgary, 5:51:41; . . .

Diving

Use a field result format.

BC-Tab-DIVE-Cda-Rslts
WINNIPEG (CP) — Results Sunday in Canadian World Cup diving:
WOMEN
Three-metre: 1. Emilie Heymans, Montreal, 877.05 points; 2. Myriam Boileau, Montreal, 876.36; . . .

Equestrian

1.   Identify events as *show jumping, dressage* or *three-day event*.

2.   Use basic field result format.

Fencing

1.   Identify events as *épée, foil* or *sabre*.

2.   Use head-to-head result format.

Football

1.   Avoid **major** as a synonym for touchdown. A major was an old scoring play worth five points. Use **touchdown** or, in subsequent references, **TD**.

2.   For results, use a bare score format.

3. Style for game summary:

BC-Tab-CFL-Sums-Tor-Ham

HAMILTON (CP) — CFL Thursday night:

SUMMARY

First Quarter

Tor — TD Clemons 15 run (Chomyc convert) 0:45

Ham — TD Winfield 27 pass from McPherson (Osbaldiston convert) 2:10

Second Quarter

Tor — Single Ilesic 55 7:18

Tor — Safety McPherson tackled 13:15

Third Quarter

Ham — FG Osbaldiston 47 4:15

Ham — TD Zatylny 95 kickoff return (two-point convert failed) 12:12

Tor — TD Harding blocked punt in end zone (Chomyc convert failed) 13:42

Tor — Safety Osbaldiston conceded 15:00

Fourth Quarter

No scoring.

Toronto	7	3	8	0—18
Hamilton	7	0	9	0—16

Attendance — 16,485.

4. Style for game statistics:

BC-Tab-CFL-Stax-Edm-Wpg

WINNIPEG (CP) — Statistics from the Edmonton-Winnipeg CFL game Friday night:

	Edm	Wpg
First downs	14	22
Yards rushing	156	88
Yards passing	255	280
Total offence	411	368
Team losses	25	15
Net offence	386	353
Passes made-tried	20-37	21-37
Returns-yards	5-95	2-22
Intercepts-yards by	0-0	2-22
Fumbles-lost	0-0	0-0
Sacks by	2	1
Punts-average	6-41	5-44
Penalties-yards	7-70	4-25
Time of possession	26:45	33:15

Net offence is yards passing, plus yards rushing, minus team losses such as yards lost on broken plays.

Individual

Rushing: Edm — Foggie 11-84, Marshall 13-54, Smith 1-11, Soles 1-8, Walling 1-minus 1; Wpg — Richardson 11-55, Dunigan 7-26, Hudson 4-7.

Receiving: Edm — Smith 8-131, Brown 4-46, Cyncar 2-24, Soles 2-17, Wright 1-11, Walling 1-10, Smith 1-8, Marshall 1-6; Wpg — House 6-17, Tuttle 3-70, Hudson 4-66, Hull 2-26, Streeter 2-17, Richardson 1-14.

Passing: Edm — Ham 20-37, 253 yds, 1 TD, 3 int; Wpg — Dunigan 18-31-286-3-0, McManus 2-2-66-1-0, Garza 1-4-15-0-1.

5. Style for rosters provided before the opening of the season, or as game lineups for the Grey Cup:

BC-Tab-CFL-Grey-Cup-Lineups
    VANCOUVER (CP) — Lineups for the CFL Grey Cup game Sunday between the Edmonton Eskimos and the Winnipeg Blue Bombers (x-denotes import):

EDMONTON
2. x-Henry Williams, wr
4. Ray Macoritti, p-k
6. x-Warren Jones, qb
9. Damon Allen, qb
14. x-Rickey Foggie, qb . . .

WINNIPEG
3. Trevor Kennerd, k
4. x-Danny McManus, qb
6. Bob Cameron, p
9. x-Sammy Garza, qb
10. x-Rod Hill, db . . .

Golf

1. Write **par 4, par-4 hole, five-iron** or **No. 5 iron, three-wood** or **No. 3 wood, 1 over par for the round, shot a 1-over-par 73, parred, birdie, birdied, bogey, double-bogey, triple-bogey 7, bogey-free** (not **bogey-less**), **bogeyed**.

2. There are two basic types of play: *match* and *medal* (or *stroke*).

In *match* play, the individual or team wins a hole by taking fewer strokes than the opponent. The entry winning the most holes wins the match. Stroke totals are not kept.

In *medal* play, the individual or team keeps a running total of strokes taken at each hole. The one taking the fewest strokes overall is the winner.

3. Match-play tournaments follow this style in head-to-head results:

    Bill Richardson, Creston, B.C., def. Ian MacDonnell, Antigonish, N.S., 3 and 2.

(Richardson had an insurmountable lead of three after 16 holes. As a result the final two holes were not played.)

    Bill Richardson, Creston, B.C., def. Ian MacDonnell, Antigonish, N.S., 1-up.

(Richardson led by one after 18 holes or after extra play. If two players are tied after 18 holes, play continues until a hole is won.)

4. Medal-play tournaments follow this style for results (lowest scores are listed first; home towns are listed, indented on a second line, for major national tournaments):

	For first round:
Cheryl Richardson Creston, B.C.	33-35—68
Heather MacDonnell Antigonish, N.S.	36-34—70

	For second round:
Cheryl Richardson Creston, B.C.	68-69—137
Heather MacDonnell Antigonish, N.S.	70-68—138

	For third round:
Heather MacDonnell Antigonish, N.S.	70-68-69—207
Cheryl Richardson Creston, B.C.	68-69-71—208

	For fourth round:
Heather MacDonnell Antigonish, N.S.	70-68-69-70—277
Cheryl Richardson Creston, B.C.	68-69-71-71—279

5. In professional tournaments, prize money is included and golfers' first names are reduced to initials to accommodate a single column results format. Some unusually long surnames may also require abbreviation.

G. Norman, $250,000	70-73-72-70—285
A. Forsb'd, $175,000	74-72-70-72—288

6. Team standings for men's and women's interprovincial competitions follow this style:

ST. JOHN'S, Nfld. (CP) — Final interprovincial team standings after play Thursday at the Canadian amateur women's golf championship (top three individual scores each day are counted):

NEW BRUNSWICK

Marilyn Smith Campbellton	70-72—142
Jennifer McDougall Sackville	68-74—142
Sandy Garson Shediac	75-75—150
Heidi Green Moncton	76-81—157
Total: 434	

SASKATCHEWAN

Bev Richards Saskatoon	73-74—147
Sally Oneschuk Prince Albert	75-72—147
Pamela Gordon Regina	79-77—156
Rosemary Hart Moose Jaw	80-77—157
Total: 450	

Gymnastics

1.   Identify events as *side horse, floor exercises, vault, rings, parallel bars, high bar, uneven bars, balance beam, team, all-round,* and ensure it's clear whether it's *team, individual combined* or *individual competition.*

2.   Use a field result format.

WOMEN

All-round: 1. Yvonne Tousek, Cambridge, Ont., 38.250 points; 2. Michelle Conway, Toronto, 37.650; 3. Julie Beaulieu, Montreal, 36.950; . . .

Hockey

1.   A three- or four-letter abbreviation is used to identify teams in slug lines and in the *penalties* section of the game summary. For team bench penalties, spell out the team name.

For the NHL, use: **Ana** (Anaheim), **Atl** (Atlanta), **Bos** (Boston), **Buf** (Buffalo), **Cal** (Calgary), **Chi** (Chicago), **Col** (Columbus), **Dal** (Dallas), **Det** (Detroit), **Edm** (Edmonton), **Fla** (Florida), **Hart** (Hartford), **LA** (Los Angeles), **Min** (Minnesota), **Mtl** (Montreal), **Nash** (Nashville), **NJ** (New Jersey), **NYI** (New York Islanders), **NYR** (New York Rangers), **Ott** (Ottawa), **Pha** (Philadelphia), **Pgh** (Pittsburgh), **Que** (Quebec), **SJ** (San Jose), **StL** (St. Louis), **TB** (Tampa Bay), **Tor** (Toronto), **Vcr** (Vancouver), **Wash** (Washington), **Wpg** (Winnipeg).

2.   For results, use the bare score format.

3.   Style for game summaries:

BC-Tab-NHL-Sums-NJ-Ott
code:4
   OTTAWA (CP) – NHL Saturday night:
                       First Period
   1. Ottawa, Daigle 11 (Cunneyworth, Yashin) 10:20 (pp)
   2. New Jersey, Carpenter 5 (Driver) 11:18 (sh)
   Penalty – Cole NJ (holding) 10:10.
                       Second Period
   3. Ottawa, Daigle 12 (Gaudreau) 14:53
   4. New Jersey, Cole 4 (MacLean, Broten) 19:38
   Penalties – Guerin NJ, Dahlquist Ott (double roughing), Huffman Ott (third man in, game misconduct) 13:35.
                       Third Period
   5. New Jersey, Richer 17 (Carpenter) 3:27
   6. New Jersey, Guerin 9 (Dean, Chambers) 16:50
   Penalties – Peluso NJ, Levins Ott (fighting) 2:55, Dahlquist Ott (interference) 14:48, New Jersey bench (too many men; served by Peluso) 18:42.
   Missed penalty shot – Daigle Ott, 6:15 third.
   Shots on goal by
New Jersey 11 16 9–36
Ottawa   8   8 6–22
   Goal (shots-saves) – New Jersey: Brodeur (W,11-8-5); Ottawa: Beaupre (L,4-18-2).
   Power plays (goals-chances) – New Jersey: 0-1; Ottawa: 0-2.
   Referee – Dan Marouelli. **Linesmen** – Pierre Racicot, Pierre Champoux.
   Attendance – 9,582.

Note 1: The number after a scorer's name is his season goal total. The *(pp), (sh)* and *(en)* notations designate *power-play, short-handed* and *empty-net* goals.

Note 2: The time of each goal is computed from the start of the period.

Note 3: The winning goaltender is the one in net when the winning goal is scored. The NHL defines the winning goal as the goal which is one more than the opposition's final total. For example, if the final score is 8-4, the fifth goal scored by the victorious team is the winner.

4.   At the end of each night's play, results are grouped by league in descending order of significance. Junior leagues are listed geographically, east to west.

BC-Tab-HKY-Grp-Rslts
Monday's list
                    By The Canadian Press
                             NHL
  Nashville 5 NY Rangers 4
  Detroit 4 Hartford 2 . . .
                             AHL
  Hershey 6 St. John's 3
  Cornwall 4 Syracuse 3 . . .
                      QUEBEC MAJOR
  Hull 4 Chicoutimi 3
  Halifax 2 Shawinigan 1 . . .

---

5. Style for standings:

BC-Tab-NHL-Stdgs-Final
code:2
National Hockey League
At A Glance

By The Canadian Press
All times EST
NHL
EASTERN CONFERENCE
Atlantic Division

	G	W	L	T	F	A	P
Philadelphia	44	24	10	10	135	87	58
New Jersey	44	25	14	5	129	117	55

Northeast Division

Toronto	46	27	16	3	152	133	57
Ottawa	45	25	14	6	133	101	56

Southeast Division

Carolina	45	20	18	7	116	112	47
Florida	44	17	16	11	110	115	45

WESTERN CONFERENCE
Central Division

Detroit	46	23	20	3	135	122	49
St. Louis	42	16	17	9	111	108	41

Northwest Division

Colorado	45	22	19	4	114	113	48
Edmonton	44	18	19	7	126	116	43

Pacific Division

Dallas	43	27	9	7	127	89	61
Phoenix	41	24	11	6	110	84	54

Monday Results

Dallas 5 Phoenix 3
Detroit 1 St. Louis 0 (OT)

Tonight's Games

Ottawa at Boston, 7 p.m.
Florida at N.Y. Rangers, 7:30 p.m.

Horse racing

1. Terms to watch include *colt* (an uncastrated male aged four or less), *horse* (an uncastrated male aged five or more), *stallion* (an uncastrated male, especially one used for breeding), *gelding* (a castrated male of any age), *filly* (a female aged four or less), *mare* (a female aged five or more), *quarter-horse* (a horse bred to run a quarter-mile), *standardbred* (bred chiefly for harness racing; a pacer or trotter), *thoroughbred* (of pure or pedigree stock; chiefly for flat racing and steeplechase).

2. This results style is used for thoroughbred, standardbred or quarter-horse racing:

BC-Tab-HARN-Mohawk-Rslts
   CAMPBELLVILLE, Ont. (CP) — Mohawk Raceway results Wednesday night:
   First — $2,900, mile, pace

Fiddlers Belle (Sloan)	20.60	8.90	5.30
Roberto GB (Strauss)		9.40	7.30
Pet Rock (Condren)		4.30	

   Time 2:05
   Carry The Cash, dq-Wil Lor Harry, Echo Vic, Peter Puck Herbert, Wil Lor Kal also started.
   Scratched: Broadway Star.
   dq-disqualified, finished 3rd, placed 5th, lapped on break.
   Second — $6,600, mile, trot

Mauras Pride (Davies)	7.40	5.50	3.70
Minto Stirrett (Gassien)		3.10	2.50
Durita Hanover (Arthur)		6.40	

   Time 2:06 2-5
   Kawartha Neon, Borne Eliminator, Darby Demon, Performance Plus, Miway Herbert also started.
               Daily Double (2-9) paid $141.10
                  Exactor (9-4) paid $25.80
   Attendance: 7,138; **handle**: $1,067,492.

---

3. Race charts are used primarily for the U.S. Triple Crown (Kentucky Derby, Preakness Stakes and Belmont Stakes) and the two major thoroughbred races in Canada (Queen's Plate and Rothmans International). The chart, provided by the *Daily Racing Form,* is copyright and must be acknowledged as such at the bottom.

BC-Tab-THBRD-Preakness-Chart

BALTIMORE, Md. (CP) — Chart of the 107th running of the Preakness Saturday at Pimlico:

Eighth Race: 1 3-16 miles for three-year-olds. Purse $200,000 added. Conditions: Stake: all 126 pounds. Value to winner $209,900. Second $40,000. Third $20,000. Fourth $10,000.

Horse	1/4	1/2	3/4	Str.	Fin.
Aloma's Ruler	1-1	1-1	1-1	1-1hf	1-hf
Linkage	4-1	3-hf	3-hd	2-6	2-6¾
Cut Away	3-hf	4-1hf	4-hf	6-5	3-2
Bold Style	2-hf	2-hf	2-1	3-hf	4-2
Laser Light	7	7	5-1hf	5-hd	5-no
s-Reinvested	5-hf	5-hf	7	4-hd	6-4
Water Bank	6-4	6-2	6-hf	7	7

s-Supplementary nomination.

Winner: Ok b or br c by Iron Ruler-Aloma by Native Charger.

Times: :23 4-5, :48, 1:12, 1:36 2-5, 1:55 2-5.

Off: 5:41 EDT. Start good, won driving. Track fast.

Scratch: Cupecoy's Joy.

Mutuels Prices:

7-Aloma's Ruler	15.80	4.60	3.60
6-Linkage		2.60	2.60
2-Cut Away			6.00

Exacta (7-6) paid $30.40

Aloma's Ruler broke in stride and was quickly angled to the rail, taken in hand and relaxed nicely while setting the pace. He turned back Bold Style entering the far turn and accelerated to increase his advantage under light rousing approaching the stretch. Aloma's Ruler then continued resolutely in response to alternate right and left handed whipping to determinedly hold off Linkage.

Linkage, reserved snugly outside, was always within striking distance. He responded willingly when set down entering the stretch and closed steadily in a game effort.

Cut Away raced along the rail, eased out between horses at the top of the stretch, split foes near the eighth pole and finished willingly.

Bold Style broke sluggishly and slightly in the air, was rushed to prompt the early pace outside Aloma's Ruler, was sent up to challenge entering the far turn and fell back.

Laser Light circled wide to reach contention midway round the far turn and weakened in the drive while bumping repeatedly with Reinvested.

Reinvested, in hand behind horses to the far turn, swung outside entering the stretch and bumped with Laser Light the final sixteenth. Water Bank was not a factor.

Copyright: Daily Racing Form Inc.

Judo

1. Weight categories are *extra lightweight* (up to 60 kg), *half lightweight* (up to 65 kg), *lightweight* (up to 71 kg), *half middleweight* (up to 78 kg), *middleweight* (up to 86 kg), *half heavyweight* (up to 95 kg), *heavyweight* (over 95 kg), *open category* (no weight limit).

2. Use field result format.

Lacrosse

Use the **Hockey** summary style.

Motorcycle racing

Follow the **Auto racing** style.

Rowing

1. A *regatta* is a knockout competition ending with a race or races between two or more finalists. A *repechage* is a second chance to qualify, used only in the preliminaries. The boats used in sculling and rowing are *shells*, not sculls.

In sculling (*singles, doubles* or *four-member crews*), each competitor rows with two oars called *sculls*. In rowing (*pairs, fours, eights*), each competitor uses one oar.

Fours and eights are *crews*, never teams. The competitors are *scullers* or *oarsmen* or *oarswomen*, never rowers. The terms *rowing* and *oars(wo)men* may be used in a general sense referring to regattas and the scullers who take part.

2. Identify events as *single sculls, double sculls, coxless pairs, coxed pairs, coxless fours, coxed fours, coxless eights, coxed eights.*

3. Use a field result format.

Rugby

1. Carry scores on major international matches only.

2. Use a bare scores result format. List the home team first in international matches.

Shooting

1. Identify events as *free pistol, fullbore, rapid-fire pistol, skeet, smallbore rifle* and *trap.*

2. Use a field result format.

Skating, figure

1. Most figure-skating competitions comprise *men's singles, women's singles, pairs* (man-woman) and *ice dance* (man-woman). *Singles* consists of two segments — a short program of required elements and a free-skating long program. The short program is worth one-third and the free-skating segment two-thirds. In the short program, skaters must attempt predetermined jumps or movements in not more than two minutes 40 seconds. In free skating, competitors put together their own combination of jumps, spins and steps, with time allowed varying between three and 4 1/2 minutes depending on whether it's a men's or women's competition and on the age group. Skaters select their own music for both the short and long programs. Judges assign two marks, one for technical merit and one for artistic impression.

Pairs skating consists of a short program in which several elements (jumps, spins, lifts, etc.), announced in advance, must be attempted, and a free-skating portion which contains moves similar to singles skating but executed simultaneously by both competitors. Free skating accounts for two-thirds of the final mark and varies in length from three to four minutes, depending on the age group.

Ice dancing, in simple terms, is ballroom dancing on ice. It is easily distinguished from *pairs* skating in that there are no jumps or lifts above the waist. The couple seldom separate. The program has three elements — compulsory dances (variations of such dances as the waltz, tango and foxtrot) skated to designated rhythms and patterns; the original dance (three repetitive sequences of steps), and the free dance in which competitors select their own moves, steps and music.

2.   Some of the more common jumps (named after their inventors and, therefore, capitalized):

Axel: Skater, facing forward, takes off on the outside edge of either foot, rotates up to four times and lands on the outside edge of the other foot, facing backward.

Lutz: Skater, facing backward, takes off on the outside edge of either foot and, after up to three reverse rotations, lands on the outside edge of the other foot, facing backward.

Salchow: Skater, facing backward, takes off from the inside edge of either foot and, after up to three rotations, lands on the outside edge of the other foot, facing backward.

3.   Use a field result format.

Skating, speed

1.   Speed skating consists of *outdoor* (long track) and *indoor* (short track) events. Race distances include 500, 1,000, 1,500, 3,000 (women only), 5,000 and 10,000 metres (men only).

2.   Use a field result format.

Skiing

1.   Skiing is divided into four categories: *alpine, nordic, biathlon* and *freestyle*. Alpine includes downhill, slalom, giant slalom, super giant slalom and a combined event. Nordic includes cross-country, ski jumping and a combined event. Biathlon combines cross-country skiing with rifle shooting. Freestyle includes acro, moguls and aerials.

2.   Use a field result format.

BC-Tab-SKI-WCup-Rslts
   KITZBUEHEL, Austria (CP) — Results and standings following a World Cup men's downhill ski race Saturday:
   1. Pirmin Zurbriggen, Switzerland, two minutes 6.68 seconds; **2. Rob Boyd, Calgary, 2:07.01; 3. Brian Stemmle, Aurora, Ont., 2:07.12**; . . .
   Downhill standings: 1. **Boyd, 95 points**; 2. Zurbriggen, 80; 3. Leonard Stock, Austria, 77; . . .
   Overall standings: 1. Stock, 110; 2. Conrad Cathomen, Switzerland, 105; **3. Boyd**, Zurbriggen, **95 each**; . . .

Note: When a competitor appears a second time in standings, his first name and country are dropped.

Soccer

1.   British standings and results lists require some team abbreviations to ensure material does not spill over on to a second line. The necessary abbreviations are:

English League: Bristol City (**Bristol C**), Bristol Rovers (**Bristol R**), Crystal Palace (**Crystal P**), Manchester City (**Man City**), Manchester United (**Man United**), Nottingham Forest (**Notts F**), Queen's Park Rangers (**QPR**), Sheffield United (**Sheffield U**), Sheffield Wednesday (**Sheffield W**), West Bromwich Albion (**West Brom**), Wolverhampton (**Wolves**).

Scottish League: Dundee United (**Dundee U**), East Sterling (**E Sterling**), Glasgow Celtic (**Celtic**), Glasgow Rangers (**Rangers**), Hearts of Midlothian (**Hearts**), Queen of the South (**Queen of S**).

2.   For scores, the home team is listed first in British and European play.

Results style is as follows:

BC-Tab-SOC-British-Rslts
      LONDON (CP) — British soccer results Saturday:
                        ENGLISH LEAGUE
                        Premier League
      Aston Villa 4 Chelsea 3
      Man United 1 Everton 2 . . .
                        Division 1
      Derby 1 Chelsea 0
      Leicester 0 Leeds 1 . . .
                        SCOTTISH LEAGUE
                        League Cup
                  Quarter-finals, first leg
      Celtic 4 Partick 0
      St. Mirren 1 Hearts 1 . . .
                        Premier League
      Kilmarnock 2 Motherwell 1
      Dundee 1 Dundee U 2 . . .

---

3.   For standings, use this style (note order for *T* and *L* reversed from standard North American tables):

BC-Tab-SOC-British-Stdgs
      LONDON (CP) — British soccer standings following play Saturday:
                        ENGLISH LEAGUE
                        Premier League

	W	T	L	F	A	P	
Chelsea	21	6	3	73	24	69	
Aston Villa	18	4	9	60	37	58	
Man United	14	9	6	39	25	51	. . .

                        Division 1

Wolves	18	7	6	56	33	61	. . .

                        SCOTTISH LEAGUE
                        Premier League

Aberdeen	20	4	4	59	21	44	. . .

Squash

Use head-to-head format.

Swimming

1.   Identify events as *men's 100-metre freestyle, women's 4x100-metre medley relay,* etc.

2.   Use a field result format.

Tennis

1.   Use head-to-head results format. Grouped results should be graded in order of seedings. See example page 399.

2.   Tiebreakers are used to avoid marathon sets. The first player to win six games wins the set, unless the opponent has won five games. In that case, the player with six games may take the set by winning the next game. If that player loses it, (a) play can continue until either player wins two straight games, or (b) a tiebreaker may be played in which the winner is the first player to score seven points with at least a two-point lead. If the score reaches 6-6 in the tiebreaker, play continues until one player leads by two points.

Track and field   (Athletics)

1.   Olympic and other international events are measured in metric, although some imperial distances are still raced in the United States. Distances and heights in such field events as the high jump, long jump, pole vault, shot put, discus, hammer and javelin should be reported in metres. But the 100-yard dash, for example, is not converted to the 91.44-metre dash.

2.   Use the metric distance for marathons — 42.195 kilometres (not 26 miles 385 yards).

3.   Use a field result format. See example page 399.

Volleyball

Use head-to-head result format.

BC-Tab-VLBL-Rslts
Friday's list
By The Canadian Press
WORLD LEAGUE
Canada def. Brazil 3-2 (15-12, 16-14, 8-15, 12-15, 15-10).

Weightlifting

1.   Olympic and most other amateur competitions are divided into 10 weight categories: *52 kg, 56 kg, 60 kg, 67.5 kg, 75 kg, 82.5 kg, 90 kg, 100 kg, 110 kg* and *over 110 kg.*

2.   Use a field result format.

Wrestling

1.   There are eight weight categories for men and six for women. The eight men's classes are: up to 54 kg, to 58 kg, to 63 kg, to 69 kg, to 76 kg, to 85 kg, to 97 kg, to 130 kg. The women's divisions are: to 46 kg, to 51 kg, to 56 kg, to 62 kg, to 68 kg, to 75 kg.

2.   Identify events as Greco-Roman or freestyle for men. Women compete only in freestyle.

3.   Use head-to-head formats.

Yachting

1.   Following are Olympic-sanctioned yacht classes: *Soling* (three-person keel boat), *Star* (two-person keel boat), *Tornado* (two-person catamaran), *Laser* (one-person dinghy), *Finn* (one-person dinghy), *International Europe* (one-person dinghy), *470* (two-person dinghy), *49er* (two-person high-performance dinghy) and *Mistral One-Design* (windsurfer).

The *470* and *Mistral* classes feature separate men's and women's competition. *Finn* is for men while *Laser* is for women. The rest are open to both men and women.

2.   The America's Cup is a *formula* class event. For a yacht to qualify for this challenge series, its size must not exceed a given limit. That limit, which approximates the length of the boat, is arrived at using a complicated mathematical formula that factors in such things as length, draft and sail area. In 1992 a 24-metre limit was set.

3.   Where names of yacht classes include an imperial measure (e.g. *Whatsis 30:* a 30-footer), a sentence of explanation may be necessary if there's a risk of confusion.

4.   Some races are still measured in nautical miles. Convert these to kilometres but retain an initial nautical-mile equivalent in parentheses. A nautical mile is equivalent to 1.852 kilometres.

News for cable and online services

General

Many Canadians get their news and information directly from The Canadian Press through World Wide Web sites and cable television "screen" news.

Basic CP principles apply to all news services, but some style allowances are made to meet different requirements.

Cable (on screen) news

Up-to-the-minute news, weather and sports are available in households and offices across the country on the cable news service, displayed in text form on television screens.

Cable news goes directly to the public, and CP editors face the challenge of informing viewers of breaking news before others can get on the air or in print.

With the exception of story size, filing the cable service is similar to handling other news services — get it to the reader quickly and accurately.

The cable editor is faced with a very tight format. This is tough. To quote Jim Poling, former CP editorial vice-president, "anyone can write long. Too few people can write short with the punch and brilliance that raises eyebrows and makes ears twitch with alertness."

Some cable formats can handle nothing more than a three-line item. Others can take two or three paragraphs. Both must inform the reader without leaving out essential information.

Tight writing is crucial, and editors employ a variety of tricks to keep stories short:

• Avoid generalities — screen space is at a premium. All sentences need substance. Don't tell the reader that the federal government brought down a budget today. Go right to the contents of the budget.

• Cable writing must be conversational. It's a hybrid between news written for the eye (newspaper) and that written for the ear (radio and television). Try reading it as though you were telling a story to another person. Lengthy attributions at the end of a sentence don't work. A chain of clauses is too ponderous for the reader/viewer.

• Stories work best if they can be summed up in one screen — so a viewer can see the entire story at once. Top or exceptional news stories can run more than one screen if the particular format allows it, but the names of anyone being quoted should be repeated in the second screen. The cable reader may have missed the first screen, where the person's name first appeared, or have forgotten it.

- Although quotes are permitted in cable reports, they can eat up a lot of space without providing much information. Paraphrase or keep them pithy.

- Brevity allows for some casualness in style, but try to be consistent. If abbreviations must be used, keep to familiar ones. Don't interchange **Tto**, **Tor** and **T.O.** for **Toronto**.

- Numbers below 10 don't need to be written out. **First** becomes **1st**, and so on.

- Some cable formats are all-caps and this adds a further wrinkle. Acronyms and short forms such as UN take periods (U.N.).

Online news

News for Internet readers is at the other end of the spectrum, with virtually no space limitations. This doesn't mean, however, that long overblown copy is acceptable. Some tips:

- Headlines need to be enticing yet still make clear what the story is about.

➤ See **Headlines**, page 369.

- **Premier makes speech** doesn't cut it. As with all headlines, they need to be focused on the interesting part of the story. In many online news menus, readers decide whether they want to pull up a story based on the information on the "hot key" — usually a headline and the top of the story. So headlines should not make false promises about what a story may be about; this will only irritate a reader who takes the time to pull it up on his screen.

- The first paragraph of the story may not give enough information for that hot key and may need to be combined with the second or even third paragraph. Check to make sure that what appears on the hot key is complete.

- Longer stories need subheads — good subheads. Look for an interesting quote, expression or anecdote to feature in a subhead.

- Cutlines on pictures should not repeat information that's in accompanying stories. Usually, the online reader is looking at the story alongside the picture and doesn't need to be told the same thing twice.

News releases

Newsrooms are inundated with news releases every day. Most of them go straight into the garbage. But a few will become the basis of a news story, especially if they are announcing genuine news. A well-written news release, like a well-written news story, can help that process by grabbing an editor's attention.

What makes a good news release? Accurate information, clearly presented, that answers all the basic questions a reporter or reader might have. Although the purpose of a news release is quite different from that of a news story, many of the same writing principles apply.

Content

1. Write in everyday English. Forget the bureaucratic or scientific jargon. Explain unfamiliar terms. Prefer **begin** to inaugurate, **best** to optimum, **less than ideal** to sub-optimal, **carry out** to implement, **final result** to bottom line.

2. Don't hide bad news under fancy words. The layoff of 150 workers is just that; it's not consolidation or downsizing. Be specific and save the reporter a phone call.

3. If you must use unusual technical terms, explain them.

4. Try to answer the questions all readers ask: *Who? What? When? Where? Why? How?* What is happening? Who says? Who is involved? When will it happen? And where? How or why is it happening?

5. Don't try to answer all six questions in the first sentence. Put what you consider the most important news in the first paragraph.

> **Not:** At a news conference today, Atlas Mines president John W. Merryweather said he was "happy to announce that the company has signed a $100-million, five-year agreement" with Karasawa Industries of Tokyo to produce coal for the Japanese metallurgical company, which would "necessitate the reopening of the Dovetail mine and the creation of 250 jobs at the coal face and in surface installations."

> **But:** The Dovetail coal mine, which has been closed for 20 years, is to be reopened as part of a $100-million, five-year contract with a Japanese company. Some 250 miners and surface workers will be hired.

The details can be added in subsequent paragraphs.

6. How much detail? That's a matter of judgment. Put yourself in the reader's place and try to answer all pertinent questions. What network will the show be on and when? How soon will the new vaccine be in drugstores? What prize did your prize-winning author win? The Pulitzer? Or the Grade 10 English award? The union is pressing for $1 an hour more. What is the current rate?

7. Give some background on the organization or company involved in

the news. Make sure it is factual and doesn't give the wrong impression. Resist hyperbole. Don't say the company had its highest revenues ever in the last year without also mentioning that profits were down.

8. Include the source of the news. The person quoted should be someone in authority – the company president, the coach, the chief fund-raiser, the researcher who made the discovery. Include phone numbers. Most reporters like to get their own quotes; broadcast reporters will need quotes on tape.

9. Make sure time elements are clearly presented. Specify when the book is going to be released. If it is a tour, provide specific details. If the ballet company is going to Europe, include cities, dates, theatres and hotels so news coverage can be arranged.

10. Include the person's age and birthplace in biographical material. Tracking down such small but important facts can consume a lot of a reporter's time. If people from across the country are involved in a news event, include home towns.

Format

Certain conventions should be followed, no matter if the release is being delivered by fax, regular mail or electronic mail:

1. Put a date at the top of the release. Specify at the top if the news item can be used at once. If it is to be released at a specific time, add that information: For release at 8 p.m. EST Monday, Dec. 23.

2. Headlines can be useful, especially in lengthy announcements. They don't need to be fanciful – just a clear summary of the main news is fine.

Not: Royal Bank president speaks to Canadian Club.

But: Royal Bank president predicts bank mergers won't proceed.

3. At the top or bottom of the release, give the names and titles of people who can be contacted for more information, their phone numbers and the name of the organization and address. Make sure they will be at those numbers when the release is distributed.

4. Gimmicks might get an editor's attention for a minute or two, but they are no substitute for solid information tied to a genuine news event. Samples or other free material are not usually wanted. Exceptions would be cases where the product is needed to write a story – a new book or video, for instance.

Pictures

Pictures are usually a welcome addition to a news release. Like the written information, they should be new or in some way unusual, or relate to a live news topic. They attract attention because of human interest and appeal to the emotions, or they can relate to some important person, event or place.

The print must have a sharp, sparkling quality. Avoid busy

backgrounds and low, "artsy" lighting. Colour is preferred. Captions should identify everyone in the picture.

Who gets it?

1. Keep a contacts list up to date. It is always best to direct a release to the beat reporter, but make sure that person is not on holidays or out of town. Next best is the appropriate editor, such as the entertainment editor for an announcement on music awards. An urgent release during off-hours should be directed to the news desk.

2. The president, publisher or other top executives of a news organization rarely attend news conferences or assign staff to cover them, so nothing is gained by sending them a copy of a news release.

3. Don't blanket news organizations with the same release. It is only going to get reported once. The bank president may be taking his speech on a cross-country tour, but a national news organization is only going to carry one story, preferably the first time he makes it.

Bibliography

These works have been consulted in the preparation and shaping of the *CP Stylebook:*

Barber, Katherine (ed.). *The Canadian Oxford Dictionary.* Oxford University Press. Toronto, 1998.

Barzun, Jacques. *Simple & Direct: A Rhetoric for Writers.* Harper & Row. New York, 1975.

Bernstein, Theodore M. *The Careful Writer: A Modern Guide to English Usage.* Atheneum. New York, 1973.

Brown, Lesley, C.T. (ed.). *The Shorter Oxford English Dictionary.* Oxford University Press. Oxford, 1993.

Burchfield, R.W. (ed.). *The New Fowler's Modern English Usage.* Oxford University Press. Oxford, 1996.

Canadian Encyclopedia. McClelland and Stewart. Toronto, 1998.

Canadian Trade Index. The Canadian Manufacturers' Association. Toronto, 1990.

Collins-Robert French-English English-French Dictionary. William Collins Sons & Co. (Glasgow) and Dictionnaires Le Robert (Paris), 1987.

Colombo, John Robert (ed.). *The Canadian Global Almanac.* Macmillan Canada. Toronto, 1998.

Copperud, Roy H. *American Usage and Style: The Consensus.* Van Nostrand Reinhold. New York, 1980.

Crane, David. *A Dictionary of Canadian Economics.* Hurtig Publishers. Edmonton, 1980.

Eerdmans' Handbook to the World's Religions. William B. Eerdmans Publishing. Grand Rapids, Mich., 1982.

Fee, Margery and McAlpine, Janice. *Guide to Canadian English Usage.* Oxford University Press. Toronto, 1997.

Evans, Harold. *Editing and Design; Newsman's English.* Heinemann. London, 1973.

Goldstein, Norm (ed.). *The Associated Press Stylebook and Libel Manual.* The Associated Press. New York, 1994.

Guide du journaliste. La Presse Canadienne. Montreal, 1992.

Jacobi, Ernst. *Writing at Work: Dos, Don'ts and How Tos.* Hayden Book Co. Rochelle Park, N.J., 1976.

Jordan, Lewis (ed.). *The New York Times Manual of Style and Usage.* New York Times Books. New York, 1979.

Kidd, Paris M. and Huber, Wolfgang. *Living With the AIDS Virus.* HK Biomedical Inc. Berkeley, Calif., 1990.

Manser, Martin H. *Good Word Guide*. Bloomsbury Publishing. London, 1988.

Manual of Style. U.S. Government Printing Office. Gramercy Publishing. New York, 1986.

McFarlane, J.A. and Clements, Warren. *The Globe and Mail Style Book*. McClelland and Stewart. Toronto, 1998.

Metric Press Guide. Metric Commission Canada. Ottawa, 1981.

Nickles, Harry G. *Dictionary of Do's and Don'ts*. McGraw-Hill. New York, 1975.

Robertson, Stuart M. *Robertson's Newsroom Legal Crisis Management*. Hallion Press. Dunedin, Ont., 1991.

Rose, Turner. *Stylebook for Writers and Editors*. U.S. News and World Report. Washington, 1984.

Ross-Larson, Bruce. *Edit Yourself*. W.W. Norton. New York, 1982.

Sabin, William. *A Reference Manual*. McGraw-Hill Ryerson. Toronto, 1978.

Shaw, Harry. *Dictionary of Problem Words and Expressions*. McGraw-Hill. New York, 1975.

Skilling, Marjorie E. and Gay, Robert M. *Words Into Type*. Meredith Publishing. New York, 1964.

Strunk, William Jr. and White, E.B. *The Elements of Style*. Macmillan Publishing Co. New York, 1979.

Timmons, Christine and Gibney, Frank (eds.). *Britannica Book of English Usage*. Doubleday. Garden City, N.Y., 1980.

The World Almanac and Book of Facts. Primedia Reference Inc. New Jersey, 1998.

Worth, Sylvia (ed.). *Rules of the Game*. St. Martin's Press. New York, 1990.

Acknowledgments

What more appropriate for a co-operative news agency than a co-operative stylebook. CP staff across the country have traditionally shared in the updating and revising of this book through many editions. For many, it is work fitted around their regular workload. People from every bureau and desk toss in ideas for improvements. All recognize the importance of making the CP Stylebook as authoritative and helpful as possible.

The greatest debt for any new edition of the CP Stylebook is undoubtedly to the past. The earliest workers and managers at The Canadian Press established the traditions of quality, integrity and consistency for the news agency.

Beginning more than 50 years ago, style rulings were first gathered into book form. Senior managers of the past like Gillis Purcell, Charles Bruce and John Dauphinee put their various personal – and sometimes eccentric – stamps on CP style. Later, Bob Taylor contributed an enviable knowledge and a distinctly human touch to regular updatings of the stylebook. More recently, Peter Buckley co-ordinated a major revision and his sensible voice on style and ethics issues continues to reverberate throughout the book.

In this most recent update, the following CP people contributed their time and expertise: Dean Beeby, Neil Davidson, Ross Hopkins, Pierre LeBrun, Paul Loong, Malcolm McNeil, Ron Poling, Lorraine Turchansky, Sheryl Ubelacker, John Valorzi, Kevin Ward and Scott White.

Once again, Mike Fuhrmann's editing and proofreading skills kept embarrassing mistakes and inconsistencies from creeping into the book.

Sean Vokey of CP's Graphics Department designed the book's new cover, the first one in 10 years. Harold Herschell, also of CP's Graphics Department, and Graeme Roy, CP Picture Editor, co-ordinated the graphics and pictures. Wendy MacDonald, CP's manager of marketing, helped with production decisions.

Stuart M. Robertson of O'Donnell, Robertson and Sanfilippo continues to provide crucial advice for all legal revisions.

The editor salutes them all and takes full responsibility for any shortcomings or errors in the finished work.

Index

Notes

Notes

Notes

Notes

Notes

Also available from The Canadian Press

CP Command News

With Command News you can have access to the same newswire service accessed by reporters at nearly 100 Canadian newspapers and 500 radio and television stations at the same time they do.

Command News is a subscription-based service accessed through the Internet and can be customized to deliver just the news you need.

If you need to stay on top of the news—as a writer or for competitive reasons—this service is for you!

CP Picture Archive

The CP Picture Archive is a digital collection of more than 150,000 images including contemporary news and sports images and a historical collection that dates back to 1840. Subscribers to the CP Picture Archive can quickly and easily search, browse and download pictures through the Internet. Photos are available for use in marketing brochures, flyers, reports, presentations, conventions, books or other publications.

If you work with pictures, you'll want access to the CP Picture Archive.

CP Photo Assignment Services

Need commercial photography services? CP has a network of more than 500 highly skilled news, studio and specialty photographers across Canada and around the world. That means we can have your pictures shot in just about any major city in the world, then processed, scanned, transmitted or e-mailed to any location.

If you need commercial photography services, including business portraiture, corporate events, studio work or major news and sports events, we can help.

To find out more about the above products and services, call 416-507-2129 or e-mail sales@cp.org.

Printed in Canada
Design and cover art by Sean Vokey, The Canadian Press.
Printed by Image Plus Graphics, Toronto, Ont.
Printed on recycled paper

The Canadian Press
The Last Word. First.

CP Books order form

The CP Stylebook is an all-purpose writing guide. (450 pages)
(CP) Caps and Spelling lists hundreds of tricky names and spellings. (181 pages)
(CP) Caps and Spelling on disk is a help file that contains
the contents of the book in a searchable onscreen format.
Guide du journaliste is for French-language writing. (200 pages)
BN Style Guide is for broadcast writing. (265 pages)

Mail to: Book Orders, The Canadian Press, 36 King St. E., Toronto, Ont., M5C 2L9
Phone: 1-800-434-7578 416-507-2091 (Credit card orders) **Fax:** 416-507-2071
E-mail: books@cp.org

Name:_____ Organization:_____

Address:_____

_____

Phone:_____ Fax: _____ E-mail: _____

I would like to order the following:

____ copies of the CP Stylebook ($32 each)   _____
____ copies of (CP) Caps and Spelling ($19 each)   _____   _____
____ copies of (CP) Caps and Spelling, book plus disk ($29 each) _____   Total
____ copies of Guide du journaliste ($20 each)   _____
____ copies of the BN Style Guide ($23 each)   _____   add 7% GST
Bulk Rates available (call for details)
                                                                          _____
                                                                         Total enclosed

----

Name:_____ Organization:_____

Address:_____

_____

Phone:_____ Fax: _____ E-mail: _____

I would like to order the following:

____ copies of the CP Stylebook ($32 each)   _____
____ copies of (CP) Caps and Spelling ($19 each)   _____   _____
____ copies of (CP) Caps and Spelling, book plus disk ($29 each) _____   Total
____ copies of Guide du journaliste ($20 each)   _____
____ copies of the BN Style Guide ($23 each)   _____   add 7% GST
Bulk Rates available (call for details)
                                                                          _____
                                                                         Total enclosed

----

Note: Rates include Canada Post shipping for orders of three books or fewer. Shipping
costs are added for larger orders. Call for details.